THE ISLAND of Cyprus was conquered from its Byzantine ruler by Richard I of England in 1191 during the Third Crusade, and remained under western rule until the Ottoman conquest of 1570–1. From the 1190s until the 1470s the island was a kingdom governed by members of the Lusignan family. The Lusignans, who hailed from Poitou in western France, imposed a new, European landowning class and a Catholic ecclesiastical hierarchy upon the indigenous Greek population. Nevertheless, their regime provided long periods of political stability and, until the late fourteenth century, a considerable period of prosperity. In the thirteenth century the island was closely linked to the Latin states in Syria and the Holy Land by political, social and economic ties and, with the fall of the last Christian strongholds to the Muslims in 1291, it became the most easterly outpost of Latin Christendom in the Mediterranean.

This new study, which is based on original research, traces the fortunes of Cyprus under its royal dynasty and its role in the crusades and in the confrontation of Christian and Muslim in the near East until the 1370s when it was severely weakened in a war with Genoa. It is both a major contribution to the history of the crusades in the Levant and the only scholarly study of medieval Cyprus currently available.

The Kingdom of Cyprus and the Crusades, 1191–1374

The Kingdom of Cyprus
and the Crusades, 1191–1374

PETER W. EDBURY

University of Wales College of Cardiff

CAMBRIDGE
UNIVERSITY PRESS

Published by the Press Syndicate of the University of Cambridge
The Pitt Building, Trumpington Street, Cambridge CB2 1RP
40 West 20th Street, New York, NY 10011–4211, USA
10 Stamford Road, Oakleigh, Melbourne 3166, Australia

First published 1991
First paperback edition 1994

British Library cataloguing in publication data
Edbury, P. W.
The Kingdom of Cyprus and the Crusades, 1191–1374.
1. Cyprus, history
I. Title
956.45

Library of Congress cataloguing in publication data
Edbury, P. W. (Peter W.)
The Kingdom of Cyprus and the Crusades, 1191–1374
Peter W. Edbury.
p.   cm.
Includes bibliographical references and index.
ISBN 0 521 26876 1
1. Cyprus – History. 2. Crusades. I. Title.
DS54.6.E33   1991
956.45–dc20   90–40488   CIP

ISBN 0 521 26876 1 hardback
ISBN 0 521 45837 4 paperback

Transferred to digital printing 2000

For my parents

CONTENTS

FIGURES

PREFACE

IN 1841 the Académie des Inscriptions et Belles-Lettres announced an essay competition on the 'history of Cyprus under the rule of the princes of the house of Lusignan'. What was wanted was not a simple narrative but 'a more accurate account of events with some discussion of the geography, laws and customs and of the religious, political and civil institutions of the kingdom'. In the event the prize was shared. One of the winners was Count Louis de Mas Latrie, a French aristocrat who subsequently, in the course of the following half century, proceeded to lay the foundations of all modern research into Cyprus in the period of the crusades. Mas Latrie died in 1897 after a varied and prolific career. But there were few who followed in his footsteps, and it was not until the 1940s that the most appreciable English contribution to the subject appeared. This was Sir George Hill's four-volume *History of Cyprus* which covered the island's history from prehistoric times to the British colonial administration. Volumes II and III, which deal with Lusignan and Venetian Cyprus, are notable for their careful scholarship and in general have stood the test of time better than the others. However, in recent years it has been another Frenchman, Professor Jean Richard, who has donned Mas Latrie's mantle and, through a series of articles and editions of sources, has greatly enriched our knowledge of the island's history in the later middle ages. Richard has blazed the trail for what can now be clearly seen as a revival of academic endeavour. I would single out three scholars in particular: Count W. H. Rudt de Collenberg, who has laboured long in the archives of the Vatican in the furtherance of his prosopographical enquiries; Dr D. M. Metcalf, who has made substantial advances in investigating Lusignan numismatics and monetary history, and Dr Benjamin Arbel, whose work on Cyprus under Venetian rule promises to overturn many long-held assumptions.

Since the 1950s there has been an upsurge in research into the crusading movement. Our knowledge of the kingdom of Jerusalem has been considerably enhanced, not least by a succession of major studies by British scholars. But no one since Hill, whose book for all its merits is now showing its age and in any case has long been unobtainable, has attempted a general reappraisal of the history of Cyprus under the Lusignans in the light of recent scholarship. The present contribution is intended to go some way towards filling this gap. My emphasis is on the political history of Cyprus within the context of the crusading endeavours in the eastern Mediterranean. I had originally planned to include chapters on the social and economic fabric of the kingdom, but after much heart-searching I decided that such topics would be better dealt with elsewhere. In any case I am not at all sure that in the 1990s people will want to read academic monographs from cover to cover if they are much over two hundred pages long! Nevertheless I have tried to satisfy the terms of reference set by the Académie des Inscriptions all those years ago, even if the end-result is a century and a half too late for consideration by that august body.

One scholar more than any other has me in his debt. Professor Jonathan Riley-Smith was the man who first introduced me to the study of the crusades when I was a student at St Andrews University, and his friendship and encouragement ever since have been of immense value. My researches into Cypriot history began as far back as 1969 when, under Jonathan's direction, I was preparing my undergraduate dissertation, and over the years he has patiently chivvied me along when other concerns have threatened to prevent my work on Cyprus ever seeing its way into print. There are many other scholars who at different times have helped me in one way or another. It is a matter of great sadness that neither Dr L. H. Butler nor Dr R. C. Smail are living to see this work come to fruition, but on a happier note I am pleased to be able to thank the four historians referred to at the end of the opening paragraph, Jean Richard, W. H. Rudt de Collenberg, Michael Metcalf and Benjamin Arbel, all of whom have been most generous in sharing their opinions with me. I have also profited from the wisdom of, among others, Bernard Hamilton, Robert Irwin, David Luscombe, Tony Luttrell and Christopher Tyerman, while at the same time I have been most fortunate to have had the benefit of the company of David Bates and Clive Knowles as colleagues here in Cardiff. The British Academy gave me some most welcome financial support to enable me to further my research, and my thanks go also to the Governing Body of Christ Church, Oxford. As for the dedicatees, they alone know how much I owe them.

P.W.E.

Cardiff, 1990

ABBREVIATIONS

Annales ESC	*Annales Économies Sociétés Civilisations.*
AOL	*Archives de l'Orient latin.*
BEC	*Bibliothèque de l'École des Chartes.*
BEFAR	Bibliothèque des Écoles françaises d'Athènes et de Rome.
BF	*Byzantinische Forschungen.*
BIHR	*Bulletin of the Institute of Historical Research.*
CS	*Crusade and Settlement.* Edited by P. W. Edbury, Cardiff, 1985.
CSFS	Collana storica di fonti e studi. General editor G. Pistarino. Genoa, 1969–
DOP	*Dumbarton Oaks Papers.*
DVL	*Diplomatarium Veneto-Levantinum.* Edited by G. M. Thomas and R. Predelli. 2 vols. Venice, 1880–99.
EHR	*English Historical Review.*
EKEE	*Ἐπετερίς τοῦ Κέντρου Ἐπιστημονικῶν Ἐρευνῶν.*
Hill	G. Hill, *A History of Cyprus.* 4 vols. Cambridge, 1940–52.
HC	*A History of the Crusades.* General editor K. M. Setton. 6 vols. Philadelphia and Madison, 1955–89.
MAHEFR	*Mélanges d'archéologie et d'histoire de l'École française de Rome.*
MEFR	*Mélanges de l'École française de Rome.*
Outremer	*Outremer: Studies in the History of the Crusading Kingdom of Jerusalem.* Edited by B. Z. Kedar, H. E. Mayer and R. C. Smail. Jerusalem, 1982.
PAPS	*Proceedings of the American Philosophical Society.*
PBSR	*Papers of the British School at Rome.*
PL	*Patrologiae cursus completus. Series Latina.* Edited by J. P. Migne. 217 vols. Paris, 1844–64.
Potthast	*Regesta pontificum Romanorum inde ab anno post Christo nato 1198 ad annum 1304.* Compiled by A. Potthast. 2 vols. Berlin, 1874–5.

PPTS	Palestine Pilgrims Text Society. 13 vols. London, 1896–1907.
RHC	*Recueil des historiens des croisades.* 16 vols. Paris, 1841–1906.
Arm.	*RHC Documents arméniens.* 2 vols. 1869–1906.
Lois	*RHC Lois. Les assises de Jérusalem.* 2 vols. 1841–3.
Oc.	*RHC Historiens occidentaux.* 5 vols. 1844–95.
RHF	*Recueil des historiens des Gaules et de la France.* Edited by M. Bouquet *et al.* 24 vols. Paris, 1737–1904.
ROL	*Revue de l'Orient latin.*
RRH	*Regesta Regni Hierosolymitani (1097–1291).* Compiled by R. Röhricht. Innsbruck, 1893. *Additamentum.* 1904.
RS	Rerum Brittanicarum Medii Aevi Scriptores (Rolls Series). 251 vols. London, 1858–96.
Setton, *PL*	K. M. Setton, *The Papacy and the Levant (1204–1571).* 4 vols. Philadelphia, 1976–84.
ZDPV	*Zeitschrift des deutschen Palästinavereins.*

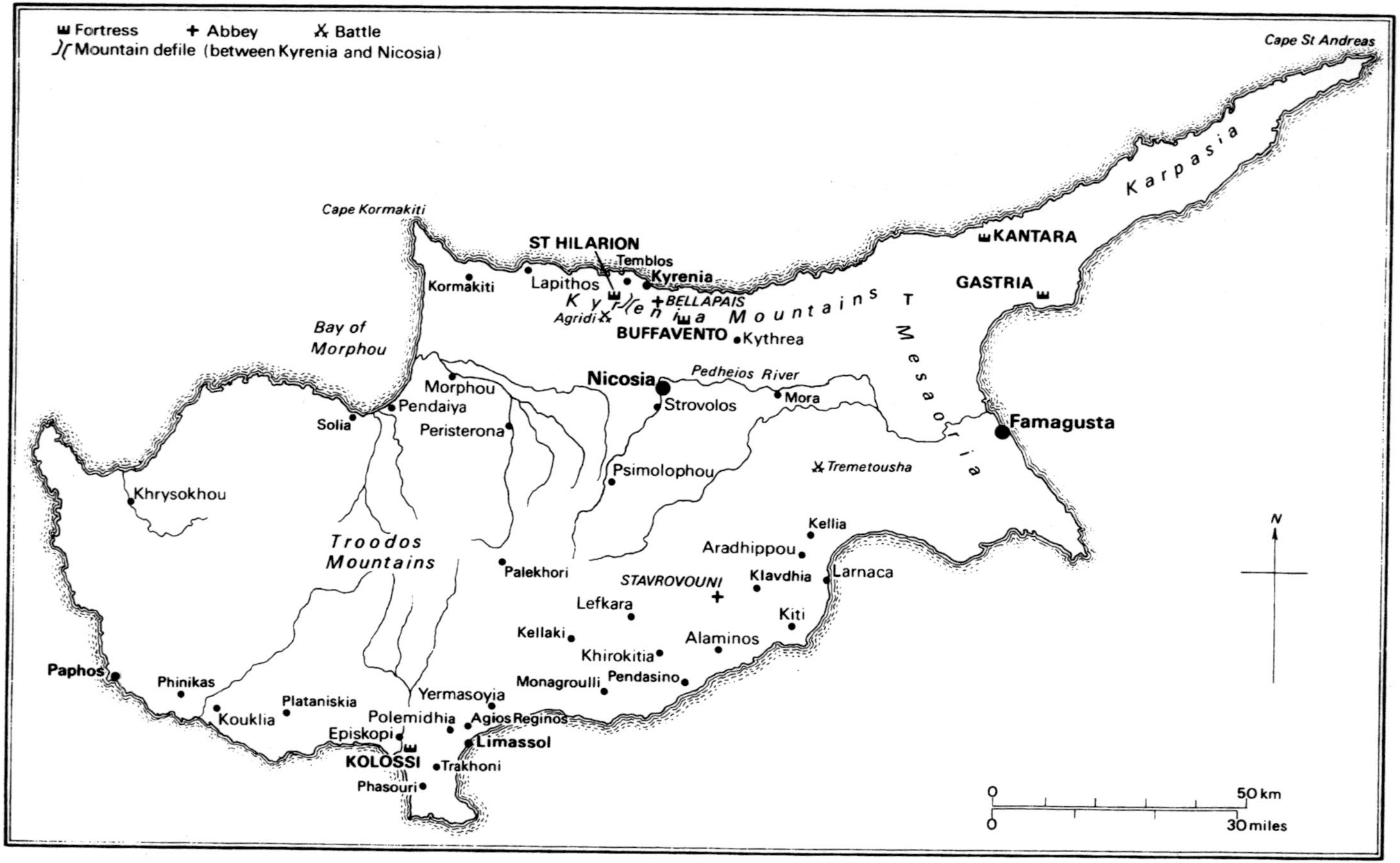
Fortress
Abbey
Battle
Mountain defile (between Kyrenia and Nicosia)
Cape St Andreas
Karpasia
KANTARA
GASTRIA
Cape Kormakiti
ST HILARION
Temblos
Kyrenia
Kormakiti
Lapithos
BELLAPAIS
Kyrenia Mountains
Agridi
BUFFAVENTO
Kythrea
Mesaoria
Bay of Morphou
Nicosia
Pedheios River
Mora
Morphou
Strovolos
Pendaiya
Solia
Peristerona
Famagusta
Psimolophou
Tremetousha
Khrysokhou
Kellia
Troodos Mountains
Aradhippou
Palekhori
STAVROVOUNI
Klavdhia
Larnaca
Lefkara
Kiti
Kellaki
Alaminos
Khirokitia
Paphos
Monagroulli
Pendasino
Phinikas
Yermasoyia
Plataniskia
Kouklia
Polemidhia
Agios Reginos
Episkopi
Limassol
KOLOSSI
Trakhoni
Phasouri
0
50 km
0
30 miles
N

Map 1 Cyprus

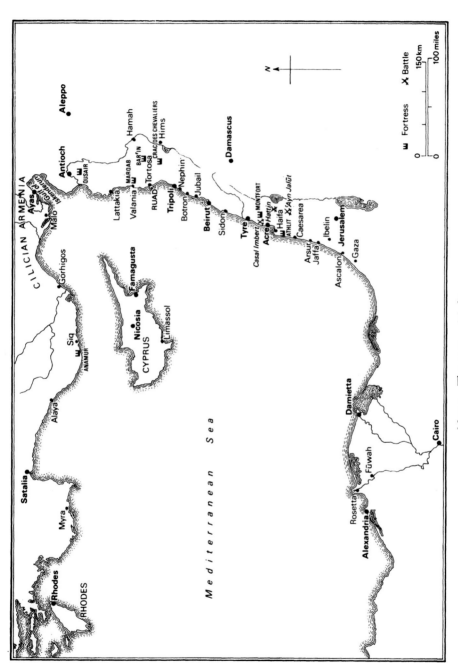

Map 2 The eastern Mediterranean

1

CONQUEST

FOR 380 years, from its conquest by King Richard I of England in May 1191 until the fall of Famagusta to the Turks in August 1571, Cyprus lay within the orbit of western European expansionism. A century before Richard's invasion, at the time of the First Crusade (1095–9), the Franks, or Latins as the occidentals were often known, had burst in spectacular fashion upon the lands around the eastern basin of the Mediterranean. Aflame with enthusiasm to wrest the Holy Places in Jerusalem from Muslim control, their determination reinforced by hope of salvation and lust for adventure, large numbers of knights and pilgrims had marched through Europe and Asia Minor and had conquered significant areas of Syria and the Holy Land. In their wake came settlers and merchants, and with their help the conquerors consolidated their hold on the territories they had occupied. But in 1187 the Muslims won back Jerusalem and most of the other western-held areas. Christian Europe responded with a new crusade, the Third. Among those who came to the East in this fresh expedition was King Richard the Lionheart, and in the course of his campaigns he added Cyprus to the lands under Latin rule.

In important respects Cyprus differed from the territories conquered during and after the First Crusade. The island had been a Byzantine province and so was won not from the Muslims but from Christian Greeks, and Cypriot society, although subject henceforth to western domination, remained largely Greek in culture, language and ritual. The crusaders' seizure of territory peopled by Christians under Christian rule and not under direct Muslim threat marked a new departure, and it was to be repeated on a far larger scale after the capture of Constantinople by the army of the Fourth Crusade in 1204. From 1192 a crusading family of Poitevin origin, the Lusignans, governed Cyprus. Their rule brought prosperity – at least until the economic collapse of the later fourteenth century – and saw the introduction of an array of European institutions and influences.

Although the Lusignan regime owed its origins to the crusaders, it far outlasted the crusading expeditions to the Holy Land. The Christian states in Syria and Palestine survived until 1291, though for most of the thirteenth century the Muslims retained Jerusalem itself. During that time Cyprus became intimately linked to the mainland states by dynastic, military and commercial ties and so came to be involved in the crusades to the East and acquire a strategic role in the confrontation between western Christendom and Islam. Indeed, the early decades of Lusignan rule coincided with the apogee of crusading activity in the eastern Mediterranean. But as the thirteenth century progressed, the likelihood of recovering Jerusalem receded and obstacles to the launching of new crusades multiplied. The loss of Acre and the other Christian possessions in Syria in 1291 marked the end of an epoch. Cyprus was now the sole outpost of western Christendom in the eastern Mediterranean and had to find a way of living at peace with the Muslim rulers of the mainland coasts opposite and at the same time making the most of its commercial prosperity. True, talk of crusades and crusade projects continued well into the fourteenth century and beyond, but little was actually done. In the 1360s King Peter I of Cyprus took the initiative and embarked on a flurry of aggression against the Mamlūk sultanate, which for over a century had been ruling in Egypt, Syria and the Holy Land. His efforts, however, ended with his murder in 1369. Then in 1373–4 the Genoese invaded Cyprus. They seized Famagusta, the principal port, and placed the island under tribute. After that any further significant role for Cyprus in crusading history was out of the question. The island remained under Lusignan control until the 1470s and in 1489 was formally annexed by the Venetians. But by then the days of the crusades to the Holy Land were long past. It is with the years 1191–1374, when Cyprus was directly affected by the crusading movement, that this study is concerned.

To understand the background to Richard's conquest, we must consider both the earlier history of Cyprus and the changing fortunes of the crusader conquests in Syria. Comparatively little is known about the island between the seventh century and the end of the eleventh. Until 965, when the Byzantines took complete control, the Greeks and Arabs had ruled jointly in a condominium. At the time of the First Crusade Cyprus would seem to have been a backward province of little importance in which governors and prelates sent out from Constantinople lorded it over an indigenous population that was predominantly Greek-speaking but retained traces of its earlier contacts with the Arab world.[1] In the twelfth century, however, its fortunes revived, thanks partly to the economic stimulus provided by the creation of the Latin states in Syria and

[1] For the condominium, R. J. H. Jenkins, 'Cyprus between Byzantium and Islam, A. D. 688–965' in G. E. Mylonas (ed.), *Studies Presented to David Moore Robinson* (St Louis, 1951–3), II, 1006–14; P. Lemerle, 'Séance de clôture de la Section médiévale', Πρακτικὰ τοῦ Πρώτου Διεθνοῦς Κυπρολογικοῦ Συνεδρίου, II (Nicosia, 1972), 153–6. For Cyprus in the eleventh and twelfth centuries, C. Mango, 'Chypre carrefour du monde byzantin', *Rapports et co-rapports du XVe congrès international d'études byzantines*, v. *Chypre dans le monde byzantin*, part v (Athens, 1976).

Palestine. The successes of the First Crusade encouraged the Italian maritime republics to trade in the eastern Mediterranean, and Cyprus benefited from its position on the sea-routes from the West. In 1126 the Venetians obtained trading concessions in the island, and there was clearly a western European community resident in Limassol by the time Richard arrived in 1191.[2]

This revival of Cyprus was part of a wider pattern of Byzantine resurgence in the East which lasted until the 1170s. The First Crusade had helped make possible a partial recovery of Greek power in Anatolia, and in the middle years of the twelfth century the emperors John and Manuel Comnenus were able to consolidate their control of the south coast of Asia Minor and assert Byzantine suzerainty over the Latin principality of Antioch. Successive emperors shared the ambition of bringing the conquests of the crusaders within their sphere of influence, and they made use of Cyprus and Cypriot resources to obtain this end. But in the 1170s and 1180s the Byzantine position in the eastern Mediterranean declined radically. The Greek defeat at the hands of the Turks at Myriokephalon in 1176 was symptomatic of a more general malaise and signalled the effective end of Byzantine intervention in the Christian states in Syria and Palestine. The imperial fleet, which for much of the reign of Manuel Comnenus (1143–80) was frequently to be seen in the East, was allowed to decay to the extent that it could no longer even contain piracy in the Aegean. The consequent falling off of Greek influence was further aggravated by the political instability which reappeared in the empire after Manuel's death. Although Cyprus seems to have been prospering, the government in Constantinople now found it no longer had the ability to defend it.[3]

In 1184 Isaac Comnenus, a member of the imperial house, seized power in the island and had himself proclaimed emperor. A great-nephew of the emperor Manuel, Isaac had been governor in Cilicia in the mid-1170s and had then spent some time as a prisoner of the Cilician Armenians, who had taken control when Byzantine authority in the region collapsed. He was released in 1182. What happened next is obscure: according to the Greek historian Nicetas Choniates, he forged letters appointing himself governor of Cyprus, but Nicetas' self-evident hostility casts suspicion on his testimony, and it has been suggested that Isaac was legitimately appointed to the office by the regents for the young

[2] *Urkunden zur älteren Handels- und Staatsgeschichte der Republik Venedig*, ed. G. L. F. Tafel and G. M. Thomas (Vienna, 1856–7), I, 124. For twelfth-century Venetian interests in Cyprus, *Documenti del commercio veneziano nei secoli XI–XIII*, ed. R. Morozzo della Rocca and A. Lombardo (Rome/Turin, 1940), nos. 74, 82. For 1191, 'L'estoire de Eracles empereur', *RHC Oc.*, II, 164.

[3] J. L. La Monte, 'To What Extent was the Byzantine Empire the Suzerain of the Crusading States?', *Byzantion*, VII (1932); H. Ahrweiler, *Byzance et la mer: la marine de guerre, la politique et les institutions maritimes de Byzance aux VIIe–XVe siècles* (Paris, 1966), pp. 234–7, 268–9, 288–92; C. M. Brand, *Byzantium Confronts the West, 1180–1204* (Cambridge, Mass., 1968), chapters 1–4 *passim*.

Alexius II in about 1183 and then rebelled after Andronicus Comnenus' *coup d'état* towards the end of that year. For support Isaac turned to the Sicilians whose invasion of the Byzantine empire in 1185 precipitated Andronicus' overthrow. In 1187 the Sicilian admiral and freebooter, Margaritone, defeated the galleys sent by the new emperor, Isaac II Angelus, to recover Cyprus. For the time being Isaac Comnenus was secure in his possession of the island, but, with the departure of Margaritone's fleet from the East in 1188 and the death of King William II of Sicily the following year, he was bereft of his one ally.[4]

The 1170s and 1180s also witnessed the almost total collapse of the Latin states in the East. In the 1160s the forces of the kingdom of Jerusalem under King Amaury had been able to take the offensive and invade Egypt in the hope of bringing it under Christian control, while further north in Syria, although Edessa had been lost in the 1140s and Muslim pressure had gradually eroded the frontiers of the principality of Antioch and the county of Tripoli, the situation was essentially stable. But Muslim unity and Christian disunity combined to lead to a complete reversal of this state of affairs. In 1174 Saladin, who had been ruling in Egypt since 1169, gained possession of Damascus, and in 1183 he added Aleppo to his rule. He was now master of all the lands surrounding the Christian possessions. Never before had the Latins found themselves confronted by a single Muslim ruler controlling all the territory beyond their own borders, and after Amaury's death in 1174 weak government and divisions among the nobility left the kingdom of Jerusalem without a consistent policy to combat the threat thus posed. In July 1187 Saladin invaded Galilee and, thanks largely to the Christian leaders' mutual distrust and indecision, was able to outmanoeuvre and overwhelm the forces of the Latin kingdom at the battle of Hattin. The king of Jerusalem, Guy of Lusignan, was taken captive together with a number of other prominent figures. The victorious Muslim army then proceeded to occupy almost all the Holy Land including Jerusalem itself without serious opposition. Apart from Tripoli and Antioch, the only major city to remain in Christian hands was Tyre, saved by the timely arrival of an able and well-connected nobleman from northern Italy, Conrad of Montferrat. Guy was released in 1188, but Conrad, who had ambitions of his own, refused to let him enter Tyre. In August 1189, undaunted by this rebuff and aided by men who had remained loyal, Guy began to besiege Acre, an important port which had fallen to the Muslims in 1187 without a blow being struck. Meanwhile Europe, led by the western emperor, Frederick Barbarossa, and by the kings of France and England,

---

[4] For Isaac, W. H. Rudt de Collenberg, 'L'empereur Isaac de Chypre et sa fille (1155–1207)', *Byzantion*, XXXVIII (1968). For Margaritone, B. Lavagnini, 'I Normanni di Sicilia a Cipro e a Patmo (1186)', *Byzantino-Sicula*, II (1974) (= *Miscellanea G. Rossi Taibbi*); E. Vranoussi, 'A propos des opérations des Normandes dans la mer Égée et à Chypre après la prise de Thessalonique (1186–6)', *Byzantina*, VIII (1976); Brand, *Byzantium Confronts the West*, p. 172.

had responded well, if rather slowly, to the appeal for a new crusade to recover the Christian Holy Places and re-establish the kingdom of Jerusalem.

The story of the Third Crusade (1189–92) has been frequently retold. Richard had taken the Cross as early as November 1187, but a series of dynastic quarrels in the period leading up to his accession to the English throne on the death of his father in July 1189 delayed his start.[5] In July 1190 he was ready to depart, and an advance party led by the archbishop of Canterbury duly arrived in Tyre in mid-September. The king was expected to arrive later that same autumn.[6] However, neither Richard nor King Philip Augustus of France, who had set off on crusade at the same time, managed to progress any further than Sicily. Richard, moving by easy stages, reached Messina towards the end of September, and there he found a situation that demanded his intervention. His sister Joanna was the widow of King William II who had died ten months earlier. William had had no children, and the new ruler of Sicily, his illegitimate kinsman Tancred of Lecce, had imprisoned her, withheld her dowry and impounded the legacy William had left to Richard's father, Henry II. By means of a series of high-handed actions Richard was able to exploit the precarious nature of Tancred's regime to force him to release Joanna and offer generous terms by way of compensation for his misdeeds. The affair ended with Tancred securing Richard's support against his rival, the Hohenstaufen emperor Henry VI. But these manoeuvrings took time, and final agreement between the two rulers was not reached until the season was too far advanced for a safe crossing to Palestine. The English and French crusaders therefore spent the winter in Sicily re-equipping their ships. It was not until 10 April 1191 that Richard's forces could resume their journey. Even then the fleet was caught in a storm. On 22 April Richard arrived at Rhodes where he fell ill, and, when on 1 May he set off again, it was only to run into more bad weather.[7]

Richard described what happened next in a letter dated 6 August:

> . . . as we were continuing our pilgrimage journey, we were diverted to Cyprus where we hoped to find the refuge of those of our number who had been

[5] For Richard's preparations, J. Gillingham, *Richard the Lionheart* (London, 1978), pp. 110–42 *passim*.

[6] 'Epistolae Cantuarienses', ed. W. Stubbs in *Chronicles and Memorials of the Reign of Richard I* (RS 38, 1864–5), II, 328.

[7] For Richard in Sicily, Gillingham, *Richard the Lionheart*, pp. 143–63. Also L. Landon, *The Itinerary of King Richard I* (Pipe Roll Society NS 13, 1935), pp. 40–8. For the journey from Sicily, Ambroise, *L'estoire de la guerre sainte*, ed. G. Paris (Paris, 1897), lines 1169–1354; 'Itinerarium Peregrinorum et Gesta Regis Ricardi', ed. W. Stubbs in *Chronicles and Memorials of the Reign of Richard I* (RS 38, 1864–5), I, 176–81; *Gesta Regis Henrici Secundi Benedicti Abbatis*, ed. W. Stubbs (RS 49, 1869), II, 162–3; Richard of Devizes, *Cronicon de Tempore Regis Richardi Primi* ed. J. T. Appleby (London, 1963), p. 35.

shipwrecked. But the tyrant [Isaac Comnenus] . . . hurriedly brought a strongly armed force to bar us from the port. He robbed and despoiled as many as possible of our men who had suffered wreck and imprisoned those dying of hunger. Not unnaturally we were spurred to revenge. We did battle with our enemy and, thanks to divine assistance, obtained a speedy victory. Defeated and fettered, we hold him together with his only daughter. We have subjected to ourselves the whole island of Cyprus with all its strong points . . . [8]

The narrative sources for the crusade, while not always in agreement with one another, enlarge on this summary. It would appear that in the storm that struck the fleet before it reached Rhodes, a few ships were separated and ran on before the gales to Cyprus where three were wrecked. The survivors were imprisoned and maltreated on Isaac's orders, a Frankish-Syrian writer preserving a seemingly fictitious account of how his intention to kill them was foiled by the self-sacrifice of a Norman mercenary in his service.[9] Next to arrive at Cyprus was a ship bearing Richard's sister, Joanna, and his bride-to-be, Berengaria of Navarre. It anchored off Limassol, and there Isaac gave further evidence of his ill-will by trying to entice the women ashore.[10] Perhaps his intention was to hold them as hostages against the eventuality of Richard attacking the island. On the evening of 5 May Richard, with the main part of his storm-tossed fleet, rejoined Joanna and Berengaria. On learning of Isaac's depredations, he resolved to take reprisals, and on the following day he landed near Limassol.

We have conflicting reports about the course of events during the next few weeks, but the following reconstruction provides an idea of the likely sequence. Isaac made some attempt to oppose the landing, but his forces were brushed aside and Richard entered Limassol. The king then defeated the Cypriots in a skirmish nearby – one source identifying the location as Kolossi – and Isaac withdrew.[11] Richard returned to Limassol where on 12 May his marriage to Berengaria was solemnized. At this point Isaac came to offer terms on the basis that he himself would serve with Richard in Palestine. Richard, whose presence at the siege of Acre was urgently awaited, seems to have been prepared to accept such an agreement, but evidently Isaac was not in earnest or had second thoughts, because no sooner had the settlement been reached than he fled.[12] It appears to have been this incident which led Richard to embark on the total

[8] 'Epistolae Cantuarienses' p. 347.
[9] 'Itinerarium', pp. 183–6; Gesta Regis, II, 162–3; La continuation de Guillaume de Tyr (1184–1197), ed. M. R. Morgan (Paris, 1982), pp. 115, 117 (for the Norman).
[10] 'Itinerarium', pp. 182, 186–8; Cont. Guillaume de Tyr, pp. 113, 115.
[11] Ambroise, lines 1449–1700; 'Itinerarium', pp. 189–94; Gesta Regis, II, 163–4; Cont. Guillaume de Tyr, pp. 117, 119; 'Eracles', pp. 163–4; Chronica Monasterii de Melsa, ed. E. A. Bond (RS 43, 1866–8), I, 257–8.
[12] Ambroise, lines 1735–1850; 'Itinerarium', pp. 196–9; Gesta Regis, II, 164–7; 'Eracles', pp. 164–7; Melsa, I, 258. 'Eracles' and the Gesta Regis place Richard's marriage after the abortive negotiations with Isaac. For a further reason for Isaac's continued resistance, see below, p. 27.

subjugation of the island. He had his fleet sail round the coast to K¡ Famagusta – again the sources differ – and he then moved inland towards Nicosia.[13] At the village of Tremetousha Isaac's forces were again defeated. Resistance was at an end. Richard occupied Nicosia and Kyrenia where he captured Isaac's daughter. At the end of May Isaac, who is variously said to have taken refuge in the castles of Buffavento or Kantara or at Cape St Andreas, surrendered. The island was now entirely in Richard's hands, the sources, for once in almost total agreement, recording the curious detail that Isaac was held in chains made of silver because Richard had promised not to put him in irons.[14]

Exactly a month after his arrival, on 5 June, Richard left Cyprus for Palestine. Less than six weeks later the Muslim garrison in Acre, which had withstood siege for almost two years, capitulated. The Christian forces were now able to extend their control to other areas of the Holy Land, but Saladin was far from beaten. Eventually in September 1192 a truce to last three years and eight months was agreed. By its terms the Christians were to hold the coastal strip from Tyre in the north to Jaffa in the south but not Jerusalem or the other inland areas. Richard had taken a leading part in the campaigns of 1191 and 1192. His departure for Europe in October 1192 marked the end of the crusade.

The sixteen months during which Richard was active in the Holy Land were crucial for Cyprus. Once his conquest was complete, he left the island in the custody of two of his men, Richard of Camville and Robert of Thornham, and appointed castellans. However, the precise nature of his dispositions is unclear. One writer asserted that Richard established a Greek as the titular ruler and associated Robert of Thornham with him to look after the royal interests and subject Cyprus to this new puppet government. But although Robert of Thornham was able to quell a rebellion led by a monk said to be one of Isaac's relatives, the king's arrangements proved short-lived.[15] Within a few weeks of his departure and before the fall of Acre, Richard sold his rights in the island to the Templars. A period of Templar domination then ensued, lasting until April 1192. It was rapacious and unpopular, and the Order sent insufficient troops to keep the populace under control. On 4 April, the day before Easter Sunday, the

---

[13] Ambroise, lines 1851–1878; 'Itinerarium', pp. 199–200 (Famagusta); *Gesta Regis*, II, 166; 'Eracles', p. 167 (Kiti).

[14] Ambroise, lines 1908–2092; 'Itinerarium', pp. 200–4 (Isaac took refuge at Kantara); *Gesta Regis*, II, 167 (Isaac at Cape St Andreas); *Cont. Guillaume de Tyr*, pp. 119, 121; 'Eracles', pp. 168–9 (Isaac captured at Buffavento); *Melsa*, I, 258–9 (Isaac took refuge at Buffavento, then fled to St Andreas). For further discussion, Hill, I, 317–20.

[15] *Gesta Regis*, II, 167, 172–3; cf. *Melsa*, I, 258–60. The Melsa Chronicle (from Meaux Abbey Yorkshire) is a fourteenth-century compilation which had generally been ignored by historians of Richard's crusades. Robert of Thornham's family, however, were associated with the abbey, and so the chronicler may have had access to a reliable tradition. See the editor's preface, I, pp. xxviii–xxxi. Richard of Camville soon died. *Gesta Regis*, II, 172.

Cypriots in Nicosia attempted to rise and massacre the garrison. The small force of Templars in the town made a sally and cut down a substantial number of the insurgents. Although this incident might have appeared as a victory, the master evidently decided that Cyprus was more than the resources at his Order's disposal could manage and surrendered the island to Richard. Richard promptly sold it again, this time to Guy of Lusignan, on terms similar to those by which the Templars had held it.[16]

The sale of Cyprus to Guy of Lusignan marked the beginning of the Latin regime which was to continue for three centuries. The creation of such a regime, however, had formed no part of Richard's programme. The king was concerned only with the immediate demands of the crusade, not with the long-term future of the island. Almost certainly his initial intention in forcing a landing at Limassol was revenge – reprisals for Isaac's treatment of the shipwrecked crusaders and his attempt to capture Joanna and Berengaria. Some chronicles, by way of providing futher justification for the invasion, alleged that Isaac's hatred of the Latins extended to an alliance with Saladin.[17] This claim was probably baseless, but even if it had been believed at the time it would probably have made no difference to Richard's course of action. However, once he had landed in Cyprus, Richard must have recognized the island's potential as a supply-base. Large quantities of money and provisions were essential for a successful campaign, and, although he had gone to considerable trouble to raise enough funds before he set out, the long delay in Sicily would have used up a sizeable proportion of his resources. In his negotiations with Richard Isaac Comnenus offered cash, supplies and men. The king had already gained much booty and was later to seize Isaac's treasury at Kyrenia. The narratives agree that when he left Cyprus he took with him an immense quantity of plundered valuables.[18]

Richard's policy, however, was not to destroy the existing institutions, but to exploit them; until the breakdown of the negotiations he had been prepared to

---

[16] Cont. Guillaume de Tyr, pp. 135, 137, 139; 'Eracles', pp. 189–91 (indicating that the sale to the Templars took place before the fall of Acre, 12 July 1191); Chronique d'Ernoul et de Bernard le Trésorier, ed. L. de Mas Latrie (Paris, 1871), pp. 285–6 (establishing the date of the rebellion); Ambroise, lines 9103–9126; 'Itinerarium', p. 351.

[17] Ambroise, lines 1389–1394; 'Itinerarium', p. 183. For a discussion of the possibility that Richard's invasion may have been premeditated, J. A. Brundage, 'Richard the Lion-Heart and Byzantium', Studies in Medieval Culture, VI/VII (1976). Cf. J. O. Prestwich, 'Richard Coeur de Lion: Rex Bellicosus' in Riccardo Cuor di Leone nella storia e nella leggenda (Accademia Nazionale dei Lincei, quaderno 253, 1981), pp. 8–9.

[18] Ambroise, lines 1667–1700, 1777–1782, 2065–2092; 'Itinerarium', pp. 193–4, 198, 202, 203–4; Gesta Regis, II, 164, 166; Cont. Guillaume de Tyr, p. 119; 'Eracles', pp. 166, 169; Arnold of Lübeck, 'Chronica', MGHS, XXI, 178; 'Imād al-Dīn al-Iṣfahānī, Conquête de la Syrie et de la Palestine par Saladin, trans. H. Massé (Paris, 1972), p. 292; Neophytus, Περὶ τῶν κατὰ χώραν Κύπρου σκαιῶν, ed. W. Stubbs in Chronicles and Memorials of the Reign of Richard I (RS 38, 1864–5), I, p. clxxxvii.

leave Isaac in control; on his departure he may have attempted to establish a Greek government under English tutelage; Roger of Howden reported that he granted a charter confirming the laws as they had been in the days of the emperor Manuel Comnenus in exchange for a levy of a half of all the possessions owned by Cypriots.[19] Initially Richard's officers in Cyprus were to forward provisions from the island to the English crusaders in Palestine, but the king very soon changed his policy and, treating Cyprus as a marketable asset, sold it to the Templars for 100,000 Saracen bezants; 40,000 were handed over at once, the balance was to be paid out of the revenues from the Order's new acquisition.[20] When in April 1192 the Templars surrendered Cyprus, it seems that Richard was able to profit from his conquest yet again. According to the most authoritative account, Richard refused to refund the Templars' original payment and, in selling the island to Guy of Lusignan, received a further 60,000 bezants. Guy, however, never paid the additional 40,000 bezants he still owed.[21] Even so, Richard had done well out of Cyprus: the island must have borne a significant proportion of the costs of his warfare in Palestine.

Richard had taken less than a month to defeat Isaac. There can be no question that tactically the English forces were superior. Isaac would have had the advantage of familiarity with the terrain, but he evidently possessed no fortified positions which were garrisoned and provisioned to withstand a siege: the possibility of his waging a defensive campaign in the hope that Richard would give up and go on to Palestine did not arise. It is also clear that Isaac did not enjoy the full support of his subjects: possibly the Armenian troops in his service were a source of friction;[22] the contemporary Greek recluse, Neophytus, roundly condemned him as a tyrant;[23] an English account noted that after his capture Isaac did not even suggest the possibility that he might be ransomed,[24] and it is doubtless significant that at an early stage in the invasion a group of Greek notables made their own peace with King Richard. Apparently the noble families from Constantinople who, it has been suggested, formed the ascendant element in Cypriot society failed to give Isaac the aid necessary to resist the catastrophe that confronted them.[25]

[19] *Gesta Regis*, II, 168.

[20] Ambroise, lines 2101–7; 'Itinerarium', pp. 204, 212; 'Eracles', pp. 189–90.

[21] *Cont. Guillaume de Tyr*, pp. 137, 139. 'Eracles' (p. 191) seems to indicate that Guy gave the Templars 40,000 bezants to compensate for their payment to Richard, but *Ernoul* (p. 286) confirms that Guy bought the island from Richard. For the superiority of the *Continuation* over 'Eracles', M. R. Morgan, *The Chronicle of Ernoul and the Continuations of William of Tyre* (Oxford, 1973). Note, however, that the latter part of the account of Richard's conquest of Cyprus in 'Eracles' (pp. 163–70) is fuller than in the text of the *Continuation* (pp. 119, 121) and contains a number of details which it lacks.

[22] Ambroise, lines 1552, 1650, 1691; *Gesta Regis*, II, 164, 166, 172.

[23] Neophytus, p. clxxxvii.   [24] *Melsa*, I, 259; Neophytus, pp. clxxxv, clxxxvii.

[25] *Gesta Regis*, II, 164–5. See Mango, 'Chypre', pp. 7–9.

The conquest proved durable. After the rising against the Templars in April 1192 no more is heard of Greek insurgents for nearly two centuries. It was not until 1570–1 that another foreign army conquered the whole island, although Cyprus suffered badly at the hands of the Genoese in the 1370s and the Mamlūks in the 1420s. However, Richard's victory left a series of claimants in its wake. King Philip of France asserted his right to a half-share in the island on the grounds that he and Richard had agreed to divide between them whatever conquests they might make during the crusade. This contention was firmly rejected.[26] Isaac's family too were to assert their claim. Isaac himself seems to have made no attempt to recover Cyprus; he was held in prison in the Hospitaller castle of Marqab in northern Syria until his release in 1193 or 1194 and died about 1195, supposedly by poison while trying to incite the sultan of Konya against Byzantium. His daughter was taken to Europe by Joanna and Berengaria, and she eventually married Thierry, an illegitimate son of Count Philip of Flanders. A decade after Richard's conquest of Cyprus, Thierry joined the Fourth Crusade and then attached himself to one of the groups which left the main army to travel to Syria. In 1203 he arrived in Cyprus on his way east. He came before the then ruler, Aimery of Lusignan, and demanded the island by right of his wife. He was curtly told to leave.[27] Another claimant who apparently derived his rights from Isaac was Duke Leopold VI of Austria. During the Third Crusade Leopold's father, Leopold V, had quarrelled with King Richard and had then made the king his prisoner when he returned to the West late in 1192. Leopold V was Isaac's second cousin, and Richard's treatment of Isaac was among the charges he levelled against him. We only learn of Leopold VI's claim, which he must have made during his participation in the Fifth Crusade in 1217–19, from a remark later attributed to John of Ibelin, lord of Beirut. John is said to have reminded the young King Henry I of Cyprus that he and his family had thwarted the duke's attempt to disinherit him while Henry was a minor.[28]

Not unnaturally the authorities in Constantinople wanted to recover Cyprus. Isaac II Angelus (1185–95) had already dispatched a fleet for this purpose in 1187, but it was defeated by Isaac Comnenus' ally Margaritone. A Byzantine embassy destined for Cyprus in 1192 came to a premature end when the ship

[26] *Gesta Regis*, II, 171, 183. Cf. *Die Register Innocenz' III*, ed. O. Hagender and A. Haidacher (Graz/Cologne, 1964–), I, 327–8.

[27] For Isaac's death and his daughter's marriage, Rudt de Collenberg, 'L'empereur Isaac', pp. 154–5, 169–72. For Thierry and Aimery, 'Eracles', pp. 256–7.

[28] For Richard's quarrel and imprisonment, Gillingham, *Richard the Lionheart*, pp. 176–8, 221–5. For Leopold and Isaac, Rudt de Collenberg, 'L'empereur Isaac', pp. 128–9 and table facing p. 128. More generally, H. Fichtenau, 'Akkon, Zypern und das Lösengeld für Richard Löwenherz', *Archiv für österreichische Geschichte*, CXXV (1966). For Leopold VI, 'Les Gestes de Chiprois', *RHC Arm.*, II, 702. For a possible allusion to his claim in a papal letter of July 1218, L. de Mas Latrie, *Histoire de l'île de Chypre sous le règne des princes de la maison de Lusignan* (Paris, 1852–61), III, 610–11.

bearing the ambassadors was captured by pirates in the Aegean, and in the same year Saladin turned down a suggestion that he and the Byzantines should mount a joint expedition against the island.[29] The Latin rulers nevertheless continued to fear a Byzantine attack. It was later claimed that it was this menace that determined Aimery of Lusignan in 1195 to seek the alliance of the western emperor, Henry VI, and make Cyprus a kingdom under his suzerainty, and early in 1199 Aimery's ambassadors at the papal court were voicing fears of a Byzantine *revanche*.[30] In 1203 the emperor Alexius III (1195–1203) turned to Pope Innocent III and tried to induce him to use the threat of excommunication to force Aimery to hand back the island, but Innocent refused to co-operate.[31] The Fourth Crusade, with its destruction of the enfeebled empire, put an end to the possibility of a Byzantine invasion. However, immediately after the Greek recapture of Constantinople in 1261 Pope Urban IV warned the government in Cyprus that the Byzantines, in conjunction with the Genoese, were planning an attack and were anticipating that the Greek population in the island would join in throwing off the Latin yoke. The pope's fears proved unfounded.[32]

To Richard Cyprus had been his by right of conquest to dispose of as he pleased.[33] Although subsequent English kings never made any serious attempt to assert their suzerainty over the island, the idea that the English had residual rights there was to reappear from time to time in historical literature. Roger of Howden declared that Richard gave Cyprus to Guy to be held for life, thereby perhaps implying that it was to revert after his death, and this idea was taken up and embroidered by the thirteenth-century author of the text known as *The Crusade and Death of Richard I*. Early in the fourteenth century, the chronicler Walter of Guisborough noted that when the Lord Edward was in the East in 1271 the Cypriot nobility told him that 'they were bound by his orders because his predecessors had formerly ruled their land and they themselves ought always to be the faithful men (*fideles*) of the kings of England'. Another fourteenth-century writer, the compiler of the Meaux Chronicle, believed that since the conquest Cyprus had been held as a dependency of the English crown and that the Cypriot kings had done homage to the kings of England until his own time. According to a French source, the *Chronique des quatres premiers Valois*, King Edward III told Peter I of Cyprus when they met in 1363 that if Peter succeeded in

[29] C. M. Brand, 'The Byzantines and Saladin, 1185–1192: Opponents of the Third Crusade', *Speculum*, XXXVII (1962), 170, 177–8; *idem, Byzantium Confronts the West*, pp. 172, 211–12.
[30] 'Eracles', p. 209 (1195); *Die Register Innocenz' III*, II, 461–2. For Aimery and Henry VI see below, p. 31.
[31] Innocent III, 'Opera Omnia', PL, vol. 214, cols. cxxiii–cxxv. The papal letter recording this episode is undated but belongs to the fourth year of Innocent's pontificate, i.e. 1203. *Vetera Monumenta Slavorum Meridionalium Historiam Illustrantia*, ed. A. Theiner (Rome/Zagreb, 1863–75), I, 56 no. 15.   [32] Mas Latrie, *Histoire*, III, 653–5.
[33] For crusaders' right of conquest, J. Riley-Smith, *The Feudal Nobility and the Kingdom of Jerusalem, 1174–1277* (London, 1973), pp. 113, 117–20.

recovering Jerusalem, Cyprus should be returned to the English. In the fifteenth century the idea that Richard the Lionheart acquired the crown of Jerusalem for himself when he gave Guy Cyprus began to make its appearance, and this idea, together with the belief that the island ought properly to belong to the English, was widely held in the sixteenth.[34] In reality Richard had had no designs on the crown of Jerusalem. The only Latin ruler of Cyprus ever to perform homage to a king of England was Guy of Lusignan; but Guy's homage was a purely personal act which in any case took place some months before the possibility arose that he might receive the island.[35] Any rights over Cyprus Richard may have possessed after 1192 would have passed by default. Even so, these stories show that later generations in western Europe kept alive the memory that Cyprus had once been an English conquest.

[34] Roger of Howden, *Chronica*, ed. W. Stubbs (RS 51, 1868–71), III, 181; *The Crusade and Death of Richard I*, ed. R. C. Johnston (Oxford, 1961), p. 38; Walter of Guisborough, *Cronica*, ed. H. Rothwell (Camden Soc. 3rd Series 89, 1957), p. 208; *Melsa*, I, 259; *Chronique des quatre premiers Valois (1327–93)*, ed. S. Luce (Paris, 1862), p. 128. Cf. Hill, II, 68. The idea that Richard acquired the crown of Jerusalem when he gave Guy Cyprus was repeated by Felix Fabri (*The Book of the Wanderings*, trans. A. Stewart (PPTS 7–10, 1892–3), III, 348–9) in the 1480s.

[35] *Gesta Regis*, II, 165.

2

SETTLEMENT

PHYSICALLY CYPRUS can have changed hardly at all since Guy of Lusignan acquired the island in the spring of 1192. At its centre, with foothills reaching down towards the southern and western coasts, rise the Troodos mountains, their highest point standing over 6,000 feet above sea-level. Along the north coast and extending into the Karpasia peninsula, that finger of land which points north-east towards the Gulf of Iskenderun, runs another line of mountains, the Kyrenia range. Between these two mountainous regions and occupying much of the rest of the island's 3,500 square miles, lies a plain, the eastern portion of which is known as the Mesaoria. Strategically the Kyrenia range has always been of greater importance than the Troodos. Admittedly it is lower – the highest peaks barely reach above 3,500 feet – but its escarpment is more pronounced, and it separates the capital, Nicosia, from the nearest point on the coast, the port and fortress of Kyrenia, sixteen miles to the north. By the time of the Latin conquest three of the summits of the Kyrenia mountains were capped by castles, from east to west: Kantara, Buffavento and St Hilarion. St Hilarion guarded the pass between Nicosia and Kyrenia, which, as the the location of Isaac Comnenus' treasury, was probably the best fortified place in the island at that time. For any ruler or conqueror, control of Nicosia, Kyrenia and St Hilarion was critical, as the civil wars of 1229–33 and 1458–64 and the Genoese invasion of 1373–4 were to demonstrate.

Cyprus lacks navigable rivers. Nicosia, which seems to have been regarded as the chief town in the island since at least as early as the end of the eleventh century,[1] cannot be reached by water and the river on which it stands, the Pedheios, does not flow continuously throughout the year. There was nevertheless a danger from flooding, as in 1330 when the Pedheios in full spate destroyed much property in Nicosia and was said to have claimed 3,000 lives.[2] More serious was the danger from earthquakes. Southern Cyprus lies along a line of major seismological activity, and from our period tremors are recorded in 1204,

---

[1] Mango, 'Chypre', p. 11.
[2] 'Chronique d'Amadi, in *Chroniques d'Amadi et de Strambaldi*, ed. R. de Mas Latrie (Paris, 1891–3), I, 404–5. For other references, Hill, II, 306.

1222, 1267 and 1303. There can be little doubt that the worst was that of 1222. Oliver of Paderborn, who also mentioned damage at Limassol and Nicosia, stated that at Paphos the city was completely destroyed together with the fortress and the harbour.[3] So great was the impression left by this calamity that Matthew Paris, writing about thirty years later at St Albans, could single out the destruction of Paphos and Limassol at that time as a divine warning presaging the loss of Jerusalem to the Khwarazmians in 1244.[4]

Contemporaries were agreed on the wealth and fertility of Cyprus at the time of the conquest. For Gislebert of Mons, the island was 'a land rich in all things'; for his near-contemporary, Wilbrand of Oldenburg, who visited the island in 1212, Cyprus was 'a most fertile island, having the very best wines'. Locusts, a persistent scourge in later centuries, are not recorded before 1351.[5] The overwhelming majority of the island's population was engaged in agriculture or viticulture – most of the vineyards being situated, then as now, on the southern slopes of the Troodos. Evidence is lacking for the exploitation of the deposits of metallic ores during the first two centuries of Lusignan rule, but the salt pans near Larnaca and at Limassol were a royal monopoly and certainly attained considerable importance.[6]

There can be no question that when Guy purchased the island, the bulk of the population lived in the countryside. The impression of Cyprus in the twelfth century is of a rural society with few urban centres, none of which was walled. Towns developed under the Latins, but even in the sixteenth century, when statistical data first becomes available, it would seem that less than a fifth of the total population dwelt in them.[7] We have no adequate means of calculating the size of the population on the eve of the conquest. A figure of 60–75,000 has been suggested for the eighth and ninth centuries, and the sixteenth-century evidence points to a rapid growth between 1500 and 1570 from around 120,000 to rather

[3] Oliver of Paderborn, 'Historia Damiatina' in *Die Schriften des Kölner Domscholasters, späteren Bischofs von Paderborn und Kardinal Bischofs von S. Sabina, Oliverus*, ed. H. Hoogeweg (Tübingen, 1894), p. 279; al-Maqrīzī, *A History of the Ayyūbid Sultans of Egypt*, trans. R. J. C. Broadhurst (Boston, 1980), p. 146; Hill, II, 87, 159, 216, cf I, 244–6, 311, III, 819–20. For striking evidence confirming the destruction of the fortress at Paphos at the time of the 1222 earthquake, A. H. S. Megaw, 'Saranda Kolones: A Medieval Castle Excavated at Paphos' in Πρακτικὰ τοῦ Πρώτου Διεθνοῦς Κυπρολογικοῦ Συνεδρίου, II (Nicosia, 1972).

[4] Matthew Paris, *Chronica Majora*, ed. H. R. Luard (RS 57, 1872–83), IV, 346.

[5] Gislebert of Mons, 'Ex Gisleberti Montensis Praepositi Hannoniae Chronico', *RHF*, XVIII, 403; Wilbrand of Oldenburg, 'Itinerarium Terrae Sanctae', ed. S. de Sandoli, *Itinera Hierosolymitana Crucesignatorum* (Jerusalem, 1978–84), III, 226–33. For locusts, R. C. Jennings, 'The Origins of the Locust Problem in Cyprus', *Byzantion*, LXVII (1987), 315–17; B. Arbel, 'Sauterelles et mentalités: le cas de la Chypre vénitienne', *Annales ESC*, (1989), 1060, 1072–3.

[6] J. Richard, 'La révolution de 1369 dans le royaume de Chypre', *BEC*, CX (1952), 113.

[7] Mango, 'Chypre', pp. 11–12; B. Arbel, 'Cypriot Population under Venetian Rule (1473–1571): A Demographic Study', Μελέται καὶ Ὑπομνήματα, I (1984), 203.

less than 200,000.[8] In common with the rest of Europe and the Near East, the upward trend in population between the ninth and sixteenth centuries was put into reverse by the Black Death of 1348 and subsequent epidemics in the fourteenth and fifteenth centuries, and it is likely that the pre-plague total was not matched again until the eve of the Ottoman conquest and quite likely not even then.[9] For 1191 an estimated population something in excess of 100,000 may therefore not be too far wide of the mark.

Communication with the outside world was liable to be slow and irregular. As a tenth-century Arab geographer, Muqaddasi, noted, it would take twenty-four hours to cross from Syria to Cyprus. However, at the beginning of the twelfth century bad weather meant that the pilgrim, Saewulf, took seven days to cross to Palestine, and in the thirteenth Louis IX of France took four days to sail from Limassol to the Egyptian port of Damietta, having already delayed embarkation for two days because of contrary winds.[10] The time taken to travel to or from the West could vary far more. In summer the journey might take as little as three to four weeks: thus in 1191 King Richard took twenty-seven days, including a delay of thirteen days at Rhodes, to come from Messina to Limassol; Frederick II in 1228 took twenty-four days to sail from Brindisi to Limassol, and in 1248 Louis IX took the same number of days to come from Aigues Mortes.[11] Winter conditions might make the journey far longer: on 16 October 1309 the papal nuncio, Raymond of Piis, set out for Cyprus from Marseilles; after seventy-eight days of buffeting by the weather he arrived at Rhodes on 3 January 1310; there he fell ill and was unable to continue his journey for about two months, eventually arriving in Famagusta on 7 March.[12] But at least he did arrive: in December 1308 a ship taking an embassy from Cyprus to the papal curia had been wrecked on Cos.[13]

Although communications might be impeded, the fact that Cyprus was an island proved a major advantage to its inhabitants. The sea formed a natural defence and preserved the islanders from the ravages of war. The only recorded attacks by Muslim shipping before the fifteenth century occurred in 1271 when a

---

[8] Mango, 'Chypre', pp. 5–6; Arbel, 'Cypriot Population', pp. 188–90, 211–14 et passim.

[9] For the Black Death, Leontios Makhairas, Recital Concerning the Sweet Land of Cyprus entitled 'Chronicle', ed. R. M. Dawkins (Oxford, 1932), I, §66; 'Amadi', p. 407. Cf. Lacrimae Nicosienses, ed. T. J. Chamberlayne (Paris, 1894), pp. 52–4, 79, 149; J. Darrouzès, 'Un obituaire chypriote: le Parisinus graecus 1588', Κυπριακαὶ Σπουδαί, XI (1951), 55 et passim. For subsequent plagues, Hill, II, 323, 411, 464–5.

[10] Muqaddasi, Description of Syria including Palestine, trans. G. Le Strange (PPTS 3, 1886), p. 82; Saewulf, 'Relatio de peregrinatione ad Hierosolymam et Terram Sanctam', ed. S. de Sandoli, Itinera Hierosolymitana Crucesignatorum, II, 8, 10; John of Joinville, Histoire de Saint Louis, ed. N. de Wailly (Paris, 1868), pp. 52–3. [11] Landon, Itinerary, p. 48; Hill, II, 94, 140.

[12] C. Perrat, 'Un diplomate gascon au XIVe siècle: Raymond de Piis, nonce de Clèment V en Orient', MAHEFR, XLIV (1927), 65–6. [13] 'Amadi', p. 267.

Mamlūk fleet was wrecked on the coast near Limassol before it could do any damage, and in 1363 when Turkish raids prompted the Cypriots to take firm retaliatory action.[14] On the other hand, the coasts were exposed to corsairs such as the Greek, who in the 1190s carried off Aimery of Lusignan's wife and children, or those, said to be from Rhodes and Monemvasia, who in 1302 captured the count of Jaffa and members of his family while they were staying on his estate at Episkopi.[15] But apart from incidents such as these and rather more serious Genoese depredations in the 1310s,[16] Cyprus enjoyed a remarkable record of immunity from attack. After the initial conquest and pacification of 1191–2, the only serious fighting in the island before the Genoese invasion in 1373 took place during the civil war of 1229–33.

For our knowledge of the Latin settlement of Cyprus as begun during the rule of Guy of Lusignan, we have largely to rely on various thirteenth-century traditions. None of these accounts is entirely trustworthy, but they do tell us what people were prepared to believe a generation or so after the settlement, or at least what the writers themselves wanted people to believe. The fullest and probably the best informed is worth quoting at length:

> After King Guy had paid the 60,000 bezants to the king of England, he went to Cyprus and took some of the knights who had been disinherited in the kingdom (of Jerusalem). As soon as he had taken seisin of the island, he sent messengers to Saladin asking his advice as to how he could continue to rule the island of Cyprus. Saladin replied that he had no great love for King Guy, but since he had asked his advice, he would give it as best he knew how ... and so he said to the messengers, 'I counsel King Guy that if he wants the island to be secure he should give it all away'. At this the messengers departed and came to Cyprus and gave this reply to the king who followed Saladin's advice closely.
>
> Now I shall tell you what King Guy did when he had taken seisin of the island of Cyprus. He sent messengers to Armenia, to Antioch, to Acre and through all the land saying that he would give generously to all those who wished to come and dwell in Cyprus so that they might live. The knights, sergeants and burgesses whom the Muslims had dispossessed heard the word of King Guy. They set off and came to him, and also young women and orphans in great numbers whose husbands and fathers were dead and lost in Syria. He gave rich fiefs, both to the Greeks and the knights he had brought with him and to shoemakers, masons and Arabic scribes so that (may God be merciful!) they have become knights and great lords in the island of Cyprus. And he had them marry the women on their arrival as appropriate to their station ... and he granted enough land away to those who would take it that he enfeoffed 300 knights and 200 mounted sergeants, not to mention the burgesses who lived in the cities to whom he gave substantial lands

[14] For 1271, Hill, II, 167. For 1363, Leontios Makhairas, §137–44, 150–2. For Muslim destruction of Christian shipping in Limassol in 1220, Hill, II, 87.
[15] Cont. Guillaume de Tyr, pp. 162–5; 'Amadi', p. 238.   [16] 'Amadi', pp. 393–5, 398.

and allowances. And when he had finished this distribution, he had not kept enough for himself to support twenty knights.[17]

It is probable that the author of this passage was a squire of Balian of Ibelin, one of Guy of Lusignan's leading opponents among the baronage in the kingdom of Jerusalem. Elsewhere in his history he had shown himself consistently hostile to Guy, and this hostility is also apparent here. The writer was an early exponent of the tradition in Christian circles that depicted Saladin as a man of high personal integrity, and in this passage, by giving Saladin the credit for suggesting Guy's policy, he was praising him at Guy's expense. The assertion that Guy surrounded himself with artisans whom he had ennobled was a more explicit example of his denigration of Guy, and he registered his horror at this affront to aristocratic exclusiveness by his pious ejaculation.[18] But neither the turning of Greeks and base-born men into great lords nor Saladin's advice can be substantiated from independent evidence, and these elements in the story may perhaps be discarded as no more than further instances of the author's partisanship.[19]

Left by itself, however, the passage does provide a grudging recognition that the settlement of Cyprus had been a success and that Guy had acted wisely in recruiting as many settlers as possible. The experience of the Templars during their brief period of rule had shown that a small garrison was not sufficient to control the population: what was needed, if Cyprus was to be held permanently, was a large number of men with a vested interest in preserving the new regime. But the numbers quoted – 300 knights and 200 mounted sergeants – may well be exaggerated. Before 1187 the entire feudal host at the disposal of the kings of Jerusalem apparently amounted to no more than 675 knights,[20] and so, despite the permanent loss of large areas of land in Syria and Palestine, it seems unlikely that Guy would be able to find dispossessed men in such numbers to go with him to Cyprus. The implausibility of these figures is underlined when considered in the light of another tradition concerning the settlement. This recorded that the knights received fiefs worth 400 white bezants annually and turcopoles (a term evidently used here as an alternative for 'mounted sergeants'), 300.[21] Assuming that these statistics were well-founded, it would seem that the Cypriot fiefs were

---

[17] *Cont. Guillaume de Tyr*, p. 139.

[18] Morgan, *Chronicle of Ernoul*, pp. 41–4 (for Ernoul, the putative author, although the attempt to identify him with Arneis of Jubail is unconvincing), pp. 102–6 (for Saladin), pp. 163–5 (for this passage, but with a differing interpretation).

[19] A contemporary Arabic source confirms that Guy was in friendly contact with Saladin immediately after his acquisition of Cyprus. M. C. Lyons and D. E. P. Jackson, *Saladin. The Politics of the Holy War* (Cambridge, 1982), p. 349.

[20] R. C. Smail, *Crusading Warfare (1097–1193)* (Cambridge, 1956), pp. 89–90.

[21] 'Eracles', p. 192.

worth appreciably less than their Syrian counterparts. If so, then Cyprus would have had little attraction for men who reckoned that they had some chance of a livelihood in Syria.[22] But however unsatisfactory particular statements in these accounts may seem, the outline is clear enough: there was no attempt to colonize Cyprus before Guy took charge early in 1192, and the early settlers, like Guy himself, came from Syria and were drawn from the ranks of those men and women who had been dispossessed by the Muslims.

Few of those who accompanied Guy to Cyprus after his purchase of the island can be positively identified, but the names of some of the more prominent knights in the first decade of Lusignan rule are known from the witness lists in the handful of charters that survive.[23] Several had been Guy's associates before his acquisition of the island. His brother, Aimery, Humphrey of Toron, Hugh Martin, Renier of Jubail and the brothers Walter and Alelm Le Bel, had supported him during and immediately after the siege of Acre (1189–91), but it should be pointed out that some of his other supporters from those years chose to remain in Syria.[24] Other early settlers had been members of Guy or Aimery's households and in a number of instances would, like the Lusignans themselves, have originated from Poitou. But again the list of identifiable individuals is short: Hugh Martin, Fulk of Yver, Lawrence of Plessy, Massé of Gaurelle, Adam of Antioch, Guy Le Petit and Reynald Barlais.[25] Some settlers belonged to families established in the East before Saladin's conquests, although, apart from the Lusignan brothers, only Humphrey of Toron had been a major figure in the

[22] At this period fiefs in Syria were generally worth at least 300 saracen bezants. Riley-Smith, *Feudal Nobility*, p. 10. The saracen bezant, although somewhat lighter than the white bezant, had a far greater gold-content. Four hundred white bezants were therefore worth considerably less than 300 saracen bezants. D. M. Metcalf, *Coinage of the Crusades and the Latin East in the Ashmolean Museum, Oxford* (London, 1983), pp. 10, 51. According to the less authoritative accounts of the settlement, the fiefs in Cyprus turned out to be worth twice as much as anticipated. 'Eracles', p. 189 variant mss; *Ernoul*, p. 287.

[23] Five charters survive from before 1205. (1) August 1194: J. Richard, 'L'abbaye cistercienne de Jubin et le prieuré Saint-Blaise de Nicosie', *EKEE*, III (1969–70), 69–70. (2) September 1195: Mas Latrie, *Histoire*, III, 598–9. (3) May 1196: Mas Latrie, *Histoire*, II, 30; cf. *RRH*, no. 729. (4) November 1197: Mas Latrie, *Histoire*, III, 606–7. (5) March 1201: *Le cartulaire du chaptire du Saint-Sépulcre de Jérusalem*, ed. G. Bresc-Bautier (Paris, 1984), pp. 331–2.

[24] A list of Guy's supporters at Acre can be compiled from his charters. *RRH*, nos. 683–4, 690, 693, 696–8, 701–2. Hugh and William of Tiberias, Antelinus of Lucca, Thomas Chamberlain, Philip Morosini, Baldwin of Cyprus and Renouard of Nephin stayed in Syria. *RRH*, nos. 707, 716–17, 736.

[25] 'Les Lignages d'Outremer', *RHC Lois*, II, 472, 473, 474. Lawrence of Plessy was the ancestor of the Morphou family. For Reynald Barlais, 'Eracles', p. 219; *Cont. Guillaume de Tyr*, p. 191 (wrongly named William). Reynald is believed to have been related to the Berlay lords of Montreuil-Bellay on the Poitou/Anjou border. J. Richard, *The Latin Kingdom of Jerusalem* (Amsterdam, 1979), p. 199. For the Berlay see for example, 'Cartae et chronica de obedentia Mairomno' in *Chroniques des églises d'Anjou*, ed. P. Marchegay and E. Mabille (Paris, 1869), pp. 66, 72, 80–3; *Cartulaires et chartes de l'abbaye de l'Absie*, ed. B. Ledain (Poitiers, 1895), pp. 22, 27, 88. The Rivet and Cheneché families should probably be added to this list.

kingdom of Jerusalem. Philip and probably Baldwin of Bethsan were younger sons of Gremont, lord of Bethsan; Walter Le Bel had held a fief in or near Acre, and Reynald of Soissons had had one at Nablus; Elias of Robore appears to have been a vassal of the lord of Tiberias, Renier of Jubail is likely to have been descended from or identical with a man of that name who appears in 1160 and 1161 as a vassal of the lord of Caesarea; Odo of Mayre may have come from Antioch; Baldwin Hostiarius and Baldwin of Neuvillé may have been related to men with the same surnames living in the Latin kingdom at other periods in the twelfth century, while William of La Baume and his brother Roland could have been descended from a Tripolitan knight who was witnessing documents as far back as 1139.[26]

This analysis goes some way towards confirming the narrative traditions of the settlement. True, many of the early settlers known to us by name had already been associated with the Lusignans before 1192, and there is no way of distinguishing the knights who accompanied Guy to Cyprus as members of his entourage from those who came to the island in the hope of being given fiefs following an appeal for more men. But the general indications as to the origins of the settlers do find support. Knights who seem to have had connections with Antioch and Tripoli are represented as well as those from Jerusalem, and, since Toron, Nablus, Bethsan and Tiberias were among those places that remained in Muslim hands after the Third Crusade, in some cases at least they must have been disinherited by Saladin. This pattern was paralleled in the ecclesiastical sphere: the first Latin archbishop of Nicosia and the first bishop of Paphos, sees erected in 1196, had previously been archdeacon of Lydda and archdeacon of Lattakia.[27]

In the thirteenth century and later people emigrated to Cyprus directly from western Europe. Doubtless this process began almost immediately after 1192, but in its initial stages the European colonization of the island was achieved by settlers from the kingdom of Jerusalem and the other Latin states in Syria. It was these people who set the tone of the Lusignan regime. In many instances the ideas and institutions they brought with them were western in origin, even if they had already been modified by their introduction into an eastern environment. So for example, the feudal customs of Jerusalem, which were essentially western in

[26] For the Bethsan family, J. L. La Monte and N. Downs, 'The Lords of Bethsan in the Kingdoms of Jerusalem and Cyprus', *Medievalia et Humanistica*, VI (1950), 63–6. For Reynald of Soissons and Walter Le Bel, John of Ibelin, 'Livre de Jean d'Ibelin', *RHC Lois*, I, 424, 425. For Elias of Robore *RRH*, no. 583. For Renier of Jubail, *RRH*, nos. 361, 373; E. G. Rey, 'Les seigneurs de Giblet', *ROL*, III (1895), 417–18. For Odo of Mayre, *RRH*, no. 550. For a Renier Hostiarius, *RRH*, no. 1122. For a *Guago* of Neuville, *RRH*, no. 452. For a Raymond of La Baume in 1139, *RRH*, nos. 191, 192.

[27] R. Hiestand, *Papsturkunden für Kirchen im Heiligen Lande* (Göttingen, 1985), no. 181; *Cont. Guillaume de Tyr*, p. 121.

concept but conditioned by the hard struggles in the early twelfth century against the Christians' Muslim neighbours, were transplanted into Cyprus with only minor changes.[28] But although the settlers would have had their own ideas about legal, religious, administrative and economic organization, they encountered an existing system of social and political structures, the legacy of Byzantium. The result was a compromise. In certain sectors, they simply took over or adapted what they found; in others, particularly in those that had been affected most by the conquest, they introduced their own institutional ideas. Thus the exploitation of the land and the peasantry and the organization of commercial taxation seem to have gone on much as before. As for the currency, the Byzantine scyphate trachea – the debased gold coin known in Cyprus as the 'white bezant' – would have been the principal unit at the time of the conquest, and, from the time of Guy of Lusignan until the closing years of the thirteenth century, the Lusignans issued their own imitative versions of this coin.[29] But in the matter of landownership, in military and ecclesiastical organization, and in the social structure of the ruling class, the Latin conquest and settlement brought far-reaching changes.

Richard's conquest of Cyprus had been thorough, and between them he and the Templars seem to have broken the will of the population to resist. So far as is known, Guy's settlement of the island did not run into internal opposition. The fate of the former Byzantine landowners is not at all clear. According to the Greek recluse, Neophytus, many fled to Constantinople.[30] Perhaps others continued in Cyprus in straitened circumstances. Whether the Lusignans pursued a systematic policy of expropriation is uncertain, although, for what little he is worth, the sixteenth-century writer, Etienne de Lusignan, asserted that they did.[31] But there is no evidence for members of the Greek landowning class, the *archontes*, surviving under the new regime. How far their disappearance resulted from flight, death or dispossession remains open to question, but their demise has to be attributed in the first instance to the speed and effectiveness of the conquest. In Crete and the Morea, conquered after the sack of Constantinople in 1204, resistance was protracted, and the new western rulers were obliged to admit existing Greek landowners into the feudal hierarchy, although admittedly with inferior status.[32] Nothing comparable seems to have occurred in Cyprus.

[28] P. W. Edbury, 'Feudal Obligations in the Latin East', *Byzantion*, XLVII (1977), 329.

[29] Metcalf, *Coinage of the Crusades*, pp. 51–3.   [30] Neophytus, pp. clxxxv, clxxxvii.

[31] Estienne de Lusignan, *Description de toute l'isle de Cypre* (Paris, 1580), f. 77v. Writing in the mid-thirteenth century, Philip of Novara ('Livre de Philippe de Navarre', *RHC Lois*, I, 536) referred to the former properties of churches, abbeys and 'artondes' (*lege* 'arcondes', i.e. *archontes*) being given as fiefs.

[32] F. Thiriet, *La Romanie vénitienne au moyen âge* (Paris, 1959), pp. 128–33; A. Bon, *La Morée franque* (Paris, 1969), p. 88; D. Jacoby, 'The Encounter of Two Societies: Western Conquerors and Byzantines in the Peloponnesus after the Fourth Crusade', *American Historical Review*,

The thoroughness of the conquest, combined with the security afforded by the sea, also affected the way in which the Lusignans organized their own feudal dependants. Favoured vassals did not receive fortified towns or castles to be held in fief, presumably because there was no need: there were no frontiers to defend and no insurgent population to hold in check. Here again the contrast with the Morea is instructive. The princes of Achaea, who took forty years to conquer the territories to which they laid claim, were obliged to enfeoff their followers with castles and grant them extensive privileges, including the right to build new fortifications and exercise high justice within their lordships.[33] Such privileges were unknown in Cyprus. There the Lusignans retained exclusive control of defence and gave their vassals fiefs which had no strategic significance but were simply intended to provide them with their livelihood and enable them to perform their military obligations.

The conquest had destroyed the Greek landowning aristocracy, but not the Greek church. With the advent of the Lusignans, eastern orthodoxy, while retaining the support of the indigenous, Greek-speaking population, ceased to enjoy the patronage and protection of the ruling class. This divergence between rulers and ruled in their religious loyalties seems to have presented greater problems than the mere fact that Greeks had been replaced by non-Greeks in position of power and landed wealth. The introduction of a Latin hierarchy and Latin clergy to cater for the faith of the new rulers evoked resentment, and the efforts of the Latin clergy from the 1220s onwards to subordinate the Greek church to themselves provided a continuing source of friction. The Greek church was at a disadvantage, both politically and economically, for, although it had survived, the rank of society comprising the wealthiest of its benefactors had not, and the difficulties resulting from the termination of their patronage and munificence were aggravated by the loss of some at least of its existing property and endowments.[34]

Guy of Lusignan and the early Latin settlers were fortunate in that the invasion had been clear cut and so had not harmed the economy. Massacre and wanton destruction had not been a feature of Richard's success; indeed, the principal Frankish-Syrian account particularly noted the measures taken by the English king to safeguard the lives and property of the inhabitants of Limassol.[35]

LXXVIII (1973), 905 *et passim; idem*, 'From Byzantium to Latin Romania: Continuity and Change' in B. Arbel, *et al.* (eds), *Latins and Greeks in the Eastern Mediterranean after 1204* (London, 1989), pp. 3–10, 26–30. The statement in the passage quoted above (p. 16) that Guy of Lusignan gave fiefs to Greeks is unsupported and in any case would appear to refer to Greeks from Syria. The reference from Philip of Novara cited in the previous note appears to be the sole thirteenth-century allusion to Greek *archontes* in Cyprus. For a Latin-Syrian author using term *archontes* in the context of the Byzantine world, 'Eracles', p. 292.

[33] Bon, *Morée franque*, p. 87.

[34] J. Gill, 'The Tribulations of the Greek Church in Cyprus, 1196–c.1280', *BF*, v (1977).

[35] 'Eracles', p. 164.

The establishment of the new class of landowners, with its own culture and ecclesiastical organization, was the most obvious result of the conquest and Guy's subsequent acquisition of the island. The events of the early 1190s had less dramatic but nevertheless significant consequences for administration, commerce and urban society and led to important changes in the role of Cyprus in the politics of the eastern Mediterranean world. Guy of Lusignan brought knights, burgesses and clergy as settlers from Syria and Palestine, but his period of rule was only the beginning. Throughout the thirteenth century, a steady stream of men and women with previous connections with the Latin states of the mainland came to Cyprus, and as they succumbed to the superior military might of their Muslim neighbours so the island provided a refuge for the survivors. Other newcomers, including knightly adventurers, clergy and merchants, arrived from the West, and they were eventually to transform the original predominantly French-speaking ruling class into a more heterogeneous, cosmopolitan group. By the fifteenth century there was scarcely a region of western Europe that was not represented among the Latin settlers.

3

THE LUSIGNAN DYNASTY

THE LORDS of Lusignan could trace their association with the Latin East back to 1102 when Guy of Lusignan's great-grandfather, Hugh VI, fought at the battle of Ramla. In 1163, two generations later, Guy's father Hugh VIII, came from his native Poitou to Syria only to be captured by the Muslims in the following year. He never regained his freedom.[1] Hugh VIII had several sons. The eldest, also named Hugh, did not long survive him, but three of the others, Geoffrey, Aimery and Guy, all lived to acquire fame for their exploits in the East.[2] As members of the Poitevin nobility, the lords of Lusignan were from 1154 vassals of the kings of England, a connection that may help explain the support given Guy by King Richard at the time of the Third Crusade. In the twelfth century, however, the family was not conspicuous for its loyalty to the Plantagenets. Aimery, Geoffrey and Guy had all been involved in rebellions against Richard's father, King Henry II: Aimery in 1168, the others in 1173.[3] Aimery was the first to leave for the East. He must have gone soon after his rebellion, for by 1174 he was already a vassal of the young Baldwin IV. According to a tradition current in the mid-thirteenth century, his career was launched by King Amaury (1163–74) who was said to have ransomed him from captivity in Damascus.[4] In 1180 it was Aimery of Lusignan who persuaded Guy to come to Jerusalem.

In the period between the accession of Baldwin IV in 1174 and the battle of Hattin in 1187 Jerusalem was toubled both by the external threat from Saladin and by divisions among the Latin nobility. These divisions were caused and exacerbated by a constitutional situation that allowed a protracted struggle for power. When he came to the throne, Baldwin IV was a minor. He was also a

---

[1] For Hugh VI, Fulcher of Chartres, *Historia Hierosolymitana*, ed. H. Hagenmeyer (Heidelberg, 1913) pp. 437–9. For Hugh VIII, William of Tyre, *Chronicon*, ed. R. B. C. Huygens (Turnhout, 1986), pp. 873, 875; 'Epistolarum Volumen . . . ad Ludovicum VII', *RHF*, XVI, 62–3.

[2] S. Painter, 'The Lords of Lusignan in the Eleventh and Twelfth Centuries', *Speculum*, XXXII (1957), 40.

[3] Robert of Torigny, 'Chronicle', ed. R. Howlett, *Chronicles of the Reigns of Stephen, Henry II and Richard I* (RS 82, 1884–9), IV, 235, 257; *Gesta Regis*, I, 46.

[4] *RRH*, no. 518; Philip of Novara, p. 569; John of Ibelin, pp. 429–30.

leper. There would have to be a regency until he came of age; then a period of unforeseeable duration in which the debilitating effects of the disease rendered him progressively less able to govern; finally, with his death, an uncertain succession, since he would have no direct heir of his own. Baldwin's father, King Amaury, had married twice. On his accession in 1163 he had divorced his first wife, Agnes of Courtenay, the mother of Baldwin and his eldest child, Sibylla. His second wife was a Byzantine princess, Maria Comnena, and she bore him another daughter, Isabella. Both women survived their husband, and they and their daughters provided the foci for the opposing groups. Particularly close to Agnes were her brother, Joscelin titular count of Edessa and from 1176 seneschal of Jerusalem, Reynald of Châtillon, formerly prince of Antioch and now, by marriage, lord of Oultrejourdain, Eraclius, from 1180 patriarch of Jerusalem, and Gerard of Ridefort, from 1185 master of the Temple. Among those who eventually found themselves ranged against them were Balian of Ibelin, Maria Comnena's second husband, his brother Baldwin and Count Raymond III of Tripoli, husband of Eschiva of Bures, lady of Tiberias.

Shortly after the beginning of Baldwin's minority Raymond of Tripoli seized power. During his period as regent Sibylla, who at that time was regarded as heiress-presumptive to the throne, married William, marquis of Montferrat. This union, which should in due course have led to William's acceptance as king by right of his wife, apparently won widespread approval, but in 1177, only a few months after his marriage, he died. By now Agnes and her supporters were in control, and it was they who were faced with the task of finding a new husband for Sibylla. The task was far from easy. They approached the duke of Burgundy, but he was hesitant. Aimery of Lusignan thereupon suggested his brother Guy, who at that time was still in the West. He brought him to Jerusalem, and at Easter 1180 Guy and Sibylla were married. At about the same date Aimery became constable of the kingdom.[5]

The Lusignan brothers' meteoric rise to prominence only served to deepen the divisions. It seems that Baldwin IV's permission for the marriage to take place came about more as an attempt to forestall the possibility of Raymond determining whom Sibylla should marry than as a sign that Guy was regarded as an ideal candidate. Raymond was threatening to seize power again, and allegedly Baldwin of Ibelin entertained ambitions to have Sibylla as his bride. As the protégé of one faction, Guy inevitably incurred the resentment of the other. William of Tyre's remark that King Baldwin could have found someone of greater importance, wisdom and wealth than Guy to marry his sister suggests further grounds for the unpopularity of the match: although the Lusignans were

[5] For politics in Jerusalem in the 1170s and 1180s, Riley-Smith, *Feudal Nobility*, pp. 101–12; Richard, *The Latin Kingdom*, pp. 49–57, 164–74. Aimery became constable after the death of Humphrey of Toron in April 1179 (William of Tyre, p. 999) and before March 1181 (*RRH*, no. 601).

an influential family in Poitou, Guy, as a younger son, lacked the reserves that a powerful magnate could have brought to strengthen the Latin East against Saladin, and he also lacked the sort of reputation that would draw men from the West to serve with him in the field. He was no substitute for the marquis of Monteferrat or the duke of Burgundy.[6]

In 1183 Baldwin's leprosy forced him to give up his control of the government. Despite the misgivings of Guy's opponents who feared the consequences for the kingdom of his inexperience and foresaw their own eclipse by Agnes and her supporters, Guy was appointed the king's lieutenant. But within a few months Baldwin and Guy had quarrelled, and Guy had seriously lost face over his conduct during a campaign against Saladin. So strong was the current of opinion, that Baldwin was able to dismiss him and attempt to bar him from succeeding to the throne altogether. The king designated Sibylla's infant son by William of Montferrat, also named Baldwin, as his successor and had him crowned king immediately. Raymond of Tripoli was appointed regent for the rest of Baldwin IV's reign and for Baldwin V's minority. In the event Baldwin IV died in 1185 and Baldwin V in 1186. On the young king's death, however, thanks to decisive action by Joscelin of Edessa, Reynald of Châtillon and Gerard of Ridefort, Raymond was ousted from power. Sibylla was proclaimed queen, and she and Guy were anointed and crowned in Jerusalem. Raymond and his supporters toyed with the idea of proclaiming Sibylla's half-sister, Isabella, queen in opposition, but this scheme came to nothing when Isabella's husband, Humphrey of Toron, did homage to Guy as king. Reluctantly Guy's opponents submitted. Only Baldwin of Ibelin, who preferred voluntary exile in Antioch, and Raymond of Tripoli, who retired to Tiberias, remained unreconciled. But even greater fluctuations in fortune were in store. In the summer of 1187 Guy and Raymond came to terms; almost at once Saladin entered Galilee and on 4 July defeated the Christian army at Hattin. The consequences are well-known: Guy fell captive; his field-army was destroyed; the Muslims overran the Latin kingdom.

When in the summer of 1188 Guy was restored to freedom, he found that control of Tyre, the one city in his realm remaining in Christian hands, had been usurped by Conrad of Montferrat. Conrad's prompt action had saved Tyre from falling to Saladin in 1187, and he now had the support of the surviving members of Raymond of Tripoli's circle. Raymond himself and Baldwin of Ibelin were now both dead, and the leadership of their group had passed to Baldwin's brother Balian, his wife, Maria Comnena, Pagan lord of Haifa and Reynald lord of Sidon. But despite the ill-feeling that had attended him since his arrival in the East, despite the defeat at Hattin and the loss of Jerusalem, and despite the

---

[6] William of Tyre, p. 1007; *Ernoul*, pp. 48, 56–60. For Guy's position in the period leading up to Hattin, R. C. Smail, 'The Predicaments of Guy of Lusignan, 1183–87', *Outremer*, pp. 159–76.

months in captivity, Guy still enjoyed the loyalty of a substantial section of the community in the Latin East. Matters came to a head in 1189 when Guy arrived before Tyre with an army he had recruited in Tripoli. Conrad refused to recognize him as king and denied him entry.[7] Rather than try to force him to submit, Guy responded by going on to the offensive against the Muslims, thereby re-asserting his kingship, and, aided by the western crusaders who were now starting to arrive in the East, he began to besiege Acre. Had his efforts met with early success, his reputation would have been restored and Conrad's ascendancy in Tyre would have collapsed. As it happened, the siege dragged on inconclusively through 1190. The mortality due to disease in the Christian army was heavy. In the Autumn of 1190 Queen Sibylla and her two small daughters died. Guy's opponents seized their opportunity. Guy was the anointed king, but he derived his rights from his wife. Now that Sibylla was dead and there was no issue surviving from the marriage, it could be argued that his kingship had lapsed and that the throne should pass to Sibylla's next of kin, her half-sister Isabella. Isabella's marriage to Humphrey of Toron was thereupon dissolved, and she was married to Conrad. The faction led by her mother, Maria Comnena, and her step-father, Balian of Ibelin, accepted her as queen and did homage. Guy, however, refused to give way and continued to regard himself as the true king. He and his army persevered in the siege of Acre, while Conrad and his supporters held Tyre. The situation remained unchanged until the arrival of the kings of France and England the following year.[8]

The intense rivalry that already existed between King Richard of England and King Philip Augustus of France found ample scope for expression in the East. Both kings were determined to recover territory lost to the Muslims, and they also expected that, as commanders of powerful military contingents, they would have a hand in ordering the reconstituted Latin states. It was predictable that they should find themselves on opposing sides in the dispute over the throne. King Philip arrived in the East on 20 April 1191, and he at once made clear his sympathies for Conrad. Richard was slower to leave Sicily, where both he and Philip had wintered, and then, as we have seen, delayed in Cyprus. With Philip and Conrad joining in the siege of Acre, Guy's position was highly vulnerable. A successful assault would end with his opponents elbowing him aside and taking custody of the town for themselves; their assumption of power would thereby be assured, and Guy would lose all hope of retaining the throne. In what was evidently a desperate attempt to avoid this eventuality, Guy and a group of his leading supporters left the siege and sailed to meet Richard in Cyprus. Their purpose was to secure his support and speed his arrival in Syria. They had only limited success: when on 11 May they found the English king at Limassol, Richard took their homage, thus committing himself to their cause, and gave

[7] Riley-Smith, *Feudal Nobility*, pp. 112–14.   [8] *Ibid.*, pp. 114–16.

Guy a generous subsidy. But he was set on reducing Cyprus to submission and had Guy assist him in his campaign. Isaac Comnenus' decision to break off his negotiations with Richard was allegedly taken at the instance of one of Guy's Syrian enemies, Pagan of Haifa, who presumably was hoping that Isaac would delay Richard and so give Conrad and King Philip more time to capture Acre on their own.[9] It was not until 8 June, almost a month after Guy had first met him, that Richard arrived in Acre; he had not allowed himself to be hurried, but neither had Acre fallen in the meantime.

The events of the following months do not need to be recounted in detail. Acre fell on 12 July, and almost at once Philip returned home, having secured for Conrad both the revenues of Tyre (and the as yet Muslim-held Beirut and Sidon) and, on Guy's death, the expectancy of the crown for himself and his heirs by Isabella. Not content with this solution, Conrad and his followers plotted for control of Acre and Guy's total exclusion from power while Richard was away campaigning against the Muslims. Had it not been for the English king's continued backing, Guy's position would have crumbled completely. During the siege of Acre Gerard of Ridefort, Joscelin of Edessa and Patriarch Eraclius, his three most influential allies among the Syrian leaders, had all died. His only other supporters of any consequence in the East seem to have been his own brothers, Aimery the constable of Jerusalem and Geoffrey, who in 1191 was made count of Jaffa.[10] The death of Queen Sibylla could well have loosened the ties of loyalty between him and his Jerusalemite vassals, and his entourage may well have come to consist principally of his Poitevin retainers. The weakness of his position was illustrated early in 1192 when Conrad's party came near to seizing Acre; Conrad's efforts were thwarted by the spirited resistance of the Pisans, who inclined to Guy largely, it is assumed, because their rivals, the Genoese, supported his opponents, and then by the timely arrival of the king of England. Matters were brought to a head in April when news reached Richard which convinced him of the need to return to Europe. It was already apparent that the Christian forces were inadequate to recover Jerusalem. A gathering of the leaders of the crusade convened by Richard to discuss his departure came out strongly in the opinion that one man should rule all the lands of the kingdom of Jerusalem that were restored to Christian control, and that that man should be Conrad and not Guy.[11] Richard could appreciate the wisdom of this view. For him it would mean an abrupt change of policy and the end of the support for his protégé. But he was able to avoid putting himself in a false position: a completely

[9] Ambroise, lines 1701–34, 1832–41, 1969–2008; 'Itinerarium', pp. 195, 199, 201–2; Gesta Regis, II, 165–6.

[10] Das Itinerarium peregrinorum, ed. H. E. Mayer (Stuttgart, 1962), pp. 313–14, 307; 'Itinerarium', p. 235; Gesta Regis, II, 147.

[11] 'Itinerarium', pp. 321–3, 333–5; cf. Ambroise, lines 8601–36.

independent development had opened the way for Guy to be compensated handsomely.

On 4 April 1192 the Cypriots rose in rebellion against the Templars. The insurrection failed, but the Order was sufficiently shaken to return the island, for which it still owed 60,000 bezants, to King Richard. Thereafter events moved rapidly. Presumably Richard already knew that the Templars were giving up Cyprus when he decided to accept Conrad as king-designate. He gave Guy the opportunity to purchase the island for 100,000 bezants and allowed him two months in which to find 60,000 bezants as a down payment. Guy's chancellor, Peter of Angoulême, had no difficulty in raising the money from merchants in Tripoli in less than a month.[12]

Cyprus had become available at an opportune moment, but the struggle for power on the mainland was not over. On 28 April, even before Guy had taken possession of his new domain, Conrad was murdered. But any hopes Guy may have had of recovering his position were dashed, when, with unseemly haste, Conrad's widow, Queen Isabella, was married to the leading French crusader still in the East, Count Henry of Champagne. As a grandson of King Louis VII of France and his first wife, Eleanor of Aquitaine, Henry was close kinsman of both Richard of England and Philip of France, and he enjoyed the full support of the English and the French leaders in the East as well as of Conrad's partisans among the Syrian baronage. Guy, however, refused to be content with Cyprus and became involved with the Pisans in a plot to seize Tyre. The details are obscure, but it would seem that this scheme had the result of souring his relations with Richard. Reportedly the king of England, who to begin with had not pressed Guy for a speedy payment of the 40,000 bezants he still owed, even went so far as to promise Henry of Champagne that he should have Cyprus as well as the Christian possessions in Palestine. This promise, if indeed it were ever made, was not fulfilled, although Richard did give Henry his rights to collect the balance outstanding on the sale of the island.[13]

In September 1192 the Christians and Muslims agreed on a truce, and early the following month Richard departed for the West. Guy had taken those of his followers who so wished to Cyprus, and their departure probably helped lower the tension between the political factions. But one other incident occurred that illustrates the continuing ill-will. Henry took reprisals on the Pisans for their part in the plot to seize Tyre, and when Aimery of Lusignan intervened on their behalf Henry imprisoned him. This action evoked protests from some prominent figures in the kingdom, and the upshot was that Henry released

---

[12] Cont. Guillaume de Tyr, pp. 137, 139.

[13] Ibid., pp. 139, 143, 145, 151, 153. Guy's breach with Richard was noted by a contemporary Muslim observer. Lyons and Jackson, Saladin, p. 349.

Aimery, in return for relinquishing his office of constable of Jerusalem, and allowed him to join his brother in Cyprus.[14]

The twelve years that had elapsed between Guy's arrival in the East and his purchase of Cyprus had been marked by incessant factional disputes. In his settlement of the island, he naturally turned to his supporters during the previous years and raised them to positions of prominence. But, for the followers of Raymond of Tripoli, Conrad of Montferrat or Henry of Champagne, there was no place there at all. Towards Henry Guy was irreconcilable, and he continued to lay claim to the kingdom of Jerusalem until his death, which took place at about the end of 1194.[15] It is difficult to obtain a balanced view of his career since the narrative sources are violently partisan. It may be significant, however, that a well-informed English writer suggested that he was rather naïve in the midst of intrigue but praised him for his conduct of the siege of Acre, and that Saladin's Muslim biographer, Imad al-Dīn, mentioned his good administration in Cyprus.[16]

Guy of Lusignan had designated his brother Geoffrey as his successor in Cyprus, but Geoffrey, who had been one of the heroes of the Third Crusade, showed no interest. It seems that he preferred his Poitevin lands to either Cyprus or his county of Jaffa and returned home, probably in 1192. So Guy's vassals chose his other brother, Aimery, to be their lord.[17] As Aimery was Guy's elder brother, his accession was not strictly speaking a matter of hereditary right, but, with his long experience of the East, he was undoubtedly a sensible choice; indeed, he must have seemed the obvious choice.

Within three years of Guy's death, Aimery had two notable achievements to his credit: the establishment of a Latin ecclesiastical hierarchy and the elevation of Cyprus to a kingdom with himself as first king. Aimery's initiatives began in 1195 when he sent the archdeacon of Lattakia to the pope with letters concerning the future of the Church in the island. Pope Celestine III commissioned a plan to be drawn up, and in December 1196 he issued a bull formally inaugurating the Latin diocesan establishment. An archbishop of Nicosia was to have suffragans at Paphos, Limassol and Famagusta – an arrangement that was to last until the Turkish conquest in the sixteenth century. The first archbishop was Aimery's chancellor, and the first bishop of Paphos, his emissary of the previous year.[18] It

[14] *Cont. Guillaume de Tyr*, p. 159. 'Eracles' (p. 208) preserves what seems to be a garbled account of this incident.
[15] For his title, 'Guido per Dei gratiam in sancta civitate Iherusalem Latinorum rex VIII et Cipri dominus', Richard, 'L'abbaye cistercienne', p. 69. Cf. W. H. Rudt de Collenberg, 'Les Lusignan de Chypre', *EKEE*, x (1980), 93.   [16] 'Itinerarium', pp. 350–1; 'Imād al-Dīn, p. 377.
[17] *Cont. Guillaume de Tyr*, pp. 159, 161, 173; 'Eracles', pp. 192, 209.
[18] Hiestand, *Papsturkunden im Heiligen Lande*, nos. 173, 176, 181.

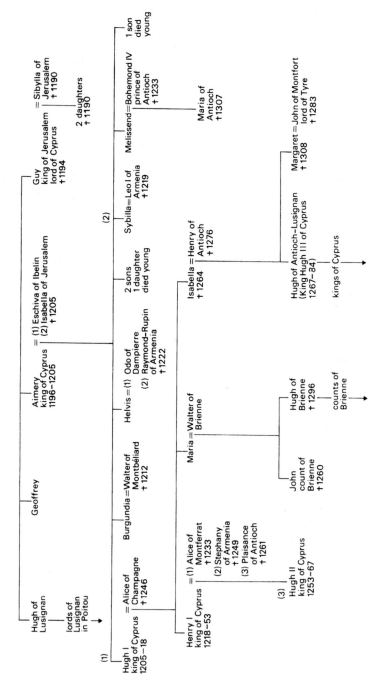

Figure 1   The Lusignan dynasty to 1267

is probable, as one writer hinted, that the creation of a Latin hierarchy was seen by contemporaries as a prerequisite for acquiring a crown.[19] Certainly the idea of a king, himself of the western rite but with no Latin bishops in his kingdom, would have been unthinkable, not least because he and his successors would have been in the unsatisfactory position of having to rely on visiting clergy or on the Greek bishops for their coronation.

Aimery's royal title was acquired from the western emperor, Henry VI of Hohenstaufen. In 1195 Henry had taken the Cross, and he was planning to lead a crusade to the East in 1197. He was an ambitious man. He had already conquered Sicily, and he intended, besides crusading in Syria, to bring Byzantium into subjection. The idea of Cyprus as a kingdom under imperial suzerainty fitted in well with his schemes.[20] For his part, Aimery had much to gain by the elevation of his island domain to the status of a kingdom, even if it did mean accepting Henry's overlordship. Possession of a crown would enhance his own prestige and help ensure that Cyprus would continue to be ruled by his descendants. Furthermore, the potential diplomatic advantages were considerable. Allegedly it was fear of a Byzantine attack on Cyprus that had prompted him to make overtures in the first place, and in Henry Aimery had found an ally who was unquestionably hostile to Constantinople. By becoming a king Aimery would also put an end to any idea that Cyprus might be regarded as a dependency of Jerusalem, perhaps a potent consideration in view of the poor relations that prevailed between the Lusignans and Henry of Champagne. Furthermore, the emperor's overlordship would in itself guarantee that when he arrived in the East in person he would not overturn the regime in Cyprus, even although it had been established under the auspices of his enemy, King Richard of England.

At about the same time as the archdeacon of Lattakia had set off to Rome to open negotiations with the pope for a Latin ecclesiastical hierarchy, Aimery had sent his vassal, Renier of Jubail, as his ambassador to the emperor. Henry agreed to his requests, took his homage as Aimery's proxy and dispatched the archbishops of Trani and Brindisi with the royal regalia. The archbishops appear to have arrived in Cyprus in April or May 1196, and Aimery may have styled himself king from that time. The actual coronation was postponed until 1197, as the emperor hoped to be present in person. But then rebellion in Sicily and illness delayed his departure, and eventually an advance party including the imperial chancellor, Conrad bishop of Hildesheim, left without him. It arrived in the East in September 1197, and Conrad crowned Aimery king of Cyprus.[21] In

[19] 'Eracles', p. 209.   [20] Brand, *Byzantium Confronts the West*, pp. 191–3.
[21] Hill, II, 48–9. The arrival of the archbishops of Trani and Brindisi is dated from a charter mentioning the presence of the former and giving trading concessions to Trani. Mas Latrie, *Histoire*, II, 30. As printed, the text is corrupt, but the charter is nonetheless genuine. See *RRH*, no. 729. Aimery was described as king in papal letters dated December 1196 and January 1197. Hiestand, *Papsturkunden im Heiligen Lande*, nos. 176, 181.

the same month Henry died. His crusade ground to a halt, and early in 1198 those crusaders who had reached Syria returned home. The empire plunged into an extended period of civil war, and for almost three decades Henry's successors were unable to intervene in the East or make their suzerainty over Cyprus effective. Aimery had obtained his crown, but the hoped-for alliance against Byzantium was still-born.

Aimery's fears of a Byzantine *revanche* were genuine, but, although threats were made, no campaign was ever launched.[22] On the other hand, there was no mistaking the inevitability of Muslim expeditions against the truncated Latin Kingdom of Jerusalem once the truce expired in 1196. It was almost certainly this danger that led Henry of Champagne's vassals to urge an accommodation with Aimery. As individuals they may well have had other reasons for wanting an end to the ill-feeling that prevailed: some, such as the Bethsan family who were specifically mentioned as working for a *rapprochement*, had interests in both kingdoms, and several of the leading figures in the Latin Kingdom were related to Aimery's first wife, Eschiva of Ibelin, and so could have had family reasons for wishing to heal the split. In 1197 Henry was persuaded to visit Aimery in Cyprus; the two rulers were formally reconciled, and they then forged an alliance, the basis of which was that Aimery's three sons by Eschiva were to marry Henry's three daughters. The accounts of the terms are somewhat confused, but it seems that the dowries were to consist of Jaffa, which was to be put into Aimery's custody immediately, and the remission by Henry of the balance still owed to him for the purchase of Cyprus in 1192. Even before the two rulers had parted, news reached them that a Muslim invasion was beginning. Aimery sent Reynald Barlais with a small force to take seisin of Jaffa, which, as the most southerly outpost of the kingdom of Jerusalem, was known to be an object for attack. He had done well out of the deal: he had secured the cancellation of his debt to Henry and had thereby ended any lingering claim Henry may have had on Cyprus; it is possible that at the same time he was restored to the office of constable of Jerusalem; he had also obtained Jaffa, although in the event his garrison was unable to resist the Muslim siege and the town was lost; above all, he had secured recognition from the most powerful of the other Christian rulers in the East for his position as king of an independent kingdom. The marriage agreements, however, did not work out as expected.[23] All the children were still too young to be married immediately, and two of Aimery's sons and one of Henry's daughters died in childhood. But eventually, in 1210, Hugh, Aimery's sole surviving son, married Henry's daughter, Alice. The importance of the 1197 reconciliation deserves to be stressed: it marked the end of the faction fighting that had bedevilled Latin Syrian politics since Guy of Lusignan's arrival in the

[22] Above, p. 11.

[23] *Cont. Guillaume de Tyr*, pp. 177, 191, 193; 'Eracles', pp. 208–9, 218–19, 308–9. The possibility that Aimery recovered the office of constable as part of the agreement is suggested by his use of the title in a document of November 1197. Mas Latrie, *Histoire*, III, 606.

East, even though it was not many years before new disputes and new alignments were to make their appearance. Furthermore, the admittedly ineffective defence of Jaffa was the first instance of a Lusignan ruler of Cyprus coming to the assistance of the Latin Kingdom of Jerusalem.

On 10 September, within a few weeks of the reconciliation and shortly before the surrender of Jaffa to the Muslims, Henry of Champagne fell from a first floor window to his death. Once again Isabella, the heiress to Jerusalem, was a widow. The demand was immediately voiced that she should remarry and that her new husband, her fourth, should govern the kingdom. Some people wanted her to wed the seneschal of Jerusalem, Ralph of Tiberias, but they were overruled by others including the military Orders, the German crusaders who had arrived in the East shortly after Henry of Champagne's death and the chancellor of Jerusalem, Archbishop Joscius of Tyre, all of whom pressed for King Aimery whose wife, Eschiva of Ibelin, had recently died. His Cypriot resources would have made Aimery an attractive candidate in the eyes of those who were looking for someone who could bring reinforcements to the defence of the East, and the Germans doubtless favoured him since he was already ruling an imperial client-kingdom. The archbishop of Tyre appears to have negotiated the match, and it would seem that the couple were married or at least betrothed by mid-October. The choice of Aimery, we are told, was almost unanimous. Initially the patriarch of Jerusalem had scruples about the marriage's canonical validity, but he then appears to have withdrawn his objections, since it was he who conducted their coronation service. The new king of Cyprus was now king-consort of Jerusalem as well.[24]

Aimery of Lusignan ruled over Cyprus and the kingdom of Jerusalem until his death in April 1205. The two realms were linked only by the person of the monarch; otherwise they retained their separate identities and their own institutions. Each had its own High Court and its own chancery.[25] If the list of witnesses to the one surviving Cypriot royal charter issued by Aimery after he had acquired his second crown can be taken as a guide, he did not follow a policy of rewarding his Jerusalemite followers with fiefs and offices in his island kingdom.[26] On the other hand, he was prepared to use his Cypriot forces in the

---

[24] *Cont. Guillaume de Tyr*, pp. 193, 199; 'Eracles', pp. 220–4. For Joscius' role, the patriarch's changing attitude and the near unanimity in choice, *Die Register Innocenz' III*, ii, 753, cf 662. Joscius was given an estate in Cyprus in November 1197, presumably in appreciation of his efforts. Mas Latrie, *Histoire*, iii, 606–7. For possible canonistic objections to the marriage, Riley-Smith, *Feudal Nobility*, p. 152.

[25] The only document which purports to show Aimery making a grant of Cypriot lands and trading concessions in the High Court of Jerusalem is a fabrication. H. E. Mayer, *Marseilles Levantehandel und ein akkonensisches Fälscheratelier des 13. Jahrhunderts* (Tübingen, 1972), pp. 43–9, 186–8.

[26] *RRH*, no. 780 (March 1201). There is only one witness to this charter who did not attest a charter issued by Aimery in 1197 (*RRH*, no. 737), and this man, Rostain Aymar, is not known to have been a vassal in the kingdom of Jerusalem.

military campaigns fought in the interests of Jerusalem. Cypriot knights and sergeants were present at the siege of Beirut in October 1197, and in 1204 the combined strength of Cyprus and Latin Syria participated in a naval raid on the coast of Egypt.[27] Aimery's rule, however, was for the most part a period of peace. The truce with the Muslims was renewed in July 1198 to last for five years and eight months. In the West yet another crusade was prepared, but the main part of the expedition never reached the East. Instead it diverted to Byzantium. The crusaders sacked Constantinople and set up the so-called Latin Empire in its ruins. We are not told how Aimery reacted to these events, although the sour comments of a later writer in the East suggest that they were viewed there with resentment and dismay. But on the expiry of the truce there was little conflict, the most notable engagement being the naval raid of 1204, and in September of that year the truce was again renewed, this time for six years.[28] Aimery's reign had been a time of consolidation. The Muslims had been held at bay and the Latin kingdom had achieved a new stability. The only incident to have endangered its internal tranquillity occurred when Aimery forced Ralph of Tiberias, his rival for the hand of Isabella, into exile after an attempt on the king's life in which he was alleged to have been implicated. Some of Ralph's fellow vassals in the kingdom of Jerusalem protested, but to no avail, and the affair seems to have had no lasting repercussions. Indeed, Aimery's reputation stood high among those later generations of lawyer-barons in whose eyes Ralph too was esteemed for his legal ability.[29]

Guy and Aimery of Lusignan had established permanent western rule in Cyprus, but, although they both occupied the throne of Jerusalem, they had failed to establish a Lusignan dynasty in the mainland kingdom as well. Aimery was father to the only son born to Queen Isabella, but the child predeceased him, dying in February 1205. Aimery himself died on 1 April of that year, and, when Isabella followed him to the grave shortly afterwards, the throne of Jerusalem passed to her eldest daughter, Maria, the child of her marriage to Conrad of Montferrat.[30] In Cyprus Aimery was succeeded by his son Hugh. Hugh was the only surviving son of his marriage to Eschiva of Ibelin and reigned from 1205 until his death in 1218. He was followed by his own only son, Henry I (1218–53), and then by Henry's son, Hugh II (1253–67). In 1267 the line of

---

[27] For 1197, 'Eracles', p. 224. For 1204, 'Gestes', p. 663; 'Annales de Terre Sainte', ed. R. Röhricht and G. Raynaud, AOL, II (1884), 435; Hill, II, 65 note 6.

[28] For the truces, Richard, The Latin Kingdom, pp. 207, 210, cf. p. 201. For an eastern comment on the Fourth Crusade, 'Gestes', p. 663.

[29] For this incident, Riley-Smith, Feudal Nobility, pp. 151–2, 156–9; G. A. Loud, 'The Assise sur la Ligece and Ralph of Tiberias', CS, pp. 206–10. For Aimery's later reputation, Philip of Novara, pp. 523, 544, 569–70; John of Ibelin, pp. 429–30.

[30] 'Anonymi Continuatio appendicis Roberti de Monte ad Sigebertum', RHF, XVIII, 342; 'Eracles', p. 305. Cf. Innocent III, vol. 215, col. 699.

Aimery's direct male descendants came to an end, and the succession passed to the son of one of Hugh I's daughters.

Henry I and the two Hughs were all minors at the time of their accession. Heirs, whether to fiefs or to the throne, came of age in the East at fifteen, but although the age of majority was comparatively low, no less than thirty-two out of the sixty-two years between the death of Aimery in 1205 and the death of Hugh II in 1267 were years of royal minority. It is hardly surprising therefore that none of these kings left a strong personal impression on the politics of the age. Hugh I was perhaps the ablest. A brief character-sketch by a near contemporary spoke of him being ready to embark on anything that might redound to his honour, being fond of the company of knights and being easily angered and stirred to violence.[31] Henry I was less than a year old when his father died, and his long minority was marked by worsening relations between his mother, the regent Philip of Ibelin and a group of knights opposed to Philip. As we shall see, this three-cornered struggle led eventually to a civil war which ended in 1233, the year after Henry came of age, with a complete victory for the Ibelin faction. For the next twenty years Henry ruled Cyprus without ever, it would seem, holding the limelight in the politics of the Latin East of his day. Hugh II, like his father, was only a few months old at his accession. The regency was held first by his mother, Plaisance of Antioch, and then after her death in 1261 by his cousin, another Hugh, who is known to historians as Hugh of Antioch-Lusignan. In 1267, still a minor, the young king died.

Hugh II's death without direct heirs contributed to what was an already complex dynastic dispute developing in the Latin East. Initially the dispute had concerned the kingdom of Jerusalem, and its background and wider implications will be considered later.[32] In 1267 there were two claimants to the Cypriot throne: the sons of Henry I's two sisters, Maria and Isabella. Maria, the elder sister, had married Count Walter of Brienne; Isabella, the younger sister, had married Henry of Antioch, the brother of of Prince Bohemond V of Antioch. Each couple had a son named Hugh: respectively Hugh of Brienne and Hugh of Antioch-Lusignan. Hugh of Antioch-Lusignan, the son of the younger sister, was older than Hugh of Brienne, the son of the elder sister. The question of which of them was the nearer heir of Hugh II had been debated earlier in the 1260s in the context of arguments over who should exercise the regency in the kingdom of Jerusalem. On that occasion the High Court of Jerusalem had come down on the side of Hugh of Antioch-Lusignan. In 1267, therefore, Hugh of Antioch-Lusignan was regent in Acre, and he was also regent in Cyprus where Hugh of Brienne had not previously asserted his claims. Not surprisingly it was Hugh of Antioch-Lusignan, the candidate already in effective control, who was recognized as king of Cyprus in preference to his cousin. He was crowned on

---

[31] 'Eracles', p. 360.   [32] Below, pp. 89–90.

Christmas Day 1267 and reigned as King Hugh III. Rebuffed and frustrated, Hugh of Brienne departed for the West.[33] He took service with Charles of Anjou, Hugh III's most formidable enemy in Europe, and in about 1275, perhaps with Charles' assistance, he was trying to organize an army to win the island by force. However, he was unable to press his claim, and in 1289 he was attempting to sell his rights to the throne of Cyprus to King Alphonso III of Aragon.[34] Final echoes of the affair are heard in the early fourteenth century when the French publicist, Peter Dubois, suggested that the French monarchy should purchase the Brienne claim from Hugh's heir as a prelude to endowing a younger son of King Philip IV with the island, and in 1331 when rumours reached the pope that King Robert of Naples might be encouraging the Briennes to acquire the island.[35]

In 1268, with the execution of Conrad V of Hohenstaufen, the senior branch of the royal family of Jerusalem died out, and King Hugh III, as a descendant through his maternal grandmother of Queen Isabella and Henry of Champagne, mounted the throne of the mainland kingdom. Once again Cyprus and Jerusalem shared the same monarch, and henceforth the kings of Cyprus took their title from both kingdoms, even though the remaining Christian possessions on the Syrian littoral passed into Muslim control in 1291. By the late 1260s the kingdom of Jerusalem, or what was left of it, needed a period of strong and vigorous rule if Muslim encroachments were to be resisted. Hugh III saw the need and made a valiant effort to meet the threat, but he found himself incapable of uniting the various interests in Latin Syria behind him. In 1276 he despaired and retired to Cyprus. Part of the trouble was that his title to the throne of Jerusalem was in dispute. An unmarried cousin, Maria of Antioch, had also put forward a claim, and, like Hugh of Brienne, she too turned to Charles of Anjou, the king of Sicily. Charles bought her claim for himself, and, in 1277, after Hugh's departure, his officers took control in Acre.

Hugh III died in 1284. He was succeeded by his eldest surviving son, John, who in his turn died the following year, and then by his next son, Henry II, who reigned until 1324. In 1286 Henry regained control of Acre for the Lusignans – a success made possible by the rebellion of 1282 known as the Sicilian Vespers which had the effect of putting an end to the expansionist aims of the Sicilian Angevins. But in 1291 Acre and the other Christian-held ports were lost to the

[33] 'Gestes', p. 769; Ibn al-Furāt (Ayyubids, Mamlukes and Crusaders: Selections from the Tārīkh al-Duwal wa'l Mulūk, ed. and trans. U. and M. C. Lyons with historical introduction and notes by J. Riley-Smith (Cambridge, 1971), II, 129) indicates that he was in Cilicia at the time of Hugh II's death.

[34] Gregory X and John XXI, Registres, ed. J. Guiraud and L. Cadier (Paris, 1892–1960), no. 832; E. Lourie, 'An offer of the Suzerainty and Escheat of Cyprus to Alphonso III of Aragon by Hugh de Brienne in 1289', EHR, LXXXIV (1969), 101–3.

[35] Peter Dubois, 'Opinio cujusdam suadentis regi Francie ut regnum Jerosolimitanum et Cipri acquireret pro altero filiorum suorum, ac de invasione regni Egipti', ed. C.-V. Langlois in Peter Dubois, De recuperatione Terre Sancte (Paris, 1891), p. 140; N. Housley, 'Charles II of Naples and the Kingdom of Jerusalem', Byzantion, LIV (1984), 533.

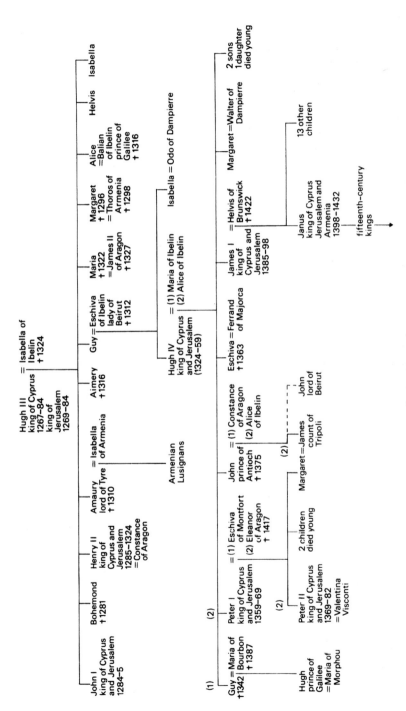

Figure 2   The Lusignan dynasty, 1267–1398

Muslims, and Henry and the bulk of the survivors retreated to Cyprus. Much of the rest of Henry's thirty-nine year reign – his was the longest of any of the Lusignan kings – is a dismal story of quarrels with the nobility, futile gestures of hostility towards the Muslims and inconsequential diplomacy. The king himself was frequently ill and was almost certainly impotent.[36] On his death the throne passed to his nephew, Hugh IV (1324–59). The accession of neither Hugh IV nor his son, Peter I (1359–69), passed unchallenged, but the reigns of these two kings are generally regarded as the period in which Lusignan Cyprus reached the apogee of its power and prosperity. Under Peter I the dynasty enjoyed a brief moment of military glory. But during the reign of his son and successor, Peter II (1369–82), the kingdom suffered a crippling invasion by the Genoese, who were to occupy Famagusta from 1373 until 1464. Thereafter political and economic decline proceeded apace. Under James I (1382–98) the dynasty acquired a third crown, that of Cilician Armenia – a purely titular honour since Cilicia itself had succumbed to Muslim invasion a few years earlier. In King Janus' reign (1398–1432) the Mamlūks invaded Cyprus from Egypt, causing considerable devastation and placing the island under tribute. After the death of John II in 1458, civil war broke out between the supporters of his heiress and those of his bastard son, James. James was eventually victorious and ruled until his death in 1473. His only legitimate son died in infancy the following year, and with his death the dynasty had all but ended.[37] James' widow, the Venetian noblewoman Catherine Cornaro, reigned in her own right under Venetian tutelage until in 1489 she was induced to abdicate and allow Venice to assume outright sovereignty. With her departure for the West that same year the Cypriot monarchy had ceased to exist.

[36] For Henry's ill-health, see for example Mas Latrie, *Histoire*, III, 703, 704; 'Amadi', pp. 248–9, 254. There is little evidence for the widely repeated belief that he was an epileptic. But see Domenico Malipiero, 'Annali Veneti dall'anno 1457 al 1500', ed. A. Sagredo, *Archivio Storico Italiano*, VII (1843–4), 593. For his presumed impotency, Mas Latrie, *Histoire*, III, 718; W. H. Rudt de Collenberg, 'Les dispenses matrimoniales accordées à l'Orient latin selon les registres du Vatican d'Honorius III à Clément VII (1223–1385)', *MEFR*, LXIX (1979), no. 88 (pp. 74–5).

[37] For other, illegitimate branches of the Lusignan family surviving in the 16th century, Rudt de Collenberg, 'Les Lusignan', pp. 240–67.

4

THE HOUSE OF IBELIN

THE IBELIN family was the most prominent noble house in Cyprus during the centuries of Lusignan rule. Its pre-twelfth-century origins are unknown: a tradition found in an early fourteenth-century source linked the family with the viscounts of Chartres, but this claim cannot stand critical scrutiny, and onomastic evidence points to a presumably less exalted Italian background, perhaps in Pisa or Sardinia.[1] The founder of the Ibelins' fortunes in the East was a certain Barisan or Balian 'the Elder', who by the second decade of the twelfth century had become castellan of Jaffa. In the early 1140s King Fulk granted him the castle and lordship of Ibelin (the modern Yavne) to hold as a fief in the county of Jaffa. Marriage to an heiress brought Barisan another important fief in the same county, the lordship of Ramla, and thereafter he and his descendants were numbered among the leading barons in the kingdom of Jerusalem. In the next generation Barisan's three sons, Hugh, Baldwin and Balian, came to the fore. Balian advanced the family's standing still further when in 1177 he married Maria Comnena, the widow of King Amaury of Jerusalem and the mother of the future Queen Isabella I (1192–1205).[2] So by the end of the twelfth century, with Balian's two sons by Maria the half-brothers of the then queen, the Ibelins' lasting pre-eminence in the kingdom of Jerusalem was assured. It was during the first half of the thirteenth century that they achieved a comparable position in Cyprus, and the story of their rise provides a unifying theme in the island's history during the reign of Hugh I, the minority of his son, Henry, and the civil war of 1229–33.

The Ibelins had not figured among the original Latin settlers of Cyprus. In the period before the Christian defeat at Hattin and the loss of Jerusalem the two surviving brothers, Balian and Baldwin, had been noted opponents of the Lusignans, although in 1186 they were helpless to prevent the *coup d'état* that

[1] J. Richard, 'Un évêque d'Orient latin au XIVe siècle: Guy d'Ibelin, O.P., évêque de Limassol, et l'inventaire de ses biens (1367)', *MAHEFR*, LIX (1949), 98–9. W. H. Rudt de Collenberg ('Les premiers Ibelins', *Le moyen âge*, LXXI (1965), 473–4) suggested an origin in Norman Sicily.

[2] For the twelfth-century genealogy, H. E. Mayer, 'Carving up Crusaders: the Early Ibelins and Ramlas', *Outremer*. For the origins of the Ibelin lordships, S. Tibble, *Monarchy and Lordships in the Latin Kingdom of Jerusalem, 1099–1291* (Oxford, 1989), pp. 43–6.

brought Guy of Lusignan to power. Rather than come to terms with the new regime, Baldwin chose exile in Antioch and apparently remained there until his death.[3] After Hattin Balian continued his opposition to Guy and joined forces with Conrad of Montferrat. In 1190, as a ploy to deny Guy his rights as king, he took the lead in marrying Maria Comnena's daughter Isabella, who was now heiress-presumptive to the throne of Jerusalem, to Conrad. Balian ended his days in about 1193 as a leading vassal of Henry of Champagne.[4] With records such as these it is scarcely surprising that evidence for members of the Ibelin family accompanying Guy of Lusignan to Cyprus and receiving lands there after his acquisition of the island is altogether lacking.

After the deaths of Guy of Lusignan and Balian of Ibelin the way stood open for an improvement in relations between the two families. In Cyprus Guy's successor, his brother Aimery, had as wife Eschiva, the daughter of Baldwin of Ibelin. The circumstances and date of their marriage are unknown, but this union meant that the Ibelins were close kinsmen of the new dynasty. Eschiva of Ibelin had died in the mid-1190s, and in 1197 Aimery married Queen Isabella of Jerusalem. This marriage also furthered his connections with the Ibelin family, since John and Philip of Ibelin, the sons of Balian, were Isabella's uterine half-brothers. But Aimery's attitude towards his brothers-in-law is difficult to assess, and it may well be that he was less than friendly. Not only were they the sons of two of his former leading opponents, but John of Ibelin had received the post of constable of Jerusalem from Henry of Champagne after Aimery himself had been forced to relinquish it.[5] In 1198 John, who at the time can have been aged no more than twenty, was one of those lords who tried to oppose Aimery when the king exiled Ralph of Tiberias.[6] Towards the end of Aimery's reign John resigned his office of constable in exchange for the lordship of Beirut, which, if we are to believe words attributed to him many years later, was 'totally destroyed, so much so that the Templars and Hospitallers and all the barons of Syria had refused it'.[7] In the long term the exchange worked to John's advantage, but it is possible that at the time Beirut was seen as inadequate compensation for the constableship which Aimery then presented to his new favourite and son-in-law, Walter of Montbéliard. But whether or not the Ibelin brothers enjoyed amicable relations with the king, it remains true that there is no indication whatever for Aimery establishing John or Philip of Ibelin – his first wife's cousins and his second wife's half-brothers – in Cyprus.

The Ibelins might have lacked wealth or influence in Aimery's island realm, but

---

[3] Baldwin was living in Antioch in June 1187. *Cont. Guillaume de Tyr*, p. 44, cf. pp. 33–5; *RRH*, no. 649.

[4] Riley-Smith, *Feudal Nobility*, pp. 109–11, 114–15. Balian is last known in May 1193. *RRH*, no. 713.   [5] *Cont. Guillaume de Tyr*, pp. 159, 161.   [6] Above, p. 34.

[7] 'Gestes', pp. 678–9. The evidence for persistent ill-feeling between John and Aimery is not conclusive. John later expressed his respect for Aimery's expertise as a jurist. Philip of Novara, pp. 515, 544.

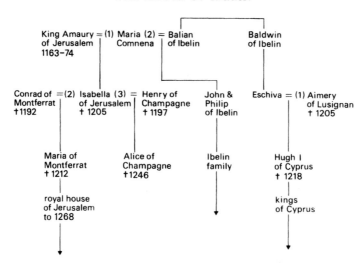

Figure 3   The relationship of John and Philip of Ibelin to the royal families of Jerusalem and Cyprus.
Note: After the death of Eschiva of Ibelin, Aimery of Lusignan married Isabella of Jerusalem whose fourth husband he was. Hugh I of Cyprus married Alice of Champagne

in the kingdom of Jerusalem they attained the highest possible position short of the throne itself. When in April 1205 Aimery died, Queen Isabella accepted John of Ibelin as her vassals' choice to rule on her behalf as her lieutenant. He continued to govern after her death later that same year and held power until the arrival of John of Brienne in 1210 to marry the new queen, Maria of Montferrat.[8]

In Cyprus it was a man of very different background who assumed control in 1205. Walter of Montbéliard was the second son of Amé of Montfaucon, count of Montbéliard, and had spent his early life in the West. In 1199 he had taken the Cross in response to the preaching of the Fourth Crusade, but in the spring of 1201 he left the main body of crusaders to join his kinsman Walter of Brienne to pursue ambitions in southern Italy. It would appear that it was only then that he came to the East. King Aimery gave him his daughter Burgundia in marriage and made him constable of Jerusalem. Although the date of his arrival cannot be fixed precisely, at the time of the king's death he cannot have been living in the East for more than two or three years.[9]

[8] 'Eracles', p. 305. J. L. La Monte, 'John d'Ibelin: The Old Lord of Beirut, 1177–1236', *Byzantion*, XII (1937), 424–5.

[9] Geoffrey de Villehardouin, *La Conquête de Constantinople*, ed. E. Faral (5th edn Paris, 1973), I, 6, 35; 'Eracles', pp. 234–5, 316; J. Longnon, *Les Compagnons de Villehardouin* (Geneva, 1978), pp. 20–1. It is not known whether Walter had visited the East before the Fourth Crusade, but the marriage and grant of the constableship cannot have been before October 1200 since the office was then held by John of Ibelin. *RRH*, no. 776.

Hugh, Aimery's sole surviving son, would have been aged nine at the time of his father's death. Later in the thirteenth century elaborate rules for determining who should exercise the regency during a minority and what powers the regent should wield were evolved in the Latin East, but in 1205 it is likely that ideas about what to do in such circumstances were still fluid. This was the first occasion on which there had been a royal minority in Cyprus, and precedents from Jerusalem were limited. But some aspects of the future customs were already being followed. In 1174 Raymond of Tripoli had argued that he should be regent for the young Baldwin IV because he was the nearest relative of the royal line present in the East.[10] In 1205 more or less the same principle was applied. Hugh's nearest relative – indeed at the time the heiress to the throne – was his sister Burgundia, and it was her husband, Walter of Montbéliard, who acquired the regency. On the other hand, a later rule, and one that had already found expression in the arrangements for the minority of Baldwin V agreed in 1183, that the regent who was himself the next heir to the throne should not have the custody of the person of the minor, was not observed in 1205: Walter had custody of both the kingdom and the king.[11]

There can be no doubt that Walter of Montbéliard was vigorous and ambitious. The most important port on the southern coast of Asia Minor was Satalia (the present-day Antalya), and, with the collapse of Greek power in the area after the destruction of the Byzantine empire by the Fourth Crusade, various interests sought to gain possession. The new Latin regime in Constantinople granted it to the Templars, and the Order obtained confirmation of this benefaction from both the papal legate in the East and Pope Innocent III.[12] But Satalia lay far beyond the area the crusaders controlled, and this grant, which thus conveyed no more than theoretical rights, availed the Templars nothing. By 1207 possession of the city was disputed between the Seljuk sultan of Rūm and the actual occupant, an Italo-Greek freebooter named Aldobrandino. When the Seljuks besieged him, Aldobrandino appealed to Cyprus for aid. Walter mounted what appears to have been a major expedition and succeeded in driving off the attackers. Exactly what happened next is unclear, but the Greeks in Satalia evidently turned against Walter and called in the Turks to expel the Cypriot forces. It can only be assumed that the regent had tried to use the opportunity to seize the place for himself.[13] Later in the thirteenth century it was believed that Walter had also attempted to win another piece of Byzantine territory, the island of Rhodes.[14] Control of Satalia and Rhodes would have meant control of an essential trade route in the eastern Mediterranean, since it would have established Cypriot rule in all the major ports of call between Crete and northern Syria. Had Walter achieved this objective, the economic and strategic advantages would have been considerable and his own

---

[10] Riley-Smith, *Feudal Nobility*, pp. 102, 185–6. Baldwin's sister Sibylla was a closer relative, but she would have been ruled out as a woman and an unmarried one at that.

[11] 'Eracles', p. 305. Cf. Riley-Smith, *Feudal Nobility*, pp. 38, 108, 187.

[12] Innocent III, vol. 215, cols. 1019–20.   [13] Hill, II, 74–5.

[14] 'Document relatif au service militaire', *RHC Lois*, II, 428.

political position would have been considerably strengthened. But success eluded him.

Walter also tried to enhance his standing by the creation of a nexus of marriage alliances. But here again his achievements fell short of his intentions. It would seem that he married his wife's sister, Helvis of Lusignan, to one of his own kinsmen, Odo of Dampierre. But although Odo later claimed that the marriage had been consummated, the couple were separated, and Helvis then married the Armenian prince, Raymond Rupen.[15] A marriage of far greater importance was that of King Hugh I to Alice of Champagne. As already mentioned, in 1197 Aimery of Lusignan and Henry of Champagne had agreed that Aimery's sons should marry Henry's daughters, but one of Henry's daughters and all but one of Aimery's sons died in childhood. In 1206, at Walter's request, the pope wrote to the patriarch of Jerusalem instructing him to look into the accounts of the 1197 agreement that had reached him, and, especially if it was to the advantage of the Latin East, to see to it that the proposed union be implemented.[16] At the time Alice was heiress to the throne of Jerusalem – she was a half-sister of Queen Maria of Montferrat – and it may well be that, in pressing for the marriage, Walter was hoping to extend his own influence to the Holy Land. There were other interests that could see advantages in the marriage of Alice and Hugh. Alice had a claim to her father's lands in France, and Blanche of Navarre, the countess of Champagne and mother of the infant Count Thibaut IV, was keen that she should be married in the East in the hope that she would thus be less likely to come to Europe and assert her rights. In 1207 Blanche sent out a representative who in effect bribed Alice's guardians, her uncles John and Philip of Ibelin, to give effect to the 1197 agreement.[17] But the Ibelins may have needed no persuasion. If Walter imagined he could benefit by the marriage of his ward to Alice, so might they in their turn hope for advantage from the marriage of their ward to Hugh. And so it turned out, for the Ibelins were to acquire considerable influence in Cyprus, thanks in part it may be assumed to their kinship with Hugh's queen, while the union did Walter no good whatever in Jerusalem. The marriage took place in 1210. In what is the first recorded instance of their having set foot in the island, John and Philip conducted their niece to Cyprus for her wedding.[18]

[15] Innocent III, vol. 216, cols. 466–7 (October 1211). Odo had complained to the pope about the break-up of his marriage and his wife's illicit union with Raymond Rupen. It looks as if Walter had promoted the match, and then, when he fell from power, Helvis married elsewhere. For the kinship of the Dampierre and Montbéliard families, 'Lignages', p. 455 note 3.

[16] Innocent III, vol. 215, cols. 829–30.

[17] *Thesaurus novus anecdotorum*, ed. E. Martène and U. Durand (Paris, 1717), I, cols. 806–7. Cf. Mas Latrie, *Histoire*, I, 175–7.

[18] 'Eracles', 308–9. There is some confusion as to the date of the marriage, but 'Eracles' indicates that it was just before the expiry of the Muslim truce in September 1210 and the arrival of John of Brienne. 'Annales' (p. 436) and 'Gestes' (p. 664) place the marriage in 1211. 1208, a date frequently cited, is unwarranted.

Hugh's marriage to Alice was the first of a rapid series of events that transformed the politics of the Latin East. In September 1210 the Muslim truce came to an end. In the same month John of Brienne arrived to marry Maria of Montferrat, the young queen of Jerusalem. Ironically this marriage, in which Walter of Montbéliard is not known to have had any hand, did work to his advantage; John was his cousin and provided a refuge for him after his fall from power in Cyprus. September 1210 also witnessed King Hugh's majority; the immediate aftermath of this milestone in his career was dramatic:

> It came to pass that when King Hugh came of age, Walter of Montbéliard, who had been regent for six years, surrendered his regency. As soon as he had done this, Hugh called him to account and said that he would require him to hand over the treasure that his father, King Aimery, had left – at least 200,000 white bezants, money which Walter had held – and to pay the 40,000 white bezants that he (Hugh) had spent during the regency owing to the hardship he had inflicted on him. For he should have been provided for out of his own as becomes a king and certainly not as becomes a boy, such was the state of deprivation in which he had been kept. Walter of Montbéliard said he would seek counsel and would reply next day. When he had gone back to his house, people came and told him that the king was being advised to break with him and seize as much of his goods as he could find. Walter believed this report, and so, when night fell, he, his wife and his household got up, and, carrying off as much gold and silver as they could, they went to a castle belonging to the Templars called Gastria and from there sought boats and a galley from Tripoli. The prince (Bohemond IV of Antioch-Tripoli), who loved him greatly, sent them to him. He embarked his horses and equipment, assembled his men, and set off for Acre where he found his nephew, his sister's son, King John, who received him with great joy. It was said that he had carried off at least 200,000 Saracen bezants, money that he had had from his regency of Cyprus over and above the considerable expenses he had incurred. And it could well be so, for he kept a good forty knights in his service for a whole year, and then he incurred very great expense when he went to take Satalia and even then it was the same as before. From King John he only had the 5,000 bezants for his surrender of the office of constable. For King Aimery had given it to him as well as extensive lands in Cyprus at the same time as he gave him his daughter Burgundia.[19]

It is possible to raise objections to this story – for example, the kinship between John and Walter is wrongly stated – and in any case the details of the charges are not independently attested. But stories of regents using their office to line their own pockets or of guardians keeping their wards short of funds are perfectly credible. Walter's own version of the incident as retailed to Pope Innocent III was that Hugh 'had expelled him from the kingdom and confiscated his lands without the judgement of his court'.[20] Unfortunately we are denied Walter's

---

[19] 'Eracles', pp. 315–16.
[20] Innocent III, vol. 216, col. 466. In the late 1220s Walter's daughter and heiress had substantial estates in Cyprus, and so presumably his estates were later restored. 'Eracles', p. 376.

explanation of why Hugh should have done this to him. For one account to claim that he fled while the other asserted that he was expelled can be dismissed simply as the result of special pleading. That Walter should have fled or should have been forced into exile at all is evidence not so much for the truth of the allegations made against him as for the fact that he can have had little or no support in the island; either by his personality or by his policies he must have alienated the other leading figures in Cyprus.

It is open to question whether Hugh, newly entered into his inheritance at the age of fifteen, would have had the capacity to determine his political actions for himself. There is no direct evidence that he was dominated by his advisers, but it is unlikely that he would have been able to act without them. Exactly who had been advising him to break with Walter and seize his property is not recorded, but a small group of royal privileges surviving from the period immediately after these events preserves the names of some twelve of Hugh's vassals who were in attendance at the court at that time.[21] The overwhelming majority were either men who had been prominent in Cyprus since the 1190s or members of families long settled in the Latin East. For example, the same four head each list: Walter of Caesarea, Aimery of Rivet, Reynald of Soissons and Walter of Bethsan. Of these the two Walters, though not previously known as members of the Cypriot High Court, were sprung from families that had held lordships in the kingdom of Jerusalem since early in the twelfth century, while Aimery and Reynald had careers in the island stretching back at least as far as the accession of King Aimery.[22] If, as seems probable, it was these men and men like them who had engineered Walter of Montbéliard's fall, the inference would be that what had taken place was a reaction against an interloper from the West by the older nobility.

Whatever the precise circumstances of Walter's fall from power in Cyprus, the incident had wide-ranging repercussions. Walter was able to embarrass Hugh by complaining to Pope Innocent III about his own treatment and also about an irregularly conducted episcopal election in Cyprus – a complaint which eventually brought the king a sharp papal rebuke.[23] In Syria John of Brienne welcomed Walter, and from 1210 until his death, apparently in 1212, he was active in raiding Muslim territory on John's behalf.[24] The beginning of Hugh I's personal rule was accompanied by a reversal of Walter's policies with regard to Cypriot foreign relations. Instead of continuing to try to win Satalia by force,

[21] RRH, nos. 844, 846; P. W. Edbury, 'The "Cartulaire de Manosque": A Grant to the Templars in Latin Syria and a Charter of King Hugh I of Cyprus', BIHR, LI (1978), 175.

[22] J. L. La Monte, 'The Lords of Caesarea in the Period of the Crusades', Speculum, XXII (1947), 154–5; La Monte and Downs, 'Lords of Bethsan', pp. 63–6. For Aimery and Reynald, RRH, no. 737 (1197). Aimery is first found in Cyprus in 1194. Richard, 'L'abbaye cistercienne', p. 69.

[23] Innocent III, vol. 216, cols. 466, 494. At the same time Odo of Dampierre complained about the break-up of his marriage.   [24] Hill, II, 77 and note 4.

Hugh negotiated a commercial agreement with its ruler, the Seljuk sultan of Rūm, guaranteeing the safety of both Turks and Cypriots engaged in trade between Cyprus and the ports under the sultan's control on the southern coast of Anatolia.[25] In the northern parts of the Latin states in Syria, Prince Bohemond IV of Antioch-Tripoli, supported by the Templars, was engaged in a war over the succession to Antioch with Leo of Armenia and his grand-nephew, Raymond Rupen, who in their turn enjoyed the support of the Hospitallers. As the passage describing his exile proves, Walter had been on good terms with both Bohemond and the Templars. Hugh favoured their opponents. In 1210, presumably immediately after Walter's fall, Hugh married two of his sisters to Leo and Raymond Rupen, clear evidence for where his sympathies lay in this struggle.[26] With the Hospitallers, Hugh seems to have had particularly close relations: in 1210, at the beginning of his personal rule, he confirmed and extended their rights and possessions in Cyprus: in 1214 he sent a Cypriot force to join them in an expedition in Syria, and on his death in 1218, presumably in accordance with his own wishes, he was buried in a Hospitaller church.[27]

The accession of John of Brienne to the throne of Jerusalem and the welcome he afforded his cousin, Walter of Montbéliard, marked the beginning of a new period of tension between Jerusalem and Cyprus. The earliest clear evidence for strained relations dates to early 1213 when the pope wrote to Hugh accusing him of helping rebels against John's authority and maltreating and imprisoning a group of his vassals who had taken refuge in Cyprus while escaping from some Muslim shipping.[28] As the preparations for the Fifth Crusade (1217–21) proceeded, the pope became more anxious that the Christians in the East should end their differences, and in 1215 or 1216 he wrote to both Hugh and King Leo of Armenia telling them to make peace with King John and hold ships in readiness for the Crusade.[29] By the time the first crusaders arrived (September and October 1217), Hugh and John were sufficiently reconciled for Hugh to bring a Cypriot

[25] C. Cahen, 'Le commerce anatolien au début du XIIIe siècle' in *Mélanges d'histoire du moyen âge dédiés à la mémoire de Louis Halphen* (Paris, 1951), pp. 93–4.

[26] Hill, II, 76. Helvis of Lusignan had married Raymond Rupin as early as September 1210. Rudt de Collenberg, 'Les Lusignan', pp. 98–9. Hugh I's support for the Armenians against Bohemond would seem to be a return to his father's policy. 'Eracles', p. 314.

[27] *Cartulaire général de l'Ordre des Hospitaliers de St-Jean de Jérusalem*, ed. J. Delaville Le Roulx (Paris, 1894–1906), no. 1354; Edbury 'Manosque', p. 175. For the 1214 campaign, C. Cahen, *La Syrie du Nord à l'époque des croisades et la principauté franque d'Antioche* (Paris, 1940), pp. 620–1. For Hugh's burial, 'Eracles', p. 325; 'Amadi', p. 104.

[28] Innocent III, vol. 216, cols. 736–7. The leading figure among the group that sought refuge in Cyprus was a relative of John designated in the papal letter by his initial as 'O'. Odo of Montbéliard, a nephew of Walter and John's first cousin once removed, is the only known relative of John in the East with this initial. (Odo was Walter's nephew and not his son as frequently stated. 'Lignages', p. 455 note 3.)

[29] Potthast, nos. 5178–9. The letters are undated but belong to the period 22 February 1215–6 July 1216.

force including a number of his leading vassals to join an expedition into Galilee. Then disputes arose between John of Brienne on the one hand and Hugh and King Andrew of Hungary on the other. Towards the end of 1217 Andrew decided to go home. Whether Hugh was intending to abandon the crusade at the same time is not clear; he accompanied Andrew as far as Tripoli, and there at the beginning of 1218 he died.[30]

It was against this background of diplomatic re-alignment and strained relations between the kingdoms of Cyprus and Jerusalem, that the Ibelins came to prominence in Cyprus. Unfortunately it is not possible to trace their rise in detail. We can be certain that the family had not been numbered among the first settlers in the 1190s; we know that Hugh I and his wife were both closely related to John of Ibelin, lord of Beirut, and his brother Philip; we also know that in September 1217 the brothers took precedence over all the other liegemen when for the first time they are named in a surviving document issued in the Cypriot High Court. In October 1217 they were listed among the participants in the opening campaign of the Fifth Crusade in such a way as to leave no doubt that they were included in the Cypriot contingent.[31] But although the sources do not allow us to chart the growth of the Ibelins' association with Cyprus before 1217, it is possible to suggest a context for this development.

From 1205 to 1210 John of Beirut was regent of the kingdom of Jerusalem; he rounded off his tenure of that office by attending John of Brienne's coronation at Tyre in October 1210. His younger brother, Philip, seems also to have enjoyed a certain prominence during this period and was entrusted with the defence of Acre while the other magnates were away at the coronation.[32] The evidence of the surviving royal diplomas shows that the brothers then withdrew from public life. John of Beirut never appears in any formal document emanating from the king's chancery during John's reign; Philip appears in only one, in 1211.[33] In other words, they were not in regular attendance on the king, and it may be that their apparent disappearance from the royal entourage is to be explained as the result of a quarrel with King John.

Support for this view is to be found in a group of papal letters dated January 1213 which speak of unnamed rebels against John's authority receiving encouragement from King Hugh. What the rebellion amounted to is not known since the episode found no echo in the narrative sources for the period. But we can glimpse its pretext. John of Brienne's wife, Maria of Montferrat, had died in 1212, and, as the information that had reached the pope made clear, once the queen was dead some people had challenged John's continuing authority.[34] The

[30] Hill, II, 82.   [31] RRH, no, 900, cf. no. 903; 'Eracles', p. 322.

[32] 'Eracles', pp. 311–12. For Philip, RRH, nos. 812, 823, 841a.

[33] RRH, no. 853. RRH, no. 855 is a forgery. Mayer, Marseilles Levantehandel, pp. 189–91, cf. pp. 50–55, 113–15.   [34] Innocent III, vol. 216, cols. 736–9.

situation was not unlike that of 1190. Then Guy of Lusignan had been faced by a party who claimed that with the death of his wife, Sibylla of Jerusalem, his own power should lapse.[35] The difference was that, unlike Guy and Sibylla, John and Maria had a surviving child of their marriage – the future Queen Isabella II – and in fact John continued to rule as king-regent for his daughter until her marriage in 1225. King Hugh's support for John's opponents is understandable. If in 1212 John of Brienne had stood down from the throne, the regents for his daughter, the child-heiress to Jerusalem, would presumably have been her next heir, her aunt Alice of Champagne, and her husband, the king of Cyprus. It is not too far-fetched to suggest that the Ibelin brothers figured prominently among the disaffected nobles. In 1190 it had been their parents, Balian of Ibelin and Maria Comnena, who had led the assault on Guy's rights to rule, and it could well be that memories of their attitude and reasoning had passed to their sons. If these suppositions are correct, then it would seem that Hugh I and the Ibelins were making common cause against John of Brienne, and it can be assumed that, when the opposition movement in the kingdom of Jerusalem failed, the Ibelins either entered Hugh's service in Cyprus or, if they were already his vassals, transferred their allegiance more fully.[36]

Hugh I died on 10 January 1218.[37] His son and heir, Henry I, was aged eight months, and his long minority can be seen as falling into two parts: ten years of growing tension followed by five years of civil war. Whereas the problem for understanding the politics of Hugh I's reign is lack of sources, for Henry I's minority the difficulty is not so much the shortage of materials as the bias they exhibit in favour of the Ibelins. Both the principal narratives, 'L'Estoire de Eracles' and the memoirs of Philip of Novara, were written from their standpoint. Philip of Novara was particularly notable for the partisanship of his writings. He was a vassal of the Ibelins, and his account of Cypriot history in the years 1218–33, much the fullest that has survived, is both a panegyric of his successive lords, John of Beirut and his eldest son Balian, and a vehicle for boasting about the role that he himself played in the events described. Philip was

---

[35] Above, p. 26.

[36] Quite likely a key figure in these years was the Ibelins' brother-in-law, Walter of Caesarea, the husband of their sister Margaret and the son of Juliana, lady of Caesarea. In the 1190s and 1200s he was an active member of the High Court of Jerusalem but from 1210 was in regular attendance on King Hugh. RRH, nos. 721, 722a, 740b, 746, 812, 844, 846, 896, 900, 903; 'Eracles', p. 322. There is good reason to suppose that there was antipathy between him and King John over his inheritance of Caesarea. His mother lived until the mid-1210s when Walter was probably aged about forty. For much of his adult life, Caesarea was controlled by his stepfather, Aymar of Laron, a close adherent of the king. Not only was Walter being kept waiting for his inheritance longer than was usual, but he had to watch Aymar burdening the lordship with debt. Then, after his mother's death, he evidently had difficulty in obtaining possession of his inheritance; he had still not gained custody of Caesarea itself at the time of its destruction by the Muslims in 1219. La Monte, 'Caesarea', pp. 153–4; Tibble, *Monarchy and Lordships*, pp. 125–8.

[37] 'Gestes', p. 670; 'Eracles', p. 325; 'Amadi', p. 104.

obviously conscious of the need for his narrative to entertain; its style resembled that of a prose romance with heroes cast in conventional mould and the villains lampooned in the guise of characters out of *fabliaux*. As a result his interpretation of events and the details of his information must be treated with a considerable degree of circumspection.[38] There is no anti-Ibelin chronicle that can be used as a counter-balance to Philip's work, and even the non-narrative sources such as formal documents and letters are more useful for building up a picture of events from the Ibelin side than for illustrating the activities of their opponents.

Hugh was survived by his widow, Alice of Champagne, and by his three children: the infant Henry I and two young daughters, Maria and Isabella. The immediate task in 1218 was to make orderly arrangements for the regency. Three versions of what was done at that time have been preserved. According to the anonymous author of the relevant section of 'L'Estoire de Eracles', Alice the queen-mother received homage as regent from the Cypriot vassals and then appointed Philip of Ibelin her lieutenant, enjoining the vassals to obey him until Henry I should come of age. Philip of Novara also related how Alice received homage as regent and claimed that the vassals then urged her to appoint Philip as her lieutenant in accordance with the wishes Hugh I was said to have expressed on his death-bed; Philip then governed while Alice enjoyed the profits from the royal revenues. From papal letters of February 1226 it would seem that Pope Honorius III had been told that the nobles, barons, knights and people of Cyprus had chosen Philip of Ibelin to be regent, and that since the death of Hugh he had ruled with Alice and would continue to do so until either Henry came of age or Alice made a suitable marriage. In each case these accounts reflect subsequent developments, but it is nevertheless possible to see the principles that lay behind the decisions taken in 1218. Just as the wardship of the fiefs of minor heirs was exercised by a surviving parent, so the regency of the kingdom for an under-age king passed, as in this case, to his mother. So Alice was accepted as regent. But the idea that a woman should herself exercise royal power in the kingdom was unacceptable, and so she appointed Philip to govern on her behalf.[39]

By about 1223 or 1224 Philip and Alice had quarrelled.[40] Alice resolved to get

---

[38] For Philip's history, G. Paris, 'Les mémoires de Philippe de Novare', *ROL*, IX (1902); C. Kohler, introduction to 'Les Gestes des Chiprois', *RHC Arm.*, II, pp. ccxxviii–ccxxix; Philip of Novara, *The Wars of Frederick II against the Ibelins in Syria and Cyprus*, trans. J. L. La Monte (New York, 1936), pp. 3–21; J. Bromiley, 'Philip of Novara's Account of the War between Frederick II of Hohenstaufen and the Ibelins', *Journal of Medieval History*, III (1977). The difficulty in using Philip's work is aggravated by textual problems. The 'Chronique d'Amadi' includes an Italian translation of what was apparently a better version of the text with details lacking in the unique French ms.

[39] 'Eracles', pp. 360–1; 'Gestes', p. 670; Honorius III, *Regesta*, ed. P. Pressutti (Rome, 1888–95), nos. 5824–5.

[40] Hill's explanation for the quarrel (II, 88) is ill-founded. The chronology of the mid-1220s is confused. See La Monte, 'John d'Ibelin', p. 426 note 7; Hill, II, 88 note 3.

rid of him, but he was too firmly entrenched to be ousted easily. So the queen-mother then went to Tripoli where she married Bohemond, the son and eventual successor of Prince Bohemond IV. In 1205 the regency had been awarded to the husband of Burgundia of Lusignan, the member of the royal family closest to the throne. There was thus a precedent for investing the consort of a female relative of a minor king with effective control, and Alice evidently hoped that the Cypriots would allow her to install Bohemond as governor of Cyprus in place of Philip. The 1226 papal letter certainly envisaged just such an eventuality. But Bohemond was not acceptable. According to Philip of Novara, the Cypriot vassals were unanimous in opposing him on the grounds that they feared for the safety of their young king should he fall into Bohemond's clutches. In other words, they stood by Philip of Ibelin. The pope then reduced Bohemond's chances of taking power in the island still further by ordering an enquiry into the allegation that his marriage was inadmissible in canon law since he and Alice were too closely related to each other. Bohemond's father, Bohemond IV, had long been at odds with the papacy, and Pope Honorius would have been reluctant to countenance the growth of Tripolitan influence in Cyprus.[41]

There is no direct evidence that Alice ever attempted to get formal acceptance for Bohemond from the Cypriots; reaction to the news of her marriage perhaps convinced her that such a move was bound to end in failure. She therefore tried a different tack. Philip was her appointee; she would simply announce that she had dismissed him and tell the Cypriots to receive his replacement. Her choice was Aimery Barlais, a Cypriot knight known for his opposition to the Ibelins. But Philip of Ibelin's grip on the situation was sufficient to thwart Aimery's appointment. Neither of the two accounts of this episode questioned the fact that Alice was the lawful regent and Philip her lieutenant, and so it might be supposed that legally he was removable at will. But one source recorded that Philip rejected Aimery on the grounds that he himself had been appointed for the duration of Henry's minority, while the other, which stated that Philip had actually resigned at this point, claimed that Aimery found the Cypriots solidly behind the Ibelins and withdrew leaving Philip in control. But was his appointment in 1218 intended to last for the whole of the minority? It is impossible to be sure. Alice evidently thought not. Philip's refusal to bow to Alice's wishes and stand down could well have put the legitimacy of his rule in doubt in the eyes of all but his most loyal supporters, and it is arguable that the vassals had put themselves in the wrong by refusing to acknowledge Alice's nominee.[42] At the beginning of 1226 the pope issued a series of letters designed to bolster the Ibelin regime: Philip was told to exercise his office for the good of the

[41] 'Gestes', p. 673; 'Eracles', p. 361; Honorius III, no. 5593. Cf. Rudt de Collenberg, 'Dispenses matrimoniales', pp. 86–7 and notes 73–4 (p. 92) (also noting a papal prohibition on Alice's proposed marriage to William of Dampierre in 1223).

[42] 'Gestes.', p. 673; 'Eracles', pp. 361–2; Riley-Smith, *Feudal Nobility*, pp. 192–3.

young king and the kingdom; the military Orders and the Cypriots were told to support Philip and King Henry; the king was placed under papal protection and commended to the emperor Frederick II and others, and the archbishop of Nicosia was instructed to publish Bohemond IV's excommunication. It is not altogether clear whether these letters were intended to strengthen Cypriot opposition to Bohemond of Tripoli or were an endorsement of the refusal to accept Aimery Barlais, but undoubtedly they would have boosted the morale of the Ibelins and their supporters and helped give Philip's position an appearance of legality.[43]

Philip of Ibelin died in 1227 or 1228.[44] His brother John, who until then had divided his time between helping Philip in Cyprus and building up his own lordship of Beirut, thereupon assumed control of the government of the island. By what authority he could do so we are not told. He was scarcely likely to have been appointed by Alice. Philip had at least been properly installed, even if he had then clung to office against the wishes of the regent. But John's right to govern can have followed from nothing more than the acclamation of the vassals of his own party in the island. To his enemies he must have seemed a usurper, maintaining himself and his followers in opposition to the lawful authority, Alice and her lieutenant-designate, Aimery Barlais. So, when in July 1228 the suzerain of the kingdom of Cyprus, the emperor Frederick II, arrived in the East, he found a situation in which the queen-mother, Alice of Champagne, had lost control, and in which power rested with a man whose entitlement to rule was dubious.

Frederick II's intervention in the Latin East in 1228 and 1229 acted as a catalyst which had the effect of transforming existing rivalries in Cyprus into a full-scale civil war. These rivalries had come to the surface in the years since the death of Hugh I. As Philip and John of Ibelin hung on to office, so opposition towards them had hardened. The sources for the period 1218–33, with their stress on the achievements of the Ibelins and their party, allow us to identify only a handful of their opponents. The nucleus of the opposition comprised a group of five knights, who were to become known as the five *baillis* – so called because in 1229 Frederick farmed the regency or *bailliage* of Cyprus to them jointly: Aimery Barlais, Amaury of Bethsan, Hugh of Jubail, William of Rivet and Gauvain of Cheneché. Other members of their party included Philip Chenard and Bertram and Hugh Porcelet.[45] Philip of Novara tried to make out that Aimery Barlais and

---

[43] Honorius III, nos. 5808, 5813, 5822, 5824–5, 5828, 5829.

[44] For the date, Hill, II, 91 note 4.

[45] 'Gestes', pp. 672, 676, 684; 'Amadi', p. 175. Apart from these eight, another seven names are recorded: Hugh *Zaboc*, Hugh of Mare, and Reynald Chamberlain ('Amadi', p. 175); Humphrey of Monaigre ('Gestes', p. 713); Baldwin of Belleme ('Eracles', pp. 361–2), and two deserters from the Ibelins, *Denises* and Martin Rousseau ('Gestes', pp. 701, 720).

his associates were no more than a troublesome pressure-group, who for military strength in the civil war were dependent on mercenaries and the Hohenstaufen forces from the West. However, at one point in his narrative of the events of 1232 he let slip the information that at that time the five *baillis* had the support of eighty Cypriot knights – evidently a significant proportion of the total.[46] It is also clear that the leaders were substantial figures. Aimery Barlais, Gauvain of Cheneché and William of Rivet had been attending the Cypriot High Court and witnessing formal documents issued there as early as 1220,[47] and in the previous generation the fathers of Aimery Barlais, Amaury of Bethsan, William of Rivet and Hugh of Jubail had been prominent royal counsellors.[48]

The leaders of this faction formed a tight-knit group. Philip of Novara, who claimed that the five *baillis* swore together to oppose the Ibelins at some point in the mid-1220s, drew attention to ties of kinship linking on the one hand Aimery Barlais and Amaury of Bethsan and on the other William of Rivet and Gauvain of Cheneché.[49] In fact the web of family connections spread far wider: Gauvain was the uterine half-brother of Philip Chenard; Hugh Porcelet's brother Bertram was Aimery Barlais' step-father; Hugh of Jubail was married to their sister, Maria Porcelet, and Amaury of Bethsan was the son of yet another member of the Porcelet family.[50] These relationships undoubtedly served to give added cohesion to their party. In addition, several of these men shared links with the county of Tripoli. Hugh of Jubail was the grandson of William II, lord of Jubail; Hugh's father, besides being a member of the Cypriot High Court, had been a man of some consequence in Tripoli, and it was there that Hugh and his descendants were to live after the end of the civil war. Bertram and Hugh Porcelet came from a well-established Tripolitan family, and, like Hugh of Jubail, Bertram took part in the affairs of the county.[51] Bertram's stepson, Aimery Barlais, had married the heiress of the former lord of Marqab, and through her had the substantial rent paid by the Hospitallers from their revenues in Tripoli in exchange for the castle and lordship.[52]

There can be little doubt that personal animosity born of victimization at the

---

[46] *Ibid.*, p. 703. Eighty knights may have represented as much as a third of the nobility. Richard, *Latin Kingdom*, p. 312 note 13 (p. 436).   [47] *RRH*, nos. 912, 929, 938.

[48] Respectively, Reynald Barlais, Walter of Bethsan, Aimery of Rivet and Bertrand of Jubail. Below, p. 55.

[49] 'Gestes', p. 672; cf. p. 694. Aimery and Amaury were first cousins once removed. 'Lignages', p. 463; F. Chandon de Briailles, 'Lignages d'Outre-Mer, les seigneurs de Margat', *Syria*, xxv (1946–8), 246 ('Renaud' in the last line of note 5 is a misprint for 'Aimery'). Gauvain and William's brother James had married two sisters. 'Lignages', pp. 457, 461; cf. *RRH*, no. 938.

[50] 'Gestes', pp. 694, 719; 'Lignages', pp. 458, 463; J. Richard, 'Le comté de Tripoli dans les chartes du fonds des Porcellet', *BEC*, cxxx (1972), 352–3.

[51] Rey, 'Seigneurs de Giblet', pp. 410–12; Richard, 'Le comté de Tripoli', pp. 348–66 *passim*.

[52] Chandon de Briailles, 'Margat', pp. 244–6; J. Riley-Smith, *The Knights of St John in Jerusalem and Cyprus c.1050–1310* (London, 1967), p. 68.

hands of the Ibelins played an important part in stimulating opposition. In the mid-1220s both Aimery Barlais and Gauvain of Cheneché became involved in violent incidents with retainers of Philip or John of Ibelin that led to periods of exile. As recounted by Philip of Novara, it was the Ibelins' opponent who was at fault in each case, but allowance should be made for his bias, and his version of events leaves room for alternative constructions to be placed upon them. A knight named William of La Tour accused Gauvain of wounding him; the two men fought a judicial duel in which William evidently got the better of his adversary; Gauvain went into exile complaining that William would not have dared bring the action had the Ibelins not been maintaining him. Whether or not the accusation against Gauvain was true – and it may be noted that for the case to have come to a duel he must have been prepared to deny the charge under oath – his allegations of maintenance suggest that he believed that he had not had a fair hearing and that the court under the presidency of Philip of Ibelin was less than impartial.[53]

Aimery Barlais' recorded scrapes with the Ibelins began when he attacked and seriously wounded a knight in Philip of Ibelin's retinue. It was all John of Beirut could do to rescue Aimery from his brother's wrath and protect him from immediate reprisals. Aimery spent the winter in exile in Tripoli, and then, at John's insistence, Philip reluctantly agreed to pardon him. As told by Philip of Novara, the story is designed to illustrate John of Beirut's magnanimity, and Aimery, as his foil, is shown as a dishonourable and undeserving coward. But leaving aside the literary and propagandist aspects of the account, it is clear that immediately after the deed was committed Aimery was in physical danger from Philip of Ibelin, and, irrespective of the merits of the case, the grudgingly extracted pardon was hardly likely to have reassured him. The next stage in Aimery's relations with the Ibelins followed when Alice of Champagne attempted to appoint him her lieutenant. According to Philip of Novara, Aimery found he could get no support, and, rebuffed by stern speeches from Philip of Ibelin and a retainer and kinsman of the Ibelins named Anseau of Brie, who formally accused him of breaking faith and challenged him to defend himself, he retired once again to Tripoli. Not only had Aimery been humiliated, the refusal of the Ibelins to accept him as Alice's nominee would have seemed to some people at least an illegal act only made possible by their tight hold on power in the island. Another pro-Ibelin source added a significant detail that illustrates the nature of their control: a knight by the name of Baldwin of Belleme had had the temerity on this occasion to deny Philip's rights and speak up for Alice as the only legitimate regent; Philip's supporters thereupon set on him, and he was mortally wounded. The conclusion is unavoidable: the Ibelins were prepared to use illegal and violent means to maintain their control of the government; a man

---

[53] 'Gestes', p. 674.

as important as Aimery Barlais was humiliated and obliged to go into exile; a lesser man was the victim of lynch law. Further loss of face was in store for Aimery. Philip of Novara related that he pinned his hopes for revenge on the emperor Frederick; according to Philip, Aimery returned to Cyprus and to clear his name challenged Anseau of Brie to a judicial duel in the expectation that before the battle could take place, Frederick would have arrived and put an end to the matter. Aimery apparently reasoned that the Ibelins would be overawed and that he himself would emerge high in Frederick's esteem for his persistence and courage in resisting the Ibelin regime. But Frederick did not come when expected – his sailing scheduled for the autumn of 1227 was postponed – and the battle had to go ahead. Aimery was defeated, and John of Beirut and Walter of Caesarea had to intervene to save his life. Whether or not we accept the aspersions cast on Aimery's motivation, Philip's account makes it seem that Aimery, having set himself up in opposition to the Ibelins, had been utterly discredited.[54]

According to Philip of Novara, 'My lord Philip of Ibelin governed the land extremely well and in peace, and he did much that was good, honourable, true and generous . . . '[55] As a verdict on the decade 1218–27, these words clearly require modification: political violence had made its appearance; the legitimacy of the regime had been put in doubt. The author's adulation for his heroes brought him into difficulty when he had to explain why anyone who had enjoyed the benefits of their rule should want to oppose them. He informed his readers that the hostility of the five *baillis* resulted from 'the foolishness and pride that often stem from wealth and leisure'.[56] This sententiousness is plainly unhelpful. We have seen that the leading opponents of the Ibelins had close family ties with one another; that several shared a common background in Tripoli, and that at least two of the most prominent had been humiliated and forced into exile. Maybe they began their opposition out of loyalty to Alice of Champagne when she quarrelled with Philip of Ibelin. Alice and her husband, the future Bohemond V, appear to have remained in Tripoli after their marriage, and it is likely that they fostered relations with Cypriot knights with Tripolitan connections in an attempt to build up an opposition party in the island. But evidence specifically linking Alice to the five *baillis* is limited: Aimery Barlais was her candidate to replace Philip, and William of Rivet may have acted on her behalf at the papal court in the wrangle over the legality of her marriage to Bohemond.[57] But even if the anti-Ibelin faction first took shape as a group of men who supported Alice, their loyalty to her was not lasting. After 1228 they were

[54] *Ibid.*, pp. 672–4, 675–6; cf. 'Eracles', pp. 361–2. 'Amadi' (pp. 122–3) preserves an apparently superior version of Philip's account of the duel.   [55] 'Gestes', p. 670.   [56] *Ibid.*, p. 672.
[57] Honorius III, no. 6272, cf. no. 6271. William and his colleague, an Antiochene cleric, persuaded the pope to withdraw his commission to investigate the consanguinity between Bohemond and Alice from the archbishop of Nicosia.

totally committed to the emperor whose policy was not only to supplant the Ibelins but also to disregard the queen-mother's rights to hold the regency.

A glance at the antecedents of the five *baillis* reveals what must have been a potent underlying cause of their disaffection. Aimery Barlais was the son of Reynald Barlais, the Poitevin companion of Guy of Lusignan who unsuccessfully defended Jaffa on behalf of King Aimery in 1197. William of Rivet's father was almost certainly Aimery of Rivet, one of the earliest known settlers in Cyprus in the 1190s and seneschal of Cyprus from 1197 until some time after 1210.[58] Amaury of Bethsan was the son of Walter of Bethsan, prominent in the 1210s, and nephew of two other members of the family who were living in the island in the 1190s.[59] Gauvain of Cheneché must surely have been a son or close relative of the 'Galganus' of Cheneché who, though he cannot be shown to have settled in Cyprus, may well have done so as he had been permanently in attendance on Guy of Lusignan during and after the siege of Acre (1189–92).[60] Only Hugh of Jubail, whose father, Bertrand, is first found in the island in 1217,[61] may not have been a member of a family which had been in Cyprus or in the service of the Lusignans from as far back as the 1190s. But all five were second generation vassals of the Cypriot crown. Perhaps it may not be too fanciful to suggest that, with the possible exception of Hugh of Jubail, they were conscious of traditions of service to the Lusignan rulers of Cyprus in their families stretching back much further than was true of the Ibelin family. At a time when the Ibelins were still the bitter foes of the Lusignans, their fathers had been high in the latter's counsels. Now, as they themselves achieved manhood, they had seen members of the family that they had been brought up to think of as the enemies of their lord establish themselves in Cyprus and rapidly acquire an almost unassailable position of power. What is more, much of the influence, the patronage and the favour that their fathers, as leading vassals of earlier rulers of Cyprus, would have enjoyed was being denied them. The Ibelins had displaced them as the leaders of Cypriot noble society.

To his contemporaries, as to modern scholars, the emperor Frederick II was a controversial figure. Whatever view is taken of his reign as a whole, the words of one modern historian admirably sum up his intervention in the Latin East:

> on his crusade and in his relations with the kingdoms of Cyprus and Jerusalem one is faced by a man who had a strong will and was capable of ruthless and arbitrary acts, but was motivated by conservative ideas, determined to enjoy what he took to be established imperial or royal rights . . . [62]

[58] For Aimery, *RRH*, nos. 723, 729, 737, 780, 844, 846; Richard, 'L'abbaye cistercienne', p. 69.
[59] *RRH*, nos. 723, 729, 844, 846, 900, 912, 938; 'Eracles', p. 322; 'Lignages', p. 463.
[60] *RRH*, nos. 683–4, 690, 693, 697–8, 701–2.
[61] *Ibid.*, no. 896. Cf. 'Gestes', p. 685. Renier of Jubail, Aimery's ambassador to Henry VI in 1195, was no relation.   [62] Riley-Smith, *Feudal Nobility*, p. 160.

Frederick had taken the Cross in 1215. It had been expected that he would participate in the Fifth Crusade, but he made repeated postponements, and after the capitulation of the Christian army and the surrender of Damietta in 1221 his plans were shelved. In 1225 he renewed his vows and organized an expedition timed to begin in the autumn of 1227. At the last moment he turned back, and it was not until May 1228 that he eventually set sail. But by 1228 his interest in Cyprus came a long way behind interest in the kingdom of Jerusalem. For whereas in Cyprus he had inherited rights of suzerainty, in Jerusalem he was now father to the heir to the throne. In 1225 Frederick had married Queen Isabella II of Jerusalem, the daughter of John of Brienne. The following year he sent one of his most trusted Italian officers to Acre to take charge there on his behalf. Then, shortly before he was due to leave for the East, the queen died having just given birth to a son named Conrad.

In 1196 Frederick's father, Henry VI, had established Cyprus as a kingdom under his suzerainty, but the turmoil in Germany and Italy during the two decades after his death meant that Frederick can have had little thought of asserting his rights over the island before the 1220s. As suzerain Frederick now claimed that the regency necessitated by Henry's minority should be his, that the king and the vassals owed him homage,[63] and that the profits from the royal revenues during the minority belonged to him. His demand for the regency posed problems arising from a conflict between the customs of the Western Empire and of the Latin East: while in parts of the West it was normal for the lord to hold the wardship of the lands of a minor heir, in the East it was the next of kin who exercised this right.[64] In 1205 and 1218 the young king's relatives had taken charge without, so far as is known, making reference to the emperor, but at some point during the 1220s Frederick wrote to Alice of Champagne asserting his claims and telling her that she held the regency on his behalf and at his pleasure.[65] But for as long as Frederick was far away in Europe, he could be ignored by the authorities in Cyprus. It was only when he turned up in the East with a crusading army that his demands had to be taken seriously.

In July 1228, when Frederick first set foot in Cyprus, he was already predisposed to regard the Ibelin regime in the island with hostility. He accepted that John of Beirut was the effective ruler, but, no doubt anxious to maintain an adequate supply of funds for himself during his crusade, he demanded that John render account for the previous ten years of Henry I's minority and hand over the profits. Evidently there were none. An Italian Ghibelline writer hints that the Ibelins were guilty of peculation. John's own explanation as recorded by Philip of Novara was that his brother Philip had merely run the day-to-day affairs and

[63] 'Eracles', p. 367.
[64] A later jurist in Latin Syria allowed the lord rights of wardship only if there was no parent or relative qualified to exercise it. James of Ibelin, 'Livre de Jacques d'Ibelin', RHC Lois, I, 461.
[65] 'Gestes', p. 672.

that the profits had gone to the regent, Alice of Champagne, who had spent them as she wished. In view of the tension between Alice and the Ibelins during the years immediately before Frederick's arrival, this explanation might be thought disingenuous. Indeed, the fact that Philip of Novara repeated on no less than three occasions that Alice had had the money may in itself suggest that he was suspiciously over-anxious to rebut charges that the Ibelins had lined their own pockets during this period.[66]

But finance was only one of the issues that concerned the emperor. In 1225 the Ibelins had the young king crowned without giving Frederick prior notification. The emperor was enraged at what in his eyes was a flagrant disregard for his authority over the island.[67] However, it is not necessarily true that the Ibelins intended the coronation as a deliberate snub; it is equally likely that they wanted to avoid criticism nearer home if they delayed. But Frederick's distrust of their regime may have dated from that time, and his attitude towards them was no doubt reinforced by the activities of their Cypriot opponents. Gauvain of Cheneché, in exile after his clash with William of La Tour, took service with the emperor some time before the beginning of 1226. William of Rivet seems to have made contact with Frederick when he visited the papal court in 1227. Aimery Barlais, we are told, based his hopes for a political recovery on the emperor in the expectation that he would put an end to the Ibelin ascendancy, and he and his supporters wrote letters and in 1228 even went part of the way by sea to meet him in their attempts to secure his good will. They were not to be disappointed.[68]

The arrival of Frederick II placed John of Beirut in a dilemma. He would have been well aware that the emperor was less than friendly, and the temptation to keep out of his way and refuse to co-operate must have been strong. On the other hand, Frederick was generally welcomed by the Latins in the East, and John may not have anticipated much support outside his immediate circle if he resisted. Nor could he risk giving the impression that he wanted to prevent the recovery of the Holy Land by his own non-co-operation. Furthermore, Frederick's military resources were large enough to compel respect. John's only hope was to attempt to work as fully as possible in collaboration with the emperor in the hope that in return Frederick would not undermine his position. So when, shortly after his arrival, Frederick summoned John to join him at a banquet in Limassol and bring his sons, his friends and the young King Henry as well, John rejected the advice of those who feared that this was a trick to get them all into the emperor's power and complied. As described by Philip of Novara, the banquet formed a spectacular back-drop for a highly dramatic incident. During the meal the

---

[66] Ibid., pp. 669, 670, 678–9; 'Breve chronicon de rebus siculis', ed. J. L. A. Huillard-Bréholles in Historia diplomatica Frederici secundi (Paris, 1852–61), I, 900.

[67] 'Gestes', p. 672. For the date, Hill, II, 90 note 5.

[68] For Gauvain, RRH, nos. 974–5; 'Gestes', pp. 674, 675. For William, Honorius III, nos. 6271–2. For Aimery, 'Gestes', pp. 673–4, 675–6.

Cypriots were surrounded by the emperor's men-at-arms. Then Frederick made his demands: John must surrender his lordship of Beirut on the grounds that he held it illegally, and he must hand over the profits from the Cypriot regency for the period since the death of King Hugh I. John stood his ground: his title to Beirut was good, and he would answer for it in the proper place, the High Court of Jerusalem; by Cypriot custom the regent of Cyprus was Queen Alice: she had had the profits of the regency, and John was prepared to defend his own conduct in the Cypriot High Court. He had answered bravely, but his gamble had failed. Any hope he may have had that the emperor would respond favourably to his apparent willingness to co-operate had proved unfounded. Frederick's demands had been too great. Called to render account and faced by the threatened loss of his Syrian lordship, John had had to defend himself if he was to prevent his total ruination. But in defending himself he necessarily antagonized the emperor irrevocably. Frederick made John surrender two of his sons and have twenty leading Cypriot vassals pledge themselves and their possessions as security for his appearance before the High Court of Jerusalem.[69]

John of Beirut had at least retained his own liberty. The next morning, or at nightfall – the sources differ – he and his supporters rode off to Nicosia. He provisioned the castle of St Hilarion, where he sent the wives and children of his men, and he had the rest of his men-at-arms and his horses brought over from Syria. After some delay Frederick followed him. He was accompanied by the Ibelins' Cypriot opponents and a number of Latin Syrian nobles including the prince of Antioch, who had with him a force of sixty knights as well as sergeants and footmen. In mid-August the emperor's party occupied Nicosia while John shut himself up in St Hilarion. Philip of Novara tried hard to make out that John was acting with the utmost propriety by taking care not to take up arms against the emperor, the suzerain of the kingdom of Cyprus, in person, but he was unable to conceal the fact that John had embarked on what amounted to armed resistance. Frederick evidently decided that it would be unwise to try to besiege St Hilarion, and at the beginning of September the two antagonists came to an agreement. In practical terms John had lost. He had secured the release of his sons, and the knights were freed from their pledges for his appearance in court, but these were almost the only concessions Frederick granted. A compromise was worked out over the regency: the emperor took the fealty of the Cypriots in his capacity as suzerain, accepting the argument that having done homage to Alice as regent they would be breaking faith if forced to do homage to himself. But he saw to it that he was to have the all-important profits from the royal revenues. The young king was to have nominal control of the fortresses in the island, and Cypriot liegemen were to have custody of them until he came of age.

---

[69] 'Gestes', pp. 676–80; 'Eracles', pp. 367–8. The sources differ as to which of John's sons the emperor held.

But here again Frederick had outmanoeuvred John of Beirut, for Henry was obliged to appoint castellans from among Frederick's allies in Cyprus. John of Beirut was promised that he should not be deprived of anything that was his without judgement of the High Courts of Cyprus or Jerusalem, but he had to accompany Frederick to Syria and serve him, together with his men, for as long as he remained there. Two of his sons, Balian and John, were, it would seem, kept under the emperor's direct surveillance.[70]

Frederick had ended Ibelin rule in Cyprus, at least for the time being. But fortunately for John and his supporters, the following months saw an abrupt change in the emperor's fortunes. Shortly before his departure for the East he had been excommunicated by the pope who disapproved of his Italian policies and the postponement of his crusade in 1227. News of his excommunication turned many leading members of the Latin Syrian community including the patriarch of Jerusalem against him. By his patronage of the Teutonic Knights he then alienated the Templars and Hospitallers. By his high-handed actions in confiscating or withholding fiefs, he provoked hostility from the nobility – hostility so determined that in at least two instances he had to back down. His treaty of February 1229 with the ruler of Egypt, al-Kamil, restored Jerusalem to Christian control but did nothing to ingratiate him with the growing number of his detractors. Then news from Europe that the former king of Jerusalem, John of Brienne, was invading his lands at the head of a papal army made it imperative that he return home The Syrian Franks were still recalcitrant, and by the time Frederick left the Holy Land in May 1229 the political standing of his most prominent opponent in the East, John of Beirut, was high.[71]

Aimery Barlais and his associates had not gained control in Cyprus directly after the collapse of John's power in the summer of 1228. At some point during the following winter Frederick sent Count Stephen, one of his trusted western officers, with a force of Italians to take charge in the island on his behalf. Count Stephen then seized the Cypriot castles, thereby breaking the agreement between Frederick and John of Beirut that the strongpoints should be held by Cypriot liegemen until King Henry's majority. According to Philip of Novara, the wives and children of the pro-Ibelin knights whom Frederick had made accompany him to Syria went in fear for their safety; some took refuge in religious foundations; others fled to northern Syria.[72] But towards the end of his stay in

---

[70] 'Gestes', pp. 680–2; 'Eracles', pp. 368–9; 'Breve chronicon de rebus siculis', p. 900. Frederick had arrived in Cyprus on 21 July, moved to Nicosia on 17 August and left on 2 September. The banquet at Limassol was clearly soon after his arrival, and his departure followed close on the settlement. John's defiance in St Hilarion cannot therefore have lasted for more than ten days.

[71] J. Riley-Smith, 'The Assise Sur La Ligece and the Commune of Acre', *Traditio*, XXVII (1971), 191–4; *idem, Feudal Nobility*, pp. 165–73; T. C. Van Cleave, *The Emperor Frederick II of Hohenstaufen. Immutator Mundi* (Oxford, 1972), pp. 215–28.

[72] 'Gestes', pp. 682–3. For Count Stephen's identity, p. 682 note c.

Acre the emperor arranged to farm the regency of Cyprus to a consortium consisting of Aimery Barlais and his four leading companions. They were to hold it jointly for three years, at the end of which Henry would come of age, in return for a payment to the emperor's representatives in Syria of 10,000 silver marks. Frederick's western officers were to retain custody of the castles until the money was handed over. The five *baillis*, as they were now known, were given a force of western mercenaries whom they undertook to pay, and, according to Philip of Novara, they were made to swear that, far from allowing the Ibelins to return to the island, they would dispossess them. On his way back to Europe Frederick stopped at Limassol where he handed over the young king, whom he married to Alice, a daughter of his Piedmontese vassal William of Montferrat, and delivered custody of the island to the five *baillis*.[73]

The emperor had left the *baillis* in a difficult position. To obtain effective control they had to find the money, but a rapacious policy would have added to their unpopularity. The Ibelins and their dependants who had either been deprived of their fiefs or feared dispossession were opposed to them, and John of Beirut's power-base in Syria remained intact. The *baillis* seem to have tried to do the best they could under the circumstances. Philip of Novara described how they made a clumsy attempt to persuade him to join them – a mixture of cajolery and intimidation. The clear implication of his story was that he himself had been able to remain in Cyprus up to that time and had not been dispossessed. But other evidence suggests that knights in John of Ibelin's company may have lost their lands: Klavdhia, which had belonged to an Ibelin adherent named John of Mimars and which in June 1229 the *baillis* gave to the emperor's most dependable allies in the East, the Teutonic Knights, was almost certainly part of their spoils. Aimery Barlais and his associates had been told to destroy the Ibelin party in Cyprus completely; if the Ibelins were to recover anything in the island, they in their turn would have to overthrow the five *baillis*.[74]

The stage was set for the opening of hostilities. In little over a month after Frederick's departure the Ibelins, spurred on by news of the sequestration of their fiefs and the plight of their womenfolk, set sail from Acre and landed at the Templar fort of Gastria to the north of Famagusta. From there they marched on Nicosia. On 14 July battle was joined outside the capital. As recorded by Philip of Novara, the chief feature of the engagement was the deeds of prowess performed by John of Beirut, his sons and their kinsman, Anseau of Brie. The constable, Walter of Caesarea, and Gerard of Montagu, the nephew of the

---

[73] *Ibid.*, p. 684; 'Eracles', p. 375. For Alice's relationship to the Hohenstaufen and to the other members of the Montferrat family connected with the East, see the table in T. S. R. Boase, *Kingdoms and Strongholds of the Crusaders* (London, 1971), pp. 250–1.

[74] 'Gestes', pp. 684–6; 'Eracles', p. 376. For John of Mimars and Klavdhia, *Tabulae ordinis Theutonici*, ed. E. Strehlke (Berlin, 1869), p. 56; *RRH*, no. 1049. The Mimars were vassals of the Ibelins.

archbishop of Nicosia, were among the slain, but despite these losses victory went to the Ibelins. The *baillis* escaped from the field of battle and defended themselves in the fortresses of Kyrenia, St Hilarion and Kantara. Kyrenia soon fell, but Kantara, defended by Gauvain of Cheneché and then, after his death during the siege, by Philip Chenard, and St Hilarion, where the other *baillis* held the king, resisted for about ten months, capitulating in April or May 1230.[75]

John of Beirut had won the first round of the civil war, but it remained highly likely that the emperor would return or would send further troops to the East. Apparently the defenders of St Hilarion and Kantara had waited to see whether relief from Europe would arrive in the spring of 1230 before surrendering.[76] Fear of renewed imperial interference in Cyprus may have lain behind the policy of conciliation that John now pursued towards his defeated opponents. He offered the emperor's garrison at Kyrenia generous terms to induce it to capitulate and paid a high price to get it off Cypriot soil. After the surrender of St Hilarion and Kantara, Aimery Barlais and his followers were made to swear not to oppose the Ibelins ever again, but otherwise they were not penalized. They kept their fiefs and, although some of their partisans refused to lay aside their bitterness, John of Beirut and his sons, so we are told, went out of their way to treat them with honour and respect.[77] John was clearly conscious of his own vulnerability. He had overthrown the emperor's officers in Cyprus and expelled his garrisons. For ten months he had besieged a castle containing the king, and, although pro-Ibelin apologists could claim that Henry was virtually the prisoner of the *baillis*, an alternative view would have been that John had taken up arms against the person of his monarch. No amount of appealing to due judicial process, as in 1228, would dissuade Frederick from treating John as a traitor and a rebel if and when he could re-assert his suzerainty in the island or gain effective control of the kingdom of Jerusalem where John and several of his supporters also had fiefs.

After the surrender of St Hilarion and Kantara, Ibelin ascendancy in Cyprus survived unchallenged for over a year. It was not until the autumn of 1231 that the emperor was able to set about restoring his control in the East. He appointed the imperial marshal, Richard Filangieri, to take overall charge on his behalf, although it is not entirely clear whether he intended him to act as his lieutenant in Cyprus.[78] A substantial army sailed from Europe with Richard following. News of its coming brought John of Beirut hurrying from Syria, and he and the forces at his disposal took up positions in Cyprus to prevent the imperial troops from landing. The emperor's spokesman demanded that King Henry should expel John of Beirut together with his sons and other relatives from the island. These demands were rejected, and John, in what he presumably intended as a

---

[75] 'Gestes', pp. 688–95; 'Eracles', pp. 376–7; Hill, II, 103–6. For the date of the battle and the length of the siege, Hill, II, 104 note 1, 106 note 1.

[76] 'Eracles', p. 377. They also sought help in Armenia where William of Rivet died. 'Gestes', p. 694.

[77] 'Gestes', pp. 690, 694–5, 699–700.   [78] 'Amadi' (p. 147) asserts that he did.

conciliatory gesture, offered once more to defend himself against any charges in the Cypriot High Court. The imperial fleet then departed for Syria and made for John's lordship of Beirut. The army occupied the town of Beirut and was already intent on besieging the citadel when Richard Filangieri arrived. There can be little doubt that he had instructions from Frederick to crush Ibelin power in the East and to do so by whatever means necessary.[79]

The decision to attack John in Syria rather than in Cyprus may have been prompted by the belief that John's position was weaker there. In 1229 Frederick had left two Syrian nobles, Balian of Sidon and Garnier L'Aleman, to act as his deputies in Acre. Their close associate was the constable of Jerusalem and nephew of the former regent of Cyprus, Odo of Montbéliard. Before 1225 all three had been counsellors of John of Brienne to whom both Balian and Odo were related by marriage. In view of King John's long estrangement from the Ibelins, it may well be that they felt no particular call to make common cause with John of Beirut in his opposition to the emperor. At the time of Richard Filangieri's arrival they had between them been serving Frederick in a vice-regal capacity for much of the period since 1225.[80] Richard now expected these men to work with him, even although he had been sent to supersede them as the emperor's lieutenants in Syria. But his behaviour, while not driving them directly into alliance with John of Beirut, had the effect of alienating them. His army was attempting to dispossess a liege man of his fief without prior judgement of the High Court; he then had Tyre, the second most important royal city in the kingdom, occupied on his behalf, and only after that did he go to Acre where he convened the High Court and presented his letters of appointment. It would appear that the Latin Syrian nobles accepted him as the emperor's lieutenant in the kingdom, but, according to an admittedly pro-Ibelin source, Balian of Sidon delivered a strongly worded protest against his illegal attack on Beirut. Undaunted, Richard Filangieri pressed on with the siege, and, when two knights who had been sent to Balian of Sidon and the other nobles in Acre arrived at Beirut to see what was going on, they found that the imperial troops were unmoved by Balian's stance. What happened next was that the Ibelin sympathizers in Acre formed themselves into a sworn association consisting of both feudatories and burgesses with the aim of resisting Richard Filangieri and preventing him from extending his control over the rest of the kingdom. This movement developed within the framework of a pre-existing confraternity, the Confraternity of St Andrew, and came to be known as the Commune of Acre.[81]

[79] 'Gestes', pp. 700–1; 'Eracles', pp. 385–8.

[80] Riley-Smith, *Feudal Nobility*, pp. 166–73 *passim*. Odo was related to John of Brienne through John's mother; Balian was married to John's niece. W. H. Rudt de Collenberg (Rüdt-Collenberg), *The Rupenides, Hethumides and Lusignans: The Structure of the Armeno-Cilician Dynasties* (Paris, 1963), table IX(B); above, note 28.

[81] Riley-Smith, *Feudal Nobility*, pp. 175–82.

John of Beirut's reaction to events in Syria was predictable: he would use his Cypriot resources to raise the siege of Beirut. Two accounts survive of the scene in the High Court of Cyprus at which he received promises of assistance. In one John's request for help was couched in terms of a formal feudal petition to his lord, King Henry: his fief was under attack; Henry should bring his feudal host to its defence. But this version of what was said fails to convince. Henry was not yet of age, and so it is difficult to see how he could summon his host, and in any case he was under no formal obligation to come to John's aid since Beirut was not held from him but from the king of Jerusalem. According to Philip of Novara, the author of the other account, John made an impassioned appeal to the king and his fellow vassals 'as my brothers and dear friends' to come to his aid. Philip gave no reference to the notion of feudal obligation, but while he may have preserved the gist of the speech made on that occasion, he had clearly embellished it in line with his literary affectations with the result that this account too is of questionable value. Both writers agree that the king and all the Cypriot vassals, whether friendly towards John of Beirut or not, were induced to accompany his expedition. But the recorded behaviour of John's opponents provides a further reason for not accepting either account at face value. Aimery Barlais and his followers wanted to oppose him but dared not do so; they tried to wriggle out of going; they deserted at the earliest opportunity, and they claimed that, as King Henry was a minor and in someone else's control, their prime loyalty lay with the emperor as overlord. The picture is of a situation in which John of Beirut had used his preponderant power in the island to compel even his enemies to join him. There may have been a formal request as a propagandist exercise, but the reality was that neither the Cypriot vassals nor the king had any choice but to fall in with his wishes. Moreover, John was so determined to stake his position in Cyprus on the successful outcome of his campaign that he almost denuded Cyprus of his supporters.[82]

The expedition began early in 1232 and met with one setback after another. Getting the army from Nicosia to Famagusta was hard because of the weather. At Famagusta the Cypriots were held up for an appreciable length of time owing to storms. As soon as the fleet reached the coast of Syria, Aimery Barlais and some eighty supporters deserted – John of Beirut's attempts to conciliate them had failed. A number of ships were then wrecked on the coast at Botron with the loss of the army's tents, and this reverse was followed by further desertions. John then turned to Acre for support, where he apparently invoked an interpretation of the law known as the *Assise sur la ligece* that allowed the peers of a vassal who had been deprived of his fief without a judgement in his lord's court to take violent action if necessary to re-instate him. But despite strenuous efforts by his nephew, John lord of Caesarea, only forty-three knights

---

[82] 'Gestes', pp. 701–2, 703; 'Eracles', pp. 392–3.

esponded, while Balian of Sidon, Odo of Montbéliard and a number of other leading members of the Latin community tried to negotiate for peace. John was unable, moreover, to raise the siege; he managed to get supplies of provisions and reinforcements through the blockade, but he evidently lacked the strength to risk a pitched battle or force the emperor's men to withdraw. So he abandoned the attempt and went back to Acre.[83] At this point his fortunes changed. John's presence in Acre brought a new vitality to the Commune which elected him its mayor, and it then achieved a notable success in seizing the imperial ships that were wintering there. At the same time John enlisted the support of the Genoese who had their own quarrel with the emperor, and with their help he was able to mount an attack on Tyre. Richard Filangieri thereupon raised the siege of Beirut. But the Ibelin re-occupation of John's principal city in Syria was followed by a set-back in which the Cypriot troops guarding the main route from Tyre to Acre were taken unawares and defeated by Filangieri's men at Casal Imbert. This defeat, the military significance of which seems to have been exaggerated by the principal narratives of the period, coincided with the coming of age of the king of Cyprus, Henry I.[84]

After Casal Imbert a political stalemate that was to last for about ten years developed in Syria: Richard Filangieri held Tyre, and his opponents, among whom were now numbered Odo of Montbéliard and Balian of Sidon, held Acre.[85] The main theatre of action shifted to Cyprus. At about the time of John of Beirut's unsuccessful attempt to regain Beirut, Aimery Barlais and his followers had returned to the island and seized control. They found few Ibelin supporters to resist them: the *bailli* of the *secrète*, Arneis of Jubail, and the castellan, Philip of Caffran, held St Hilarion, while Guinart of Conches and Balian of Ibelin's wife, Eschiva of Montbéliard, defended themselves in the nearby castle of Buffavento. Aimery Barlais occupied the rest of the island and laid siege to St Hilarion. After his victory at Casal Imbert, Richard Filangieri evidently believed he had the Ibelins contained in Acre, and, leaving a garrison in Tyre, brought the majority of his forces to Cyprus to help reduce the two remaining strongholds. But he may well have overestimated the straits to which his enemies were reduced. Balian of Ibelin had now re-occupied Beirut, and the Ibelin party retained control of Acre and the costal cities to the south. Thanks partly to the sacrifices made by his nephews, John of Caesarea and John the son of Philip of Ibelin, in selling lands to the military Orders, John of Beirut was able to re-equip his army and arrange for it to be transported back to Cyprus. It would appear that the shipping consisted of the imperial vessels seized in Acre

[83] 'Gestes', pp. 702–6; 'Eracles', pp. 393–5; Riley-Smith, *Feudal Nobility*, pp. 182–3. News of John of Beirut's failure to raise the siege of Beirut led to the suspension of negotiations with Bohemond IV of Antioch for an alliance to be cemented by the marriage of one of his sons to a sister of King Henry. 'Gestes', pp. 706–7.   [84] 'Gestes', pp. 707–10; 'Eracles', pp. 395–8.

[85] Riley-Smith, *Feudal Nobility*, pp. 199–209.

and manned by local seamen, to whom King Henry now gave fiefs which were to be burdened with naval services, together with Genoese ships acquired by promises of commercial concessions in Cyprus to Genoa.[86]

The fleet set sail from Acre at the end of May and after calling at Sidon disembarked on the rocky islets that protect the harbour at Famagusta. Famagusta itself was seized in a surprise attack by night, and the imperial garrison withdrew to Nicosia. The Genoese were duly rewarded with the trading privileges which henceforth were to form the basis of their rights in the island. John of Beirut's forces then advanced to Nicosia and prepared to raise the siege of St Hilarion. This castle guarded the defile through the mountains separating Kyrenia from Nicosia, and on 15 June at the southern end of this pass near the villiage of Agridi (Aghirda) the Ibelin army encountered the enemy. The imperial forces had the advantage of being able to charge downhill, but the Ibelins' tactics and strategy were superior. Their cavalry appears to have been better disciplined and more effectively deployed, and their foot-soldiers gave able support in killing or capturing any knight who became unhorsed. In the end Richard Filangieri and some of the survivors fled back to Kyrenia, while others were cut off and scattered. The Ibelins had won the battle and could bring relief to their supporters in St Hilarion.[87]

The civil war in Cyprus now moved into its final phase. Imperial supporters still held Kyrenia. At first the Ibelin investment was inadequate owing to their inability to blockade the castle from the sea, and the defenders were free to come and go in their attempts to find reinforcements. It was only with the appearance of a new Genoese fleet and a formal military alliance with Genoa in December 1232 that the castle could be fully besieged by both land and sea. Resistance continued until sometime after Easter 1233. Eventually the commander, Philip Chenard, surrendered on terms: the garrison was to go free to Syria, and there was to be an exchange of prisoners. The war in Cyprus was over; the Ibelin victory was complete.[88]

With the surrender of Kyrenia Cyprus entered an extended period of internal peace. Now that Henry I had come of age, Frederick had lost his chief pretext for intervening as suzerain in the affairs of the island, and his preoccupations with Italian politics and relations with the papacy prevented him from sending any further expeditions to the East. In 1242 the Ibelins and their allies expelled

[86] 'Gestes', pp. 707, 710–12; 'Eracles', pp. 398–9. For the Ibelins selling properties to the Hospitallers, RRH, nos. 1036, 1036a.

[87] 'Gestes', pp. 712–17, 718; 'Eracles', pp. 400–1. For the Genoese privilege, dated 10 June 1232, Mas Latrie, Histoire, II, 51–6.

[88] 'Gestes', pp. 717–21, 724; 'Eracles', pp. 401–2. For the text of the Genoese alliance, Mas Latrie, Histoire, II, 56–8. Although the treaty is dated December 1233, the indiction would point to 1232 as the correct year. P. W. Edbury, 'Cyprus and Genoa:The Origins of the War of 1373–1374', Πρακτικα τοῦ Δευτέρου Διεθνοῦς Κυπριολογικοῦ Συνεδρίου, II, (Nicosia, 1986), 110 note 9.

Frederick's garrison from Tyre, thereby depriving him of his one remaining stronghold in Syria. The final seal was placed on the repudiation of the emperor's overlordship in Cyprus when in 1247 Pope Innocent IV formally absolved Henry from any oaths he may have sworn to Frederick.[89] No more is heard of Cyprus as a client-kingdom of the Western Empire.

Even before the siege of Kyrenia was over, King Henry had convened the High Court to pass judgement on those Cypriot knights who were at war with him. All who had taken up arms against his authority since he came of age were deprived of their fiefs and banned from the kingdom. At the head of the list stood the names of Aimery Barlais, Amaury of Bethsan, Hugh of Jubail and Philip Chenard.[90] Some of the vanquished subsequently made their way to Apulia where the emperor took them into his service; Philip Chenard in particular had a distinguished career there.[91] Hugh of Jubail and Aimery Barlais remained in Syria. By an ironic change of fortune one of Aimery's sons married John of Beirut's great-granddaughter and for a while in the years around 1280 would have had custody of the lordship of Beirut.[92] Gauvain of Cheneché and William of Rivet had both died before Henry's majority, and their heirs escaped dispossession. Gauvain's descendants, however, were sentenced to live in exile from Cyprus. Later in the thirteenth century his fiefs passed to the Ibelin family when Balian of Arsur, a grandson of John of Beirut, married Gauvain's granddaughter.[93] In most cases, however, the families of the defeated party were disinherited. Indeed, the civil war seems to have stimulated a change in the law concerning forfeitures: Philip of Novara made the observation that before the war children already born to men who were sentenced to dispossession could succeed to their fathers' fiefs, but afterwards this ceased to be so.[94]

The war had been costly. Admittedly the list of Cypriot nobles known to have died in the fighting is short: Walter of Caesarea and Gerard of Montagu in the battle of Nicosia in 1229; Gauvain of Cheneché at the siege of Kantara; Anseau

---

[89] Innocent IV, *Registres*, ed. E. Berger (Paris, 1881–1921), no. 2441.

[90] 'Gestes', p. 719; 'Amadi', pp. 174–5.

[91] E. Bertaux, 'Les Français d'outre-mer en Apulie et en Epire au temps des Hohenstaufen d'Italie', *Revue historique*, LXXXV (1904).

[92] 'Lignages', pp. 449, 468; W. H. Rudt de Collenberg, 'Les Ibelin aux XIIIe et XIVe siècles', *EKEE*, IX (1977–9), 136–7.

[93] 'Gestes', pp. 694, 695; 'Amadi', p. 175; 'Lignages', pp. 449, 457; Rudt de Collenberg, 'Les Ibelin', p. 143. Two of John of Beirut's sons, Baldwin and Guy, married respectively Alice of Bethsan and Philippa Barlais, the daughters of two of the *baillis*. 'Lignages', p. 449; Rudt de Collenberg, 'Les Ibelin', pp. 158, 178. It is not known when these marriages took place. They may belong to the period of attempted reconciliation in 1230–1, but, if they were later, it could be that Baldwin and Guy were expecting to gain possession of their fathers-in-law's fiefs. In 1247 a marriage dispensation was issued for a grandson of John of Beirut to marry a member of the Rivet family 'ad sedendas discordias et contrahendas amicitias'. Rudt de Collenberg, 'Dispenses matrimoniales', pp. 58–9 no. 5.   [94] Philip of Novara, p. 498.

of Brie, mortally wounded at the siege of Kyrenia in 1233.[95] But loss of life during the civil war nevertheless appears to have been considerable. The battle of Nicosia was a bloody affair, and although sixty knights of Richard Filangieri's imperial army were said to have been killed at Agridi as against only one in the Ibelin army, there is evidence that the death toll among the Cypriots during the siege of Kyrenia was high.[96] It is difficult to assess the cost in terms of damage to property and loss of wealth. Large areas of the island would have escaped, but the area around Kyrenia and St Hilarion must have suffered during the sieges, and we read of wanton destruction elsewhere, in particular at Kythrea where the mills were wrecked in 1232. Philip of Novara made much of the outrages committed by the emperor's supporters against the civilian population, but it is uncertain how much allowance should be made for exaggeration.[97] Normal government crumbled under the impact of war, and even after Henry had come of age and had gained the upper hand at the battle of Agridi, it is clear that his control of the whole island was uncertain. Thus, when in December 1232 during the siege of Kyrenia King Henry and the Ibelins made an alliance with the Genoese, they did so not as the rulers of an independent kingdom but as a group of named individuals; the treaty was between the Genoese representative and about fifty men of whom the king was one.[98] The breakdown of recognizable central control that this implied is further illustrated by an incident in 1231 in which thirteen Greek monks were martyred for refusing to conform to western practices concerning the eucharist. The government was normally careful to protect the indigenous church from attack by over-zealous Latin clerics, and it is doubtless significant that this, the only recorded atrocity of its kind, took place at a time of civil war when the authorities were otherwise preoccupied.[99]

Quite apart from the cost of the war in terms of loss of life, damage to property and social dislocation, it is apparent that the strain on the resources of the crown was heavy. Philip of Novara noted that at the end of the war King Henry was poor; he owed his men for their fief-rents and their provisions, and he was still faced with claims for unpaid debts dating from the time of his minority.[100] At the same time tithes went unpaid, and after the war Henry found himself obliged to alienate royal lands to the archbishop of Nicosia in compensation.[101] The closing stages of the war seem to have been particularly

[95] 'Gestes', pp. 689, 694, 718, 720; 'Eracles', pp. 376, 377, 402–3. Henry I's bride, Alice of Monteferrat, died in Kyrenia during the siege of 1232–3.

[96] 'Gestes', pp. 689, 716–17, 719, 721; 'Eracles', p. 401.

[97] 'Gestes', pp. 683, 684, 686, 710–11, 714, 718.

[98] Mas Latrie, Histoire, II, 56–8. For the date, above, note 88.

[99] Hill, III, 1049–51; Gill, 'Tribulations of the Greek Church in Cyprus', pp. 79–80.

[100] Philip of Novara, pp. 515–16; cf. John of Ibelin, pp. 383–4. The case of Philip of Jubail described by John of Ibelin (p. 236) is probably further evidence for non-payment of fief-rents at this period.

[101] Mas Latrie, Histoire, III, 631, 633–6; 'A Register of the Cartulary of the Cathedral of Santa Sophia of Nicosia', ed. J. L. La Monte, Byzantion, V (1930), nos. 30–4, 39–40, 42.

difficult. Whereas in 1229 John of Beirut was able to bear the cost of hiring mercenaries and equipping the fleet for the expedition that led to his triumph at the battle of Nicosia, in 1232 King Henry had to buy support with promises of fiefs. He evidently possessed no ready money and so was having to dissipate his domain. Genoese assistance was obtained at the cost of giving Genoa important commercial and legal franchises. At the siege of Kyrenia expenditure on the wages of the foot soldiers and on the ships involved in the blockade was high, and the king was forced to levy some form of *taille* to maintain the siege. The forfeitures taken from Aimery Barlais and his party had to be regranted immediately as rewards for loyalty.[102]

Why then did the Ibelins win? There can be little doubt that John of Beirut enjoyed genuine popularity and through his network of kinsmen and clients could command the loyalty of a substantial section of the knighthood of both Cyprus and Jerusalem. He seems also to have won the confidence of his great-nephew, the young king of Cyprus. The resources at the Ibelins' disposal consisted of their lands and revenues in Cyprus as well as of their lordships in the kingdom of Jerusalem. Walter of Caesarea and then his son John held the lordship of Caesarea; Philip of Ibelin and his son John, the future jurist and count of Jaffa, also had lands in Syria. John of Beirut himself had fiefs at Acre and held the lordship of Arsur as well as Beirut. In the 1220s he was developing the commercial potential of the port of Beirut, and he had been issuing his own coins there; indeed, it may well be that his lordship in effect slipped out of the *mouvance* of the kings of Jerusalem at this period.[103] Furthermore, because the Ibelins had controlled the kingdom of Cyprus during Henry's minority, especially since the rupture with Alice of Champagne, they would have controlled the sources of royal patronage and so could strengthen their own position accordingly. John of Beirut thus had widespread support and extensive financial assets. In the later stages of the war he could also turn to the Genoese who were prepared to make common cause with him against the emperor. However considerable the opposition may have been within Cyprus, there can be no question that his opponents there were in a minority and had far less wealth to sustain their efforts. Admittedly there is no means of measuring the value of the Ibelins' Cypriot fiefs against those of Aimery Barlais and his associates, but it is likely that the latter's resources in Syria were tiny by comparison. What Aimery Barlais' party did have was imperial support, but this proved inadequate. In 1229 the Emperor Frederick installed the five *baillis* in power and then left them with insufficient military muscle. They were incapable of warding off an Ibelin recovery. In 1232 Aimery Barlais enjoyed the backing of Richard Filangieri and his forces but suffered defeat nonetheless. The imperial

---

[102] 'Gestes', pp. 688, 711–12, 719, 721; 'Eracles', p. 399.
[103] Riley-Smith, *Feudal Nobility*, pp. 66, 76–8; Metcalf, *Coinage of the Crusades*, pp. 25–6 and plate 7.

army that arrived in the East in the autumn of 1231 held the upper hand at first –
John of Beirut was unable to raise the siege of Beirut for several months and
suffered defeat at Casal Imbert – but after the defeat at Agridi Richard Filangieri
received no more reinforcements from the West and was clearly at a
disadvantage.

It is impossible to arrive at any satisfactory appreciation of the relative size of
the military forces involved in the war. Various figures were recorded: for
example, Philip of Novara claimed to have commanded 150 men at the battle of
Nicosia; the Ibelin forces at the siege of St Hilarion were said to have been
organized in three shifts, each of a hundred knights serving one month on and
two off; one set of figures for Richard Filangieri's total forces in 1231 was 600
knights, 100 mounted squires, 700 foot soldiers and 3,000 armed marines; when
the Ibelins returned to Cyprus in May 1232, their forces numbered 233 mounted
men, whereas their opponents' cavalry was estimated at 2,000.[104] The Ibelins
won two pitched battles in Cyprus, Nicosia (1229) and Agridi (1232), and
sustained three lengthy sieges, St Hilarion and Kantara (1229–30) and Kyrenia
(1232–3). How far the victories in battle resulted from superior numbers and
how far from superior generalship is unclear. At Nicosia clouds of dust proved a
problem, but we are not told whether either side derived any advantage from
them. At Agridi the imperialists seem to have been poorly commanded, but the
fact that they made a strategic withdrawal at the coming of the Ibelins rather
than going out to meet them may tell against the impression given by Philip of
Novara that the Ibelins were seriously outnumbered. The sieges placed far
greater strain on the Ibelins' ability to organize their forces. In the winter of
1229–30 the effectiveness of the siege of St Hilarion was impaired because too
many men on the Ibelin side had gone home, and at Kyrenia the problem lay in
finding and paying for the naval support necessary to blockade the castle from
the sea.[105]

The surrender of Kyrenia marked the culmination of the rise of the Ibelin family
in Cyprus. Whenever possible they had sought to surround their actions with a
cloak of legalism, but much of their behaviour, especially at moments of greatest
threat, had been violent and high-handed. The refusal to allow the appointment
of Aimery Barlais as Alice of Champagne's lieutenant, the lynching of Baldwin
of Belleme, John of Beirut's armed defence of St Hilarion against the emperor in
1228, and the use of war to overthrow the acknowledged suzerain's duly
appointed officers provide ample evidence that beneath this cloak, and despite
the efforts of Philip of Novara to conceal the fact, the Ibelins were determined to
maintain their ascendancy by any means at their disposal. It is true that many of

---

[104] 'Gestes', pp. 686, 689, 692, 700, 712. 'Eracles' (pp. 385–6) gives Filangieri's forces as 300 knights
and 200 crossbowmen and mounted sergeants.   [105] 'Gestes, pp. 689–95, 712–21.

their acts were in response to opponents who were prepared to use equally violent or illegal means to dislodge them from their positions of power, but it is also true that on occasion the Ibelins gratuitously defied convention and legality and employed violent means to further their ambitions. A good example of this sort of behaviour is provided by the circumstances surrounding the marriage of John of Beirut's eldest son, Balian. In about 1230 Balian had married Eschiva of Montbéliard. Eschiva was the daughter of Walter of Montbéliard, the regent in the 1200s, and widow of Gerard of Montagu, killed in 1229. One contemporary writer noted that she had 'grant terre en Chypre': in marrying her Balian was clearly making a 'good marriage'. But the couple were related within the prohibited degrees, and the marriage was contracted *clandestine*. Consequently the archbishop of Nicosia excommunicated the couple. But far from leading to their separation, the excommunication resulted in the archbishop being hounded from his see and taking refuge in Acre. The episode nevertheless ended with a dispensation for the marriage to be legitimized. Balian had secured a rich widow, defied canon law, intimidated the archbishop and got his own way. Significantly, his vassal and apologist, Philip of Novara, made only a single, oblique reference to the affair.[106]

After 1233 the Ibelins were firmly entrenched, and there was no one to challenge them. Their supremacy within the ranks of the Cypriot nobility was to last until the third quarter of the fourteenth century when the remaining branches of the family each failed in the male line. John of Beirut had five sons of whom four lived to have descendants of their own: Balian, who succeeded to Beirut, held fiefs in both Cyprus and Jerusalem; his brother John, who was given the lordship of Arsur as part of a family pact on the death of his father in 1236, may not have had any lands in Cyprus, but the other brothers, Baldwin later seneschal of Cyprus and Guy later constable, seem to have had interests exclusively in the island. Philip of Ibelin's son John, later count of Jaffa, held extensive estates in both kingdoms. As the Christian possessions in Syria were lost to the Muslims, so the interests of all five branches of the family (the four descended from John of Beirut and the one descended from Philip) came to be concentrated in Cyprus. Members of the family were invariably to be found numbered among the kings' counsellors and intimates. Between the 1240s and the 1290s all the constables of Cyprus were Ibelins, and the family supplied all the seneschals of Cyprus until the 1360s. Hugh III, Hugh IV and also Hugh IV's father and one of his sons married into the family, thereby renewing the already close ties of kinship between the Ibelins and the reigning dynasty in succeeding generations.

The precise nature of the relationship between the kings of Cyprus and the

---

[106] Mas Latrie, *Histoire*, II, 62–3, III, 629–30; 'Gestes', p. 715; 'Eracles', p. 376; Rudt de Collenberg, 'Dispenses matrimoniales', pp. 58–9 no. 2 and note 2 (p. 88).

Ibelins after 1233 is open to differing interpretations. It is possible to see the Ibelins as over-mighty subjects attempting to dominate the crown, or alternatively as loyal counsellors and close kinsmen to whom kings would turn as a matter of course for advice and service. The history of the years before 1233 might lead one to suppose that the Ibelins were out to establish themselves as 'mayors of the palace', intent on controlling and exploiting the crown for their own advantage. In fact the political developments in Cyprus during the remainder of the thirteenth century make it look as if the second alternative – that the Ibelins were loyal counsellors – was nearer the truth. There is no record of any differences between the Ibelins and Henry I, although unquestionably they took the lead in his council and at the High Court. Balian of Ibelin and then his brother Guy held the office of constable; Baldwin became seneschal and in 1247 was entrusted with command of the Cypriot contingent defending Ascalon; Guy and Baldwin led the Cypriot troops on St Louis' crusade to Damietta in 1248.[107] But although Henry may have been a pliant king, and although in the 1240s and 1250s the Ibelins took full advantage of royal weakness in the kingdom of Jerusalem to enhance their wealth and power there, there is no evidence to suggest that they set about dismantling royal authority in Cyprus.[108] The circumstances under which Henry I appointed Baldwin and Guy as seneschal and constable of Cyprus – both appointments seem to date to the mid-1240s – are a matter for speculation; perhaps their promotions coincided with other grants Henry seems to have made in his efforts to secure control of Acre as regent for the absentee Hohenstaufen king of Jerusalem.[109] But any suggestion that these offices were extorted from the king as the price of political assistance is at best unproven, and Guy of Ibelin was evidently a worthy occupant of the constableship. Joinville, who met him during St Louis' crusade, described him as 'one of the most accomplished knights I have ever seen' – high praise indeed from a seneschal of Champagne and intimate of the king of France![110]

The pattern of intermarriage with the Lusignans certainly does not suggest that the Ibelins were manipulating the ruling dynasty for their own ends. Apart from the marriage of Aimery of Lusignan and Eschiva of Ibelin back in the twelfth century, the earliest example of a marriage between an Ibelin and a member of the royal family was in or soon after 1255; the fact that the man concerned was the future Hugh III is of little immediate significance since at that date his accession to the throne would not have been thought likely. At the time of his death in 1267, Hugh II was betrothed to the lady of Beirut, but otherwise there are no further examples of intermarriage between the two houses until

---

[107] Rudt de Collenberg, 'Les Ibelin', pp. 130, 157–8, 177–8.
[108] After the seige of Kyrenia John of Beirut intervened in the Cypriot High Court to protect the crown from a procedural innovation which, had it been established, would have strengthened the position of the vassals against the king. Philip of Novara, pp. 515–16; John of Ibelin, pp. 383–4.
[109] Riley-Smith, *Feudal Nobility*, pp.214–15.   [110] Joinville, p. 119.

1291 when the pope issued a dispensation for a great-granddaughter of John of Beirut to marry a younger son of Hugh III.[111] In the question of appointments to high office it can be shown that although the Ibelins monopolized the seneschalcy and constableship, these offices did not become hereditary in any one branch of the family, and so the kings were not limited in their choice of appointees. The comparative absence of constitutional crises and the lack of more positive evidence for a systematic exploitation of the royal resources to enhance still further the family's standing provide an adequate indication that the relationship of the Ibelins to successive kings was normally that of faithful vassals enjoying the rewards that royal patronage would bring them.

As the descendants of John of Beirut and his brother Philip proliferated, the unity that had been a powerful Ibelin attribute began to weaken. The first major conflict in which members of the family found themselves ranged on opposing sides was the War of St Sabas which broke out in Acre in the 1250s between the rival Italian communes.[112] In Cyprus it was as late as 1306 that tensions within the family first emerge clearly in our sources. King Henry II had been relying on the counsel of his maternal uncle, the seneschal Philip of Ibelin, to the exclusion of his other vassals, and, for a variety of reasons of which this was one, Henry's brother Amaury with the support of the overwhelming majority of the nobility including all the other members of the Ibelin family seized control of the government. But in the course of the next few years some of the Ibelins went over to the king with the result that when Henry was restored to power in 1310 and took reprisals on his enemies, it was only the descendants of Baldwin the Seneschal and Philip of Ibelin the regent who suffered.[113]

The earliest unmistakable instance of a member of the Ibelin family attempting to thwart Lusignan power dates from 1271. In that year James of Ibelin, the son of John count of Jaffa, acted as spokesman for the Cypriot knights who were trying to claim that they did not owe military service in Syria. James, as will be seen, failed in his efforts on their behalf, but towards the end of his speech he made a claim that serves as evidence more for his family's self-esteem than for his historical accuracy or the strength of his case: ' . . . the men of the kingdom of Cyprus have more often served the house of Ibelin outside the kingdom than they have the king or his ancestors . . . '[114] Nothing could be more

[111] Rudt de Collenberg, 'Dispenses matrimoniales', pp. 58–61 nos. 8, 9, 18b (cf. 18a).

[112] Riley-Smith, *Feudal Nobility*, pp. 215–17; H. E. Mayer, 'Ibelin *versus* Ibelin: The Struggle for the Regency of Jerusalem, 1253–1258', *PAPS*, CXXII (1978), 48–51. Mayer's attempt (pp. 31ff.) to demonstrate that John of Ibelin lord of Arsur was at odds with the other members of his family from the early 1230s is not convincing. P. W. Edbury, 'John of Ibelin's Title to the County of Jaffa and Ascalon', *EHR*, XCVIII (1983), 130–3. Cf. Mayer's rejoinder, 'John of Jaffa, his Opponents and his Fiefs', *PAPS*, CXXVIII (1984), 135–9.

[113] Below pp. 130–1. A certain Balian of Ibelin 'Mal guarnito' or 'Malgarny' whose place on the Ibelin family tree is unknown supported the king in 1306. 'Amadi', p. 252.

[114] 'Document relatif au service militaire', p. 434. Below pp. 92–3.

natural than that the Ibelins should take pride in their achievements and pre-eminence, and it was this pride that at some point before the opening years of the fourteenth century led to the fabrication of the spurious pedigree which asserted their descent from the viscounts of Chartres.[115]

---

[115] The claim is found in the version of the 'Lignages' (p. 448) which belongs to the first decade of the fourteenth century. P. W. Edbury, 'The Ibelin Counts of Jaffa: A Previously Unknown Passage from the "Lignages d'Outremer"', *EHR*, LXXXIX (1974), 604–5.

5

THE DEFENCE OF LATIN SYRIA

DURING THE century that elapsed between the conquest of Cyprus in 1191 and the loss of the last strongholds in Latin Syria in 1291 it was common for Cypriot resources to be deployed in the defence of the remaining Christian possessions on the mainland. The kings of Cyprus allowed their island's material wealth and military capacity to be used in efforts to regain the Holy Places and safeguard the territory under Christian rule. It was in their own interest to ward off Muslim encroachments, especially as for long periods they themselves were recognized as having political authority in whatever was left of the kingdom of Jerusalem. Indeed, in the thirteenth century the politics of Cyprus and Jerusalem became so closely intertwined that it is impossible for the historian to treat either kingdom in isolation.

For crusaders, pilgrims or merchants travelling by sea to the Holy Land, Cyprus was a natural stopping place, and the island was soon recognized as a suitable port-of-call for crusaders to take on supplies, regroup, refit and even consult with the leaders of Latin Syria about strategy for their forthcoming campaign. In practice, however, less use was made of Cyprus in the course of the crusading expeditions to the East than might be expected. Pope Honorius III wanted the participants in the Fifth Crusade to assemble there in 1217, and in 1237 a group of prominent people in the East were advising Thibaut of Navarre to go no further than Limassol where they would meet him to discuss plans for the crusade he was leading. But neither proposal was adopted, and on each occasion the crusaders and the Christians settled in the East held their deliberations in Acre.[1] By contrast, in 1227 the leading figures in the East

---

[1] Mas Latrie, *Histoire*, II, 36: Honorius III, nos. 672–3; 'Eracles', pp. 322–3 (1217). *Thesaurus novus*, ed. Martène and Durand, I, col. 1012; 'Gestes', p. 725; 'Eracles', pp. 413–14 (1237). For the date of the letter to Thibaut, S. Painter, 'The Crusade of Theobald of Champagne and Richard of Cornwall, 1239–1241', *HC*, II, 471. During the Fifth Crusade reinforcements from the West were going to Egypt via Cyprus, and in 1221 the island was a staging post for crusaders evacuated from Damietta. *Lettres de Jacques de Vitry*, ed. R. B. C. Huygens (Leiden, 1960), p. 138 (cf. p. 140 where the island is mentioned as a source of building-stone for construction-work at Damietta); Caesarius of Heisterbach in R. Röhricht (ed.) *Testimonia minora de Quinto Bello Sacro* (Geneva, 1882), p. 344.

assembled at Limassol where they expected to meet the Emperor Frederick II, only to discover that his sailing was delayed until the following year.[2] Other crusaders, for example the Lord Edward and his followers in 1271, certainly stopped in Cyprus,[3] but it was St Louis – Louis IX of France – who during the earlier of his two crusading expeditions took the fullest advantage of the island's strategic potential. By the time the French king arrived in Cyprus in September 1248, his officers had amassed large quantities of supplies in the island. He camped near Limassol, where he remained for over eight months and where he was joined by the stragglers from his own expedition and by a contingent from the Frankish principality of Achaea. King Henry and his leading nobles gave the crusaders a warm welcome. The master of the Templars, the lieutenant master of the Hospitallers and some Latin Syrian knights visited the host, and together they agreed to attack Egypt.[4] During Louis' sojourn in Cyprus Christian hopes were raised by diplomatic contacts with the Mongols,[5] but any beneficial effect this may have had on morale was more than offset by an epidemic which carried off a number of crusaders, some nobles among them, before the army could set sail on its ill-fated expedition to Damietta at the end of May. Memories of this mortality were to lead some later publicists to discourage future crusaders from using Cyprus as a staging post.[6]

On a number of occasions Cypriot knights shared in crusading expeditions. In 1197 King Aimery brought his forces to join the German crusaders in the capture of Beirut; in 1217 Hugh I led a Cypriot contingent to Acre to take part in the initial stage of the Fifth Crusade; later, in 1219, we find Cypriot knights serving although without distinction at the siege of Damietta; in 1228 they seem to have anticipated joining Frederick II's Crusade, although the circumstances under which they eventually accompanied him reflected more the emperor's ability to compel their obedience than any willingness on their part to assist his campaign. In 1239 there were Cypriots on the Crusade of Thibaut of Navarre, and in 1249 King Henry took his men to Egypt with St Louis. On this last occasion the king himself returned to Cyprus soon after the capture of Damietta, leaving 120 knights under his seneschal and constable, the brothers Baldwin and Guy of

---

[2] 'Eracles', p. 364.

[3] Thomas Wykes, 'Chronicon' in H. R. Luard (ed.), *Annales Monastici* (RS 36, 1864–9), IV, 244–5.

[4] For Louis in Cyprus, Hill, II, 140–5; J. R. Strayer, 'The Crusades of Louis IX', *HC*, II, 493–5. For the location of his camp, J. Richard, *Chypre sous les Lusignans. Documents chypriotes des archives du Vatican (XIVe et XVe siècles* (Paris, 1962), p. 79 note 10. For the consultation, 'Gestes', p. 741.

[5] D. Sinor, 'The Mongols and Western Europe', *HC*, III, 522–3; J. Richard, 'La lettre du Connétable Smbat et les rapports entre Chrétiens et Mongols au milieu de XIIIème siècle' in D. Kouymjian (ed.), *Armenian Studies in memoriam Haïg Berbérian* (Lisbon, 1986), 683–96. Cf. P. Jackson, 'The Crisis in the Holy Land in 1260', *EHR*, XCV (1980), 483–4.

[6] A. S. Atiya, *The Crusade in the Later Middle Ages* (London, 1938), pp. 102, 122; Hill, II, 141 and note 2.

Ibelin.[7] But although Cypriots normally joined in the expeditions when crusaders were in the East, only twice before 1291, before the start of the Fifth Crusade and at the time of the Crusade of Louis IX, are we explicitly told that they themselves took crusading vows and so became crusaders in the strict sense.[8] There can, however, be no doubt that they accepted that they shared in the Christian duty of defending the Holy Land. According to Philip of Novara, in 1228 John of Beirut told Frederick II that the Cypriots would follow him to Syria 'in the service of God', and much later James of Ibelin was to use a similar phrase when recalling their involvement in the Crusade of Thibaut of Navarre as well as in St Louis' Crusade.[9]

There were a number of crusades to the East during the first century of Latin rule in Cyprus, but most of the campaigns were comparatively short and there were sometimes lengthy periods between them. Indeed, after St Louis' departure from the East in 1254, there was only one further crusading expedition in Syria of any moment before the *dénouement* of 1291. There were thus long intervals in which any Cypriot assistance in the defence of the Latin states in Syria had of necessity to take alternative forms. From time to time rulers sent contingents to join in other military campaigns in Syria or Palestine, and, particularly when the Lusignans had control of Acre, they would make available their Cypriot resources as well as their own political influence. In addition, there were many corporations and individuals based in Latin Syria who owned estates in Cyprus and so could use their income to bolster their position on the mainland.

The list of Latin Syrian ecclesiastical institutions which were able to augment their endowments by acquiring property in the island is lengthy. For example, the Augustinian canons of the Templum Domini owned property at Nicosia and at an unnamed rural settlement between 1195 and 1233.[10] In 1197 King Aimery gave one of the several places in Cyprus named Livadi to Archbishop Joscius of Tyre as a personal possession, presumably as a reward for his services in helping arrange his marriage to Queen Isabella of Jerusalem that same year. On Joscius' death the estate was to pass to his nephew and then to the church of Tyre, and

---

[7] 1197: 'Eracles', p. 224. 1217 and 1219: Oliver of Paderborn, pp. 162, 214; 'Document relatif au service militaire', p. 428 §§11–12; 'Eracles', pp. 322–5, 339–40; Philip of Novara, p. 525. The Cypriots subsequently withdrew from Damietta. *Lettres de Jacques de Vitry*, p. 135. 1228: 'Document relatif', p. 428 §13, p. 432 §9; 'Gestes', pp. 677, 681–2; 'Eracles', p. 369. 1239: 'Document relatif', pp. 428–99 §15, p. 432 §10. 1249: 'Document relatif', p. 429 §16, p. 432 §12; Hill, II, 145. For a Cypriot drowned at Mansourah (1250), Cod. Vat. lat. 4789 fo. 289 col. 2 correcting 'Lignages', p. 464. Matthew Paris (*Chronica Majora*, V, 308) noted that in 1252 Henry assisted Louis with Cypriot forces in the Holy Land.

[8] Mas Latrie, *Histoire*, II, 65 n; *Lettres de Jacques de Vitry*, pp. 89, 94–5. For the paucity of references to Christians settled in the Latin East taking crusading vows, J. Riley-Smith, 'Peace Never Established: The Case of the Kingdom of Jerusalem', *TRHS*, 5th ser., XXVIII (1978), 87–8.

[9] 'Gestes', p. 677; 'Document relatif au service militaire', p. 432 §§10–11, cf. p. 430 §3.

[10] Mas Latrie, *Histoire*, III, 598–9, 636–7.

Aimery further granted that no customs would be levied on produce from it being taken to the mainland. In the event the estate was sold, apparently in 1222, to the archbishop of Nicosia.[11] The Latin patriarch of Jerusalem and the canons of the Holy Sepulchre also had possessions in Cyprus. In 1201 they were granted Pendasino and in 1210 an unidentified place in the diocese of Paphos called *Lacridon*. In 1290 Pope Nicholas IV exempted the Holy Sepulchre from paying tithes on its properties in the island to the local bishops for five years.[12] Rents in Cyprus as well as properties in Paphos and Nicosia were owned by the abbey of St Mary and All Saints at Acre,[13] and St Lazarus of Bethany had a dependent priory in Cyprus by the 1260s.[14]

In the case of the patriarchate of Antioch, the papacy intervened to provide money from Cypriot sources for purposes of defence. In 1254 Pope Innocent IV committed the administration of the archbishopric of Nicosia to the patriarch, Opizo dei Fieschi, so that the revenues could compensate him for the damage done in his patriarchate by the Turcomans. This order apparently remained a dead letter as Archbishop Hugh of Nicosia who had previously abandoned his see had returned in the meantime. A few months later the pope ordered that a tithe of ecclesiastical revenues from Cyprus and Antioch be levied for three years to pay for the fortifications of the patriarch's castle of Qusair near Antioch, and he gave instructions that the patriarch should be given the custody of some other see within his patriarchate or in Cyprus in order to supplement his income still further. In 1256 Pope Alexander IV duly assigned Opizo the administration of the newly vacant diocese of Limassol, whence the patriarch continued to enjoy the revenues until in 1280, long after the fall of Antioch in 1268 and the capture of Qusair in 1275, he was provided with revenues in western Europe.[15]

The other ecclesiastical institutions with assets in Cyprus for use in the defence of the Latin states in Syria were the Military Orders. The Templars and the Hospitallers each owned a fortress, respectively at Gastria to the north of Famagusta and at Kolossi near Limassol. Both had been acquired before 1210,[16] but neither can have been of much military significance, and they should be seen as administrative centres rather than as defensive strongholds. The Hospitallers also had a tower at Limassol, and their house at Nicosia was evidently

---

[11] *Ibid.*, pp. 606–7, 617. For Joscius, above, p. 33. For the date of the sale, La Monte, 'Register of Nicosia', p. 452 note 4.

[12] *Cartulaire du Saint-Sépulcre*, nos. 174, 178; Nicholas IV, *Registres*, ed. E. Langlois (Paris, 1886–1905), no. 2093. For Pendasino, Richard, *Chypre sous les Lusignans*, pp. 81, 120.

[13] Gregory IX, *Registres*, ed. L. Auvray (Paris, 1890–1910, tables 1955), no. 4013.

[14] Urban IV, *Registres*, ed. L. Dorez and J. Guiraud (Paris, 1892–1929, tables 1958), nos. 210–11; H. E. Mayer, *Bistümer, Klöster und Stifte im Königreich Jerusalem* (Stuttgart, 1977), p. 384.

[15] Hill, III, 1057 note 3; B. Hamilton, *The Latin Church in the Crusader States: The Secular Church* (London, 1980), pp. 232–3, 237, 283–4. There was strong resistance in Cyprus to paying the tithe. In 1267 it was being suggested that the pope should grant tenths from the church in Cyprus for the defence of Acre. G. Servois, 'Emprunts de Saint Louis en Palestine et en Afrique', *BEC*, 4th series, IV (1858), 293.   [16] *Cart. gén. Hospitaliers*, no. 1354, 'Eracles', p. 316.

defensible, while the Templar house at Limassol seems to have been fortified and there were minor fortifications on the Templar estates at Yermasoyia and Khirokitia.[17] After the suppression of the Templars, most of their properties in Cyprus passed to the Hospitallers. But whereas it is likely that a majority of the estates listed by later writers as belonging to the Hospital were acquired by one or other of the two Orders before 1291,[18] it is not always possible to be sure who held what. Of the identifiable localities, the Hospitallers had Plataniskia, Kolossi, Monagroulli, Phinikas, Palekhori, Kellaki and Trakhoni before 1291 as well as property in Nicosia, Limassol and at Mora to the east of Nicosia,[19] while Templar estates included Khirokitia, Yermasoyia, Phasouri, Psimolophou, Gastria and presumably Temblos, as well as houses at Nicosia, Paphos, Famagusta and Limassol.[20] Both lists are far from complete. The surplus income from these estates would have been employed in furthering the Orders' activities in Syria. The only recorded disturbance of this pattern occurred in 1279 when King Hugh III confiscated the Templar properties and destroyed their houses in Limassol and elsewhere in retaliation for the master's support for his rival for the throne of Jerusalem, Charles of Anjou. Allegedly the properties were withheld until 1282. Ill-feeling between the Order and the Lusignan dynasty persisted long afterwards.[21]

Of the other military Orders, the Teutonic Knights never had many possessions in the island, thanks largely it must be assumed to the unpopularity

[17] A. T. Luttrell, 'The Hospitallers in Cyprus after 1291', Πρακτικὰ τοῦ Πρώτου Διεθνοῦς Κυπρολογικοῦ Συνεδρίου, II (Nicosia, 1972), 169–70.

[18] Mas Latrie, Histoire, III, 502–3; Florio Bustron, 'Chronque de l'île de Chypre', ed. R. de Mas Latrie in Collection des documents inédits sur l'histoire de France: Mélanges historiques, V, 170–1, 246–7. Bustron's lists purport to be of Templar properties given to the Hospitallers, but in fact are lists of Hospitaller (and Templar) properties. See Richard, Chypre sous les Lusignans, p. 111. For Templar estates not given to the Hospitallers, J. Richard, 'Le casal de Psimolofo et la vie rurale en Chypre au XIVe siècle', MAHEFR, LIX (1947), 122–3.

[19] Cart. gén. Hospitaliers, nos. 1354, 2174; E. Papadopoulou, Οι προτες εγκαταστασεις Βενετων στην Κυπρο', Συμμεικτα του Κεντρου Βυζαντινων Ερευνον, V (1983), 313, 314, cf. pp. 309; Riley-Smith, Knights of St John, pp. 505–6; Edbury 'Manosque', pp. 175, 179. The document published by Papadopoulou mentions Balian lord of Beirut (pp. 313, 315) and so is datable to the years 1236–47. 'Rogera' listed by Riley-Smith (p. 505) among the unidentified estates is almost certainly Louvaras (= 'Logara'; Florio Bustron, p. 171).

[20] 'Amadi', pp. 214, 287, 288, 290–1. Temblos, subsequently a Hospitaller possession, evidently derived its name from the Order. T. Papadopoullos, 'Chypre: frontière ethnique et socio-culturelle du monde byzantin', Rapports et co-rapports du XVe congrès international d'études byzantines: V. Chypre dans le monde byzantin, part V (Athens, 1976), p. 39 note 110. For Psimolophou, Richard, 'Psimolofo', pp. 122–3. For Yermasoiya and Phasouri, Papadopoulou, pp. 313, 314, cf. pp. 309, 312.

[21] Veterum Scriptorum et Monumentorum ... Amplissima Collectio, ed. E. Martène and U. Durand (Paris, 1727–33), II, 1300; Mas Latrie, Histoire, II, 108–9, 131; 'Gestes', p. 784; 'Annales', p. 457; Marino Sanudo, 'Liber Secretorum Fidelium Crucis', ed. J. Bongars, Gesta Dei per Francos (Hanover, 1611), II, 228; 'Amadi', p. 214.

there of their patron, Frederick II,[22] and the English Order of St Thomas of Canterbury, which had an estate near Limassol and a church dedicated to St Nicholas in Nicosia, was of even less importance. Until 1291 the Order of St Thomas had had an establishment in Acre, and presumably these Cypriot properties would have helped sustain it. In any case the Order's contribution to the defence of the Latin East was slight.[23]

A number of important nobles whose principal interests lay on the mainland held fiefs in Cyprus. The famous jurist, John of Ibelin, who was count of Jaffa from the mid-1240s until his death in 1266, had valuable estates in Cyprus including Peristerona in Morphou and Episkopi.[24] His cousins, Balian of Ibelin lord of Beirut, who died in 1247, and John lord of Caesarea, who died c. 1240, also held Cypriot properties.[25] Odo of Montbéliard, constable of Jerusalem and, at the time of his death in 1244, lord of Tiberias, had an estate at Tarsis in the diocese of Paphos.[26] In the 1230s King Henry I made generous landed settlements for the husbands of his two sisters, Walter of Brienne, who had custody of Jaffa until his capture in battle with the Muslims in 1244, and Henry of Antioch, the younger brother of Prince Bohemond V of Antioch-Tripoli, who died in 1276.[27] There can be little doubt that all these men would have used at least some of their revenues from Cyprus to maintain their position in Syria, thereby following in the footsteps of John the 'Old Lord' of Beirut, who in 1228 had told Frederick II that he had been using his Cypriot revenues to refortify his mainland lordship.[28] Lesser men too held fiefs in both kingdoms. Geoffrey le Tor, a member of a long-established Jerusalemite knightly family, had been born in Syria but went to live in Cyprus, where he received a large fief from King Henry, presumably as a reward for his part in the civil war of 1229–33.[29] Another knight of Latin Syrian origins, Baldwin Bonvoisin, seems to have acquired his fief at Kellia at about the same time.[30] On the other hand, some of the knights who had opposed the Ibelins in the civil war and who had fiefs on the mainland returned there after their defeat and dispossession in the early 1230s,[31] and in Philip of Novara we

[22] For exhaustive treatment, W. Hubatsch, 'Der Deutsche Orden und die Reichslehnschaft über Cypern', Nachrichten der Akad. der Wissenschaften in Göttingen, Philol-Hist. Kl. (1955).

[23] Richard, Chypre sous les Lusignans, pp. 69, 84, 102. More generally, A. J. Forey, 'The Military Order of St Thomas of Acre', EHR, XCII (1977), 481–503.

[24] Edbury, 'The Ibelin Counts of Jaffa', pp. 605–6.

[25] Balian of Beirut and John of Caesarea inherited their fathers' lands. Both attended the Cypriot High Court. RRH, nos. 1054, 1071, 1078, 1092; La Monte, 'Register of Nicosia', nos. 38, 39, 42, 45.   [26] Gregory IX, no. 4551.   [27] 'Gestes', p. 706; 'Eracles', p. 403.

[28] 'Gestes', pp. 678–9.   [29] 'Eracles', p. 406.

[30] Ibid., p. 394; 'Lignages', pp. 451, 470. The family was of Genoese origin and was already in the East in 1187. Urkunden Venedig, II, 386, cf. p. 377; RRH, no. 665.

[31] Above, p. 66; Rey 'Seigneurs de Giblet', pp. 410–11; Chandon de Briailles, 'Margat', pp. 247–9; H. E. Mayer 'Die Kreuzfahrerherrschaft 'Arrābe', ZDPV, XCIII (1977), 198–212.

have an example of a knight who only received his fief in the kingdom of Jerusalem some time after he had risen to prominence in Cyprus.[32]

The extent to which Latin Syrian barons with fiefs in Cyprus would have been able to employ men and money from the island in the defence of their mainland lordships was small by comparison with the contribution the Lusignan dynasty was able to make in preserving the remaining Christian-held territories in Syria and Palestine. King Aimery's use of his Cypriots to garrison Jaffa in 1197 and to stage a naval raid on Egypt in 1204 has been mentioned earlier.[33] Other examples from the first half of the thirteenth century of kings sending their forces to the mainland include the expeditions of 1214, when Cypriots joined a combined Christian military demonstration towards Hamah and Hims, and of 1235, when a force of a hundred Cypriot knights assisted the Hospitallers in their attack on Bar'in (Montferrand).[34] Most Cypriot assistance for Frankish Syria, however, came in those periods when the then ruler of Cyprus was also ruler of the Latin kingdom of Jerusalem and, in particular, had custody of Acre. King Aimery had been king of both Cyprus and, by right of his wife, of Jerusalem in the years 1197–1205, and in 1269 his descendant, Hugh III, became king of Jerusalem in his own right after the extinction of the Hohenstaufen dynasty the previous year. Henceforth he and his heirs regarded themselves as kings of both kingdoms. Hugh allowed Acre, the only major city remaining to the royal domain, to slip from his grasp in 1276–7, but his son, Henry II, recovered it in 1286 and held it until the Mamlūk conquest in 1291. The years 1276–86 were thus a period of strained relations between the Lusignans and the rulers of the Latin kingdom, just as earlier relations had been poor in the years 1192–7 when Henry of Champagne was at odds with Guy and Aimery of Lusignan and in the years after 1210 when there was tension between Hugh I and John of Brienne.[35] However, in addition to the periods when the king of Cyprus was also king of Jerusalem, members of the Cypriot royal family acted as regents in Acre for the absentee Hohenstaufen kings for much of the time between 1242 and 1269, and so for large parts of the last half century of the Latin kingdom of Jerusalem's existence the Lusignans had a direct role in its government.

In 1233 the Ibelin victory over the imperial forces put an end to Hohenstaufen power in Cyprus but left the situation that had developed on the mainland

---

[32] 'Gestes', p. 732. For other examples of knights with interests in both kingdoms, Mayer, 'Ibelin versus Ibelin', p. 34.   [33] Above, pp. 33–4.

[34] Cahen, *Syrie du Nord*, pp. 620–1 (1214); 'Gestes', p. 724; 'Eracles', pp. 403–5; 'Annales', p. 439 (1235). There is some confusion as to the date of the Bar'in expedition. It was evidently before the death of John of Ibelin lord of Beirut (early 1236) and about the time of the departure of Henry of Nazareth and Philip of Troyes as emissaries to the papal court in 1235. 'Eracles', p. 406; Riley-Smith, *Feudal Nobility*, pp. 204–7.   [35] Above, pp. 28–9, 32, 46–8.

unchanged.[36] Frederick was still regent for his infant son, Conrad IV, the titular king of Jerusalem, and was attempting to rule through his lieutenant, Richard Filangieri. The Ibelins and their supporters held Acre, Beirut, Sidon, Arsur, Caesarea and Jaffa, while Filangieri had control of little more than Tyre and Jerusalem, but he did enjoy support from the Hospitallers and the Teutonic Knights. There was little change until 1242, when Conrad, who by now was aged fourteen, wrote to the people in the East announcing that he had come of age. He attempted to appoint his own lieutenant, but the Ibelin-dominated regime in Acre refused to accept the appointment of a man who was obviously Frederick's nominee. At the same time a group of inhabitants in Tyre let it be known that they would co-operate in seizing the city by force from its Hohenstaufen garrison. For a number of reasons, not least that Filangieri had come close to taking control of Acre the previous year, the anti-Hohenstaufen barons were only too happy to avail themselves of this opportunity, but, rather than lay themselves open to the accusation that they were acting illegally, they devised arguments to justify their assault on Tyre. Frederick, they asserted, was no longer regent since his son was now of age; the regent for an absentee heir who was of age should be – although in fact there was no precedent – the heir's closest relative present in the East; that person should govern until Conrad himself should come and be accepted as king; in the meantime, if the imperial garrison at Tyre would not acknowledge that person's rule, then force could legitimately be used to bring it to submission. The Ibelins were clearly banking on the assumption that Conrad would never find himself in a position to inflict retribution on them for what in his eyes must have seemed a further act of insubordination and rebellion. As things turned out, they were right; no Hohenstaufen king ever again set foot in Latin Syria.

Conrad's closest heir in the East was his great-aunt, Alice of Champagne, the widow of King Hugh I of Cyprus and the mother of King Henry. She was the eldest surviving half-sister of Maria of Montferrat, Conrad's grandmother, and, as a daughter of Queen Isabella I, could claim descent from the twelfth-century kings of Jerusalem. She was willing to accept the role chosen for her – indeed she had tried to get herself made regent as early as 1229 – and is reported to have given Philip of Novara, who acted as her counsel in the formal hearing of the High Court at which her rights were recognized, a handsome reward. Philip later claimed, probably with some exaggeration, to have conceived the whole scheme. In June 1242, immediately after Alice had been accepted as regent in Acre, the Ibelins, with Venetian and Genoese assistance, duly seized Tyre. But Alice

[36] For what follows, P. Jackson, 'The End of Hohenstaufen Rule in Syria', *BIHR*, LIX (1986), 20–36; D. Jacoby, 'The Kingdom of Jerusalem and the Collapse of Hohenstaufen Power in the Levant', *DOP*, XL (1986), 83–101. Both authors argue persuasively that the Ibelin capture of Tyre occurred in 1242 and not in 1243 as has hitherto generally been believed.

cannot be said to have taken control. Even before Tyre had been captured, she and her husband, Ralph of Coeuvres, a brother of the count of Soissons, had been left in no doubt as to their true position. It had been stipulated in advance that all the fortresses of the kingdom should be held not by the regent but by Balian of Ibelin, lord of Beirut, and his cousin, Philip of Montfort lord of Toron, and at the siege of Tyre, when Ralph of Coeuvres succeeded in capturing Richard Filangieri, he was induced against his will to give up his prisoner to Balian of Ibelin, who used him as a hostage to secure the surrender of the citadel. So Balian and Philip took control of Tyre, and when Ralph and Alice formally requested that they hand it over to them, they refused. Ralph went back to France in digust, leaving Balian of Ibelin with custody of Tyre and Philip of Montfort and a prominent lawyer named Nicholas Antiaume in possession of the royal castle in Acre. Instead of passing to Alice, effective power had gone to the Ibelins and their supporters who had used her in a decidedly cynical fashion to give a specious legality to this latest phase in their struggle against Frederick II and his officers in the East; at the same time they induced her to rescind all Frederick's grants and appointments. As a crowning piece of legalistic hypocrisy they argued that the castles should be held by the liegemen and not by the regent, since there was a danger that a regent might usurp the rights of the heir.[37]

Alice died in 1246. Powerless though she had been in practice, her period in office had established the principle that Conrad's regent should be his closest heir in the East. She was succeeded in the regency by her son, King Henry I. But Henry was not Conrad's nearest relative; his aunt, Melisende of Lusignan, a half-sister of Queen Alice and widow of Prince Bohemond IV of Antioch, was closer, and in fact Melisende made a bid to become regent herself. It is unfortunate that no account of the circumstances of Henry's acquisition of the regency has been preserved. As a crowned king in his own right and as a man in the full vigour of manhood – he would have been aged twenty-nine in 1246 – he must have seemed a very different proposition to the barons of Jerusalem than either his aunt or his mother. What seems to have happened is that perhaps by way of outbidding his aunt, perhaps by way of buying the assent of the barons for his accession to the regency, he made generous grants of land to the leading figures in Syria. Philip of Montfort was given custody of Tyre, Balian of Beirut an estate centred on Casal Imbert and John of Ibelin, the jurist and son of Philip of Ibelin, the county of Jaffa and Ascalon.[38] It may be that the other John of Ibelin, the lord of Arsur who was a younger son of John of Beirut and Balian's brother, was made constable of Jerusalem at the same time.[39] But besides giving

[37] 'Documents relatifs à la successibilité au trône et à la régence', RHC Lois, II, 401.
[38] Riley-Smith, Feudal Nobility, pp. 212–13, 214–15. Above, p. 72. Jaffa and Ascalon were Henry's own inheritance: Edbury, 'John of Ibelin's Title', pp. 124–5.
[39] The previous constable had died in 1244. John is first found with this office in 1251. Cart. gén. Hospitaliers, no. 2576.

away royal lands to this coterie of barons, Henry also delegated his powers as regent to them. In 1246 he appointed Balian of Beirut to be his lieutenant or *bailli*; on Balian's death in 1247 he appointed his brother John to follow him, and then in 1248, at the suggestion of Philip of Montfort, he replaced John with an otherwise unknown knight named John Foignon. The next year Henry reinstated John of Arsur, who then remained in office until after Henry's death in 1253.[40] Taking the period 1242–53 as a whole, the Ibelins in Syria – Balian of Beirut, John of Arsur and their cousins John of Jaffa and Philip of Montfort – had done well by the king and his mother.

Theoretically grants of royal lands by a regent were only valid for the duration of the regency, but in each case the lands given by Henry were retained by their recipients or their heirs after his death. Henceforth the royal domain in Syria was in effect limited to Acre and its immediate environs. It may therefore be wondered what Henry's authority in the kingdom of Jerusalem actually amounted to. He styled himself 'king of Cyprus and lord of Jerusalem' and received recognition of this title from Pope Innocent IV.[41] The pope clearly expected him to take the lead in defending Latin Syria, reforming the Church and so on,[42] but this is evidence more for Innocent's hopes than for Henry's ability. Part of the problem in assessing Henry's position in Syria stems from the fact that his tenure of the regency (1246–53) coincided almost exactly with the Crusade of St Louis and Louis' sojourn in the East (1248–54), and, although the king of France had no constitutional status in Syria, his prestige and wealth meant that Henry was overshadowed. The silence of the sources has led many scholars to believe that Henry spent most of his time in Cyprus and allowed the kingdom of Jerusalem under its baronial oligarchy to go its own way: apart from the alienations at the beginning of his period of office and the changes of his lieutenants, as regent he is known to have concerned himself with the internal affairs of Latin Syria in only two instances and to have come in person with military support for the mainland kingdom only once, in 1252.[43]

Henry, however, did deploy Cypriot military resources in the defence of Latin Syria on several occasions. In 1244 he seems not to have responded to an appeal to send help to the beleaguered city of Jerusalem, although later that same year Cypriot knights fought in the battle of La Forbie.[44] In 1247 he sent a naval force

[40] 'Gestes', p. 741; 'Eracles', pp. 436–7; 'Annales', pp. 442–3; 'Amadi', pp. 198–9.
[41] *RRH*, nos. 1200, 1208; Innocent IV, nos. 3067–8, 5893; 'Abrégé du Livre des Assises de la Cour des Bourgeois', *RHC Lois*, II, 246.   [42] Innocent IV, no. 2531, 3068, 4105.
[43] Mas Latrie, *Histoire*, II, 66–7; *Tabulae ordinis Theutonici*, pp. 84–5; Matthew Paris, *Cronica Majora*, V, 308. But Henry was not without authority in the kingdom of Jerusalem. See Riley-Smith, *Feudal Nobility*, pp. 188–90; Mayer, "*Arrābe*', p. 207; *idem*, 'Ibelin *versus* Ibelin', p. 44 and note 101.
[44] 'Eracles', p. 428; Hill, II, 138. A letter supposedly from the patriarch of Jerusalem put the Cypriot casualties at 300 knights, but this and the other figures it gives would seem to be exaggerated. See Riley-Smith's comments in Ibn al-Furāt, II, 173.

under the command of the seneschal of Cyprus, Baldwin of Ibelin, which, sailing from Famagusta, combined with other shipping at Acre and went to the defence of Ascalon which was then under siege. The fleet managed to bring relief to the defenders, but the Muslims were still able to press their attack to a successful conclusion.[45] Then, as already noted, Cypriot forces were again in action in 1249–50 when a contingent participated in St Louis' expedition to Damietta and in 1252 when Henry brought aid to Louis in Syria. Even so, Henry's contribution to the defence of the Latin East pales when compared with Louis'; in the years 1250–4, the French king strengthened the fortifications at Acre, Caesarea, Jaffa and Sidon, and before he returned to Europe, he established a permanent French garrison in Acre.

It is not hard to see why Alice of Champagne and Henry of Cyprus should have been prepared to involve themselves in the politics of Latin Syria. In the early 1240s, despite the threats posed by the Ayyubids, the Khwarazmians and the more distant Mongols, the fortunes of the kingdom of Jerusalem were as bright as at any period during the thirteenth century. Territorially, thanks to the concessions exacted from the neighbouring Muslim rulers by Frederick II in 1229 and by Thibaut of Navarre and Richard of Cornwall in 1240–1, the kingdom was more extensive than at any time since 1187. It was also extremely wealthy. According to Matthew Paris, the Templars and Hospitallers had told Richard of Cornwall when he was in the East that the royal revenues of Acre were worth 50,000 pounds of silver annually – in other words more than the ordinary revenues of the king of England at that time.[46] The bulk of this income would have come from taxes on commerce. Acre, and to a lesser extent Tyre and the other coastal cities in Christian hands, attracted large numbers of western merchants, mostly Italians, and grew rich as entrepôts on the trade routes linking Europe with the East. But it was precisely in the period 1242–53, when Alice and Henry were regents, that the Christian position in the east began to take a turn for the worse. 1244 witnessed the final loss of Jerusalem by the Christians and a major defeat in battle at La Forbie. In 1247 the Muslims rcovered Tiberias and Ascalon. The previous year the king of Cilician Armenia and the prince of Antioch had acknowledged Mongol suzerainty. In 1250 the military high command in Egypt overthrew the Ayyubid dynasty and inaugrated the regime known to posterity as the Mamlūk sultanate. Although at first the Mamlūk rulers posed less of a threat to the Christians than their Ayyubid predecessors, it was they who in the space of just over forty years were to extinguish the Latin states on the Syrian littoral.

For a few years after the death of Henry I the nobles in the kingdom of Jerusalem were left to their own devices. Henry's lieutenant, John of Arsur,

[45] 'Eracles', pp. 433–4; 'Amadi', p. 198; cf. 'Continuation de Guillaume de Tyr, de 1229 à 1261, dite du manuscrit de Rothelin', RHC Oc., II, 565.   [46] Riley-Smith, Feudal Nobility, p. 64.

continued to exercise authority until 1254 when he was replaced by his cousin John count of Jaffa. Two years later, in 1256, he returned to office.[47] In Cyprus Henry's heir was his infant son, Hugh II, and in keeping with the precedent of Henry's own minority the regency was exercised by the queen-mother, Plaisance of Antioch.[48] In 1254 Plaisance, who cannot have been aged more than eighteen at the time of Henry's death the previous year,[49] married Balian of Ibelin, the son of the *bailli* of Jerusalem, John of Arsur. Presumably it was envisaged that Balian, himself newly dubbed knight at the hand of Louis IX and so evidently still on the threshold of manhood, would exercise effective control in Cyprus. But by the middle of 1255 the couple had separated. What seems to have happened was that Plaisance's kin objected to the marriage. The chroniclers present the quarrel as being between Balian and Plaisance's brother, Prince Bohemond VI of Antioch, and it was later claimed that Bohemond had explicitly withheld his agreement to the union. Perhaps he wanted power in Cyprus for himself; maybe his uncle, Henry of Antioch, who was married to the then heiress-presumptive to the Cypriot throne and sister of the later king, Isabella of Lusignan, was behind the rupture. The question of an annulment arose. Pope Alexander IV, who appears to have disregarded a dispensation issued by his predecessor, ruled that the marriage was inadmissible on the grounds that Balian was related within the prohibited degrees to Plaisance's previous husband: they were second cousins. Balian contested the case. It was not until 1258 that the marriage was finally declared null and he and Bohemond formally reconciled.[50] In the meantime, in 1256, Plaisance, acting presumably on her brother's advice, had taken the initiative in proposing that she should marry Edmund Crouchback, the younger son of King Henry III of England, and that her son, Hugh II, should marry one of the English king's daughters. Henry III entertained grandiose ambitions to establish Plantagenet power in the Mediterranean and was at this period intending to come to the East on crusade. But nothing came of his schemes, and the proposed marriages did not take place.[51]

In 1256 the war known as the War of St Sabas broke out in Acre between the Italian maritime republics. At first most of the lay baronage in the East, including the *bailli*, John of Arsur, appear to have supported the Genoese who enjoyed some early successes. In 1257, however, the Venetians under Lorenzo

---

[47] *Ibid.*, p. 215; Mayer, 'Ibelin *versus* Ibelin', pp. 37, 42–4. Above p. 72 note 112.

[48] 'Documents relatifs à la successibilité', p. 420; 'Nouvelles preuves de l'histoire de Chypre sous le règne des princes de la maison de Lusignan', ed. L. de Mas Latrie, *BEC*, XXXIV (1873), 55.

[49] Her parents married in 1234. 'Annales', p. 439.

[50] Alexander IV, *Registres* ed. C. Bourel de la Roncière *et al* (Paris, 1895–1959), nos. 741, 2510; 'Eracles', pp. 441, 443; 'Annales', pp. 445–6, 448.

[51] *Calendar of Close Rolls Preserved in the Public Record Office* (1254–6) (London, 1931), pp. 445–6, cf. p. 354; *Calendar of Liberate Rolls Preserved in the Public Record Office, 1251–60* (London, 1959), p. 319. Cf. S. Lloyd, *English Society and the Crusade, 1216–1307* (Oxford, 1988), pp. 226–30.

Tiepolo inflicted casualties on Genoese shipping and gained the upper hand in the street fighting in Acre.[52] At this juncture, John of Jaffa, the master of the Templars and Prince Bohemond of Antioch, all of whom had their own reasons for favouring the Venetians, attempted to force the various interests in the Latin East to act in concert and support the side that was now winning. Their ploy was to re-activate the regency principles which previously had conferred authority on Alice of Champagne and Henry I but which had been left in abeyance since 1253. The basic idea was simple: install as regent the closest heir in the East of the titular Hohenstaufen king – since Conrad's death in 1254 his infant son, Conrad V – and have the new regent order the community as a whole to help the Venetians. The situation was complicated by the fact that the person regarded as Conrad's closest heir, King Hugh II of Cyprus, was himself a minor. However, in February 1258, at the instance of John of Jaffa and the master of the Templars, Bohemond of Antioch brought his sister Plaisance and his nephew Hugh II to Acre. At a meeting of the High Court Hugh was formally recognized as Conrad's heir in the kingdom of Jerusalem, and it was agreed that his mother should exercise the regency on his behalf. Genoa's allies objected in vain to these developments, and Plaisance duly ordered the people of Acre to throw their support behind the Venetians. She then withdrew, leaving the former *bailli*, the hitherto pro-Genoese John of Arsur, as her lieutenant.[53] The pro-Venetian party among the Latin Syrian nobility had thus effected a change of policy, and this change was fully vindicated when in June 1258 the Venetians routed the Genoese fleet and forced the Genoese to abandon their quarter in Acre. Even so, warfare between the Italian communes continued to dog the Latin East for many years to come.

Plaisance held the regency for her son until her death in September 1261, but after 1258 she herself fades from view. In John of Arsur she had reappointed as her lieutenant the man who was father of her estranged husband, and in 1259, following John's death late in 1258, she installed the seneschal of Jerusalem and commander of the French garrison in Acre, Geoffrey of Sergines, as his successor. Geoffrey was a Frenchman, and his appointment can perhaps be seen as a move away from the pattern of allowing authority to be exercised by members of the Ibelin family or their clients and allies who between them had in effect governed Acre since the 1230s. It is certainly true that in the decades after Geoffrey's appointment the Ibelin family was far less prominent in the political

---

[52] For a useful account of the war, Richard, *The Latin Kingdom*, pp. 364-71.

[53] Riley-Smith, *Feudal Nobility*, pp. 215-17. Who was Conrad V's heir in 1258 depended on how the principles of inheritance were employed. P. W. Edbury, 'The Disputed Regency of the Kingdom of Jerusalem, 1264/6 and 1268', *Camden Miscellany* XXVII (1979), pp. 17-18. The arguments used in 1258 are not recorded, although, in what is clearly a corrupt passage, one source appears to indicate that Bohemond VI had to argue against the rights of Walter of Brienne's children. 'Rothelin', p. 634.

life of Acre than it had been in the preceding period, but nothing is known of the circumstances under which he acquired his office nor whether it was regarded as a significant departure at the time. Maybe Geoffrey was not so much Plaisance's choice as that of her brother Bohemond who, according to one source, had been responsible for the appointment of John of Arsur in 1258, or of her lover, John count of Jaffa, himself the leading member of the Ibelin family at that time.[54]

Plaisance's tenure of the regency coincided with a sequence of dramatic changes in the political structure of the Muslim world. In the later 1250s the Mongol armies had advanced into the Near East.[55] In 1258 they overran Baghdad and destroyed the Abbasid Caliphate; in 1259–60 they conquered Muslim-held Syria, occupying Aleppo in January 1260 and Damascus the following March before proceeding south as far as Gaza. The Christians in the East imagined that they in their turn would suffer Mongol attack. However, except for an assault on Sidon in late July or early August 1260, the blow never fell. Instead the main armies withdrew eastwards on learning of the Great Khan's death, leaving behind a much smaller force under the command of a leader named Kitbuqa whose primary task was evidently to guard their existing conquests. The Ayyubid regimes in Syria had been crushed, but the Franks had largely escaped. The Mamlūk sultanate, established just ten years earlier in Egypt, then went on to the offensive against Kitbuqa. In August Sultan Qutuz, aided by the benevolent neutrality of the Franks who allowed him to pass through their territory and supplied him with victuals, led his army into Syria. In September he defeated the Mongol commander in battle at 'Ayn Jālūt, and this victory, followed by a further success at Hims three months later, allowed the Mamlūks to take control of the Syrian hinterland and thus surround the Christian possessions. At first the Franks seem to have hoped to be able to profit from these events to make their own gains in Syria; certainly they could not have foreseen that the Mamlūks, whose previous history had been one of *coups d'état* and political instability, would find in their new sultan, Baybars, a capable leader who would remain in power until his death in 1277; nor could they have foreseen that the Mongols, having suffered these reverses at the hands of the Mamlūks, would be unable or unwilling to attempt to exact retribution. What in fact happened was that between 1263 and 1272 Sultan Baybars, fearing a Christian–Mongol alliance and fresh crusades from the West, took pre-emptive action and reduced the Latin states in the East to impotence.

It is perhaps surprising that despite the panic in Acre in 1260 when an imminent Mongol attack was feared, and despite the fact that in the wake of the Mongol defeat later that same year the Christians appealed to the West for

---

[54] For Geoffrey's appointment, 'Gestes', p. 750; 'Eracles', p. 444; 'Annales', pp. 448–9. For Bohemond's appointment of John of Arsur in 1258, 'Rothelin', p. 634. For John of Jaffa and Plaisance, Mayer, 'Ibelin *versus* Ibelin', pp. 51–5.

[55] For what follows, Jackson, 'Crisis in the Holy Land', *passim*.

military assistance to re-occupy Syrian territory, there is no record of Cypriot forces being sent to the mainland at that time. It is also surprising that after Plaisance's death in 1261 no member of the royal house of Cyprus came forward to claim the regency of Jerusalem on behalf of Hugh II for two whole years.[56] In April 1263 Baybars led his first attack on Acre, thereby bringing to an end the truce that had hitherto existed. A full-scale siege was evidently not envisaged, although the Mamlūks did manage to spread alarm and destruction, and in skirmishes outside the city the Christians were worsted and Geoffrey of Sergines wounded. It was only then that Hugh II's kin asserted their rights in the kingdom of Jerusalem. Hugh II was still under age and still regarded as the rightful regent for Conrad V. Now that his mother was dead, it was accepted in both Cyprus and Jerusalem that his heir should act as regent. His closest relative was his father's surviving sister, Isabella, but in Cyprus she had stood aside and allowed her son Hugh, known to historians as Hugh of Antioch-Lusignan, to take over the government of the island.[57] After Plaisance, the youthful widow whose rule had probably been dominated by her husband Balian of Arsur, her brother Bohemond and her lover John of Jaffa in turn, Cyprus was now being ruled by a man who in the early 1260s would have been in his mid-twenties,[58] and who was to prove to be of considerable ability. In the kingdom of Jerusalem, however, Isabella claimed the right to exercise the regency on behalf of Hugh II for herself. In 1263, after Baybars' attack, she and her husband, Henry of Antioch, came to Acre to assume control. In law her claim was indisputable. She nominated her husband to act as her lieutenant, but Henry, as a member of the princely house of Antioch, may have been regarded as an outsider, and it would appear that his appointment was resented. Seizing on the technicality that Isabella and Henry had not brought the young king of Cyprus with them, the members of the High Court refused them homage and fealty. The next year we find the pope calling on Henry, Geoffrey of Sergines, John of Jaffa and John II of Beirut to put an end to the discord among themselves that was endangering the security of the kingdom.[59] It is unfortunate that the sources give us no further information on the problems facing Henry, nor on his policy. In any case his period of authority was brief; his wife died at some point during 1264, whereupon his lieutenancy lapsed.

Isabella's death opened the way for the celebrated dispute between her son, Hugh of Antioch-Lusignan, and his cousin, Hugh count of Brienne, as to who

[56] Riley-Smith, *Feudal Nobility*, p. 217; Jackson, 'Crisis in the Holy Land', pp. 505–6.

[57] Riley-Smith, *Feudal Nobility*, p. 218; Edbury, 'Disputed Regency', pp. 4, 28, 30–1. Hugh later claimed to have been regent for 5 years 8 months. 'Document relatif au service militaire', p. 429. His regency ended with the death of Hugh II in November or December 1267 and, as Plaisance died in September 1261, there may have been a six-month gap before he took control.

[58] Hugh's parents had married *c.* 1233. 'Gestes', p. 706. The dispensation for his own marriage is dated 1255. Alexander IV, no. 71.

[59] Richard, *The Latin Kingdom*, p. 407; Riley-Smith, *Feudal Nobility*, pp. 217–18, cf. p. 190.

should exercise Hugh II's regency in Jerusalem. A verbatim record of the debate between the two cousins before the High Court of Jerusalem has been preserved, providing details of the arguments employed and also a rare insight into Latin Syrian legal dialectic. Ostensibly what was at stake was the right to exercise the regency of Jerusalem on behalf of Hugh II until the young king should come of age and so be able to take over the government in person. Hugh would have reached his majority round about the beginning of 1268, and so a period in office of no more than three to four years can have been envisaged. But the dispute had wider implications that would have been clearly understood at the time: whoever was declared the rightful ruler of Jerusalem on the young king's behalf would also be declared Hugh's heir-presumptive. As things turned out, Hugh II died late in 1267 without ever having reached his majority, and Hugh of Antioch-Lusignan, the victor in the dispute, duly succeeded him.[60]

In 1263 Baybars had given the Christians a foretaste of what was in store for them. The following year he was preoccupied elsewhere, but then his conquests began in earnest. In 1265 he captured Caesarea and Arsur and destroyed Haifa; in 1266 it was the turn of the important Templar castle of Safed in Galilee and also the fortresses at Toron and Chastel Neuf further to the north. Both years witnessed destructive raids in the vicinity of Acre that had the effect of preventing the Christians from sending out relief columns.[61] For the first time since the 1240s the kingdom of Jerusalem was sustaining serious territorial losses, and Hugh of Antioch-Lusignan reacted by doing what no ruler of Cyprus is known to have done since the early 1250s and deployed Cypriot military resources on the mainland. In 1265 he brought across 130 knights as well as mounted squires, and the next year he was back again accompanied by what was described as 'a very fine company of men at arms, knights and others'. In neither year did the Cypriots arrive in time to join the garrison of the beleaguered towns and castles; Hugh's purpose was probably to reinforce the defence of the all-important city of Acre, although in October 1266 he did participate with the military Orders and Geoffrey of Sergines' French garrison in a raid into Galilee. Whether or not Hugh was already exercising the regency in these years is of secondary importance; what is significant is that he recognised that he had a duty to defend the Latin East, and he used his men accordingly.[62]

Hugh's capacity to bring aid must have weighed heavily in his favour in the dispute with his cousin. Quite apart from the legal merits of his case, Hugh of Antioch-Lusignan had at his disposal the military strength of the kingdom of Cyprus; Hugh of Brienne, who it is true had inherited his ancestral county in

---

[60] Exactly when the dispute took place is uncertain. This is unfortunate, since it obscures the context in which Hugh of Antioch-Lusignan, already regent in Cyprus, acquired authority in Acre. See Edbury, 'Disputed Regency', pp. 4–6.

[61] J. Prawer, *Histoire du royaume latin du Jérusalem* (Paris, 1969–70), II, 461–75.

[62] 'Gestes', pp. 759, 766; 'Eracles', pp. 450, 455; Ibn al-Furāt, II, 100, cf. p. 217.

France a few years earlier, would not have been able to compete with his cousin in terms of readily available man-power. In addition, Hugh of Brienne was at a disadvantage when it came to family connections in the East. Both men were cousins of the king of Cyprus, but Hugh of Antioch-Lusignan, besides being the cousin on his father's side of the prince of Antioch, had married into the Ibelin family. As for the legal arguments themselves, the transcripts of the pleading reveal elements of muddled thinking on the part of both protagonists. The question turned on rules of descent. Hugh of Brienne, a son of Isabella of Lusignan's long-dead sister Maria, was the representative of the senior branch of the family, but was a younger man, and in the end the High Court of Jerusalem upheld Hugh of Antioch-Lusignan's contention that as the elder of the two cousins in the same degree of relationship to Hugh II he should be entitled to exercise the regency.[63]

King Hugh II died late in 1267. In Cyprus Hugh of Antioch-Lusignan thereupon ascended the throne, and on Christmas Day 1267 he was crowned in Nicosia cathedral. The following May King Hugh III, as he should now be called, crossed to Acre and asserted his claim to succeed Hugh II as regent of the kingdom of Jerusalem for the absentee Conrad of Hohenstaufen. The High Court seems to have been prepared to accept him, but his rights were challenged by his kinswoman, Maria of Antioch, on the grounds that as a nearer relative and hence closer heir of Conrad she had a greater right. Legally her case was sound; against her Hugh III employed arguments that he himself had discredited in his dispute with his cousin, and the members of the High Court, in recognizing Hugh's claims, may have salved their consciences with the technicality that by refusing their summons to come into court to hear them deliver their verdict, Maria had not presented her case properly and so was in default. Maria's problem was that she was over forty and unmarried. Hugh on the other hand already had experience of governing Latin Syria and was eminently suited to take charge. What probably swayed the High Court more than anything was the fact that earlier in 1268 Baybars, who the previous year had contented himself with a couple of military demonstrations before Acre, had captured the town of Jaffa and the Templar castle of Beaufort before going on to take the northern city of Antioch which the Christians had held continuously since 1098. In the face of these renewed losses, Hugh could utilize his Cypriot troops; Maria apparently could offer nothing.[64]

On 29 October 1268 Conrad V, the last legitimate descendant of Frederick II and Queen Isabella of Jerusalem, was executed in Naples. With the extinction of the line of Hohenstaufen kings of Jerusalem, Hugh III, whose recognition as regent in May 1268 had marked him out as heir-presumptive, succeeded to the throne. He crowned in the cathedral at Tyre in September 1269.

[63] Edbury, 'Disputed Regency', pp. 6-8, 12-15.   [64] Ibid., pp. 8-11.

Hugh was now king of both Cyprus and Jerusalem. His accession meant that for the first time since the 1220s and the reign of John of Brienne the kingdom of Jerusalem now had a resident monarch. But his inheritance was difficult, to say the least. The long interregnum had in itself created problems, and the Christians were now reeling under the impact of Baybars' inroads. One result of the lack of strong leadership and the pressures of war was that the barons and military Orders had taken to pursuing their own relations with the Muslims, making and unmaking truces independently of the government in Acre. The kingdom had thus gone a long way towards fragmenting into its component lordships. A further dimension to the disintegration of the fabric of the kingdom was provided by the Italians. Since 1258 the Venetians had excluded their rivals from Acre, and the Genoese theirs from Tyre, and conflict between them frequently disturbed the commercial and political life of the East. Hugh III attempted to revive royal authority. He was certainly an able man, and his rule was not without its successes, but to be king of the whole realm and not simply 'king of Acre' as Muslim writers called him proved impossible.

The corner-stone of Hugh's policy seems to have been based on close relations with the Montfort family in Tyre. Philip of Montfort had received Tyre from Henry I in 1246, but his legal title there was weak. Nevertheless the Montforts were a powerful family, and Tyre was an important city. Hugh was not prepared to relinquish his residual rights as king, although he knew he was not strong enough to expel the Montforts and re-absorb Tyre into the royal domain. Even before he became king it would seem that plans were afoot for Philip's son John of Montfort to marry Hugh's sister Margaret. Soon after Hugh's accession they came to an agreement: Margaret wedded John, and the king gave John Tyre to be held as a fief by him and his descendants by Margaret; for his part Philip handed over control in Tyre to his son.[65] This settlement with the Montfort family was to serve Hugh well in the future. However, it is noteworthy that in 1271 John of Montfort made his own truce with Baybars to cover Tyre,[66] thus anticipating Hugh III's truce of the following year which only covered the area around Acre. Hugh also sought to assert his rule in the other lordships of his kingdom. He regularized the unsanctioned alienations of Arsur to the Hospitallers and of Sidon to the Templars, both of which had taken place before his accession. But when in 1275 he attempted to give effect to his jurisdiction over Beirut he ran into difficulties; Baybars intervened to prevent him, claiming that by the terms of his treaty with the lady of Beirut, the lordship was under his protection.[67]

[65] 'Gestes', pp. 773–4, 775; Riley-Smith, *Feudal Nobility*, p. 224. For an example of Hugh exercising jurisdiction in Tyre, *RRH*, no. 1374b.   [66] Ibn al-Furāt, II, 154.
[67] *Ibid.*, p. 164; Riley-Smith, *Feudal Nobility*, pp. 28, 224.

After Baybars' successes in capturing Jaffa, Beaufort and Antioch in 1268, he was prepared to temporize, and the history of the next two years is of raids, counter-raids and negotiations. The sultan was afraid that St Louis' second crusade would come to the East, and that there could be a Franco-Mongol alliance against him. In the event the only crusaders to arrive were a contingent under the bastard sons of King James I of Aragon in 1269 and another under the Lord Edward (soon to be King Edward I of England) in 1271. The Mongols staged an attack on Mamlūk territory to coincide with Edward's presence in the East, but there was no effective co-operation between Mongols and Christians. The deviation of Louis' expedition to Tunis in 1270 left Baybars a free hand to resume his conquests, and he now turned his attention to the county of Tripoli. In 1271, he captured first the Templar castle at Chastel Blanc (Safita), then the famous Hospitaller castle nearby Crac des Chevaliers and finally the count of Tripoli's fortress at Gibelacar. He then moved south and in June 1271 seized the castle of Montfort, the principal possession of the Teutonic Knights in the East, so laying open the north-eastern approaches to Acre. Immediately afterwards, in an attempt to distract Hugh's attention from mainland Syria, he sent a naval expedition against Cyprus. This was Baybars' only attempted raid on the island, and it ended in disaster when most of the Muslim ships were wrecked near Limassol.[68] The Lord Edward had arrived in Acre not long before, and later in 1271 he and Hugh engaged in some raiding, most notably an attack on the castle at Qaqun. Early in 1272 Baybars concluded a truce, and henceforth Acre remained at peace with the Mamlūks until shortly before the final calamity in 1291.

Hugh III had brought Cypriot troops to Acre in 1265 and 1266. Between his accession as king of Cyprus at the end of 1267 and 1271 he did so again on two further occasions, probably in 1268, when he was recognized as regent, and in 1269, when he received the crown of Jerusalem.[69] In 1271 he summoned the Cypriot knights once more, but on this occasion they refused to serve, arguing that the king had no right to compel them to perform military service outside Cyprus itself. The dispute seems to have come to a head in July.[70] The knights were probably alarmed by the abortive seaborne attack a few weeks earlier; clearly they thought that they had been summoned to fight on the mainland rather too frequently in recent years. The whole affair provides an unmistakable indication that however keen Hugh may have been to defend what was left of his mainland kingdom, the Cypriot knights did not share his aspirations. The Lord Edward was called upon to arbitrate, although whether his intervention was intended to be binding for all time or was simply an interim measure for the year in question is not known. The depositions laid before him by Hugh on the one

[68] Hill, II, 167. Cf. Ibn al-Furāt, II, 152–4 and notes (p. 242).
[69] 'Document relatif au service militaire', p. 429 §18; Edbury, 'Feudal Obligations', p. 332.
[70] Walter of Guisborough, p. 208.

hand and by James of Ibelin, the spokesman for the knights, on the other have been preserved. Hugh claimed that theory and precedent were on his side, and he listed the occasions on which the knights had answered summons to serve outside Cyprus in the past. James, a son of the famous lawyer John count of Jaffa, tried to dispute his assertions point by point, although many of his own arguments were thin. One claim is particularly suggestive. According to Hugh, it was James' father and Philip of Montfort who had urged Henry I to use a feudal summons to induce Cypriot knights to participate in St Louis' expedition to Damietta in 1249. As prominent Cypriot vassals with lordships on the mainland, they had had a vested interest in getting the king to lead his army overseas. But by the 1270s many of those lordships had been lost. As Baybars eroded the Christian possessions, so the number of Cypriots who would have wanted to defend what was left grew less. If John of Jaffa had been a leader of the party in Cyprus in the 1240s calling for service abroad, his son, only three years after the fall of Jaffa in 1268, was spokesman for the party opposed to such service.[71] In 1273 a settlement was reached whereby the king of Cyprus could command his vassals to serve outside Cyprus for a maximum of four months in any year, and then only if led by the king in person or by the king's son. Hugh's right to summon his knights abroad had been upheld, but never again did he call on his Cypriot vassals to defend the Latin East against the Muslims.[72]

In 1276 Hugh left Acre for good, enraged and frustrated by the opposition he had encountered. Baybars' intervention in Beirut serves to illustrate the king's failure to weld his kingdom together. The dispute with his own knights was humiliating and must have destroyed the confidence the people of Acre would have had in his ability to bring aid when required. In any case, the king had been unable to wrest the initiative from the Mamlūks or recover any of Baybars' gains. However, at the heart of Hugh's problems was the fact that his right to the throne of Jerusalem was contested. Maria of Antioch, who had unsuccessfully challenged his rights to the regency in May 1268, persisted in her contention that she, and not Hugh, was the righful heir of Conrad V. Whether she made a formal request for the throne in the High Court after Conrad's death is not known, but she did demand to be crowned by the patriarch of Jerusalem, and, when this demand was ignored, she had a clerk and notary interrupt Hugh's coronation ceremony at Tyre. She then appealed to Rome. Litigation was protracted. Her suit was before the curia by 1272, and Hugh was sending procurators to answer her in 1273. She subsequently withdrew her case and at the beginning of 1277, with papal approval, sold her claims to the king of Sicily, Charles of Anjou. Maria would not have been able to contribute anything to the defence of Acre,

---

[71] 'Document relatif au service militaire', pp. 427–34; Edbury, 'Feudal Obligations', pp. 332–5; H. E. Mayer, *Mélanges sur l'histoire du royaume latin de Jérusalem* (Paris, 1984), pp. 106–13.

[72] 'Eracles', pp. 463–4; Marino Sanudo, p. 225. In an undated letter apparently of 1273 or 1274, the pope congratulated Hugh on the conclusion of the agreement. Gregory X, no. 810.

but Charles was in an altogether different position. A younger brother of St Louis who himself had done so much for the security of the Latin East, Charles had become ruler of Sicily in 1266. He was a man of boundless ambition whose influence was felt throughout the Mediterranean world, and to some sections of opinion he would have seemed to have been able to offer far more in terms of military aid and political and diplomatic influence than Hugh III. It is not known when the idea that Maria would make her claims over to him was first mooted, but it is likely to have been well before 1277. Certainly Charles had already been concerning himself with the East. In 1269 and again in 1271 he had been negotiating with Baybars for a truce in the Latin East, and these activities, together with the statement of a Muslim writer that as early as 1269 Hugh III was frightened of him, might suggest that his ambitions dated from that time.[73]

There were three main groups in the East to whom Charles of Anjou could look for support: the French garrison in Acre, paid for by his nephew, King Philip III of France, the Venetians and the Templars. In fact there is no evidence that the French garrison was opposed to Hugh before 1276, although it proved to be firmly behind Charles' representatives during the following decade. When Hugh first left Acre, a delegation of prominent people including the garrison's commander, William of Roussillon, followed him to Tyre where they begged him to appoint a regent and other officers to take control during his absence. These men obviously still regarded Hugh as the legitimate source of authority. By contrast, at the time when others had been urging Hugh not to leave Acre, the Venetians and the Templars had made out that they did not care whether he stayed or went. Clearly they were hoping he would go.[74] The opposition of the Venetians can probably be attributed to Hugh III's close relationship with the lord of Tyre, John of Montfort. A truce between the Genoese and Venetians had been established in 1270, and the Genoese were re-admitted to Acre. Hugh enforced the restitution of certain of their properties that had been occupied by the Venetians, although the Genoese never recovered their old quarter in its entirety.[75] The Venetians, however, were not re-admitted to Tyre. It was doubtless the result of the favourable treatment of their rivals and the fact that the Montforts had been responsible for their expulsion from Tyre in the first place at the time of the War of St Sabas that turned the Venetians against the king.[76] But the group which more than any other undermined his position in Acre was the Templars. So long as the master, Thomas Berard, was alive they

[73] 'Eracles', p. 461; Ibn al Furāt, II, 130–1, 157. For Maria's claims and Hugh's departure from Acre, Hill, II, 163–5, 172–3; Riley-Smith, *Feudal Nobility*, pp. 222–4, 225–6.
[74] 'Eracles', p. 474. For William, 'Gestes', p. 780.
[75] D. Jacoby, 'L'expansion occidentale dans le Levant: les Vénitiens à Acre dans la seconde moitié du treizième siècle', *Journal of Medieval History*, III (1977), 228 and note 9 (pp. 254–5).
[76] For evidence that Hugh had offered the Venetians franchises in Cyprus but had not fulfilled his promise, 'Nouvelles preuves' (1873), pp. 54–6.

seem to have accepted Hugh's rule,[77] but his successor, William of Beaujeu, who was elected in 1273, was a relative of the French royal family and for a brief period before his election had been Templar commander in Apulia.[78] Not surprisingly he supported Charles of Anjou. The Templars' unsanctioned acquisition of property near Acre, together with disturbances in Acre itself involving the military Orders and their client confraternities, was what finally convinced Hugh that his position was untenable, and, when Charles of Anjou's officers arrived the following year, it was the Templars who eased their take-over of power.[79]

Hugh III left Acre in October 1276. In March 1277 Maria of Antioch completed the sale of her rights to Jerusalem to Charles of Anjou, and within a matter of weeks Charles' representative, Roger of San Severino, arrived in the East.[80] At Acre Roger occupied the royal castle, bullied the liegemen into doing homage to him as Charles' deputy and appointed officials. He then seems to have proposed taking over Tyre but was dissuaded when the Venetians pointed out that this could lead to conflict. As Hugh III's brother-in-law, John of Montfort had good cause to regard the new regime in Acre with anxiety. Accordingly, in July 1277, helped by the mediation of William of Beaujeu, he re-admitted the Venetians to their third share of his lordship of Tyre in return for an explicit recognition of his title. It was a heavy price, but the concession was guaranteed by the Templars as well as by a number of other leading ecclesiastics and laymen. With Roger's principal allies in the East now committed to upholding his rights, John's position was secure.[81] Nevertheless there is no direct evidence that he ever recognized Charles of Anjou as king of Jerusalem or Roger of San Severino as his lieutenant.

Hugh III had abandoned Acre, washing his hands of responsibility for its defence and government, and in 1277 he seems to have made no attempt to stop Roger's assumption of control. But his attitude soon changed. In 1279 he made the first of two attempts to re-occupy the city. He brought a large force of Cypriots to Tyre, evidently hoping that a show of strength coupled with bribery in appropriate quarters would bring about the restoration of his power. William of Beaujeu, however, remained firmly opposed, and it was largely thanks to him that Hugh's efforts were thwarted. At the end of four months, when by the compromise of 1273 Hugh's right to compel his own vassals to serve in Syria expired, his army broke up and the king retired to Cyprus. There, by way of

---

[77] Edbury, 'Disputed Regency', p. 47; 'Eracles', p. 463.
[78] 'Gestes', pp. 779–80; M. L. Bulst-Thiele, *Sacrae Domus Militiae Templi Hierosolymitani Magistri* (Göttingen, 1974), pp. 259–60, 263–5.
[79] 'Eracles', pp. 474, 478.
[80] 8 May ('Eracles' p. 478 note a) or 7 June (Marino Sanudo, p. 227; 'Amadi', p. 214). September ('Gestes' p. 783) is clearly too late as it post-dates John of Montfort's agreement with the Venetians.   [81] *Urkunden Venedig*, III, 150–9; 'Gestes', p. 784; 'Eracles', p. 478.

reprisal, he seized the Templars' properties and destroyed their fortifications.[82] His second attempt to reassert his authority on the mainland followed in 1283. Encouraged no doubt by the rising the previous year in Sicily against Charles of Anjou – the Sicilian Vespers – and the subsequent recall of Roger of San Severino, he brought a force said to number 250 knights to Syria. His first landfall was at Beirut, and from there he proceded to Tyre. But again he failed. Odo Poilechien, the new Angevin lieutenant in Acre, had just renewed the truce with the Mamlūks, and it is possible that Hugh may have feared Mamlūk intervention had he sought to displace Odo by force. The Templars seem to have remained staunchly behind the Angevins: Odo's truce covered the Templar lordships of Athlit and Sidon as well as Acre and Haifa, and it was believed that it was they who had instigated a Muslim ambush on that section of Hugh's army which in 1283 had gone from Beirut to Tyre by land. On 24 March 1284, still in Tyre, Hugh died.[83]

Thus it was that the Angevins controlled Acre and were supported by the Templars, whose possession of Athlit and Sidon gave them a major role in the defence of the remaining Christian territories in the Latin kingdom. On the other hand, at Tyre and Beirut Hugh had continued to be recognized as the rightful king of Jerusalem. John of Montfort allowed Hugh to use Tyre as his base in both 1279 and 1283. His younger brother, Humphrey, was married to Eschiva of Ibelin who succeeded to the lordship of Beirut on the death of her sister Isabella in about 1280.[84] But after 1277 Hugh was in no position to do anything constructive in the diplomatic or military sphere to help the Latins in their dealings with the Mamlūks, although there is some evidence to suggest that he intended bringing assistance to the Mongols when they attempted to invade Syria in 1281.[85] So the king, who in the 1260s looked as if he was going to provide the Latin East with positive political leadership backed up by military aid from Cyprus, spent the last eight years of his career unable to govern the one remaining royal city in Syria.

Hugh was succeeded by his eldest surviving son, John, who was crowned king of Cyprus in Nicosia in May 1284. John died almost exactly a year later and was succeeded by his brother, Henry II, who in his turn was crowned in June 1285.[86]

---

[82] Above p. 78 note 21.

[83] 'Gestes', pp. 789–91; 'Annales', p. 458; Marino Sanudo, p. 229; 'Amadi', pp. 214–16. For the Mamlūk treaty, P. M. Holt, 'Qalāwūn's Treaty with Acre in 1283', *EHR*, XCI (1976), 802–12; D. Barag, 'A New Source Concerning the Ultimate Borders of the Latin Kingdom of Jerusalem', *Israel Exploration Journal*, XXIX (1979), 197–217.

[84] 'Gestes', p. 790, cf. p. 774. It is not known when Isabella died. Her third husband died in 1277, but she survived to marry a fourth. 'Eracles', p. 479; Rudt de Collenberg, 'Les Ibelin', pp. 136–7.

[85] Hill, II, 175–6.

[86] 'Gestes', pp. 791, 792; Marino Sanudo, p. 229; Leontios Makhairas, §41; 'Amadi', p. 216. The belief that John went to Tyre where he was crowned king of Jerusalem is first found in the sixteenth century. Lusignan, *Description*, f. 137v.

Henry renewed his father's efforts to recover Acre where it would seem the climate of opinion was now much more favourable to the Lusignans than previously. Presumably the continuing problems facing the Angevins in Italy had convinced people that no help was likely from that quarter. Even William of Beaujeu was prepared to change sides, and the groundwork for Henry's recognition in Acre was laid when his ambassador, a knight named Julian Le Jaune, reached an agreement with William. In June 1286 Henry sailed for Syria and made his entry into Acre where he was enthusiastically acclaimed by the population as a whole. Only the Angevin governor, Odo Poilechien, and the French garrison remained opposed to him. As these men occupied the royal castle it was essential for the king to dislodge them. After five days of blockade and negotiations the castle was surrendered on the understanding that no reprisals against the French would be taken and that if their paymaster, the king of France, held that Henry had behaved wrongfully in expelling them from it, he would hand the castle back to them.[87] Henry then travelled to Tyre where he was crowned king of Jerusalem on 15 August. The coronation was followed by lavish celebrations with jousts and other entertainments – 'the best that had been seen for a hundred years'. In November he returned to Cyprus leaving his maternal uncle, Baldwin of Ibelin, as his lieutenant in Acre.[88]

Once again there was a Lusignan reigning in both Cyprus and the kingdom of Jerusalem. The new king of Sicily, Charles II, was unable to respond to Henry's success in regaining Acre, although he and his descendants continued to lay claim to the title of king of Jerusalem. By 1286 the Christians in the Latin kingdom had been living at peace with their Muslim neighbours for fourteen years. The truce of 1272 had held, and in 1283 Odo Poilechien had renewed and extended it. Since 1269 and 1271 respectively the lords of Beirut and Tyre had had their own truces. Further north relations were not so peaceable, and in 1285 the Mamlūks captured the Hospitaller castle of Marqab which hitherto had been the base for raids into Muslim territory and for attempted co-operation with the Mongols.[89] Henry's kingdom consisted of little more than the royal city of Acre, the Templar lordships of Athlit and Sidon and the lordships of Tyre and Beirut. The lady of Beirut was Eschiva of Ibelin, the younger daughter of John II of Beirut. Her husband, Humphrey of Montfort, had died in 1284 and she remained unmarried until after the loss of the lordship in 1291 when she married

[87] Hill, II, 179–81; Richard, *The Latin Kingdom*, pp. 418–19.
[88] 'Gestes', p. 793; Marino Sanudo, p. 229 (wrongly naming the lieutenant as Philip of Ibelin); 'Amadi', p. 217. Henry's coronation is thought to have occasioned an upsurge of patronage of illuminated manuscripts in Acre. H. Buchthal, *Miniature Painting in the Latin Kingdom of Jerusalem* (Oxford, 1957), pp. 86–7; J. Folda, *Crusader Manuscript Illumination at Saint-Jean d'Acre, 1275–1291* (Princeton, 1976), pp. 26, 77, 102. Baldwin of Ibelin was dead by January 1287 (1286 o.s.). Mas Latrie, *Histoire*, III, 669–70.
[89] Riley-Smith, *Knights of St John*, pp. 137 and note 2, 141, 194–5.

King Henry's brother Guy.[90] John of Montfort lord of Tyre had died childless in 1283. By the terms of Hugh III's enfeoffment, the lordship should have escheated to the crown, but Hugh was unable to find the 150,000 saracen bezants due to John's heir by way of compensation for the expenses incurred by the Montfort family in fortifying their lordship. The king therefore came to an agreement with John's next of kin, Humphrey, the husband of the lady of Beirut, whereby Humphrey should hold Tyre until Hugh paid the compensation; if Hugh had not paid by the end of May 1284, Humphrey was to have the lordship on a permanent footing. In the event both Hugh and Humphrey died before the term expired. Humphrey's heirs, however, acquired no rights in Tyre, and so presumably they were indemnified. In 1285 John of Montfort's widow, Margaret of Lusignan, the sister of Hugh III, concluded a truce with the Mamlūks to cover the lordship, and so at that point she must have been regarded as possessing legitimate authority there. But at some stage in the late 1280s Henry II conferred Tyre on his brother Amaury who remained seised until its fall in 1291.[91]

The restoration of the Lusignan dynasty on the Syrian mainland in 1286 and Henry II's successes in beginning a reconstruction of royal authority ended abruptly in 1291 with the Mamlūk conquest of Acre and the abandonment of the remaining towns and fortresses. It would appear that Henry himself spent most of the intervening years in Cyprus and governed his mainland realm through lieutenants: his uncle Baldwin of Ibelin and then from 1289 his younger brother, Amaury lord of Tyre. So far as is known he only visited Syria twice after 1286: once from April to September 1289 when he came to Acre at the time of the fall of Tripoli, and again in May 1291 when he brought Cypriot reinforcements for the final defence of the town. Nevertheless, Henry was certainly not indifferent to the needs of the Latin kingdom. In 1287 we find his lieutenant acting in concert with the military Orders to put an end to the fighting among the Italians that had done so much to damage the security of the Christian territories.[92] In 1289 Henry sent his brother Amaury to the defence of Tripoli with a force of of knights and men-at-arms then in the aftermath of the loss of Tripoli he himself came to Acre and renewed the truce with the Mamlūks, and at about the same time he sent

[90] 'Gestes', pp. 790–1; Rudt de Collenberg, 'Dispenses matrimoniales', pp. 60–1 (nos. 18a–b).

[91] 'Gestes', pp. 790, 804. For the truce, J. Richard, 'Un partage de seigneurie entre Francs et Mamelouks: les "casaux de Sur"', *Syria*, xxx (1953), 72–82. Amaury is named as lord of Tyre in a description of the events of 1289 ('Gestes', pp. 803–5) and in papal letters of 1290 (Nicholas IV, nos. 4387, 4392, 4400). Margaret's status in 1285 is problematical. Richard's suggestion ('Partage', p. 73 note 2) that Hugh III's enfeoffment was a form of jointure falls on the grounds that there would then have been no need to make a deal with Humphrey, and that Henry would not have had the escheat and so could not confer the title on his brother. Margaret died in 1308. 'Amadi', p. 271.   [92] 'Gestes', p. 799; Prawer, *Histoire*, II, 529–32.

John of Grailly, the commander of the French garrison in Acre, to Europe to seek military aid.[93]

The story of the loss of Acre in May 1291 has been retold often enough. Despite the accusations of cowardice levelled at him, Henry's personal conduct during the siege seems to have been creditable.[94] The basic problem was that the Christians lacked the military might to put up an effective resistance. Various figures are given in the sources, perhaps the most authoritative being those preserved by the so-called 'Templar of Tyre' who stated that at the beginning of the siege the Christians had 6–700 knights and 13,000 footmen including the crusaders from the West. The Cypriot reinforcements brought by Henry after the siege had begun are variously put at 200 knights and 500 footmen or 100 knights and 200 footmen.[95] The fact was that Henry's forces from Cyprus did not significantly add to the number of the defenders, let alone tilt the balance in favour of the Christians. The same explanation – lack of man-power for defence – must have lain behind the surrender of the remaining cities and fortresses along the coast once Acre had fallen. No doubt the fall of Acre was a severe blow to morale, and it has to be assumed that the Christians had put all their efforts into defending it and lacked the resources to offer worthwhile resistance elsewhere.

We do not know what the total military strength at the disposal of the thirteenth-century kings of Cyprus amounted to, but it is likely that the 250 knights brought by Hugh III to Tyre in 1283 or the 200 said to have been brought by Henry II to Acre in 1291 represent the upper limits of the forces that could be spared from garrison duties within the island. In other words, welcome though Cypriot assistance no doubt was, the resources of the Lusignan kings were limited, and their ability to aid Latin Syria was correspondingly circumscribed. It should be added that although there are plenty of instances of Cypriots being deployed in Syria, there is not a single case of their prowess or achievements catching the imagination of the chroniclers, and, as the dispute over services of 1271 makes clear, the commitment of individual knights was not necessarily wholehearted. On the other hand, the political leadership provided by the Lusignans could be energetic and sensible, but there were too many interruptions for lasting achievements to be made. Neither Henry I, Hugh III nor Henry II acquired complete control over the lay baronage, the military Orders or the French garrison in Acre. Indeed, Pope Nicholas IV, pope at the time of the fall of Acre, directed his correspondence not to Henry II as king of Jerusalem, but to a group of notables.[96] At best the Lusignans ruled by consensus and gave

[93] 'Gestes', pp. 803, 804; Marino Sanudo, p. 230; 'Amadi', p. 218; Hill, II, 182–3. For John of Grailly, Nicholas IV, nos. 2252–58.

[94] Hill, II, 184–7; Richard, *The Latin Kingdom*, pp. 425–9; Prawer, *Histoire*, II, 552–7.

[95] 'Gestes', pp. 806–7; Marino Sanudo, pp. 230–1; 'Amadi', pp. 219–20, 221.

[96] Nicholas IV, nos. 4391–4401, cf. no. 4387.

the government in Acre a measure of legal sanction. However, while we should be warned against claiming undue importance for Cyprus in the history of the crusades and the Latin East in the thirteenth century, it nevertheless remains true that Cypriot material aid in terms of economic and military assistance of one sort or another did augment the resources of the Christians on the mainland with a fair degree of reliability, and that, although ultimately they failed, the Lusignan kings of the second half of the century did their best to counter the centrifugal tendencies fostered by the absence of an adequate ruler for long periods and by the disruptive ambitions of the Italian maritime republics and other elements in political society. Hugh III and his son Henry II were the only people in a position even to contemplate such an attempt. But their successes were insufficient to prevent the victory of the aggressive, centralized Mamlūk sultanate with its far superior military might.

6

THE REIGN OF HENRY II

THE MUSLIM conquest of Acre and the other cities on the coast of Syria in 1291 transformed the political situation in the East. Whilst the loss of his mainland territories meant that King Henry no longer had to commit resources in their defence, Cyprus itself was now vulnerable as the sole outpost of western Christendom in the eastern Mediterranean. The only other Christian state in the region was the Cilician kingdom of Lesser Armenia. At Jubail the Muslims allowed the Genoese Embriaco family to retain possession under their suzerainty for a few years,[1] but otherwise, with this one minor exception, the whole of the Levantine coastlands from the Gulf of Iskenderun to Egypt and beyond had come into the control of the Mamlūk sultanate. The immediate danger was that the Mamlūks might try to follow up their successes by invading Cyprus. On the other hand, there were plenty of people in the West prepared to pay at least lip-service to the idea that a new crusade should be organized to win back the Holy Land. But in the event there was no Mamlūk invasion; nor was there a crusade to recover Jerusalem.

Cyprus had been noted as a haven for refugees from Muslim advance from as early as the 1240s,[2] and in 1291 large numbers of survivors from Syria escaped thither. Many of them, both Franks and Christian Syrians, were reduced to poverty, and their condition must have been made worse by a series of harvest failures in the mid-1290s. The king and his mother are said to have done much to alleviate distress: in 1296 Henry issued an ordinance designed to control the price of bread, and he is also reported to have recruited refugee knights and sergeants into his service. Even so, in 1295 King Charles II of Sicily was making some not altogether disinterested provision for feeding impoverished *nobiles*.[3] A number of leading families from the kingdom of Jerusalem had acquired property in Cyprus long before, but many people lost their entire means of support in the disasters of 1291. After the fall of Acre, the Templars and Hospitallers established their headquarters in the island, and Cyprus also

---

[1] R. Irwin, 'The Mamlūk Conquest of the County of Tripoli', CS, p. 249.

[2] La Monte, 'Register of Nicosia', no. 61.

[3] 'Gestes', p. 818; Marino Sanudo, p. 232; J. Richard, 'L'ordonnance de décembre 1296 sur le prix du pain à Chypre', EKEE, 1 (1967–8), 45–51; Housley, 'Charles II of Naples', pp. 530–2, 534–5.

became the home for other religious communities that had fled the Muslim conquests. Many of the non-Latin inhabitants from the Christian ports in Syria who came to Cyprus crowded into Famagusta. It has been claimed that these people, mostly Arabic-speaking Christians, may well have outnumbered the Greeks there, and without doubt the 'Suriens', as they were known, came to play a major part in Famagusta's rise as a commercial centre at this period.[4]

Once news of the fall of Acre reached the West, Pope Nicholas IV began taking measures designed to make good the losses. He called for a crusade to be ready to set out in the summer of 1293; he ordered provincial church councils to meet to consider the recovery of the Holy Land; he took up the suggestion that a new military Order be formed by merging the Templars and Hospitallers; he announced a ten-year ban on all trade with the lands of the Mamlūk sultanate; he sent envoys to the Mongols, and then, at the beginning of 1292, he was organizing aid for Cilician Armenia.[5] His death in April 1292 and the ensuing papal vacancy which lasted for over two years meant that most of these initiatives came to nothing: there was no crusade and no merged military Order, although the trade boycott continued to form a cornerstone of papal policy. However, the pope had evidently taken the threat to Cyprus seriously, and he was able to arrange for a fleet of twenty galleys to be sent to Cypriot waters. It sailed in 1292 under the command of the Genoese Manuel Zaccaria, and in the East it was joined by fifteen galleys provided by King Henry. Together they attacked Alaya on the southern coast of Asia Minor and then raided Alexandria, although in neither place did they score any great success.[6] According to the Christian writers, the raid on Alexandria provoked the sultan, al-Ashraf Khalīl, into planning a conquest of Cyprus, and they then describe how his emirs, alarmed by his ambitions and arrogance, thereupon had him murdered. The Arabic sources confirm that his death came about as the result of conflict among the military elite. An extended period of internecine feuding and blood-letting then followed with the result that a Mamlūk offensive against the island was now out of the question.[7]

So far as Cyprus was concerned, the internal political strife in Egypt was most

[4] J. Richard, 'Le peuplement latin et syrien en Chypre au XIIIe siècle', *BF*, VII (1979), 168–70; D. Jacoby, 'The Rise of a New Emporium in the Eastern Mediterranean: Famagusta in the Late Thirteenth Century', Μελέται καὶ Ὑπομνήματα, I (1984), 150–4.

[5] Nicholas IV, nos. 6778–835, 6850–6.

[6] 'Gestes', p. 820; *Annali Genovesi di Caffaro e de'suoi continuatori dal MXCIX al MCCXCIII*, ed. L. T. Belgrano and C. Imperiale di Sant'Angelo (Rome, 1890–1929), V, 143–4; J. Richard, 'Le royaume de Chypre et embargo sur le commerce avec l'Égypte (fin XIIIe-début XIVe siècle)', *Académie des Inscriptions et Belles-lettres: Comptes Rendus* (1984), 123. For evidence to suggest that only half Zaccaria's fleet was available for the raid, Richard, 'Le royaume de Chypre', note 16; this would seem to confirm Marino Sanudo's report (p. 232) that twenty-five galleys took part.

[7] 'Gestes', pp. 820–1; Marino Sanudo, p. 233; 'Amadi', pp. 229–30. More generally, R. Irwin, *The Middle East in the Middle Ages: The Early Mamluk Sultanate* (London/Sydney, 1986), pp. 79–82, 85–6.

opportune. In 1293 war broke out between Venice and Genoa, and as a direct consequence a western naval presence in the East could no longer be guaranteed. On the other hand, the military Orders were now organizing their own flotillas. In 1293 we read of two Templar galleys setting sail for Cyprus in the company of some Venetians, and at the same time the Hospitallers, with papal encouragement, were developing their naval arm. Charles II of Sicily alluded to ten galleys in Cyprus belonging to the Order, and in 1297 Pope Boniface VIII made reference to its ships engaging in conflicts with the Muslims.[8] The king too had his galleys, although clearly there were not many of them, and it could well be that at this period he was simply chartering western vessels to operate in his service as occasion demanded.[9]

One of the main tasks for these ships was the enforcement of the papal prohibition on western trade with the Mamlūks. Nicholas IV's bull had allowed that in the case of flagrant breaches of his ban the merchandise concerned should be the prize of whoever should seize it. There was thus an incentive for captains who undertook to police the seas, and it would seem that certain individuals did take advantage of the ban for their own profit. One of the roles envisaged for Manuel Zaccaria's fleet in 1292 was the interception of illicit trade, and from a lawsuit before the Genoese *podestà* in Famagusta in 1297 we learn of a Genoese privateer who had chartered a *linh* which he had armed for action 'against the Sarracens and against those going to places prohibited by the Holy Roman Church'.[10] King Henry kept a small number of galleys at sea to arrest ships trading with the Mamlūks, and they ranged as far as Corfu in search of their quarry. He maintained his patrols from the 1290s until at least as late as the second decade of the fourteenth century, but, although Cypriot sources show ships being taken and merchants incurring the automatic sentence of excommunication, the efficacy of these measures in curbing the considerable volume of European trade with Egypt and Syria must have been extremely limited.[11] Henry, in common with all crusade publicists, remained wedded to the

[8]   *Annali Genovesi*, v, 167; 'Gestes', pp. 828–9. For the Hospitaller fleet, Riley-Smith, *Knights of St John*, pp. 200–1, 330. The Hospitaller admiral first appears in 1299. For a Templar admiral in Cyprus in 1301, *Notai Genovesi in Oltremare: atti rogati a Cipro da Lamberto di Sambuceto (3 luglio 1300–3 agosto 1301)*, ed. V. Polonio (CSFS 31; Genoa, 1982), no. 413.

[9]   For instances of galleys in royal service, 'Gestes', p. 830 (1293); 'Nouvelles preuves' (1873), p. 52 (c. 1298); *Notai Genovesi in Oltremare: atti rogati a Cipro da Lamberto di Sambuceto (6 luglio–27 Ottobre 1301)*, ed R. Pavoni (CSFS 32; Genoa, 1982), no. 163 (1301).

[10] *Notai Genoevesi in Oltremare: atti rogati a Cipro da Lamberto di Sambuceto (11 Ottobre 1296–23 Guigno 1299)*, ed. M. Balard (CSFS 39; Genoa, 1983), no. 88; Richard, 'Le royaume de Chypre et l'embargo', pp. 121–2, 123; N. Housley, *The Avignon Papacy and the Crusades, 1305–1378* (Oxford, 1986), pp. 204–5. For the military Orders enforcing the ban, Mas Latrie, *Histoire*, II, 119–20; *Cart. gén. Hospitaliers*, no. 4467.

[11] Richard, 'Le royaume de Chypre et l'embargo', pp. 123–8. For examples of an excommunication and the arrest of a ship, *Notai Genovesi* (CSFS 32) nos. 13, 163; cf. *Notai Genovesi* (CSFS 31), no. 61. For other allusions to the embargo in early fourteenth-century notarial materials from Famagusta, *Notai Genovesi* (CSFS 31), no. 78; *Notai Genovesi in Oltremare atti rogati a Cipro*, ed. M. Balard (CSFS 43; Genoa, 1984), pp. 37, 347.

theory that to weaken the sultanate and so make the recovery of the Holy Land possible it was necessary to starve it of war materials, *mamlūk* slaves and other seaborne merchandise and so constrict its military capacity and general economic welfare.[12] In practice, however, notwithstanding the papal embargo and the royal patrols, trade between Famagusta and the Syrian ports under Mamlūk rule flourished.[13]

A more positive prospect for the recovery of the Holy Land lay in the hope of a Mongol alliance. Since the early 1260s the idea of co-operation between a crusade from Europe and an invasion by the Ilkhan of Persia had been prominent in western plans for expelling the Mamlūks from Syria, and it was widely imagined that the Mongol leaders themselves would embrace Christianity and hand Jerusalem back to the Franks. However, in 1269 and 1271 the Ilkhan had failed to send enough support, and in 1280–1 it was the Christians who let down their ally. There were further expectations of a Mongol campaign against Damascus at the beginning of 1291.[14] After the fall of Acre hopes for co-operation continued, but western Christendom was wholly unprepared when the Ilkhan Ghazan, with Armenian and Georgian support, invaded Syria in October 1299. Apparently it was only after his campaign had begun that he sent a messenger to Cyprus calling on the king and the military Orders to send troops. The messenger turned up in November; the Christians were unable to agree what to do; a second messenger arrived at the end of the month, urging them to hurry, but they had still made no move when on 24 December Ghazan inflicted a decisive deafeat on the Mamlūks near Hims. In January 1300 Damascus surrendered. But the following month Ghazan retired to Persia, and it was not long before the Mamlūks were able to re-occupy the territory he had seized.[15]

It was only after Ghazan's departure that Henry attempted to take advantage of the collapse of Mamlūk power in Syria. He sent two galleys and two *taridae* with forty mounted men and sixty footmen to Botron with instructions to stay there and work on the fortifications at the nearby town of Nephin until he himself could bring up the main body of his forces. However, the local Christian peasantry told the commanders of the expeditionary force that it would be easy for them to seize the fortress of Mont Pelerin at Tripoli. The Cypriots set off only to be ambushed by a much larger Muslim army. The survivors retreated to Botron and thence to Cyprus.[16] A second expeditionary force under Guy of Ibelin, count of Jaffa, and John of Antioch sailed to Jubail and Nephin

[12] Mas Latrie, *Histoire*, II, 118–25; John XXII, *Lettres secrètes et curiales relatives à la France*, ed. A. Coulon and S. Clémencet (Paris, 1906–72), no. 1690; Housley, *Avignon Papacy*, p. 200.

[13] Below, pp. 133–4, 151.

[14] J. Richard, 'The Mongols and the Franks', *Journal of Asian History*, III (1969), 52–5.

[15] 'Gestes', pp. 844–8; 'Amadi', pp. 234–5; Irwin, *The Middle East*, pp. 99–101.

[16] 'Amadi', pp. 235–6.

apparently with the intention of making contact with Ghazan. On learning that he had withdrawn, the commanders decided to stay in Jubail, which had already been seized on his own account by a Genoese sea-captain, but the local Muslim forces were able to re-group and expel them.[17] The failure of these expeditions to establish a bridgehead meant that the main Cypriot endeavour, when eventually it was ready, had to content itself with a seaborne raid. On 20 July sixteen galleys and some smaller ships – by Cypriot standards a sizeable fleet – set sail for Egypt. There they pillaged the coast near Rosetta before moving on to Alexandria, which they declined to attack, although they did seize and burn a Muslim ship coming from Alaya. They then sailed north to Acre and on to Tortosa and Maraclea where a Hospitaller shore-party was taken by surprise and lost a knight and twenty footmen. After that they returned via Armenia to Cyprus. It is difficult to understand how anyone could imagine that a naval demonstration of this kind might contribute to the prospects for a Christian recovery of the Holy Land.[18]

Ghazan's winter campaign of 1299–1300 had been a considerable, albeit temporary, success. His army had occupied Damascus and overrun Palestine as far as Gaza. In western Europe rumour magnified his achievement into a complete conquest of the Holy Land. The truth was that he could not hold his position – it has been suggested that the reason for his withdrawal was as simple and as basic as the shortage of fodder for his horses – and by May 1300 the Mamlūks were back in control.[19] The failure of the Cypriots to secure a foothold and co-ordinate their efforts was an additional, if minor, setback. Ghazan, however, was set on re-establishing his position in Syria and planned a second expedition to take place during the winter of 1300–1. This time the Cypriots were ready for him. In November 300 mounted men under Henry's brother, Amaury of Tyre, went to Tortosa. With them sailed the forces of the Templars and Hospitallers. If the figures given by the chroniclers are correct, Amaury's men numbered considerably more than the Cypriot contingent at the fall of Acre in 1291 or any other thirteenth-century expeditionary force to Syria, and it has to be assumed that it represented the maximum that the king could muster. At Tortosa they awaited the Mongols. But no Mongol invaders appeared, and, when the Cypriots started to come under attack, they withdrew to the offshore island of Ruad. It was not until the following February that the Mongols entered northern Syria. They were commanded not by Ghazan who was ill, but by his general Qutlugh-shah, and were joined by the king of Cilician Armenia and by Count Guy of Jaffa and John of Jubail who had gone from Cyprus to Armenia to await his coming. The Mongols ravaged Syria as far as Hims and then, without

---

[17] 'Gestes', p. 848.   [18] Ibid., pp. 848–9; Marino Sanudo, p. 242; 'Amadi', pp. 236–7.
[19] S. Schein, 'Gesta Dei per Mongolos 1300. The Genesis of a Non-Event', EHR, XCIV (1979), 805–19; D. O. Morgan, 'The Mongols in Syria, 1260–1300', CS, pp. 231–5.

having achieved anything in concert with the main Cypriot army, abandoned their campaign.[20]

The lord of Tyre's men returned to Cyprus leaving the Templars to hold Ruad, which later in 1301 the pope confirmed as a possession of the Order. After that nothing much seems to have happened until the following year a Mamlūk force, large enough to require twenty galleys for its transport, arrived to expel the Templar garrison and so prevent any future use of Ruad in combined operations with the Mongols. The Templars were besieged in a tower on the island and sought terms for surrender. An agreement was reached, but the Muslims went back on their word and carried off the brothers of the Order into captivity after slaying the rest of their troops. Attempts to relieve the garrison from Cyprus had been too slow.[21] When early in 1303 Qutlugh-shah once more led the army of the Ilkhanate into Syria, he was defeated near Damascus. Ghazan died in 1304, and after his death there were no further major Mongol offensives aimed at conquering Syria.

The fall of Ruad marked the end of Cypriot-based efforts to regain the Holy Land. On three occasions, in 1229, 1301 and 1303, the Mongols had entered Syria , and on three occasions there had been no effective co-operation with the Christians. But in Europe it was still anticipated that there would be other Mongol expeditions and that Christendom might yet profit by them. Diplomatic exchanges between the Ilkhans and the West continued, with Mongol embassies in Rome in 1302 and 1304. A Hospitaller memorandum of about 1307 called on the papacy to station a force of 1,000 mounted men and 4,000 arbelasters with sixty galleys in Cyprus and Rhodes to enforce the commercial blockade; in the event of a Mongol invasion of Syria, this force, it was argued, would be in place to attack Egypt. The author made the point that, as Egypt would be denuded of troops to face the Mongol threat, a direct attack would be more sensible than the deployment of Christian resources nearer the likely battle zone; when the Cypriots and military Orders had gone to Tortosa, the Muslims of Egypt had rejoiced.[22] This proposal enshrined just one of a number of divergent views which were being put forward at about this time as to the strategy to be pursued during a future crusade to the Holy Land. Writing in 1311, King Henry II also came out in favour of a direct assault from Cyprus on the centre of Mamlūk power in Egypt, whereas in 1307 Hayton of Gorhigos, an Armenian who set

---

[20] 'Gestes', pp. 849–50; Hayton, 'La flor des estoires de la terre d'orient', *RHC Arm*, II, 198–9; 'Amadi', pp. 237–8.

[21] 'Gestes', pp. 850, 852–3; 'Amadi', pp. 238–9. For the papal grant, Boniface VIII, *Registres*, ed. G. Digard *et al.* (Paris, 1884–1939), no. 4199. The Teutonic Order may also have been involved in the Tortosa expedition. *Notai Genovesi* (CSFS 31), no. 245.

[22] Housley, 'Charles II of Naples', pp. 532–3; B. Z. Kedar and S. Schein, 'Un projet de "passage particulier" proposé par l'Ordre de l'Hôpital 1306–1307', *BEC*, CXXXVII (1979), 211–26. A papal plan for a crusade drawn up in 1307 envisaged a Mongol invasion of the Holy Land. N. Housley, *The Italian Crusades* (Oxford, 1982), pp. 95–6.

great store by the prospect of collaboration with the Mongols, had argued for an expedition to enter Syria from Cilicia. A few years later the Venetian Marino Sanudo favoured a campaign against Egypt but was against using Cyprus as a base.[23]

There was, however, a consensus in the West that both Cyprus and Cilician Armenia ought to be defended against further Muslim attack. Although Cyprus had remained unscathed after 1291, Armenia was losing territory and was under considerable pressure from the Mamlūks. In 1298 and 1307 the Armenians were appealing to the West for aid, and from 1307 there is evidence for the pope sending financial assistance.[24]. What was not so clear was the western attitude to the Lusignan dynasty. In the treaty of Caltabellotta of 1302 agreed between King Charles II of Sicily and his Aragonese rivals, it was laid down that the heirs of the actual ruler of the island of Sicily, Frederick of Aragon, should be compensated with Cyprus, Sardinia or a kingdom of similar standing in return for surrendering Sicily to Charles or his successor. The parties to this agreement, and Pope Boniface VIII who subsequently ratified it, can have had little legal justification for disposing of the Lusignan regime in so casual a manner. Presumably the basis for this provision lay in the expectation that they could acquire the claim to the throne of Cyprus advanced by the counts of Brienne since 1267. In 1289 Hugh of Brienne had tried to interest the king of Aragon in his claim, and, although nothing seems to have resulted from this approach, the fact that several years later the rulers of Naples and Aragon, apparently with papal complaisance, could contemplate the removal of the Cypriot dynasty shows just how isolated Henry II had become. The idea of using the Brienne claim to justify the removal of the Lusignans was then taken up by the French royal servant and publicist, Peter Dubois, who suggested that a son of the king of France should head a combined military Order and that this man should also rule in Cyprus.[25] As events turned out, neither the French, nor the Sicilian Angevins nor the Aragonese had the opportunity to oust the Lusignans from their island kingdom. All the same, if westen Europe ever had launched a major expedition to recover the Holy Land, King Henry might well have had reason to be apprehensive.

The Lusignans' title to the crown of Jerusalem had been disputed with the Angevins of Sicily since the 1270s. In the late 1290s Charles II was using his claims to Jerusalem as a diplomatic bargaining counter in his negotiations with the Aragonese: thus in 1295 there was a suggestion that he might grant his rights to James II of Aragon, and in 1299 he was offering them as part of the dowry for his daughter were she to marry the effective Sicilian ruler, Frederick of Aragon.

[23] Mas Latrie, *Histoire*, II, 122; Hayton, pp. 248–52; Marino Sanudo, pp. 37–9.

[24] Housley, *Avignon Papacy*, p. 12 and note 9; Lloyd, *English Society and the Crusade*, pp. 252, 255.

[25] Boniface VIII, no. 5348 at col. 853; Peter Dubois, *De recuperatione Terre Sancte*, pp. 133, 140. Above, pp. 35–6. Cyprus is not known to have been mentioned in subsequent peace negotiations between the Angevins and the Aragonese.

For their part, the Aragonese were certainly interested: in 1309–11 they were trying to get Charles' successor, King Robert, to renounce his title as king of Jerusalem in Frederick's favour.[26] The popes remained neutral, refusing to address either the king of Cyprus or the king of Sicily as king of Jerusalem in their correspondence, but, with the Angevins' claims being recognized by the Aragonese as well as by their cousins, the kings of France, and with some people proposing that in future the Latin kingdom should be governed by the head of a united military Order,[27] Henry II's chances of being restored to the throne of Jerusalem should a western crusade succeed in wresting Palestine from the Mamlūks must have seemed slender.

These challenges to the Lusignans' rights to Jerusalem almost certainly goaded the fourteenth-century kings of Cyprus into asserting themselves all the more strongly. In his formal written *acta* and his diplomatic correspondence, Henry was careful to style himself *Jerusalem et Cypri rex*, and, although contemporaries might often refer to him for convenience as just 'king of Cyprus', his full title received widespread recognition in the West.[28] Henry's successors inaugurated their reigns with separate coronation ceremonies, receiving the crown of Cyprus in Nicosia and the crown of Jerusalem in Famagusta, and Hugh IV and his descendants appointed Cypriot nobles to the titular dignities of Seneschal, Constable, Marshal, Chamberlain and Butler of Jerusalem. From the mid-1340s we find the princes of the blood-royal being given the honorific titles of 'count of Tripoli', 'prince of Antioch' and 'prince of Galilee', titles redolent of their crusading ancestry. Later in the fourteenth century the kings started conferring titular Latin Syrian lordships on prominent nobles, the earliest being the county of Rouchas (or Edessa) accorded John of Morphou in 1365.[29] In addition, the kings displayed their dual title in their armorial bearings – the Cross of Jerusalem quartered with the Lusignan badge, a lion rampant on barruly field[30] – and they also expressed their rights to Jerusalem on their coinage. At some point, probably in the 1290s, Henry II introduced a new silver

---

[26] Housley, *Italian Crusades*, pp. 94–5, 97; J. N. Hillgarth, *Ramon Lull and Lullism in Fourteenth-Century France* (Oxford, 1971), p. 66 note 61.

[27] A. J. Forey, 'The Military Orders in the Crusading Proposals of the Late-Thirteenth and Early-Fourteenth Centuries', *Traditio*, XXXVI (1980), 333–5.

[28] For examples of Aragonese use, J. E. Martínez Ferrando, *Jaime II de Aragón. Su vida familiar* (Barcelona, 1948), II, nos. 138, 155; for Venetian use, Mas Latrie, *Histoire*, II, 136, cf. p. 117. Cf. *Notai Genovesi* (CSFS 32), no. 163.

[29] The titles 'prince of Antioch' and 'count of Tripoli' first appear in 1345, that of 'prince of Galilee' in 1365. Rudt de Collenberg, 'Les Lusignan', pp. 126, 130, 141. For John of Morphou, Leontios Makhairas, §172. Cf. J. Richard, 'Pairie d'Orient latin: les quatre baronnies des royaumes de Jérusalem et de Chypre', *Revue historique de droit français et étranger*, ser. 4, XXVIII (1950), 85–6.

[30] Hill, II, 69–72; W. H. Rudt de Collenberg, 'L'héraldique de Chypre', *Cahiers d'héraldique*, III (1977), 143–4.

coin, the *gros grand*, together with its half, the *gros petit*. The earliest examples show the Lusignan lion, although on a plain field, but this coinage was soon replaced by a new issue with a somewhat lower weight standard and a fresh design which not only proclaimed Henry's title to Jerusalem in the legend, but also had the Cross of Jerusalem prominently displayed on the reverse. *Gros* with the Cross of Jerusalem continued to be minted as a major element in the royal coinage until the end of Lusignan rule in the late fifteenth century.[31]

Besides the royal iconography and ceremonial, there were many other reminders of the association of Cyprus with the Latin Kingdom. After 1291 the prince of Galilee, the count of Jaffa and the lords of Beirut and Arsur, descendants of the actual occupants of these lordships, were resident in the island, and they remained there until in the course of the fourteenth century one by one the lines failed. Many other knights and lesser men had sobriquets indicative of their ancestry in the ports and cities of Latin Syria. Almost twenty years after the Mamlūk conquest of the Syrian littoral there were knights in Cyprus, for example Thomas of Picquigny and James of Fleury, who were still being referred to as 'knights of Acre', and Peter Le Jaune was being described as a 'knight of Tripoli' as late as 1323.[32] The presence of the military Orders and other religious corporations from the Holy Land added an ecclesiastical dimension. In the first half of the fourteenth century the titular Latin patriarch of Jerusalem was from time to time resident in the island, and in 1295 Pope Boniface VIII amalgamated the diocese of Tortosa in the former county of Tripoli with Famagusta.[33] James of Verona, who was visiting Cyprus in 1335, and Nicolo da Martoni, who was there in 1394, were told that the women in the island wore black in mourning for the loss of Acre and the other cities of Syria.[34] Memories of Latin Syria and its associations with Cyprus were firmly implanted in the island's consciousness.

As the reign wore on Henry's brothers and vassals became more and more exasperated by his inability to handle the difficulties facing the kingdom. In the 1290s soured relations with Genoa aggravated the problems arising from the

[31] Metcalf, *Coinage of the Crusades*, pp. 56–60. The *gros* is known from a document of June 1301, and there is a possible reference from April 1299. *Notai Genovesi* (CSFS 31), no. 413; *Notai Genovesi* (CSFS 39), no. 122. The lighter series with the Cross of Jerusalem would seem to have been introduced before 1306. D. M. Metcalf, 'The Gros grand and the Gros petit of Henry II of Cyprus', *Numismatic Chronicle*, CXLII (1982), 85–6. Amaury of Tyre issued a coin with a dimidated shield showing the Cross of Jerusalem and Lusignan lion on a barruly field. For the Cross of Jerusalem on seals, 'Amadi', p. 432; J. Richard, 'La situation juridique de Famaguste dans le royaume des Lusignans' in *Orient et Occident au Moyen Age: contacts et relations (XIIe–XVe s.)* (London, 1976), XVII, pp. 224–5.
[32] 'Processus Cypricus', ed. K. Schottmüller, *Der Untergang des Templer-Ordens* (Berlin, 1887), II, 162; 'Gestes', p. 866; John XXII, *Lettres communes* ed. G. Mollat (Paris, 1904–47), nos. 17172, 17250.   [33] Boniface VIII, no. 306.   [34] Hill, II, 188–9.

new political situation. Whether the Genoese still retained a sense of grievance against the Lusignans for their part in their defeat and expulsion from Acre during the War of St Sabas is not known, but there can be no doubt that in the early years of Henry's reign matters took a decided turn for the worse. In 1288 the authorities in Genoa managed to antagonize the king by refusing to ratify a new commercial agreement.[35] It was then Henry's turn to cause resentment, when, in 1291 directly after the fall of Acre, he granted trading privileges to Pisa and Barcelona, Genoa's rivals in the western Mediterranean.[36] In 1293 the war which five years later was to culminate in the Genoese victory over the Venetians at Curzola broke out. Several incidents in this conflict took place in or around Cyprus, and the surviving accounts leave no doubt that sympathies in the island lay with Venice. Thus, when in 1294 a Venetian fleet arrived at Limassol and damaged the Genoese tower and *loggia*, Henry, far from being outraged, is reported to have offered its commander some friendly encouragement. The Venetians then made for Famagusta where the royal castellan seems to have recognized that under the terms of their privilege he was obliged to defend the Genoese merchants, but all he would do was recommend that they take refuge in Nicosia. After that the fleet sailed on to Cilicia, attacking rival interests as it went, until in the appoaches to Ayas it suffered an overwhelming defeat at the hands of a smaller Genoese force. On another occasion, in 1297, a Venetian seized a Genoese ship from under the castle at Famagusta and set it on fire with impunity in full view of both Cypriot and Genoese, and from the following year there is further evidence for Cypriot partiality with a report of royal officials warning some Venetians of a Genoese privateer.[37]

The Genoese victory over their rivals evidently had the effect of increasing their assertiveness, and they now demanded compensation from Henry for the damage inflicted on their shipping in Cypriot waters during the war. These demands were refused, and in March 1299 the Commune ordered all their citizens, except those who had resident status as *burgenses*, to leave the island. In other words, they threatened a trade boycott. Henry responded by calling on everybody who had a claim against the Genoese to make sworn depositions before him: he may also have given instructions that no one was to do business with them, that they were to be prevented from leaving Cyprus and that their merchandise was to be confiscated. How the issues were resolved or what transpired as a result of these proclamations is not known, but trade continued, and by the early part of 1301 relations were sufficiently normalized for the

---

[35] *Annali Genovesi*, v, 91. Henry rescinded the 1288 agreement in 1292. *Liber Iurum Reipublicae Genuensis* (*Historiae Patriae Monumenta*, vols. VII, IX), II, cols. 275–6.

[36] *Memorias históricas sobre la marina, comercio y artes de la antigua ciudad de Barcelona*, ed. A. de Capmany y de Montpalau (Madrid, 1779–92), II, 56–7; *Documenti sulle relazioni delle città toscane coll'Oriente cristiano e coi Turchi fino all'anno 1531*, ed. G. Müller (Florence, 1879), pp. 108–9.   [37] Hill, II, 208–9; Edbury, 'Cyprus and Genoa', pp. 112–13.

Genoese government to appoint a new *podestà* in the island.[38] But with Genoese corsairs active in Cypriot waters and with the Cypriot government committed to upholding the papal ban on direct trade between western Europe and Mamlūk Egypt, tensions remained. Matters again came to head towards the end of 1305 when a Genoese attack was said to be imminent. Henry began by ordering Genoese nationals to leave his kingdom; he then rescinded this command, making it plain that if they wanted to continue to enjoy their privileges they would have to behave: they were to swear oaths that they would defend the interests of the kingdom and that, at the king's request, they would leave the coastal towns and reside in Nicosia. It is unclear whether any particular incident had given rise to these developments, but clearly the quarrel had reached major proportions: later in 1306 the pope had to warn the Genoese that the conflict was impeding his proposed crusade and urged them to make peace with the king.[39] When in April of that year Amaury of Tyre and the baronage suspended Henry from his royal functions, it was his failure to act on the advice of his men in dealing with the Genoese – 'like mortal enemies' they had defied the king and the people of his realm – that came high on the list of the grievances advanced to justify their seizure of power.[40]

Henry also found himself at odds with the military Orders. After the fall of Acre both the Hospitallers, or Knights of St John, and the Templars had established their headquarters in Cyprus, but relations between them and the crown had been far from easy. Both Orders were major landowners in the island; both received massive subventions from western Europe, and Henry had no control over the substantial numbers of armed men they maintained in his kingdom. Since 1291 they had been looking for a fresh role to play in the struggle against the Muslims. In the case of the Hospitallers, uncertainty and demoralization in the aftermath of the loss of Latin Syria found expression in a series of internal wrangles. But from 1306 the Order undertook the occupation of the strategically significant island of Rhodes and so regained a worthwhile sense of purpose.[41] The Templars, on the other hand, had, at least outwardly, a less

[38] Jacoby, 'Famagusta', pp. 162–3; M. Balard, 'L'activité commerciale en Chypre dans les années 1300', *CS*, p. 255. For Henry's response, 'Bans et Ordonnances des rois de Chypre', *RHC Lois*, II, 363; 'Amadi', pp. 255–6. It is not entirely certain that the description of Henry's anti-Genoese orders in 'Amadi' relates to this episode.

[39] 'Bans et Ordonnances', p. 368; *Regesti Clementis papae V*, ed. cura et studio monachorum Ordinis S. Benedicti (Rome, 1885–92), nos. 752–3; 'Documents chypriotes du début du XIVe siècle', ed. C. Kohler, *ROL*, XI (1905–8), 446; 'Amadi', p. 241. For piracy in these years, Hill, II, 210–12. (The 'Chronique d'Amadi' (p. 238), the best source for the incident, does not identify the culprits responsible for the abduction of the count of Jaffa as Genoese.)

[40] 'Texte officiel de l'allocution adressée par les barons de Chypre au roi Henri II pour lui notifier sa déchéance', ed. L. de Mas Latrie, *Revue des questions historiques*, XLIII (1888), 535; 'Gestes', pp. 859–61; 'Amadi', p. 249.

[41] Riley-Smith, *Knights of St John*, pp. 200–9; Luttrell, 'The Hospitallers in Cyprus after 1291', pp. 161–5.

difficult time after 1291, but their failure to find a new *raison d'être* left them vulnerable to the attacks in the West which were to lead to their suppression. The wealth and power of the Orders could well have given the king cause for apprehension. More immediately, the fact that they both maintained good relations with his rival, King Charles II of Sicily, would have placed their support for the regime in Cyprus in question. William of Villaret, Hospitaller master in the years 1296–1305, had been one of Charles' counsellors; James of Molay, master of the Templars from 1292 or 1293 until the suppression of the Order, was prepared to act as his agent in his distribution of largesse in Cyprus in the mid-1290s; both Orders looked to Charles' kingdom as a source of supplies for their establishments in Cyprus.[42] Relations between the Templars and the Lusignans had been acerbic since the 1270s when the then master, William of Beaujeu, had championed the rights of Charles I of Anjou to the throne of Jerusalem and King Hugh III had retaliated by seizing the Order's properties. Early in his own reign Henry had complained to the pope about continuing ill-will, and in 1298 the pope was telling James of Molay and the king to make up their quarrels. James was to come out strongly against Henry at the time of Amaury of Tyre's assumption of power.[43]

It is difficult to know how far the Orders and the king were failing to see eye to eye over military policy. In 1299, during Ghazan's first Syrian campaign, the Latins' inability to respond was said to have been the result of disagreements between Henry and the heads of the Orders, although at other times they did co-operate on raiding expeditions. Maybe the Orders were keener than the king on a forward policy against the Muslims: it was the Templars who took charge of Ruad in 1301–2, and between 1300 and 1305 the Hospitaller master, William of Villaret, led two sizeable expeditions to Armenia. On the other hand, there is evidence from 1306 that Henry had been trying to stop the Knights of St John arming ships in his kingdom.[44] What is certainly true is that both Orders found themselves in dispute with the king over domestic matters within Cyprus. The Orders' own members were themselves exempt from taxation, but in the 1290s Henry had been making their servants and the serfs on their lands pay the poll tax that he had introduced shortly before the loss of Acre. His right to do so was hotly disputed. There were also complaints that he had seized on a papal prohibition against the Orders acquiring more estates to prevent them obtaining

[42] Riley-Smith, *Knights of St John*, p. 207; M. Barber, 'James of Molay, the Last Grand Master of the Order of the Temple', *Studia Monastica*, XIV (1972), 95; Housley, 'Charles II of Naples', pp. 530–1. For Charles' export-licences for the Orders, Mas Latrie, *Histoire*, II, 91–2, 97–8; *Cart. gén. Hospitaliers*, nos. 4495, 4535–6, 4538, 4589, 4605, 4855 bis, 4855 ter.

[43] For Hugh III, above, pp. 78, 95–6. For Henry's complaint, Mas Latrie, *Histoire*, II, 108–9 (the references to Acre would point to date for this document of before 1291 rather than 1307 as suggested by Mas Latrie). For James of Molay in 1306, Barber, 'James of Molay', pp. 102–3.

[44] For 1299, 'Amadi', p. 234. For Hospitaller expeditions to Armenia, Riley-Smith, *Knights of St John*, pp. 199–200. For 1306, *Reg. Clementis V*, nos. 1247–8, cf. no. 1250.

any fresh property at all, and among the charges levelled against him in 1306 was one that he had subjected them to interminable delays in the courts.[45]

On 26 April 1306 Amaury of Lusignan lord of Tyre, the king's brother and heir-presumptive, declared Henry too ill to rule and, adopting the title of 'governor and rector' (*gubernator et rector*), assumed control of the kingdom. The majority of the leading vassals, including almost all the members of the powerful Ibelin clan, were behind him, and his seizure of power was effected without resort to violence.[46] Amaury had formulated a list of complaints to justify his action, and the theme of a speech read out for him on that day by Hugh of Ibelin, a senior member of his family, was that 'the needs of the kingdom have not been and are not being attended to as is necessary . . .'[47] This indictment and further charges drawn up subsequently to impress the pope[48] have been alluded to already: the king had failed to provide for the security and well-being of the kingdom; despite the advice of his vassals he had done nothing to avert the danger posed by the Genoese; nor had he taken action to counter the sultan's threatened naval attack or send aid to the kingdom of Armenia which had suffered much in recent years at the hands of the Muslims; he was accused of inaction in the face of hostile shipping, of allowing Cyprus to become increasingly isolated both diplomatically and militarily, and of failing to arrange food supplies at a time of famine, even when foreign corn had been on offer; everyone was concerned at the absence of military preparedness; what was more, with delays of up to twenty years, there was no justice to be had so that heirs were disinherited and the clergy and the military Orders were denied redress for injuries they had suffered. The charges are couched in rather general terms, and while it is clear that the Genoese threat had been a major preoccupation, it is impossible to know how much substance lay behind some of the other accusations. There seems, for example, to be no evidence to corroborate the belief that the Muslims were planning an attack on Cyprus at the time.[49]

It is not hard to understand why the vassals should have rallied behind Amaury. Henry's government was discredited by inconsequential military activities and an inability to deal effectively with friend and foe alike. Hugh of

---

[45] Hill, II, 198–9; Riley-Smith, *Knights of St. John*, pp. 204–5. For the Orders' numbers, Riley-Smith, *ibid.*, p. 328 and note 3. For judicial delays, 'Texte officiel', p. 536.

[46] 'Gestes', pp. 857–62; Leontios Makhairas, §§ 42–54; 'Amadi', pp. 241–50.

[47] 'Texte officiel', pp. 534–8 at p. 535. The document is reprinted from this edition as footnotes in 'Gestes' at pp. 858–60, and 'Amadi' at pp. 242–5. Cf. 'Documents chypriotes', ed. Kohler, pp. 442–3. For Hugh, a grandson of John I of Beirut and son of Baldwin the Seneschal, Rudt de Collenberg, 'Les Ibelin', pp. 173–4.

[48] For documents presented at the curia presumably at the beginning of 1308, 'Documents chypriotes', ed. Kohler, pp. 440–52.

[49] D. P. Little, *An Introduction to Mamluk Historiography: An Analysis of Arabic and Biographical Sources for the Reign of al-Malik an-Nāṣir Muḥammad ibn Qalā'ūn* (Wiesbaden, 1970), pp. 141–2.

Ibelin's speech, while maintaining a show of due deference to the crown, emphasized the idea that the feudatories were behaving responsibly in demanding the good government that had not been forthcoming and to which they felt entitled. Hugh reminded the king that for the previous seventeen years the knights had willingly allowed their fiefs to be taxed, and he assured him that his interests and the interests of his kingdom were uppermost in his vassals' minds: for the good of his kingdom and his own good, in view of his illness, he should hand over power to his brother. Lack of adequate leadership from an ailing and inactive monarch goes a long way to account for the widespread support given Amaury in 1306, but the narrative sources provide an additional explanation: Henry had relied on the counsel of his maternal uncle, Philip of Ibelin the seneschal of Cyprus, to the exclusion of all his other vassals, and this denial of their rightful role as royal advisers rankled.[50]

Unlike his brother, Amaury had a good record as a vigorous and capable leader. In 1289 he had commanded the Cypriot contingent at the defence of Tripoli. He had then acquitted himself well as Henry's *bailli* in Acre until 1291, and he later came to play a prominent role in campaigns of 1299–1301 during Ghazan's invasions of Syria.[51] Although the charges levelled at Henry do not say so in as many words, it is likely that the vassals were dissatisfied with the king's conduct of military operations at the time of the Ilkhan's expeditions: he was later accused of failing to allow supplies to be sent to Amaury's forces on Ruad, and it is noteworthy that all the Cypriot knights named as commanders or emissaries during the years 1299–1301 and who are known to have participated in the events of 1306–10 supported Amaury.[52] Despite the obvious hostility of the sources, the lord of Tyre emerges as an abler and perhaps more attractive figure than his brother. He even had the rare distinction of having a philosophical treatise dedicated to him, although it would probably be stretching the evidence too far to deduce from this that he was an educated man and patron of the arts.[53]

As heir-presumptive, Amaury would have been especially anxious that the kingdom he hoped to inherit would be safe and secure, and he would also have felt more aggrieved than the other nobles by the king's exclusive reliance on his

[50] 'Gestes', pp. 857; 'Amadi', p. 241.

[51] 'Gestes', pp. 803–4, 849–50; *Annali Genovesi*, v, 94; Hayton, pp. 199, 320–1, 328; 'Amadi', pp. 218, 220–1, 236, 237.

[52] 'Documents chypriotes', ed. Kohler, pp. 447–8. Five knights are named in the sources: Bertram Fassan ('Amadi', pp. 236, 341); Baldwin of Picquigny and Raymond Viscount ('Gestes', p. 848; 'Amadi', p. 236; Kohler, 'Documents chypriotes', pp. 442, 443); John of Antioch ('Gestes', p. 848; Kohler, 'Documents chypriotes', p. 442; 'Amadi', pp. 261, 273, 392); and John of Jubail ('Gestes', p. 850; 'Amadi', pp. 237, 261, 269, 341).

[53] A. Thomas, 'Notice sur le manuscrit latin 4788 du Vatican contenant une traduction française avec commentaire par Maître Pierre de Paris de la *Consolatio Philosophiae* de Boèce', *Notices et extraits des manuscrits de la Bibliothèque Nationale et autres bibliothèques*, XLI (1923), 30–1.

uncle, Philip of Ibelin. Later writers insinuated that he struck in 1306 because he was afraid he would be cheated of his hopes of succeeding to the throne, but commentators nearer the events are silent on this point and the charge should probably be discounted.[54] He may have had a particular concern for the kingdom of Lesser Armenia. Dynastic relations with Cyprus had long been close. Early in the thirteenth century two of King Hugh I's sisters had married into the Armenian royal family, and in 1237 King Henry I had married a sister of Hetoum I.[55] More recently there had been several more unions, and these have to be seen as a part of a process whereby common interest in the face of Muslim advance drew the two kingdoms together. Twice, in 1286 and 1290, papal dispensations were obtained for a daughter and a son of Hugh III to marry a daughter and a son of the Armenian Leo III (1269–89), and on the strength of these grants Margaret of Lusignan married Thoros, who was to reign briefly as King Thoros III in the mid-1290s, and Amaury married Isabella, Thoros' sister. Another of Hugh III's daughters seems to have married Constantine of Neghir, a brother of King Hetoum I.[56] These were difficult years for Armenia, with persistent Mamlūk incursions and protracted fratricidal struggles within the ruling house. Although the Hospitallers had given military aid to Armenia, in 1306 Henry was accused of doing nothing to help, and there is no reason to suppose that this accusation was ill-founded. Amaury's concern for the well-being of his wife's family inheritance is understandable, all the more so in the light of evidence that his own daughter by Isabella was married or at least betrothed to her cousin, the young king of Armenia, Leo IV.[57]

Henry was in no mood to acquiesce in Amaury's seizure of power, but it rapidly became apparent that he was isolated. Only his mother and her brother, Philip of Ibelin, and a cousin, John Dampierre, stood by him. Otherwise the vassals and burgesses all swore to support Amaury. Outside Nicosia the new regime was readily accepted. At Kyrenia the acting-castellan was hesitant, but even here there was no appreciable delay in recognizing Amaury's rule. Henry himself seems to have been kept under virtual house arrest. Three days after the initial

[54] John Dardel, 'Chronique d'Arménie', RHC Arm., II, 22–3 (alleging that Henry was going to resign his authority to Amaury anyway and then changed his mind); Lusignan, Description, f. 138 (claiming that Amaury feared Henry would marry and have children, thereby barring him from the throne). More reliably, in 1311 it was being said that in the absence of any surviving brothers Henry would be succeeded by his eldest sister. Martínez Ferrando, Jaime II, II, 46.

[55] Rudt de Collenberg, 'Les Lusignan', pp. 98–102.

[56] Honorius IV, Registres, ed. M. Prou (Paris, 1886–8), no. 512; Nicholas IV, no. 2667; Rudt de Collenberg, 'Les Lusignan', pp. 111–12, 116–17, 119–20.

[57] S. Der Nersessian, 'The Kingdom of Cilician Armenia', HC, II, 655–8; T. S. R. Boase, 'The History of the Kingdom' in The Cilician Kingdom of Armenia (Edinburgh, 1978), pp. 28–30; A. T. Luttrell, 'The Hospitallers' Interventions in Cilician Armenia: 1291–1375', ibid., pp. 121–3. For Leo IV and Isabella, Rudt de Collenberg, 'Les Lusignan', pp. 228–9. There is no clear evidence for the date of the betrothal; it could post-date Amaury's assumption of power.

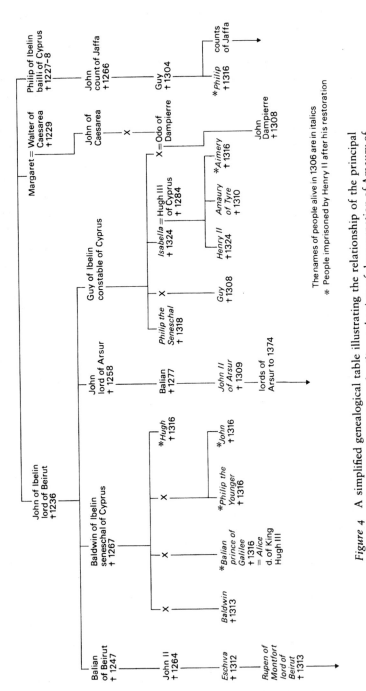

Figure 4 A simplified genealogical table illustrating the relationship of the principal members of the Ibelin and Lusignan families at the time of the usurpation of Amaury of Tyre.

move the masters of the Hospitallers and the Templars came forward to mediate. Negotiations were said to have lasted for almost three weeks, but in the end Henry came to terms. The king retained the homage and fealty of the liege men and avoided giving formal recognition to Amaury as 'governor' of the kingdom. Together the king and the 'community of vassals (*hommes*) of the said kingdom of Cyprus' issued a document recording the terms of the settlement. It consists largely of a statement of financial arrangements to meet the needs of the king and other members of the royal family together with measures to pay off Henry's debts. The king was required to sell his moveable property to satisfy his creditors and provide dowries for his unmarried sisters. He was, however, allowed a household retinue to include ten vassal knights and ten stipendiary knights. In the concluding paragraphs the parties promised to observe good faith and not to take any action to undermine the form of government ordained by the vassals, a clause which the narrative accounts of these events gloss as meaning that neither party would complain to the pope about what had been done. Amaury now took complete control of the royal administration. Philip of Ibelin and John Dampierre were obliged to swear to support the new regime, and Henry and his household withdrew to the royal estate at Strovolos where he occupied himself with his falcons.[58]

Now that his takeover was complete, Amaury had to ensure that he did not repeat Henry's mistakes. Towards the Genoese he appears to have been conciliatory. In 1308 his ambassador to the West, Hayton of Gorhigos, obtained confirmation of a peace agreement which presumably had been drafted before his departure the previous year. In November 1306 the Genoese authorities had made Amaury a substantial loan, and in 1308 their *podestà* in the island led a demonstration against the king as a token 'of the good will he had for the lord of Tyre'. Evidently relations were much improved.[59] Amaury's first recorded diplomatic move, however, was to award trading privileges to Genoa's great rival, the republic of Venice. Hitherto the Lusignans had avoided making formal concessions to the Venetians whose trading rights in Cyprus dated from Byzantine times. In the thirteenth century there had been requests for privileges, but successive governments had fobbed the Venetian ambassadors off. In 1302 the Senate had dispatched a fresh embassy, and Amaury's grant, dated 3 June 1306, should be seen as the culmination of the negotiations which had then been set in train and which it can be assumed had been begun before Henry's overthrow. Clearly Amaury was anxious to gain as much good will in as many quarters as possible.[60]

In May 1306 the Knights of St John entered into an agreement with some Genoese privateers for an expedition to conquer Rhodes. The initial discussions

[58] 'Amadi', pp. 249–53; Leontios Makhairas, §§ 51–61. For the diploma, 'Texte officiel', pp. 538–41. It is reprinted from this edition as footnotes in 'Gestes' at pp. 860–2, and 'Amadi' at pp. 245–8.   [59] Mas Latrie, *Histoire*, II, 152; 'Gestes', p. 866; 'Amadi', pp. 261–2, 280.
[60] 'Nouvelles preuves' (1873), pp. 54–6; DVL, I, 42–5; 'Gestes', p. 862.

had taken place secretly, since the most prominent of the Genoese, Vignolo de' Vignoli, was wanted by the Cypriot authorities for his depredations, but it is clear that in contrast to Henry, who had made difficulties for the Order over the arming of ships, Amaury was prepared to aid the Knights and was happy to allow them to use Cyprus as a base. A small Hospitaller force set sail from Cyprus in June 1306, and in September the Order sent to the island for reinforcements. The campaign was protracted, and mopping-up operations apparently continued until 1310. At some stage Amaury himself dispatched two galleys to help, and when a Genoese ship carrying supplies from Constantinople for the beleaguered garrison diverted from Rhodes to Cyprus because of unfavourable weather and fear of the Order's shipping, it was seized at Famagusta and handed over to the Hospitallers.[61] Whether Amaury sent much assistance to the Armenians is less clear. In 1306 the pope had made a general appeal on their behalf, and the following year they were recruiting mercenaries, presumably with official approval, in Nicosia. The regime in Armenia also looked to the Ilkhan of Persia for support, but towards the end of 1307 the young king, Leo IV, and his regent were murdered by a Mongol emir. Amaury continued to enjoy amicable relations with Oshin, Leo's uncle and successor. The new king was Amaury's wife's brother, and, although there is no direct evidence that he ever received any military support from Cyprus, Oshin readily took charge of his brother-in-law's exiled opponents.[62]

Initially Amaury was in a strong position, but with the passage of time his support began to crumble. According to the Chronique d'Amadi, Henry recovered from his illness in 1307, and from then on, as dissatisfaction with Amaury increased, so the king's own body of supporters grew. It is unclear how long the relative freedom he enjoyed at Strovolos lasted, but at some point, apparently in the early months of 1307, Amaury became alarmed by reports that individual knights had been making secret contact with the king and decided to arrest him. Henry, however, avoided his brother's men and, slipping into Nicosia, took refuge in his palace. There he remained under virtual siege until in April 1307 the bishop of Famagusta managed to smooth things over.[63] Amaury's move had been prompted by the fear that the king could still appeal to the loyalty of his vassals, and, as events were to prove, with good reason: all the knights attached to Henry's household in 1306 were to emerge as royal supporters, as did many others.[64] Although Henry had come to terms in 1306, he had refused to

[61] Riley-Smith, Knights of St John, pp. 215–16; Luttrell, 'The Hospitallers in Cyprus after 1291', pp. 164–6; idem, 'The Hospitallers at Rhodes, 1306–1421', HC, III, 283–6.

[62] For papal support, Reg. Clementis V, nos. 748–51. For recruitment in Nicosia, 'Amadi', p. 270. In a parallel passage Florio Bustron (pp. 156–7) says that Amaury sent Leo 300 cavalry and 1,000 foot.   [63] 'Amadi', pp. 253–4; Leontios Makhairas, §61.

[64] For a list of the ten vassal knights chosen in 1306 (together with the royal kinsmen, Philip of Ibelin and John Dampierre), 'Amadi', p. 252. All ten were involved in the royalist movement of 1308 ('Amadi', p. 264); two, Aimery of Mimars and Hugh Beduin, were later exiled ('Amadi', pp. 299,

accept his suspension from the exercise of royal authority and acknowledge the legality of Amaury's position. It was only after the collapse of a royalist movement early in 1308 that he agreed to accept his brother's demand to be appointed governor for life, and so blatant was the duress under which this concession was exacted that the Franciscans declined to witness the instrument recording it. Even so, Henry's retention of the vassals' homage gave rise to practical difficulties, and in August 1309 Amaury was once more demanding that Henry make a public declaration that would confer permanent legality on his rule. The issue was still unresolved in 1310 when the king was in exile in Armenia.[65] So long as Henry refused to acquiesce in his removal from power, Amaury's detractors, both at home and abroad, could label him a usurper.

In 1307 Amaury's seizure of power and Henry's continued antagonism took on a fresh dimension when both parties turned to the pope as arbiter. The *Chronique d'Amadi* claims that Amaury unjustly accused his brother of appealing to the pope and so infringing their settlement of May 1306, and that he himself then broke it by sending an embassy. But this account is biased against Amaury, and its hostility becomes ever more strident in tone as events progressed. The Cypriot narratives record that Amaury sent three embassies, one led by the Armenian nobleman and monk of Bellapaïs, Hayton of Gorhigos, which sailed in the late spring of 1307, another which ended in shipwreck the following December, and a third, comprising two knights, John of Brie and John Lombard, which had reached the papal court by February 1308.[66] On the other hand, they pass over in silence the fact that Henry also sent at least one embassy which had arrived at the papal court at some point before the end of January 1308.[67] Hayton's mission was to denigrate the king and obtain papal confirmation for Amaury as governor for life. Either he or John of Brie and John Lombard brought written evidence to demonstrate the justice of Amaury's seizure of power. This included the text of Hugh of Ibelin's speech of April 1306 and the settlement of May, together with versions of these documents in Latin and a third document, apparently concocted specifically as ammunition to be used at the papal court, which emphasized Amaury's enthusiasm for military action against the Mamlūks and Henry's indifference.[68] For his part Henry

338, 373); three others, Anseau of Brie, Reynald of Soissons and John Babin, were prominent members of the royalist party which held Famagusta after Amaury's murder ('Amadi', p. 362).

[65] *Ibid.*, pp. 266, 302–12 *passim*, 328–9; Perrat, 'Un diplomate gascon', pp. 68–70.

[66] 'Gestes', p. 871; 'Amadi', pp. 254, 267. For the date of the third embassy, *Reg. Clementis V*, nos. 2469, 2471.

[67] *Reg. Clementis V*, no. 3543. For papal indults issued in April 1308 at Henry's request, see nos. 2699, 2736.

[68] 'Amadi', p. 280. The documents survive in the Vatican archives. For the additonal document, 'Documents chypriotes', ed. Kohler, pp. 444–52. Luttrell ('The Hospitallers in Cyprus after 1291', p. 166 note 4) has drawn attention to an unpublished second version of the May settlement dated 31 January 1307.

complained that Amaury and his supporters had deprived him of the governance of his kingdom, had despoiled him of his goods and treasury and had subjected him and his adherents to a whole range of injuries. The claims and counter-claims were laid before the pope who on 23 January 1308 commissioned Archbishop Nicholas of Thebes and Raymond of Piis, a papal chaplain, to investigate and, if possible, effect a reconciliation.[69]

Hayton was well received by the pope, but although he had offered 10,000 florins and perhaps more for papal recognition, he returned to Cyprus in May 1308 having failed in his mission.[70] Amaury's representatives evidently hoped that by stressing his commitment to the crusade and to defending Cyprus against Mamlūk attack, they could convince the pope of his worthiness and so win papal approval for his government in the island. The idea of a crusade to the East lay close to Pope Clement's heart, and, as he told Archbishop Nicholas and Raymond of Piis, he regarded Cyprus as the springboard for a Christian invasion of the Holy Land. But he nevertheless stopped short of endorsing Amaury's rule.[71] It is difficult to be sure how far Amaury's espousal of crusading was a ploy to win papal support and how far it was genuine and fuelled by real fears of Mamlūk invasion plans. In the summer of 1308 a messenger from Amaury told the pope that the sultan was preparing a fleet of eighty galleys, and from a letter probably written at about the same time to the king of Aragon, we learn that the shipwrecked embassy of 1307 had been taking Amaury's detailed response to a papal request for information on conditions in the East. This same letter also spoke of the governor's hopes for action to recover the Holy Land.[72]

How much substance lay behind the 1308 invasion-scare is open to question. According to al-Maqrīzī, the Mamlūks were concentrating their military activities far away in the Yemen, although he also noted that they were refortifying the castle of Mont Pelerin at Tripoli.[73] But even if there were no immediate threat to Cyprus, it is nevertheless possible that Amaury believed that there was, and in any case the Mamlūk depredations in Armenia in recent years had been real enough. It was reportedly as a precaution against Muslim attack that work on the fortifications at Famagusta was in progress in this period, although, by a curious irony in view of Henry's alleged indifference to the defence of his kingdom, it was at his request, and not Amaury's, that in April 1308 Pope Clement issued indulgences for those assisting in this task.[74] Then in

[69] Reg. Clementis V, no. 3543.
[70] 'Amadi', 278–80; Perrat, 'Un diplomate gascon', pp. 72–3; Reg. Clementis V, nos. 2434–7.
[71] Reg. Clementis V, no. 3543; N. Housley, 'Pope Clement V and the Crusades of 1309–10', Journal of Medieval History, VIII (1982), 30–1.
[72] Vitae Paparum Avenionensium hoc est historia pontificum Romanorum qui in Gallia sederunt ab anno Christi MCCCV usque annum MCCCXCIV, ed. S. Baluze, new edn by G. Mollat (Paris, 1914–27), III, 84, cf. p. 86; Mas Latrie, Histoire, III, 680–1.
[73] al-Maqrīzī, Histoire des Sultans Mamlouks de l'Egypte, ed. and trans. M. Quatremère (Paris, 1837–45), II, part 2, pp. 278–81.
[74] Reg. Clementis V, no. 2736; 'Amadi', p. 291, cf. pp. 326–7.

August the pope took action to defend the Christians in the East by announcing a crusade. He had come to realize that the political situation in Europe precluded a large-scale expedition to recover the Holy Land, but he could channel the resources at his disposal into a more limited expedition – what crusade theorists termed a *passagium particulare* – to be commanded by the Hospitallers and designed to defend Cyprus and Armenia and prevent illegal trade with Egypt: 1,000 horse and 4,000 foot would be deployed in the East for five years, and the enterprise was scheduled to begin in the spring of 1309.[75]

The pope's reluctance to validate his rule was not the only unwelcome piece of news Hayton had to report to Amaury. He also brought papal letters, including presumably the bull *Pastoralis praeeminentiae* of November 1307, ordering the arrest of the Templars stationed in Cyprus. The initial round-up in France, the start of the train of events which ended in the Order's suppression, had occurred in October, but news of this startling development is unlikely to have preceded Hayton's return to Cyprus by more than a few weeks. Whereas the Knights of St John had on the whole remained non-committal, the Templars had consistently supported Amaury, and in recent months their senior officer then in the island, the marshal Ayme d'Oselier, had given vent to his hostility to Henry on at least two occasions.[76] Amaury must have found himself in a difficult dilemma: should he stand by the Order and incur the wrath of the pope and also of King Philip of France, or should he obey the papal instructions and turn against his allies on the basis of accusations which, as later investigations in Cyprus were to reveal, hardly anyone in the island seems to have believed? In the event he obeyed, and, as his subsequent letter to the pope makes clear, he sought to enhance his reputation at the curia by his efficiency in organizing the arrests despite the fact that the Templars in Cyprus were well armed and notwithstanding rumours of impending Muslim attack.[77] Although Amaury acted promptly, his initial approach, which appears to have been to treat the members of the Order as gently as possible while complying with the papal instructions, broke down when they proved unco-operative. At the end of May there was a brief military showdown, and they surrendered. Amaury's officers took charge of their lands, arms and moveable property, and the Templars themselves, said to number eighty-three knights and thirty-five sergeants, were confined on their estates.[78]

The arrest of the Templars would not have mattered so much to Amaury, had it not been for the fact that there was by then a sizeable backlash among the

[75] Housley, 'Pope Clement V', pp. 32–2.

[76] *Vitae Paparum Avenionensium*, III, 85. For the papal bull, M. Barber, *The Trial of the Templars* (Cambridge, 1978), pp. 73–4. For Templar support for Amaury, 'Amadi', pp. 248, 260–1, 266, cf. p. 267. Templar hostility to Henry continued after their arrest. 'Amadi', pp. 360, 392.

[77] *Vitae Paparum Avenionensium*, III, 84–6. For scepticism about the charges, Barber, *Trial of the Templars*, pp. 218–20.

[78] For a detailed account, 'Amadi', pp. 283–91. Cf. Hill, II, 233–6; Barber, *Trial of the Templars*, pp. 216–18.

Cypriot vassals against his rule and in favour of a royal restoration. In January 1308 news had reached Nicosia that about sixteen knights together with some turcopoles and footmen were setting off from Paphos to aid the king. It is not clear whether they were acting with the king's knowledge or at his bidding, but, before they could get far, Amaury had armed his followers, and Henry, fearing arrest, had put the royal palace at Nicosia into a state of defence. Amaury's supporters, including the Templars and the Genoese besieged him there. Henry's men were outnumbered, and after four days they surrendered without a fight. The *Chronique d'Amadi* names twenty-four vassals and fifteen stipendiary knights who were with the king. All the vassals were incarcerated except for the seneschal, Philip of Ibelin, who was banished to his estate at Alaminos, John Dampierre, who was sent to Karpasia, and four others whom Henry was allowed to retain in his household. Meanwhile the Paphos knights had failed to rally support at Limassol and, on learning of the situation in Nicosia, had dispersed. Twelve were later imprisoned.[79]

The Paphos rebellion had comprised vassals of middling rank – indeed, the knights at Limassol had hung back from joining when they realized that there was 'no notable leader, that is, none of the barons of the king's following' with them.[80] But soon afterwards[81] Amaury's position was impaired by the defection of two leading nobles, Rupen of Montfort and Baldwin of Ibelin. It was reported that Rupen and members of his household were plotting to capture Amaury and restore the king. Rupen denied the allegation but was nevertheless confined to his mother's estate at Lapithos. Baldwin was denounced by two knights who bore him a grudge and accused of conveying Amaury's secret plans to Henry; he too was restricted to a rural estate. Both men later supported the king, although, from the way in which the chronicler recounted these episodes, their defections would seem to have been due more to Amaury's willingness to believe stories of plots – evidence in itself for his growing sense of insecurity – than to Henry's ability to detach his brother's adherents. Rupen, as heir to the Cypriot inheritance of the lords of Beirut, and Baldwin, the senior representative of his branch of the Ibelin family, were major figures. At the same time yet more knights were rounded up. Then, in April, Amaury had Philip the Seneschal and Baldwin of Ibelin sent into exile in Armenia. Meanwhile the other notable royal supporter, John Dampierre, had died; he had been beaten up for attempting to communicate with the king.[82]

So in the early months of 1308 Amaury was taking stern measures against those he suspected of being disloyal. His policy was successful in the sense that it

---

[79] 'Amadi', pp. 259–66. Cf. 'Gestes', pp. 865–6. [80] 'Amadi', p. 265.

[81] The date is given *ibid.* (p. 267) as the end of June ('Al uscir del mese di zugno'), but this is impossible as Baldwin was exiled in April (pp. 275–6). Perhaps 'zener' (January) should be read for 'zugno'.

[82] *Ibid.*, pp. 267–9, 271–7, 329. Cf. Rudt de Collenberg, 'Les Ibelin', pp. 137–8, 157, 159–60.

put an end to overt opposition from the vassals, but the extent of the disaffection – almost seventy individuals are named as royal supporters in the chroniclers' accounts of that year – suggests widespread hostility. Against this background, the failure of his diplomatic offensive to win papal backing for his regime, not to mention the requirement that he arrest the Templars, must have come as a major setback. Although Cyprus remained quiet for the remainder of 1308 and throughout 1309, Amaury's difficulties increased. The harvests failed; two of his leading supporters, Guy of Ibelin and John lord of Arsur, died, and in April 1309 he was more or less openly rebuked from the pulpit by two Franciscans for his treatment of the king.[83] An additional concern, and one which was henceforth to preoccupy him, was the crusade proclaimed in August 1308 for the following spring. The prospect of a large force of professional soldiers arriving in Cyprus at the behest of a pope who had so far declined to recognize his government and including many, who, as subjects of the king of France or the Angevin king of Sicily, would be out of sympathy with Lusignan claims to the kingdom of Jerusalem and might well be unconvinced of the family's rights to the crown of Cyprus was alarming.[84] At the very least the crusade could lead directly to Henry's restoration and to reprisals against Amaury and his supporters; conceivably it could end with the Lusignans turned off the throne of Cyprus for good.

The crusading expedition was repeatedly postponed, and, when early in 1310 it did at last set sail, it spent its time consolidating Hospitaller control in Rhodes and never actually reached Cypriot waters at all.[85] But Amaury was not to know. In May 1309 the grand commander of the Hospital arrived in Nicosia with a papal letter informing the Cypriots that the crusade plans were well advanced and that the master of his Order, Fulk of Villaret, was to act as commander. At the end of July Amaury summoned all the vassals in the kingdom to come, but without their horses and arms, to an assembly in Nicosia. There he gave instructions for them to get ready to join in the crusade 'for the aid of the Holy Land' which was expected soon, but he added that if the crusaders proved to have other intentions, 'namely to harm us and the kingdom of Cyprus', they should be prepared to have to defend themselves.[86] Then followed a period in which Henry was subjected to considerable pressure to put the legality of Amaury's rule beyond doubt by naming him governor for life, but , despite the abuse and privations he had to suffer at this time, he resolutely refused. In September Amaury was sending more royalist knights into exile in Armenia, although by then it must have been obvious that the crusade was not going to arrive until after the winter.[87]

[83] 'Amadi', pp. 292–3, 298, 300.   [84] Above, pp. 107–8.
[85] Riley-Smith, *Knights of St John*, pp. 223–5; Housley, 'Pope Clement V', pp. 37–8.
[86] 'Amadi', pp. 298–9, 300–1.   [87] *Ibid.*, pp. 302–13, cf. p. 299.

Towards the end of 1309 the Knights of St John were moving towards outright opposition to Amaury. Early in 1308 the grand commander, Guy of Séverac, had been one of those who had forced Henry into recognizing Amaury as governor, and in August 1309 he and the marshal, Simon le Rat, had again been employed in putting pressure on Henry. But then Amaury became suspicious of Simon's good faith and stopped him visiting the king. In October stories were circulating in Armenia of plots to get Henry away from Cyprus to Rhodes and also to rescue Philip the Seneschal and Baldwin of Ibelin from Armenia and take them to Rhodes also. A similar rumour appeared in May 1310: the king was to be rescued from his place of exile in Armenia by a Genoese galley acting with the connivance of the master of the Hospitallers.[88] By now Rhodes had become a haven for royalist supporters: two knights are reported to have fled thither in March 1310; at around the same date Rupen of Montfort, who in 1309 had accompanied his mother on an unsuccessful bid to acquire the duchy of Athens, decided to remain there; in June 1310, after Amaury's death, the chronicler noted Rupen's return to Cyprus in the company of twelve other knights who had taken refuge with him.[89] So whereas in the summer of 1309 Amaury could still hope that a Hospitaller-led crusade might be content to leave him undisturbed as ruler of Cyprus, it was not long before he could be virtually certain that it would not.

By October he had decided on a change of approach. He sent his wife to arrange with her brother, King Oshin, to accept Henry as a prisoner in exile, and at the beginning of February he had the king escorted to Cilicia. He then released the royalist knights he had been holding in custody, threatening them with the confiscation of their fiefs if they tried to act against him.[90] It was a skilful move. By freeing his prisoners, Amaury was able to amake a conciliatory gesture, and, by placing Henry in custody in Armenia, he had removed the greatest threat to himself. It would be difficult for any royalist movement to prosper without the king, and, if a crusade intent on resotoring him were to come, it would have to contend with the authorities in both kingdoms. Exiling the king might not be popular, but it would serve to secure Amaury's position.

In March 1310 the papal envoy, Raymond of Piis, at last arrived in Cyprus. He had been commissioned by the pope to investigate the possibility of conciliation as far back as January 1308. Amaury is said to have feared that the crusade was following close behind him and to have redoubled the work on the fortifications of Famagusta as a precaution. In an interview with Raymond he justified his assumption of power, and explained that he dared not hand back power to Henry for the simple reason that he knew how vindictive he would be. The upshot was that Raymond undertook to go to Armenia to see the king and

[88] *Ibid.*, pp. 266, 302, 311, 312, 313–14; Perrat, 'Un diplomate gascon', pp. 70–1.
[89] 'Amadi', pp. 297, 325, 354; Perrat, 'Un diplomate gascon', p. 71.
[90] 'Amadi', pp. 314–25.

induce him to make peace with his brother. The negotiations were inconclusive – rumours that the Hospitallers and Genoese were scheming to rescue Henry and take him to Rhodes evidently perturbed Amaury so much that they prevented any progress in the discussions – and then, on 5 June, Amaury was murdered. So great had been his paranoia that, after he had been reported missing and before his body was found, his widow was prepared to believe that he had fled in fear of the coming crusade.[91]

Our heavy dependence on just one source, the anonymous compilation known as the *Chronique d'Amadi*, means that it is difficult to view the circumstances of Amaury's murder, or indeed much else that took place between 1306 and 1310, except from its standpoint.[92] Almost certainly the author of the original recension of this section was at work soon after Henry's restoration. He seems to have been closely associated with the court and the knights who had now come to prominence as royal counsellors, and his purpose was clearly to celebrate the fortitude of the king and the heroism of those of his vassals who had remained loyal. He was extremely well-informed: for example, he recounted the arrest of the Templars in 1308, Amaury's ill-treatment of the king in August and September 1309 and Henry's deportation in February 1310 in enormous detail, and his account of the period between Amaury's death in June 1310 and the king's return to Cyprus at the end of August is so full as to suggest that he or his informants must have kept a journal.[93] But for the period between February and June the narrative is much thinner, and it omits any reference to developments as important as the riot in Famagusta in which several Genoese were killed, the rumoured plot to get Henry to Rhodes, or the start of the trial of the Templars.[94]

Amaury's murderer was one of his household knights, an obscure member of a well-established family named Simon of Montolif. But although it gives a detailed account of the actual killing, the *Chronique d'Amadi* offers no discussion of his motive. There is no suggestion that Simon had acted in collusion with the king's sympathizers, and the impression is left that the royalist

[91] *Ibid.*, pp. 328–9, 330, 332; Perrat, 'Un diplomate gascon', pp. 66–71.

[92] The *Chronique d'Amadi* is an Italian translation of a lost French original and is named after Francesco Amadi, the sixteenth-century owner of the manuscript. For its relationship with the other narratives which describe the events of these years, see Kohler's introduction to 'Les Gestes des Chiprois', *RHC Arm.*, II, pp. cclii–cclviii; Leontios Makhairas, II, 8–11.

[93] 'Amadi', pp. 283–91, 302–12, 315–25, 329–79.

[94] For the anti-Genoese riot, *Reg. Clementis V*, no. 9256. The Templar process in Cyprus started in May 1310, 'Processus Cypricus', pp. 147–400. The hearings of 1–5 May (pp. 152–65), however, would appear to date to 1311 (as indicated by the text at p. 152), and not 1310 as assumed by the editor and by Hill (II, 271) and Barber (*Trial of the Templars*, pp. 218–19). Had 1310 been correct, it would have to be assumed that Philip the Seneschal and Baldwin of Ibelin were both brought to Cyprus from their captivity in Armenia for the trial, and that Rupen of Montfort and James of Montolif were both induced to forsake their refuge in Rhodes. 'Processus Cypricus', pp. 152–3, 155, 158–9. For James of Montolif in Rhodes, 'Amadi', p. 325.

knights in Famagusta who were henceforth to acquire a crucial role were as surprised as anyone by the turn of events. After the murder Simon totally disappeared. The chronicler's story is of a man acting independently and committing murder for reasons of his own. In all probability it should be accepted at face value, and Amaury's death viewed as a private homicide. It is nevertheless worth asking whether there might have been a conspiracy and then a cover-up. There could have been political reasons for someone writing shortly after these events to want to conceal royalist complicity. In his narrative the chronicler described how Simon cut off Amaury's head and then, deciding that it would be too awkward for him to carry, cut off his right hand and took that instead. But why? Was he simply a psychopath, or did he need to prove that he had done the deed?[95] Two late fourteenth-century writers believed that there had been a conspiracy. Little weight need be given to John Dardel's assertion that 'the lords of Cyprus treacherously encompassed Amaury's death' – his account is ill-informed and distorted – but Philip of Mézières' claim that the murderer acted by arrangement with other royalist knights cannot be discounted so easily.[96] However, the conspiracy theory is at best unproven. For a conspiracy to have succeeded in suborning one of Amaury's favourites, for the perpetrator to have accomplished his mission and then to have been spirited away, perhaps for good, and for the whole scheme to have been hushed up so effectively that it left hardly any clues in the surviving sources argue strongly against it ever having existed.[97]

Irrespective of whether Henry's supporters had engineered the murder, they were soon able to take advantage of it. Many of the royalist sympathizers among the knights had congregated in Famagusta. According to the *Chronique d'Amadi* Amaury had posted them there as part of his panic measures at the time of the arrival of Raymond of Piis the previous March. In Nicosia the lord of Tyre's counsellors proclaimed Aimery of Lusignan, his younger brother,

[95] 'Amadi', pp. 329–32, cf. pp. 349–51.

[96] John Dardel, p. 23; Philip of Mézières, *Le Songe du Vieil Pelerin*, ed. G. W. Coopland (Cambridge, 1969), II, 227–8; *idem*, 'Épistre lamentable et consolatoire sur le fait de la desconfiture lacrimable du noble et vaillant roy de Honguerie par les Turcs devant la ville de Nicopoli' in *Oeuvres de Froissart: Chroniques*, ed. J. M. B. C. Kervyn de Lettenhove (Brussels, 1867–77) XVI, 485.

[97] The issue is obscured still further because there were at least two men named Simon of Montolif in Cyprus in the opening decades of the fourteenth century, there were members of the family on both sides in the 1306–10 crisis, and it is not possible to reconstruct the family tree. The murderer was the son of Thomas of Montolif; in 1308 he denounced Baldwin of Ibelin ('Amadi', p. 329, cf. pp. 267–9). At about the same time another Simon of Montolif, brother of the bishop of Paphos (fl. 1302–3), was *bailli* of Paphos ('Amadi', p. 265); maybe he was the 'knight of Nicosia and Paphos' who testified in the Templar trial in June 1310 ('Processus Cypricus', pp. 385–6). In 1314 a Simon of Montolif was, with John and Thomas of Montolif, a guarantor of the terms of the marriage contract of James II of Aragon and Maria of Lusignan. Martínez Ferrando, *Jaime II*, II, 105.

governor in his place, and they immediately sent instructions to the castellan of Famagusta, John of Brie, to hold the city on their behalf. But on 6 June, the day after the murder, the knights in Famagusta, supported by representatives of the Italian communes, declared openly for the king, and John was powerless to resist them. When later in the day messengers arrived from Nicosia requiring them to swear an oath to Aimery, they refused. Instead they took the castellan and a handful of others who remained opposed to the king into custody. When news of these events reached Paphos and Limassol, the knights there also declared for the king, as did the garrison at Kyrenia.[98] Henry's partisans at Famagusta were led by Aygue of Bethsan, a descendant of the twelfth-century holders of the Jerusalemite lordship of that name who initially, in 1306, had fallen into line behind Amaury. Most of his associates were, like him, members of old-established knightly families who had emerged as royal supporters by 1308. Famagusta was placed in a state of defence and the king's banner flown. Aygue was elected 'Captain of the barons, faithful knights and communities of the kingdom of Cyprus'.[99]

The nobility was now split into two camps: Henry's partisans in Famagusta and elsewhere, and his opponents clustered around Aimery of Lusignan in Nicosia. Neither party was prepared to start a full-scale civil war; both preferred to wait and see which had the greater reserves of military strength and popular support. However, the Hospitallers were acting in close collaboration with the knights at Famagusta, and on 26 June and again a month later they brought substantial forces from Rhodes to reinforce the royalists.[100] It was their presence that undoubtedly tilted the military balance decisively against Aimery's party.

The chief problem was how to get the king away from his gaoler, King Oshin, and back to Cyprus. The initial overtures to Oshin left no doubt that Henry's release was going to require some extremely delicate negotiations. The Hospitaller grand commander, Guy of Séverac, led a delegation to Armenia from Famagusta, but the story was put about that the royalists, with Hospitaller help, had killed not only Amaury but also his wife, Isabella, who was Oshin's sister, and their offspring. As a result Guy was obliged to flee, and the king and the other Cypriot exiles held in Armenia were confined more rigorously. The royalists then formulated a scheme, the essence of which was that Henry and the others should be exchanged for Isabella of Tyre and her children. In the meantime Isabella had taken refuge in the archbishop's residence in Nicosia. On

---

[98] 'Amadi', pp. 333–6, 340–1, 343–4. For Venetian support for the royalists, *Délibérations des assemblées vénitiennes concernant la Romanie*, ed. F. Thiriet (Paris/The Hague, 1966–71), I, 296.

[99] 'Amadi', pp. 335–6. For Aygue in 1306, *DVL*, I, 42; Leontios Makhairas, §59 (where *Ἀγγε* or *Ἀγκε* should be rendered 'Aygue' rather than 'Hugh'). For a convenient though not exhaustive list of his associates, 'Amadi', p. 362; cf. pp. 252, 264, 269. For his title and its variants, Mas Latrie, *Histoire*, II, 117, 136; 'Amadi', p. 336.   [100] 'Amadi', pp. 354, 370–1.

11 June the king's supporters made contact with the queen-mother, the two papal representatives, Raymond of Piis and the legate Peter of Pleine-Chassagne bishop of Rodez, and the leading members of Aimery's party. Aimery realized that he was outnumbered and that the royalists controlled the ports, and so on 13 June he and his followers swore to work for Henry's restoration in return for the queen-mother's undertaking to do her best to secure their pardon and to get Henry to ratify various legal transactions with which they had been involved.[101]

Raymond of Piis then headed a second embassy to Oshin, but, thanks to the obstructive tactics of Isabella of Tyre, it too ended in failure. Attempts to smuggle Isabella and her children out of Cyprus and so deprive the royalists of their bargaining counter, served to heighten the tension, and the queen-mother had her work cut out to save Aimery of Lusignan and his men from the wrath of their opponents. As the royalists, reinforced by the Knights of St John and exiles returning from Rhodes, tightened their grip, so Aimery and his followers were driven to desperate measures. They tried to secure ecclesiastical protection for themselves by taking crusading vows, and then, in mid-July, they abandoned Nicosia and took refuge at Kormakiti, a village near the promontory of the same name about twenty-five miles north-west of Nicosia. Aimery's supporters were said to have included forty knights, and their entire force was put at 226 mounted men and 400 foot. Shortly afterwards the royalists took control of Nicosia. At a public gathering a letter from the king, apparently written before Amaury's death, was read out in which Henry appointed the master of the Hospitallers his deputy in Cyprus and promised pardon to all who would rally to his side. It was then announced that in the master's absence in Rhodes the government was to be headed jointly by Aygue of Bethsan and Albert l'Aleman, the Hospitaller preceptor in Cyprus; dire penalties were threatened against anyone who hindered the king's return.[102]

A third embassy to Armenia, on this occasion led jointly by the papal legate and Raymond of Piis, was more successful. On 4 August Oshin agreed to the exchange, although the negotiators had to accept clauses guaranteeing and enlarging Amaury's heirs' landed possessions and binding the king to take responsibility for most of Amaury's debts. News of the agreement was greeted with general rejoicing, and, despite the truculence and prevarications of Isabella of Tyre, the arrangements went ahead smoothly. Henry was released in return for Isabella and her children on the quayside at Ayas and landed at Famagusta on 27 August.[103]

Aimery of Lusignan and his forces remained at Kormakiti. The king sent a

[101] *Ibid.*, pp. 336–40, 344–8. For Peter of Pleine-Chassagne, *Reg. Clementis V*, nos. 4392, 4494–516. He was the papal legate on the crusade and had arrived in Cyprus shortly before Amaury's death. The archbishopric of Nicosia was vacant at this period.

[102] 'Amadi', pp. 351–69 *passim* (for the crusading vows, p. 355).

[103] *Ibid.*, pp. 366, 371–80. For the text of the agreement, Perrat, 'Un diplomate gascon', pp. 76–90.

formal summons to the vassals there to come to Famagusta, but they refused. Maybe they feared for their personal safety – a prominent member of their party, Henry of Jubail, who was in hiding in Nicosia, was murdered at about this time – and perhaps they had small hope of clemency even if they obeyed. However, resistance was short-lived. The leaders tried to arrange shipping for themselves to escape to Armenia, but, when several of them slipped away from the main encampment to make a rendezvous, the boat failed to appear. They came back to find that in the meantime the rank and file had surrendered on discovering that their commanders had deserted them. By then the king had ordered the arrest of all who had been at Kormakiti, and so they now became isolated fugitives. Balian of Ibelin, the prince of Galilee and husband of one of the king's sisters, Philip of Ibelin, count of Jaffa, Hugh of Ibelin and Walter of Bethsan allowed themselves to be taken into custody and threw themselves on the king's mercy; Aimery of Lusignan went into hiding but was discovered; Philip of Ibelin, known as Philip the Younger, was taken off a ship bound for Armenia when it put into Famagusta.[104]

Henry had no reason to be generous to his former opponents. He had been stripped of his authority and humiliated over a four-year period, and he had then had to suffer six months in exile. The Kormakiti knights had disobeyed his summons and had been in arms against him. But up to a point he was merciful: instead of having them sentenced to death as traitors and their heirs disinherited, he simply had them imprisoned. Perhaps he was content to take only such steps as were necessary to secure his return to power; maybe he was aware that if he struck any harder at what was after all a significant and well-connected section of the nobility he would provoke a fresh wave of criticism. However, in June 1316 Balian of Galilee and the other surviving leaders were put in the dungeons at Kyrenia and fed only on bread. They died within a few weeks.[105] What had prompted this treatment then is not clear. Nor is it clear why in 1318 Balian of Galilee's sisters, Alice, Maria and Eschiva, should have been locked up. All three had been closely associated with the king's former opponents: Alice was the widow of Walter of Bethsan and Maria the mother of Philip count of Jaffa, while Eschiva was said to have been the wife of Amaury of Tyre's eldest son.[106] It is difficult to avoid the assumption that the deaths in Kyrenia and the imprisonment of the women were signs of Henry's lingering vindictiveness and perhaps also of pressure from his own partisans. Even so, he did not confiscate his opponents' fiefs. That was left to his successor, Hugh IV, who in 1324 at the

---

[104] 'Amadi', pp. 380–9 passim.

[105] Ibid., pp. 385–91 passim, 397–8. Aimery of Lusignan had died some time before 19 April 1316. Mas Latrie, Histoire, III, 703. Possibly Henry had waited until his brother's death before moving against his associates. For evidence that in 1311 it was being said that Aimery would not be released, below, p. 137.

[106] 'Amadi', pp. 399–400. Rudt de Collenberg, 'Les Ibelin', pp. 163–5.

beginning of his reign had the High Court declare the fiefs of the vassals who had been at Kormakiti forfeit. But Hugh also released the remaining prisoners including the noblewomen confined in 1318.[107]

Henry's restoration and the arrest of the Kormakiti knights was not quite the end of the story. In 1311 there was a plot to take over the kingdom in the name of Amaury's eldest son, release the anti-royalist prisoners and place the government in the hands of the marshal of the Templars, Ayme d'Oselier. It was betrayed, and the authorities had little trouble in dealing with it. A number of knights were exiled, and four ringleaders were sentenced to death by drowning.[108] This episode did, however, highlight the problems that the presence of Amaury's heir might cause. In the 1310 agreement with King Oshin, the young Hugh of Lusignan's inheritance had been guaranteed and augmented. In November 1310 he and his mother, Isabella of Tyre, had returned to Cyprus from Armenia in the company of Philip the Seneschal, Baldwin of Ibelin and the other prisoners that Amaury had sent to Oshin, and who were now being repatriated. Hugh was not old enough to have played an active part in the events of 1306–10, and it would appear that Henry duly allowed him to take possession of his father's fiefs. The following May Isabella, with the king's permission, took her sons and household back to Armenia. According to John Dardel, Henry had made it plain to Hugh that he could only have leave of absence for one year; if he remained abroad any longer he would lose his fiefs, presumably on the grounds that he would not be available to perform his feudal services. But Hugh did remain abroad, and so the king carried out his threat. After that neither Hugh nor any of Amaury's other descendants were able to persuade Henry or his successors to restore their inheritance. Just as Henry had at first shown a degree of moderation in his dealings with his defeated opponents only to stike them down later, so too he began by keeping his obligations to Hugh under the 1310 treaty but then found a pretext for disinheriting him.[109]

The effects of the 1306–10 upheavals on Cypriot society are not easy to assess. The fortunes of individuals varied according to whether or not they managed to join the royalist side before it was too late, but there does not seem to have been any major shift in the overall structure of the nobility. Some great men and also a number of lesser figures lost out, but, of the leading magnate families, the Dampierres and the Montforts were unaffected, while many of the Ibelins managed to avoid retribution. The most heavily punished branch of the family were the descendants of Baldwin, the mid-thirteenth-century seneschal of Cyprus: Balian of Galilee, Philip the Younger, and John and Hugh of Ibelin all died in Kyrenia, but Baldwins's direct heir, his grandson and namesake Baldwin of Ibelin, was the man who defected to Henry in 1308 and then spent over two

---

[107] 'Amadi', pp. 401–2, 403. [108] Ibid., pp. 392–3.

[109] Ibid., pp. 390, 391–2; John Dardel, pp. 23–4, cf. pp. 24–41 passim for a self-evidently tendentious account of the family's subsequent efforts to the recover its fiefs.

years in custody in Armenia. The only other Ibelin to suffer imprisonment and death after the king's restoration was Philip of Ibelin, count of Jaffa, and here it is evident that his brother, Count Hugh, succeeded in regaining a position of wealth and prominence. Of the other branches of the clan, the descendants of Guy, the former constable of Cyprus, had almost all supported Henry from the outset, and the Ibelin lord of Arsur in 1310 was a minor and so escaped punishment.[110] After 1310 the Ibelins continued to hold high office as seneschals of Jerusalem and Cyprus, and they provided King Hugh IV with both his wives.[111] But in the course of the fourteenth century each branch failed in the male line; their eventual disappearance from the forefront of political life came about more because of this dynastic accident than because of the overwhelming support they had given Amaury of Tyre in 1306.

Among the well-established knightly families that opposed the king and suffered as a consequence, only the Mainboeufs can be pinpointed as disappearing completely from from the records after 1310.[112] On the other hand, the families whose members emerged as Henry's staunchest supporters and who were subsequently rewarded with titles and positions of trust were all established in Cyprus long before 1306, and it is not possible to identify any house coming to prominence from complete obscurity as a direct result of deeds performed during these critical years. In so far as it is possible to tell, it would seem that on the whole the vassals were politically articulate and that they were responsive to the needs of the kingdom and not simply motivated by self-interest. What was more, although feelings clearly ran high, there was remarkably little physical violence during the period between Henry's overthrow in 1306 and his return from exile. Nevertheless, the whole episode left a number of scars, and as late as 1325 King Hugh IV was seeking to set aside the enmity between two noble families which dated from the time of Amaury's rule by arranging for them to intermarry.[113]

Amaury's usurpation and the circumstances of Henry's return left a difficult series of problems in their wake. For example, provision had to be made to give retrospective legality to the routine business that had been transacted in the High Court, the office of the auditor or the *secrète*.[114] More importantly, the crown's

---

[110] Rudt de Collenberg, 'Les Ibelin', pp. 157, 159–60, 166–7, 172–4 (Seneschal branch); pp. 213–14, 215–16 (Jaffa branch); pp. 144, 147 (Arsur branch); pp. 178–9, 185–6, 190–1 (Constable branch). By 1306 the Beirut branch of the family had died out in the male line; the heir to the title was Rupen of Montfort.

[111] Rudt de Collenberg, 'Les Ibelin', pp. 117–19.

[112] For their role in 1306–10, 'Amadi', pp. 269, 275, 326, 352, 355, 359, 386, 390, 392. Cf. C. Clermont-Ganneau, 'Nouveaux monuments des croisés recueillis en Terre Sainte', AOL, II (1884), part I, pp. 458–9.

[113] Rudt de Collenberg, 'Dispenses matrimoniales', no. 58, pp. 68–9 and n. 31 (p. 90); cf. nos. 49–50, 53–4 (pp. 66–7).   [114] 'Bans et ordonnances', pp. 368–70.

finances were in serious disarray. Later in the fourteenth century Philip of Mézières alleged that Amaury had impoverished the royal domain, and he recounted the story of how Henry had declined to accept a subsidy proffered by the clergy, knights and burgesses and pursued instead a policy of financial stringency, vowing not to eat off silver or gold until he had paid all his debts; so successful was his retrenchment that within two or three years he had put the royal finances back on a sound footing. Philip had been chancellor of Cyprus in the 1360s and was presumably repeating a tradition current at that time, but it is nevertheless difficult to know how much credence his story deserves.[115] However, Amaury had been a big spender. He is reported to have seized the funds Henry had set aside for the dowries of his sisters and then to have raised a further 400,000 white bezants in taxation in 1310 as part of his preparations to defend Cyprus against the possible invasion by the crusading army that was then expected. In his 1310 treaty with King Oshin, Henry accepted the obligation to pay all but 50,000 bezants of the debts contracted by his brother, and the chronicler estimated the balance as amounting to 600,000 bezants.[116]

One debt incurred by Amaury that Henry did not repay was the sum of over 30,000 bezants outstanding from a loan of 70,000 borrowed from the commune of Genoa in November 1306.[117] As soon as the king was back in control in Cyprus, relations with the Genoese sank back to the level that had been a feature of the earlier part of his reign. Early in 1310 there had been a riot in Famagusta in which some Genoese had been killed. Amaury had promised satisfaction, but Henry refused to be bound by his brother's undertaking. Retaliation in the form of a raid by privateers on the coast near Paphos followed in 1312, and the next year the pope was calling for a cessation of hostilities and urging the emperor, Henry VII, to bring pressure to bear on Genoa. For his part, the king ordered the Genoese at Famagusta to hand in their arms and move inland to Nicosia, although he soon allowed them to resume their affairs.[118] But by 1316 the conflict had reached major proportions. A fleet of eleven galleys again raided the coast near Paphos, whereupon Henry interned all Genoese resident in Cyprus. According to an Aragonese report, the Commune's merchant galleys had ceased coming to Cyprus and trade with the West was generally disrupted. In 1317 the pope was licensing Genoese clerics beneficed in Cyprus to live away from the island, and King James II of Aragon was instructing his envoys on what to do if Henry tried to use the Genoese war as a pretext for not paying the next instalment of his wife's dower. (James had married Henry's sister Maria two

---

[115] Philip of Mézières, 'Épistre lamentable', pp. 485–8; idem, Le Songe du Vieil Pelerin, II, 228.

[116] 'Amadi', pp. 312–13, 326–7, 373; Perrat, 'Un diplomate gascon', p. 79.

[117] Mas Latrie, Histoire, II, 152, cf. p. 154 (for further unsettled loans by individuals Genoese to Amaury totalling 24,972 bezants).

[118] Reg. Clementis V, nos. 9256–7; 'Amadi', p. 393–5.

years previously.)[119] Hostilities then seem to have subsided. In 1318 the pope reported that Genoa had decided against sending a war fleet to Cyprus, and in 1319 he was enjoining a truce on the belligerents. Negotiations were begun, but, although the internees were released in 1320, the pope was still trying to get Henry to come to terms in 1323, and it was not until 1329 that the parties concluded a definitive settlement, including an agreement to repay the 1306 loan.[120]

There can be no doubt that Cypriot attempts to enforce the papal embargo on trade with the Muslims had exacerbated the escalating spiral of quarrels over unpaid debts and the depredations of privateers. Disputes arising from attempts by both Amaury and Henry to police the seas persisted far into Hugh IV's reign. Arresting ships engaged in illicit commerce inevitably led to protestations of innocence and demands for restitution and compensation as well as giving rise to violent reprisals. In 1311 King Henry sent a memorandum to the Council of Vienne on the subject of the recovery of the Holy Land in which he recounted a cautionary tale of Genoese retaliation when the Hospitallers in Rhodes had intercepted one of their galleys *en route* from Alexandria. He also described his own efforts to put a stop to trading in Muslim ports. In 1329 it was agreed that the claims of Genoese merchants who alleged they had been falsely accused of illegal trade should be referred to the pope, and, although Pope John XXII gave rulings on certain cases, others dating from the time of King Henry and his brother were still unresolved as late as 1338. From 1310 there is evidence for government officials taking pledges from merchants which would be forfeit if they then traded in ports subject to the Mamlūk sultan, and it is clear that the Cypriot authorities were taking a tough line with any Genoese they believed to be breaking the embargo.[121] On the other hand, it is clear from papal correspondence that, at least towards the end of the reign, Henry and his officers were turning a blind eye to Cypriots who traded with the Mamlūks.[122]

The advantages of enforcing the ban on western merchants going to Muslim ports while allowing Cyprus-based traders to operate freely were obvious. So long as the westerners traded in Syria, Cyprus was no more than a port-of-call where they could take on water and fresh supplies and trade in local products, but, by curtailing their access to the mainland ports, the way became open for Famagusta to become a major entrepôt. The local entrepreneurs could bring in Asiatic merchandise and there sell it for re-export to Europe. They would enrich

[119] Mas Latrie, *Histoire*, III, 706; John XXII, *Lettres communes*, nos. 2735–6; Martínez Ferrando, *Jaime II*, II, 167; 'Amadi', p. 398.

[120] For papal efforts from 1318, Hill, II, 280–1. For the settlement, Mas Latrie, *Histoire*, II, 150–8.

[121] Mas Latrie, *Histoire*, II, 119–22, 156–7, 172–3; *Notai Genovesi* (CSFS 43), p. 347; Edbury, 'Cyprus and Genoa', pp. 117–19.

[122] John XXII, *Lettres communes*, nos. 14103, 18100, 18119, 20386; Richard, 'Le royaume de Chypre et l'embargo', p. 130.

themselves, the royal treasury could levy taxes, and the Cypriot economy as a whole, stimulated by the demand for services to cater for this trade, would flourish.[123] On the other hand, the king and his advisers were well aware of the military value of starving the sultanate of war materials and in particular of the *mamlūk* slaves who were taken to Egypt as youths and trained to form the elite corps in the army. Many of these slaves originated from central Asia and were shipped to Egypt from the Black Sea ports on Christian vessels. In his crusade memorandum of 1311 King Henry inveighed against the 'evil and false Christians' who transported slaves, wood, iron, pitch, victuals and other necessities to the Muslims, and he went on to mention that in the previous summer his own patrols had intercepted a Genoese galley taking timber from Asia Minor to Egypt. The prevention of European ships transporting slaves was a theme that was to be echoed in a second memorandum which the Cypriot ambassadors presented at the papal court in 1323.[124] Henry was also prepared to confront Muslim shipping. In 1311 he claimed that his galleys had had numerous successes, and among the events of 1318 the chronicler recorded that a flotilla sent out against the Muslims burnt one of their merchantmen.[125]

The problem was that Cyprus lacked the resources to police the seas adequately, let alone weaken the Mamlūk sultanate on land. The memoranda produced in 1311 and 1323 were both based on the premise that western assistance was necessary for any effective Christian military action in the East, and both advanced the view that a strong naval presence to dominate the waters of the eastern Mediterranean and prevent supplies reaching the Mamlūks was an essential prerequisite before a general passage to recover the Holy Land could be launched. It was a view which had been incorporated into the original plan for the Hospitaller crusade of 1309–10. But it was also taken for granted that the French royal family would take the lead in any major campaign in the East. The legacy of St Louis lay heavy upon the last Capetians with the result that the whole ethos of their kingship was inextricably bound up with the rhetoric of crusading. At the Council of Vienne in 1312 King Philip IV of France announced that he would lead a crusade to recover the Holy Land, and the following year he and his sons took the Cross for an expedition which was to start by the spring of 1319. However, for a variety of reasons a full-scale crusade was never a practicable proposition, and all that happened in 1319 was that King Philip V fitted out ten galleys which he intended to send to Cyprus where they would be deployed against ships trading with Egypt. At this point the Angevin king of Sicily intervened and persuaded the pope to allow him to make use of these ships

---

[123] E. Ashtor, *Levant Trade in the Later Middle Ages* (Princeton, 1983), 39–42; Edbury, 'Cyprus and Genoa', pp. 116–17.

[124] Mas Latrie, *Histoire*, II, 119, 122; John XXII, *Lettres secrètes*, no. 1690. Cf. M. Balard, *La Romanie génoise (XIIe–début du XVe siècle)* (Genoa, 1978), 289–310 *passim*.

[125] Mas Latrie, *Histoire*, II, 121–2; 'Amadi', p. 399.

in an attack on Genoa, and they were then lost in a naval battle in the course of the ensuing campaign.[126] In 1323 Philip's successor, Charles IV, set about organizing a second fleet, but the plans went awry, the king found himself at odds with the papacy over funding, and, although ships were assembled, the project foundered when towards the end of the year conflict between France and England flared up in a dispute over Gascony.[127]

The abortive preparations in 1323 took place against a background of disturbing news from the East. In 1315 the sultan had doubled the tribute paid by the king of Lesser Armenia since 1297, but repeated defaults led to punitive raids, and in 1322 the Mamlūks overran Ayas, the kingdom's principal port. Henry sent help, and his ships were able to ferry some of the survivors from Ayas across to Cyprus. The Armenians had been appealing to the pope for aid for some time; now, with the Mamlūks threatening to invade Henry's kingdom in retaliation for his assistance, the Cypriots too sent appeals to the West. At the end of 1322 Pope John XXII authorized the preaching of the crusade in support of Cyprus and Armenia throughout western Christendom. Really what was needed was a permanent western naval presence in the East to stop illegal trade, lend aid to Armenia and prevent any invasion of Cyprus. But all Charles IV was proposing was an interim measure whereby a squadron would be sent to the East for just one year. As contemporaries pointed out, such an expedition would be in eastern waters for a few months at most and was hardly likely to achieve anything significant; its presence would only serve to antagonize the sultan still further. In the event there was no expedition, and in 1323 the Armenians and Mamlūks agreed a truce. Ayas was recovered, the refugees returned home, and the threat to Cyprus receded.[128]

Henry's military assistance for Armenia in 1322 is particularly striking in view of the bad relations which had prevailed between the two kingdoms since his release in 1310. The circumstances of his captivity provide sufficient explanation for Henry's hostility, and instances such as the refuge at Ayas afforded the Genoese ships which had raided Paphos in 1312 must have aggravated the situation. Perhaps commercial rivalry between Ayas, which was the only Christian-held town of any consequence on the whole of the Levantine littoral, and Famagusta also contributed to the ill-feeling. In about 1318 the two kingdoms came to blows. What happened is not recorded, but in 1319 and again in 1320 John XXII was enjoining Henry and Oshin to abide by a truce that had been agreed, and in 1321 he alluded to a war between Cyprus and Armenia

[126] Housley, *Italian Crusades*, pp. 100–1; *idem, Avignon Papacy*, pp. 14–18, 20–2; C. J. Tyerman, 'Sed Nihil Fecit? The Last Capetians and the Recovery of the Holy Land' in J. Gillingham and J. C. Holt (eds.), *War and Government in the Middle Ages* (Cambridge, 1984), 170–6.

[127] N. J. Housley, 'The Franco-Papal Crusade Negotiations of 1322–3', *PBSR*, XLVIII (1980), 166–85; Tyerman, 'Sed Nihil Fecit?', pp. 176–81.

[128] Housley, 'Franco-Papal Crusade Negotiations', pp. 168–74, 181; Irwin, *The Middle East*, p. 120.

which had prevented the execution of papal mandates issued four years earlier. As late as 1323 he was trying to get Henry and the new king of Armenia, Leo V, to reach a peace agreement.[129] Closely bound up with this conflict was Henry's refusal to abide by the undertakings he had made in 1310 with regard to Amaury's widow and heirs. They were deprived of their lands in Cyprus , and from a papal letter it would appear that in 1319 Henry had still not fulfilled his promise to pay off Amaury's debts. His non-adherence to the 1310 treaty was still a bone of contention in 1323.[130]

These tensions between the two kingdoms may well have contributed to strained relations between the Knights of St John and the Armenians. The Hospitallers had been staunch supporters of Henry at the time of his imprisonment, and in 1310 King Oshin had been prepared to believe that they had been responsible for Amaury's death. In 1318 the pope intervened to stop him harassing the Order, but it later transpired that he had seized its Armenian estates. Although the Knights evidently recovered some of their properties, and although they had helped in the defence of Armenia in 1322, other properties were still being withheld several years later.[131] They were, however, more than compensated by their acquisition of the Templar estates in Cyprus. The investigation into the Templars detained in Cyprus began in 1310 and apparently continued in 1311; later that year the pope had ordered a fresh trial, but it is not known whether any conclusion was ever reached. The Order was formally abolished at the Council of Vienne in March 1312, and in November 1313 letters announcing its suppression and the transfer of its property to the Hospital were read out at an assembly convened in Nicosia cathedral. It is no doubt testimony to the good relations that the Hospitallers enjoyed with King Henry that, in sharp contrast to what happened in many places in the West, the transfer seems to have been effected promptly. This windfall meant that the Knights of St John had become by far the largest landholders in the island after the king; in 1317 the Preceptory of Cyprus owed an annual responson of 60,000 bezants to the Order's headquarters in Rhodes.[132]

The Order also actively promoted the most significant diplomatic initiative of

---

[129] John XXII, *Lettres communes*, nos. 9953, 12389, 13975, 18098–9; John XXII, *Lettres secrètes*, no. 1227; Luttrell, 'The Hospitallers in Cilician Armenia', pp. 126–7; W. H. Rudt de Collenberg, 'Les *Bullae* et *Litterae* adressées par les papes d'Avignon à l'Arménie cilicienne, 1305–1375 (d'après les Registres de l'Archivio Segreto Vaticano)' in D. Kouymjian (ed.), *Armenian Studies in memoriam Haïg Berbérian* (Lisbon, 1986), p. 712 no. 7, cf. nos. 3–4.

[130] John XXII, *Lettres communes*, nos. 9953, 18104; C. Kohler, 'Lettres pontificales concernant l'histoire de la Petite Arménie au XIVe siècle', *Florilegium Melchior de Vogüé* (Paris, 1909), pp. 314–15. Above, p. 128.

[131] Luttrell, 'The Hospitallers in Cilician Armenia', pp. 124–8; Rudt de Collenberg, 'L'Arménie cilicienne', p. 710.

[132] 'Amadi', p. 395; Luttrell, 'The Hospitallers in Cyprus after 1291', pp. 167–9; Hill, II, 272–4; Barber, *Trial of the Templars*, pp. 231–8.

the later part of Henry's reign, the negotiations with Aragon which in 1315 led to the wedding of the king's sister, Maria, to King James II. It would seem that the idea for this marriage grew out of conversations between the Aragonese and Cypriot envoys to the papal court in 1311. There then followed an exchange of embassies, in which leading Hospitallers featured prominently, and which in May 1314 led to a contract of betrothal.[133] What attracted the Aragonese was the prospect that Maria would inherit the throne on Henry's death. By the early 1310s the king was over forty and still unmarried. There was little likelihood of his having children of his own. In theory, his heir was his one remaining younger brother, Aimery. But Aimery was kept under lock and key from 1310 until his death, probably early in 1316, and in 1311 the Cypriot ambassador at Avignon made it clear that he was not going to be let out alive. After Aimery, Henry's next heir was Maria, the eldest of his sisters. The Aragonese negotiators were explicitly told to establish whether the customs of the kingdom of Cyprus would give the throne to one of Henry's nephews, a son of one of his deceased brothers, in preference to his sister, and they evidently received favourable assurances on this point.[134] Had all gone to plan, after Henry's death James would have ruled Cyprus as Maria's consort, and in due course the throne would have passed to their descendants; James' heir by an earlier marriage would inherit Aragon, but Cyprus, like the island of Sicily and the kingdom of Majorca, would come to be governed by a cadet branch of the Aragonese royal house. To make an Aragonese succession even more probable, it was suggested in the course of the negotiations that another of Henry's sisters could marry James' son Alphonso, although in the event nothing came of this proposal.[135]

From the Cypriot point of view there was much to be said for marrying Maria to James. With the demise of Henry's heir-presumptive, Amaury of Tyre, in 1310 provision had to be made for the succession to the throne, and no one would have relished the prospect of the kingdom being ruled by an ageing spinster. The Aragonese wanted to extend their political influence throughout the Mediterranean, and their merchants were keen to increase their share of east–west trade. The marriage would give them a direct interest in the well-being of Cyprus and would mean that they would bring assistance at times of danger. On the other hand, they were the bitter foes of the French, and a close understanding between Aragon and Cyprus could serve to deter a French-led crusade to the East from threatening the Lusignan regime. James II had long since adopted a pragmatic approach in his dealings with the Mamlūks, and, although there was a break between 1306 and 1314, in the course of his reign he had sent a number of

---

[133] Martínez Ferrando, *Jaime II*, II, 46–7, 76–9, 81–3, 89–95, 100–1, 104–5, 106–8; A. T. Luttrell, 'The Hospitallers in Cyprus: 1310–1378', Κυπριακαὶ Σπουδαί, L (1986), 156–8.

[134] Martínez Ferrando, *Jaime II*, II, 76, cf. p. 46. Cypriot feudal custom favoured a sister as a closer heir than a nephew.   [135] *Ibid.*, pp. 82, 91, 107.

embassies to Cairo. Among other things he had urged that he be allowed the role of protector of the Christian Holy Places and the Christian inhabitants of the sultanate. Relations generally were good, and Catalan merchants frequented Egyptian ports; indeed, in the 1290s James had encouraged his merchants to trade with Egypt, although later, when political pressures in Europe forced a change, he pocketed the fines imposed on them by the Church for breaking the embargo.[136] Unlike the French, whose crusading plans threatened to leave Cyprus exposed to Mamlūk reprisals once their campaign had ended, James was not going to go out of his way to antagonize the sultan, and his contacts with the government in Cairo must have encouraged the belief that an Aragonese alliance was one of the surest ways of guaranteeing the island's security against the possibility of Muslim attack.

Maria of Lusignan's marriage to the reigning monarch of one of the most powerful Mediterranean kingdoms was arguably the best match ever made by a member of the Cypriot royal house. But it was not a success. There were no children, although, as she would seem to have been born during the 1270s, this is scarcely surprising. Indeed, in view of her age, it is perhaps odd that the Aragonese should have gone ahead with the union at all. James' correspondence with Cyprus after 1315 gives no hint that he was disappointed with his bride, but later, after her death, he complained that she had been too old and had not proved companionable.[137] She died in 1322. Aragonese hopes of obtaining the throne of Cyprus had thus come to nothing. There is no record of any tangible advantage for Cyprus being derived from her marriage, and formal contacts between the two kingdoms were chiefly concerned with Henry's procrastinations over paying the balance owed on her dower.[138] On the other hand, Maria's marriage evidently paved the way for links with two junior branches of the Aragonese royal house. In 1316 Isabella of Ibelin, the daughter of Henry's uncle Philip the Seneschal, married Ferrand, the younger son of King James I of Majorca. But Ferrand, who by virtue of a previous marriage was laying claim to the principality of Achaea, died in battle against his rivals in the Morea within a month of the wedding.[139] Then in 1317 Henry himself married Constance,

---

[136] A. S. Atiya, *Egypt and Aragon: Embassies and Diplomatic Correspondence between 1300 and 1330 A.D.* (Leipzig, 1938), *passim*; Ashtor, *Levant Trade*, pp. 20–2, 33–7.

[137] See in particular James' letter to the bishop of Tusculum written shortly after her death. Martínez Ferrando, *Jaime II*, II, 290–1, cf. pp. 142–3, 288–9. Rudt de Collenberg ('Les Lusignan', pp. 115–16) suggests she was born in 1273, although without giving reasons; a date in 1270s is indicated by the fact that at least three younger daughters were born to her father, Hugh III, who died in 1284. James clearly had misgivings about Maria's age: in 1312 he instructed his ambassadors to enquire about the ages of Henry's sisters, and they then seem to have tried to persuade the Cypriots to have Henry's youngest sister designated as his heir and let James marry her. Martínez Ferrando, *Jaime II*, II, 76, 82.

[138] Martínez Ferrando, *Jaime II*, II, 151–3, 154–5, 160–3, 164–5, 166–8, 174–5, 206–7.

[139] 'Nouvelles preuves' (1873), pp. 56–64; 'Amadi', p. 397; Rudt de Collenberg, 'Les Ibelin', pp. 192–3. For Ferrand, P. Topping, 'The Morea, 1311–1364', *HC*, III, 110–14.

daughter of King Frederick of Sicily. Isabella of Ibelin gave birth to a posthumous son, but Henry's marriage, like Maria's, was childless. According to James of Aragon, writing in 1326, Henry was impotent: Constance's virginity had remained intact.[140]

Despite the failure of these dynastic unions to leave their mark on future developments, Cyprus was clearly moving into the Aragonese sphere of influence at this period. In addition, the island continued to enjoy good relations with Venice.[141] But generally Henry's rule in Cyprus after 1310 makes a sorry spectacle. If the long-running disputes with Genoa and Armenia were not enough, in April 1323 we find the pope telling the patriarch of Jerusalem to make peace between Henry and the Hospitallers. It appears that Henry had also incurred excommunication for failing to proceed against illegal trade with the Muslims, and for detaining clerics and suppressing papal letters.[142] It was reported to James of Aragon that he spent too much time on hunting and hawking and not enough on governing his realm, with the result that evil flourished. Previously, in 1316 an Aragonese envoy, Francis des Forn, had regaled King James with a portrait of a sickly king, difficult of access and guarded by his confessor, a Franciscan friar named Aimery; his court was dominated by a coterie made up of the queen-mother and her brother Philip of Ibelin the seneschal, the man whom an earlier visitor had described as a 'fomentor of rancour and slander', together with Brother Aimery and Hugh Beduin, a knight. It should, however, be born in mind that Francis' mission was to extract the arrears of Maria of Lusignan's dower from the king, and he was having to explain away his lack of progress to his master.[143]

Hugh Beduin is a good example of a knight who had supported Henry during Amaury of Tyre's rule and had thereafter remained high in his service. In 1314 he held office as *bailli* of the *secrète* and took part in an embassy to Aragon; in 1322 he was captaining the king's galleys and then, in the early years of Hugh IV's reign, bore the title of admiral of Cyprus.[144] Another knight with a similar record was Bartholomew of Montolif. Like Hugh, Bartholomew had supported the king in opposition to Amaury of Tyre; in 1317 he had been entrusted with the responsibility of bringing Henry's bride, Constance, to Cyprus, and then in 1324

---

[140] Mas Latrie, *Histoire*, III, 718; 'Amadi', pp. 398–9.

[141] See, for example, Mas Latrie, *Histoire*, II, 137.

[142] John XXII, *Lettres communes*, nos. 18100–1, 18103, 18106, cf. no. 18119. Other papal letters written at this time concern the pope's efforts to make peace between Cyprus and Armenia and between Cyprus and Genoa (nos. 18098–9, 18102, 18104). For tension between Henry and the Hospitallers in 1316, Luttrell, 'The Hospitallers in Cyprus: 1310–1378', p. 158.

[143] Martínez Ferrando, *Jaime II*, II, 294; Mas Latrie, *Histoire*, III, 703–7. For Philip, Perrat, 'Un diplomate gascon', p. 69.

[144] Mas Latrie, *Histoire*, II, 150, 162; *DVL*, I, 210, 214; Martínez Ferrando, *Jaime II*, II, 101, 105, 107; 'Amadi', pp. 252, 253, 264, 299, 338, 390, 395, 397, 400, 401. For other references, 'Nouvelles preuves' (1873), p. 63; John XXII, *Lettres communes*, nos. 14681, 16909.

he acted as Hugh IV's procurator at the formal hearing at which Hugh claimed the throne; the new king then gave him the post of chamberlain of Cyprus.[145] But in 1321, in the middle of what was clearly a distinguished career as a royal servant, Bartholomew was accused of extortion. Sometime earlier there had been a riot which had resulted in the Greek bishops in Cyprus being imprisoned; the pope ordered their release, but allegedly Bartholomew, to whom the papal letters had been entrusted, demanded a substantial sum of money from the bishop of Solia before he would deliver them.[146]

If true, this allegation must reflect badly on Henry's choice of counsellors and calls to mind the comment made in 1316 by Francis des Forn who said of him 'there is no lord poorer . . . in counsel than he'. Indeed there was much for which the king could be criticized.[147] He had failed to remain on good terms with the Genoese and the Armenians; he had even quarrelled with his allies, the Knights of St John; in an attempt to develop links with the Aragonese, he had contracted two marriages, one for himself, one for his sister, which he must have known would not be consummated. His lack of competence had already led to his suspension from the exercise of authority, and it would seem that in the closing years of his reign things were no better. But despite Henry's personal shortcomings, the reign witnessed some important developments. The fall of Acre and the loss of Latin Syria had not led to Muslim attacks on Cyprus. Instead the Lusignan regime had had to adjust to the new circumstances in which it found itself, and the king, by his raids and by his attempts to enforce the embargo, had given visible expression to his desire to play a full part in any future crusade. In addition, the regime had survived a major political crisis which could easily have ended in civil war and even in the removal of the dynasty. That there should have been tensions within the ruling class and quarrels with Genoa and Armenia was perhaps inevitable and cannot be attributed solely to Henry's unimpressive performance as a monarch; to some extent they were part of the legacy of the disasters of 1291. Coming to terms with that legacy was not easy. What perhaps made it less of a problem was the fact that Henry's reign marked the beginning of a period of commercial prosperity unparalleled in the island's history.

[145] Mas Latrie, *Histoire*, II, 167, 178; 'Documents relatifs à la successibilité', pp. 419, 421; John XXII, *Lettres communes*, nos. 28468, 62662; 'Amadi', pp. 269, 362, 397, 399, 402.
[146] *Acta Ioannis XXII (1317–1334)*, ed. A. L. Tăutu (Città del Vaticano, 1952), no. 36 at p. 74.
[147] Mas Latrie, *Histoire*, III, 706.

7

DYNASTIC POLITICS, COMMERCE AND CRUSADE, 1324–1369

HENRY II died before dawn on 31 March 1324 at Strovolos. Later that same day a hastily arranged gathering of liege men swore to protect the rights of his nephew, Hugh of Lusignan, against all challengers until such time as he could be proclaimed king. Henry was buried next day, and then on 2 April, using Bartholomew of Montolif as his spokesman, Hugh claimed the throne at a meeting of the High Court. The assembled vassals formally recognized him as his uncle's successor and did homage. Coronation as king of Cyprus followed on 15 April in Nicosia cathedral. A month later there was a second coronation ceremony, this time at Famagusta: as the unnamed author of this section of the *Chronique d'Amadi* explained,

> the vassals and the prelates had decided that since he could not be crowned in the city of Tyre as the Saracens held the land, there was no better place in Cyprus for him to receive the crown of Jerusalem . . . [1]

The new king – not to be confused with his namesake and cousin, the eldest son of Amaury of Tyre – was the son of Guy, another of Henry's brothers. Guy had died when Hugh was three years old, and the king had brought him up in the royal household. In about 1318 he was appointed to the post of constable of Cyprus, the office once held by his father, and, although it is nowhere stated explicitly, it is likely that by the end of the reign Henry was intending that Hugh should succeed him.[2] In any case, Hugh was the only male member of the royal family resident in the island at the time of his uncle's death and so was a strong natural contender for the throne.

The chronicler tells of speedy action to effect his accession but glosses over the fact that his right to be king was open to dispute. As someone writing later in the century was to note, the High Court recognized that Hugh should have the kingdoms of Cyprus and Jerusalem in preference to the late king's sisters, Alice and Helvis. The text of Bartholomew of Montolif's speech to the Court on 2 April has been preserved. In it he made no direct reference to Hugh's two aunts but

---

[1] 'Documents relatifs à la successibilité', p. 419; 'Amadi', pp. 401–3 at p. 403.
[2] Rudt de Collenberg, 'Les Lusignan', pp. 113, 121.

instead devoted the bulk of what he had to say to setting out arguments from precedent to show that a male claimant to the throne was to be preferred to a female even if she were the closer relative of the previous monarch: thus in 1185 Baldwin V, and not his mother, had succeeded Baldwin IV of Jerusalem; in 1261 Hugh of Antioch-Lusignan had taken the regency of Cyprus in preference to his mother, and in 1269 Hugh of Antioch-Lusignan (now Hugh III of Cyprus) had become king of Jerusalem instead of Maria of Antioch. Objections could probably have been raised against the use of any of these instances as precedents for the legal principle that was being asserted – indeed, it is clear that Bartholomew had either misunderstood or deliberately misrepresented the accounts of the decisions taken in the 1260s – but the High Court must have been satisfied, and it accepted Hugh as the rightful king.[3]

As many people must have realized, the succession principle being advanced in 1324 directly contradicted the view taken only a decade earlier. When in 1315 James II of Aragon married Maria of Lusignan, Henry's eldest sister, it had been accepted that he was marrying the heiress to the throne. Furthermore, despite Bartholomew's assertions to the contrary, in the past it had been accepted that the rules governing the succession to the kingdom were the same as those governing the succession to fiefs, and in feudal custom a sister was regarded as a closer relative of the deceased, and hence a nearer heir, than a nephew.[4] But did either of Hugh's aunts actually want the crown? Maybe they were content to waive their rights, and the specious arguments put up by Hugh and his procurator served only to salve the consciences of all concerned. In any case Hugh must have seemed a much more attractive prospect than either of them. Alice, the elder sister, was the widow of Balian of Ibelin, prince of Galilee; Helvis, the younger, had never married; both women would have been in their forties.[5] It is not surprising therefore that the vassals should have rallied to him. However, there may have been a deeper reason for their support. Balian of Galilee had been a leading supporter of Amaury of Tyre and had suffered in consequence, dying in Kyrenia castle in 1316. As has been seen, the divisions caused by Amaury's usurpation and its aftermath long persisted, and it could well be that the knights who had stood by Henry in 1306–10 and who had been high in his favour ever since feared a reversal of their fortunes should Alice come to power. What was more, Alice's accession might provide the cue for Amaury's surviving sons to return to Cyprus. Like Hugh, they were nephews of the late king, and their restoration to their father's lands in the island could well have been a prelude to their eventual accession.

---

[3] John of Ibelin, pp. 3–4; 'Documents relatifs à la successibilité', pp. 419–22. For the 1260s, Edbury, 'Disputed Regency', pp. 4–19 passim.

[4] For James II, above pp. 137–8. For Latin Syrian inheritance custom, Riley-Smith, Feudal Nobility, pp. 14–16. For an instance of precedents from feudal succession used to establish rights to the regency (and hence to the throne), Edbury, 'Disputed Regency', pp. 12–13.

[5] Rudt de Collenberg, 'Les Lusignan', pp. 117–19.

In 1324, however, they were in no position to mount a challenge for the throne. Hugh, the eldest, had died a few years earlier, and in 1323 the second brother, Henry, together with his mother, had been killed in one of the periodic outbursts of blood-letting to which the Armenian royal family were prone. The next brother, Guy, was away in Byzantium where he was to have a distinguished period of service; eventually, in 1342, he became king of Armenia only to fall victim to an assassin two years later. But despite his varied career, Guy never posed any real threat to his cousin in Cyprus, and neither he nor any other member of his house were able to regain possession of their patrimony.[6] One of Hugh IV's first recorded actions on becoming king was the institution of judicial proceedings against the vassals who in 1310 had been at Kormakiti and had resisted the restoration of Henry II. These proceedings ended in the confiscation of their fiefs, and it could well be that the main purpose of this exercise was to ensure that there was no chance of Amaury's erstwhile supporters forming the nucleus of an opposition party around his sons.[7]

King Hugh married twice. His first wife was Maria of Ibelin, a daughter of Count Guy of Jaffa, and she bore him a son also named Guy. She died, and in 1318 Hugh obtained a dispensation from the pope to take as his second wife her distant kinswoman, Alice of Ibelin. Alice gave birth to at least eight children, five of whom grew to maturity: the future Peter I was born on 9 October 1329; John, later prince of Antioch, seems to have followed fairly quickly, while James, who was to reign as King James I (1382–98), was evidently several years younger and was probably born during the 1340s.[8] With four sons and also two daughters Hugh had ample opportunity to forge dynastic links with western European royalty. Hitherto the Lusignans had had little success in this respect. Negotiations with the English royal family in the 1250s had come to nothing, as had attempts to marry one of Henry II's sisters to King Philip IV of France after the death of his wife in 1305. The only royal marriages had been with the house of Aragon, and then, as has been seen, to no great effect.[9] But Hugh did better: one of his sons married into the French royal house; three of his other children renewed the association with the Aragonese.

In January 1330 Guy, Hugh's eldest son, married Maria, the daughter of Louis of Clermont duke of Bourbon.[10] Since 1316 Louis, who was a grandson of St Louis

<hr/>

[6] For Amaury's sons, Rudt de Collenberg, 'Les Lusignan', pp. 220–8. According to the late and unreliable John Dardel (p. 23), Henry had designated Amaury's eldest son, Hugh (d. 1318/23), as his successor.   [7] 'Amadi', p. 403.

[8] Rudt de Collenberg, 'Les Ibelin', pp. 186–7, 212–13; idem, 'Les Lusignan', pp. 122–3, 124–40. For Peter's date of birth, William of Machaut, La prise d'Alexandrie ou chronique du roi Pierre Ier de Lusignan, ed. L. de Mas Latrie (Geneva, 1877), p. 5.

[9] Above, pp. 85, 137–8. For negotiations with Philip IV, Martínez Ferrando, Jaime II, II, 46.

[10] O. Troubat, 'La France et le royaume de Chypre au XIVe siècle: Marie de Bourbon, impératrice de Constantinople', Revue historique, CCLXXVIII (1987), 4–6. See Mas Latrie, Histoire, II, 140–2, 144–9, 158–65.

and a second cousin of the then king of France, had been at the centre of French crusade plans as the prospective leader of a preliminary *passagium*.[11] It must have seemed that in marrying his heir-presumptive to the child of this leading western enthusiast for an expedition to recover the Holy Land, Hugh had achieved a notable success. Not only would the royal dynasties of Cyprus and France be joined henceforth by ties of blood, but Louis would now have an added incentive to press for a crusade, since his new son-in-law stood to inherit the crowns of both Cyprus and Jerusalem. Furthermore, the marriage meant that in the event of a French-led expedition regaining the Holy Land, Hugh would be in a stronger position to press his claim to a revived Latin Kingdom against the rival claims of that other cadet line of the French royal family, the Angevin kings of Naples. As it happened, Louis of Clermont's dreams of a crusade came to naught; with the fresh outbreak of war with England in 1337 – the start of the so-called Hundred Years War – all thoughts of a French campaign were shelved. Nor did Guy's marriage to Maria work out according to expectations. At first all went well: in the late 1330s Guy was beginning to take part in state affairs, and from 1338, if not earlier, he held the office formerly occupied by his father and grandfather of constable of Cyprus.[12] But then in 1343 he died. He left Maria a widow – she was to live until 1387 – and a son named Hugh.[13]

In 1337 a papal dispensation was obtained for Hugh IV's daughter, Eschiva, to marry Ferrand, the younger half-brother of King James II of Majorca. Once again there was to be a link between the royal houses of Cyprus and Aragon.[14] Ferrand already had close associations with Cyprus: as the son of Ferrand of Majorca the elder and Isabella of Ibelin, he was the king's second cousin. But this marriage too failed to fulfil expectations. The wedding took place in 1340, whereupon Hugh and Ferrand quarrelled so violently that Ferrand believed his life to be in danger. The matter came to the attention of King Peter IV of Aragon and Pope Benedict XII, both of whom made it clear to Hugh that he could expect Aragonese reprisals if any harm befell him.[15] Then, at some point after the middle of 1342, Ferrand left

[11] C. J. Tyerman, 'Philip V of France, the Assemblies of 1319–20 and the Crusade', *BIHR*, LVII (1984), 19–20; idem, 'Philip VI and the Recovery of the Holy Land', *EHR*, C (1985), 37–8; Housley, *Avignon Papacy*, pp. 21, 26, 233–4, 235–6.

[12] Mas Latrie, *Histoire*, II, 178. A Venetian document of c. 1336 names him as marshal. *I libri commemoriali della republica di Venezia regesti (1293–1778)*, ed. R. Predelli and P. Bosmin (Venice, 1876–1914), II, 69.

[13] For a papal letter of condolence dated September 1343, Clement VI, *Lettres closes, patents et curiales se rapportant à la France*, ed. E. Déprez et al. (Paris, 1901–61), no. 423, cf. no. 422. For Maria's later career, Troubat, 'Marie de Bourbon', pp. 6–17.

[14] Benedict XII, *Lettres communes*, ed. J.-M. Vidal (Paris, 1903–11), no. 4833, cf. nos. 7088–9, 7330–32.

[15] For Peter IV, J. Zurita, *Anales de la corona de Aragon*, vol. VII, ch. 55 (vol. II, fo. 148 of the Saragossa edn of 1610); Mas Latrie, *Histoire*, II, 203–6. For Benedict XII, *Annales Ecclesiastici*, ed. C. Baronius and O. Raynaldus, new edn by A. Theiner (Bar-le-Duc/Paris, 1864–82), 1341, §44; Benedict XII, *Lettres closes et patentes intéressant les pays autres que la France*, ed. J.-M. Vidal and G. Mollat (Paris, 1913–50), no. 3220, cf. no. 2508.

for western Europe where he died a few years later. His widow and infant daughter remained in Cyprus. In a lengthy memorandum written before his departure, he catalogued the indignities he had suffered at Hugh's hands. It is an extraordinary story of petty vindictiveness and humiliation, of threatened violence to Ferrand and actual violence against members of his household. Bound up with the attacks on himself were attacks on the Franciscans and on his own mother and step-father, Count Hugh of Jaffa. Ferrand recounted how he himself was accused of treason and forcibly separated from his wife.[16] There was doubtless another side to the story, but evidence is lacking which might explain matters from the king's point of view. It may be significant, however, that at the same time as he wrote to Hugh IV warning him of the possible consequences if the rift were not healed, the pope also wrote to Ferrand enjoining him to moderate his youthful intemperance and show due deference to his father-in-law.[17] The memorandum seems to suggest that the quarrel may have begun with a dispute over Eschiva's dower, but what, if anything, lay behind the charge of treason remains a mystery.

Despite, or perhaps because of, this unhappy episode, Hugh then arranged a second marriage with the house of Aragon. In 1343 he petitioned for and was granted a papal dispensation for his son John to wed Constance of Sicily.[18] Constance had been aged about fourteen when in 1317 she had married Henry II. After his death her re-marriage had been the subject of considerable discussion. Among the possible suitors were Humphrey of Montfort, King Hugh's half-brother and lord of Beirut, and Peter, count of Ribargoza, a son of James II of Aragon. The pope refused the necessary dispensation in both instances. Eventually, in 1331, she married King Leo V of Armenia, only to be widowed a second time when Leo was assassinated in 1341. By 1343 she would have been aged about forty, and, especially in view of the fact that there had been no children of her second marriage, there can have been little expectation that she would bear any children for her third husband, a youth who cannot then have been aged more than about twelve or thirteen. Two considerations may have motivated Hugh. He no doubt intended that John should be provided for out of Constance's dower income in Cyprus and Armenia and hence at no cost to himself, and it is possible that in promoting the marriage he was hoping to repair some of the damage his quarrel with Ferrand may have done to his relations with the Aragonese. In all events, Constance seems to have died within a few years, and by 1350 John was free to marry again. His second wife was drawn from the Cypriot nobility.[19]

[16] Mas Latrie, *Histoire*, II, 182–203; Hill, II, 295–7.

[17] Benedict XII, *Lettres closes . . . les pays autres*, no. 3221. There is corroborative evidence for Hugh accusing Ferrand of trying to escape from Cyprus. Mas Latrie, *Histoire*, II, 204–5. The fact that in 1345 the pope reissued Ferrand's marriage dispensation could be evidence for earlier attempts to impugn its validity. Rudt de Collenberg, 'Dispenses matrimoniales', p. 90 note 40.

[18] Rudt de Collenberg, 'Dispenses matrimoniales', pp. 74–5 no. 88 and note 47 (p. 90).

[19] Rudt de Collenberg, 'Les Lusignan', pp. 110, 130–1. Cf. R. O. Bertrand, 'Jean XXII et le mariage de Constance de Chypre avec l'infant Pierre d'Aragon', *Annales de Midi*, LXIII (1951).

A third and far more significant marriage between one of Hugh IV's children and a member of the Aragonese royal family occurred in 1353 when Peter married Eleanor, the daughter of the Infante Peter of Ribargoza. Hugh had previously arranged for him to marry his cousin, Eschiva of Montfort. In 1339 the pope had turned down a request for a dispensation on the grounds that the couple were too closely related to each other and that Eschiva was appreciably older than Peter, but in 1342 the new pope, Clement VI, acceded to the king's petition thanks to the intervention of a cardinal who happened to be a distant kinsman of Eschiva. Eschiva was a wealthy heiress whose inheritance included the Cypriot land of the lords of Beirut, and, as in the case of his other son, the king had clearly been aiming to provide Peter with a livelihood without dipping into his own resources. At the time of this first marriage, Peter had been a younger son, but by the early 1350s he was regarded as Hugh's heir – he was even spoken of, wrongly, as *primogenitus*. By then he was widowed. It was important that his new bride should be of an age to be able to provide him with a successor; more immediately, his enhanced status meant that his father could use his marriage to further Cypriot interests in the wider context of international diplomacy.[20]

It is not difficult to understand why King Hugh should have sought to marry his children to Aragonese royalty. Through its various branches it controlled Sardinia, Sicily and the Balearic islands, besides Aragon itself, and had suzerainty over Athens. Merchants from the Aragonese lands were thrusting and ambitious and were regular visitors to Cyprus. Hugh clearly recognized the advantages to be had from uniting his family with one with so wide a nexus of power and influence. What was more, the Aragonese shared the Lusignans' antipathy to the Angevin kings of Naples and to the Genoese. But it is noticeable that Hugh's offspring married members of cadet lines and not into the king of Aragon's immediate family. The kingdoms of Majorca and Sicily were of far less weight politically than Aragon itself, and just as Guy, Hugh's heir in 1330, had married a member of a junior branch of the Capetian house, so Peter, Hugh's heir in 1353, married into a junior branch of the Aragonese. Hugh evidently valued these diplomatic links, but even during his reign, when Cyprus is generally thought to have been at the height of its prosperity, the Lusignans could not deal with the royal houses of France and Aragon quite on equal terms.

Largely because the narrative sources for Cypriot history fall almost silent for much of his reign, Hugh IV himself remains a somewhat shadowy figure. Visitors to the island could regard him as a pious ruler and lover of justice,[21] but to set against their reports there is Ferrand of Majorca's depiction of him as a vicious tyrant. Ferrand's portrait would seem to find support in the chroniclers' accounts

---

[20] Rudt de Collenberg, 'Dispenses matrimoniales', pp. 72–3 no. 87; pp. 86–7 no. 8 and note 80 (p. 93).

[21] Hill, II, 304–6. Cf. P. L. M. Leone, 'L'encomio di Niceforo Gregora per il re di Cipro (Ugo IV di Lusignano)', *Byzantion*, LI (1981).

of a later episode. In 1349 Hugh's two eldest sons, Peter and John, much against their father's wishes, left Cyprus secretly to visit western Europe. Hugh went to considerable trouble and expense to bring them back and on their return shut them up in Kyrenia castle. According to Leontios Makhairas he only kept them there for three days, but William of Machaut tells of Peter being in prison for two months and nine days, and the fact that the pope is known to have intervened to secure his release may suggest that William's report is nearer the truth.[22] Peter had been created count of Tripoli in the mid-1340s, probably at the same time as his brother John became prince of Antioch. But apart from his marriages and the 1349 escapade, little is known of his career before he became king. William of Machaut reports that he had founded his chivalric order, the Order of the Sword, before his accession, which, if true, would suggest an early beginning for his interest in martial exploits and his appreciation that, if he were to wage a successful war against the Muslims, he would need to appeal to western knights and their values.[23]

On 24 November 1358 Hugh had Peter crowned king of Cyprus.[24] Coronation in the life-time of the previous monarch seems to have been without precedent in the kingdom, although it was a practice that had been used extensively in earlier centuries in France and had occurred once, in 1183, in Jerusalem. It has to be assumed that the ceremony was brought forward in an attempt to pre-empt a claim to the throne from the king's grandson, Hugh of Lusignan. Ever since Guy's death in 1343 the problem had been looming as to who was now the rightful heir to the throne: was he Peter, the king's eldest surviving son, or Hugh, the son of his deceased first-born? In Cyprus, as earlier in the Kingdom of Jerusalem, feudal inheritance custom favoured the surviving son on the grounds that he was a closer relative than a grandson to the last in seisin. However, according to Hugh and his mother's relatives in the West, his parents' marriage contract had contained a clause explicitly guaranteeing the rights of any son born to them to inherit the throne in the event of Guy dying before his father, and in 1344 they had induced Pope Clement VI to bring this provision to King Hugh's notice. But it is not at all clear that their contention was valid: the text of the contract as published by Mas Latrie contains no such clause.[25] What does seem certain is that there was no love

[22] Leontios Makhairas, §§79–85; William of Machaut, p. 18. For papal concern, Clement VI, *Lettres closes, patents et curiales intéressant les pays autres que la France*, ed. E. Déprez and G. Mollat (Paris, 1960–1), nos. 2278, 2494.

[23] Rudt de Collenberg, 'Les Lusignan', pp. 126, 130. For the Order of the Sword, William of Machaut, pp. 11–16; D'A. J. D. Boulton, *The Knights of the Crown: The Monarchical Orders of Knighthood in Later Medieval Europe, 1325–1520* (Woodbridge, 1987), pp. 241–8.

[24] Leontios Makhairas, §86. The same writer (§90) then says that he was crowned on Sunday 24 November 1359, but it is likely that this later date is a rationalization, making the coronation follow Hugh's death in October.

[25] Clement VI, *Lettres closes . . . France*, no. 825. The pope qualified his endorsement of the claim with the words 'sicut fertur'. For the contract, Mas Latrie, *Histoire*, II, 144–9. For an echo of the claim, *Chronographia Regum Francorum*, ed. H. Moranvillé (Paris, 1891–7), I, 276.

lost between Hugh and his daughter-in-law and grandson. After Guy's death the king had been reluctant to allow Maria of Bourbon and her child to leave Cyprus, and in 1344, at the instance of her family, the pope wrote asking Hugh to settle her dower and let her go to the West. Maria eventually left the island in 1346. The following year she married Robert of Taranto, prince of Achaea and titular Latin emperor of Constantinople. Hugh appears to have gone to Europe with his mother and to have lived there until after his grandfather's death. The king seems not to have held himself bound to provide for them: disputes over the payment of Maria's dower in Cyprus continued to the end of her life, and, although in the 1350s the pope wrote to King Hugh more than once asking him to provide an income for his grandson, so far as is known these requests fell on deaf ears.[26]

Hugh IV died on 10 October 1359, and on Easter Day, 5 April 1360, Peter was crowned king of Jerusalem in Famagusta by Peter Thomas, a Carmelite friar who was the papal legate in the East.[27] Meanwhile news of the old king's death reached the West. Hugh of Lusignan complained to Pope Innocent VI about Peter's accession, arguing once more that by the terms of his parents' marriage contract he himself should have become king. Hugh, who could number the king of France among his supporters and whose step-father was well-regarded as the papal curia, had a sympathetic reception, and in May 1360 Innocent wrote a strongly worded letter to Peter demanding an explanation.[28] At this juncture a Cypriot mission led by a knight named Raymond Babin arrived in Avignon to inform the pope of Peter's accession and protest about the papal legate whose insensitivity towards the Greeks had stirred up inter-communal violence in the island. According to Leontios Makhairas, Raymond made the best defence he could against Hugh's claim and lectured the pope on the principles of Cypriot law. Innocent then wrote to Peter again, this time taking a softer line: he was to rule well, and he was to do justice to Hugh. The fact that Peter had received coronation at the hands of the legate must have weakened the pope's position, but he nonetheless continued to favour Hugh, conferring on him the office of Senator of Rome.[29]

Peter responded to these developments by dispatching an embassy led by the marshal of Cyprus, John of Morphou. It had reached Avignon by November 1361, and by the following January John had made contact with the king of France.

[26] Clement VI, *Lettres closes . . . France*, nos. 825, 2455–6, 2458; Innocent VI, *Lettres secrètes et curiales*, ed. P. Gasnault et al. (Paris 1959–), nos. 863, 2014, 2372; Troubat, 'Marie de Bourbon', pp. 6–8, 16–17.

[27] Philip of Mézières, *The Life of St Peter Thomas*, ed. J. Smet (Rome, 1954), pp. 91–2; Leontios Makhairas, §104.

[28] *Annales Ecclesiastici*, 1360, §§15–16; N. Jorga, *Philippe de Mézières (1327–1405) et la croisade au XIVe siècle* (Paris, 1896), pp. 115–16.

[29] *Annales Ecclesiastici*, 1360, §§13–14; Leontios Makhairas, §§101–2, 105–8. For the chronology, Jorga, *Philippe de Mézières*, p. 117 note 4. For Hugh as Senator (12 August 1360), Rudt de Collenberg, 'Les Lusignan', p. 141. For Maria of Bourbon's antipathy towards Peter Thomas on account of his role in Peter's coronation, Philip of Mézières, *St Peter Thomas*, p. 94.

Evidently the ambassadors were able to make some progress towards achieving a settlement on the basis that Hugh would renounce his claim in return for a substantial annual pension.[30] It would seem, however, that there was no final agreement. Leontios Makhairas says that the French king pressed the pope to re-open the case and that Peter was summoned to defend himself in person; if Leontios is to be believed, it was this summons rather than Peter's wish to rally support for his military ambitions that lay behind his departure to the West in October 1362. However, letters of the newly elected Pope Urban V dated 29 November 1362, in which Peter was urged to treat Hugh generously on condition that he accept him as king, belie this version of events while confirming that the dispute was still not ended: it would appear that the pope, ignorant of Peter's impending visit, envisaged that the remaining differences could be resolved by a further embassy. In the event the king arrived in Avignon in March 1363, and there he and Hugh were eventually reconciled.[31] Hugh was to receive an annual income of 50,000 bezants, much of which was provided by assigning him the important rural centre of Lefkara. By the beginning of 1365 Peter had also conferred on him the honorific title of prince of Galilee. Hugh was present on the Alexandria crusade, and then at the end of 1367 he accompanied his uncle on his second visit to the West. After that he seems to have stayed in Europe, only returning to Cyprus shortly before his death in the mid-1380s.[32]

There is not the slightest hint that Hugh's claim to the throne found any support within Cyprus itself. At the time of his grandfather's death he had been living in Europe for a number of years, and so he must have been virtually unknown in the island. Once Peter had been crowned he would have had no realistic prospect of supplanting him. On the other hand, Hugh could still prove an embarrassment, and failure to reach a satisfactory composition might well have cost Peter dear in terms of diplomatic and military support. Both the pope and the king of France were prepared to believe that Hugh had a good case, and Cypriot practice was by no means general in the West: when in 1377 precisely the same dynastic situation arose in England, it was accepted that the grandson of the late king and not his eldest surviving son should ascend the throne. No king would want to have a pretender lurking on the side lines, especially if he was as well connected as Hugh of Lusignan, and there could well be something to be said for the suggestion that Peter's enthusiastic espousal of the crusading project that was being aired at the time of his arrival in Avignon in 1363 arose, at least in part, from his determination

[30] Mas Latrie, *Histoire*, III, 741; Leontios Makhairas, §108. For the date of the embassy's presence at Avignon, W. H. Rudt de Collenberg, 'Les grâces papales, autres que les dispenses matrimoniales, accordées à Chypre de 1305 à 1378', *EKEE*, VIII (1975–7), 233, 243.
[31] Leontios Makhairas, §§129, 131; Urban V, *Lettres secrètes et curiales se rapportant à la France*, ed. P. Lecacheux and G. Mollat (Paris, 1902–55), nos. 119–20.
[32] Richard, *Chypre sous les Lusignans*, p. 66 and note 3; Rudt de Collenberg, 'Les Lusignan', pp. 141–2.

to ingratiate himself with the papacy and thereby ensure papal endorsement for his rule in the face of Hugh's challenge.[33]

By the 1320s the fear that the Mamlūk sultanate would follow up its conquest of Latin Palestine with an invasion of Cyprus had ceased to be a major preoccupation. A generation had passed since the fall of Acre, and there had been no attack. Such seaborne depredations that there were had been the work of Christian, not Muslim, shipping, and, far from receiving papal subsidies to help in defence, there was a steady flow of funds out of Cyprus to the *curia* to help meet the requirements of successive popes. Indeed, it has been calculated that between 1328 and 1343 the papal collectors raised a total of 55,750 florins in taxes on the Church in the island.[34] On the other hand, awareness that the king of Cyprus was also by rights king of Jerusalem remained ever present. As has been mentioned, Hugh IV, Peter I and Peter II had each had separate coronations at which they had received the crown of Jerusalem; the titles of Prince of Antioch, Count of Tripoli and Prince of Galilee were revived for princes of the royal blood; members of the aristocracy were appointed to the fine-sounding, but, it is presumed, entirely ceremonial grand sergeantries of Jerusalem. We have seen that in the time of Henry II there had been raids on Syria and Palestine and attempts to co-ordinate military efforts with the Mongols, and that on at least two occasions Henry's ambassadors at the papal curia had submitted proposals for bringing about the destruction of the Mamlūk sultanate. Henry had also tried to enforce the embargo on trade by policing the seas, even if the effectiveness of his measures was limited. Western merchants trading with the Muslims often had the acquiescence, if not the connivance, of their home governments, and Henry too had been prepared to allow his merchants to trade in the Muslim-held ports of the mainland.

In the first few years of Hugh's rule some important changes can be detected. The 1320s see the beginning of papal licences permitting traders to buy and sell in the Mamlūk lands. In 1318 Cypriot naval patrols had relieved a Genoese merchant operating from Chios of a cargo of mastic apparently destined for Egypt, but in 1320 and again in 1322 and 1325 the Genoese lords of Chios were obtaining indults from the pope which specifically allowed them to export this commodity to Alexandria, and in 1326 the Genoese received permission to trade in Lattakia over a two-year period.[35] Whereas Henry II and his officers had been censured by Pope John XXII in the early 1320s for their failure to act against illicit trade, in 1326 we

[33] Atiya, *Crusade in the Later Middle Ages*, pp. 322–3.

[34] Housley, *Italian Crusades*, p. 204, cf. pp. 178, 184, 220–1.

[35] Mas Latrie, *Histoire*, III, 720 note 1; John XXII, *Lettres communes*, nos. 15644, 21494; J. Delaville Le Roulx, *Les Hospitaliers à Rhodes jusqu'à la mort de Philibert de Naillac (1310–1421)* (Paris, 1913), pp. 367–8, cf. pp. 9–10; Balard, *Romanie génoise*, p. 745. At the same period absolutions for merchants involved in illicit trade became more readily available. J. Trenchs Odena, ' "De Alexandrinis" (El comercio prohibido con los muslmanes y el papado de Aviñón durante la primera mitad de siglo XIV)'. *Anuario de estudios medievales*, X (1980).

find Hugh IV being allowed to send Cypriots to the sultanate with merchandise, and there are a number of other examples of papal licences exempting Cypriots from the trading prohibitions in the following decades. In 1329 the new patriarch of Jerusalem who was then about to set out for Cyprus, was empowered to absolve forty persons from the automatic sentence of excommunication incurred for breaking the embargoes. Eventually, in the mid-1340s the Venetian state galleys began to trade with Egypt on a regular basis, and from then on it would seem that the popes were far more concerned with the fees for licences or for absolutions for trading without licences than with maintaining the economic blockade.[36] Under these circumstances it is scarcely surprising that Hugh appears to have stopped his uncle's practice of employing a naval flotilla in an attempt to impose the embargo.

There is no doubt that in the reigns of Henry II and Hugh IV Cyprus enjoyed considerable prosperity. Ludolf of Sudheim's description of the opulence of the island in about 1340, the numerous churches in Famagusta which can be dated to the first half of the century and which survive to this day in varying stages of decay, and the numismatic evidence which points to an abundance of silver being available to the mints all attest this fact.[37] Equally, there can be no doubt that this wealth owed much to the advantageous position of the island in the pattern of international trade. As explained in a previous chapter, after the fall of Acre Asiatic spices and other goods that were in demand in western Europe were acquired by Famagusta-based middle-men from the ports of Cilicia and Syria and then re-sold to western merchants in Famagusta itself. It was a flourishing commerce which owed something of its success to the papal attempts to ban Latin merchants from trafficking direct with the Muslims, and it was encouraged by the authorities in Cyprus who in making some attempt at enforcing the ban could channel east–west trade through the ports under their control. With Asiatic goods changing hands in Cyprus, there was a far greater opportunity for the island to prosper than formerly when westerners came simply to take on fresh supplies and buy such agricultural products or manufactures – foodstuffs, salt, cloth – as were available. Dealings in local produce had always contributed to the general level of prosperity; what was new was that from the end of the thirteenth century Famagusta became a major entrepôt and not just a port of call for ships *en route* for Syria.[38]

Patterns of commercial activity, however, are never static, and around the middle of the fourteenth century there were two significant developments. The

[36] Richard, 'Le royaume de Chypre et l'embargo', pp. 131–3; Housley, *Avignon Papacy*, pp. 206–9.
[37] For Ludolf, Mas Latrie, *Histoire*, II, 210–17. For the churches of Famagusta, C. Enlart, *Gothic Art and the Renaissance in Cyprus*, trans. and ed. D. Hunt (London, 1987), pp. 210–303. For mint output, D. M. Metcalf, 'The Gros grand of Henry II', (1983), pp. 198–200; *idem*, 'The Gros grand and the Gros petit of Hugh IV of Cyprus', *Revue numismatique*, 6th ser., XXVII (1985), 156–7.
[38] Ashtor, *Levant Trade*, pp. 38–42, 54; Jacoby, 'Famagusta', *passim*.

first concerned trade routes. There is no way of quantifying the value of commerce on the various routes between Asia and the West, but there is reason to believe that the Cypriot share in this trade was beginning to show signs of dwindling. Goods from India and the Far East could come by ship up the Red Sea, across to Alexandria and thence to Europe, or alternatively overland through Persia either to Trebizond on the Black Sea or to the ports of Cilicia and northern Syria. But political changes, in particular the end of Ilkhanid rule in Persia in 1335, made these latter routes insecure. How far political instability impeded the merchant caravans bound for the Mediterranean is not clear, but if less merchandise was finding its way to the ports on the mainland opposite Cyprus, Famagusta would suffer in consequence. The route through Tabriz to Trebizond was certainly disrupted, and this in turn seems to have prompted western merchants to make greater use of Alexandria and so be all the readier to take advantage of any relaxation of the papal prohibitions on trading there.[39]

In the 1330s and early 1340s, however, Famagusta's commerce would appear to have remained buoyant. The evidence for the Venetian state galleys in this period shows that the numbers of ships and the level of investment on the Famagusta route were only slightly less than on the route to Constantinople.[40] Once the Venetian government stopped sending galleys to Ayas, Famagusta's Armenian competitor, in 1334, and especially after Ayas fell to the Mamlūks in 1337, east–west trade through northern Syria and Cilicia would have been concentrated even more on Cyprus. But from 1345 the republic's state-sponsored galleys, now sailing with papal permits for commerce with the Muslims, began going regularly to Alexandria. Henceforth Venice was sending about the same number of galleys to the East each year as previously – usually between six and eight – but now only half were bound for Cyprus, the others being destined for Egypt. In the three years 1357–9 a total of fourteen galleys were equipped for Alexandria and only nine for Famagusta.[41] The Venetian state galleys would have carried only a fraction of the total trade between East and West. But in all probability the re-routing of a part of this traffic from Cyprus to Alexandria was symptomatic of a more general trend away from the island. If so, it would confirm the impression that less merchandise was available for sale there, and imply that Cyprus was now less attractive as a destination for European investors and ship-owners.[42]

The other significant change with implications for the island's prosperity was

[39] Ashtor, *Levant Trade*, pp. 64–6.

[40] *Ibid.* pp. 54–5 and table II; P. Racine, 'Note sur le trafic Veneto-Chypriote à la fin du moyen âge', *BF*, V (1977), 312–13.

[41] P. W. Edbury, 'The Crusading Policy of King Peter I of Cyprus, 1359–1369' in P. M. Holt (ed.), *The Eastern Mediterranean Lands in the Period of the Crusades* (Warminster, 1977), pp. 96–7; Ashtor, *Levant Trade*, pp. 69, 78–80 and table III; Racine, 'Note sur le trafic', pp. 315–17.

[42] The continuing re-export of Asiatic goods through Cyprus in the early 1360s is attested by the notarial register of Nicola de Boateriis. *Nicola de Boateriis, notaio in Famagosta e Venezia (1355–1365)*, ed. A. Lombardo (Venice, 1973). Cf. Ashtor, *Levant Trade*, pp. 80–1.

the mid-fourteenth-century demographic catastrophe which overtook the entire Mediterranean world, not least Cyprus itself. There can be no doubt that in 1348 the Black Death struck the island extremely hard, and, although no statistics survive, it is likely that here, as elsewhere, the mortality resulted in a reduction of the population by between one third and one fifth. Thereafter epidemics broke out in the island from time to time – the next recorded outbreaks being in 1362 and 1363 – and the population continued to fall. It was a trend which was to continue until late in the fifteenth century.[43] The precise effect of the Black Death and later plagues on commercial activity is a matter for some debate, but, with fewer producers and fewer consumers throughout the Mediterranean world, the region's economy undoubtedly contracted. Individual families or communities may have been better off and so better able to purchase foreign goods, but, even so, the volume and hence the value of international commerce diminished. The population loss would have affected all aspects of economic activity, and everywhere there would have been vacated properties and a shortage of labour. In Cyprus, Famagusta – never a healthy place and with its economy heavily dependent on seaborne trade – would have been particularly hit.

The changing trade routes combined with the economic effects of the Black Death must have meant a significant reduction in the overall volume of the trade passing through the island. It is therefore likely that even before Peter I began his war with the sultanate in 1365 and before the Genoese invasion of 1373, Cyprus and in particular the port of Famagusta were showing signs of recession. Numismatic evidence indicates that mint output per year in Peter's reign was less than in the early part of the century, and this too would suggest that the economy was slowing down.[44] One immediate consequence of the decline in the value of trade would have been the fall in the revenues from tariffs and other commercial charges flowing into the royal coffers. It is against this background that relations between Hugh IV and Peter I and the western merchant communities have to be considered. Cyprus needed the westerners. If they stopped coming; the island's prosperity would suffer. But they were also important from the point of view of security: the commercial revenues they generated helped pay for defence; their ships could be employed against marauders or hired to bring in arms and men. If for any reason Cyprus ceased to attract merchants from the West, then western Europe would no longer have a stake in protecting the island from Muslim attack. Any indication that overseas commerce was in decline would therefore have been a matter for considerable anxiety, and it is not surprising that relations between the government and the merchants were a matter of the utmost delicacy.

During the central decades of the fourteenth century the Cypriot authorities

---

[43] For 1348, above, p. 15 note 9. For 1362–3, Leontios Makhairas, §135; Philip of Mézières, *Saint Peter Thomas*, pp. 97–100. Cf. Arbel, 'Cypriot Population', p. 184.

[44] D. M. Metcalf, 'A Decline in the Stock of Currency in Fourteenth-Century Cyprus?', CS, pp. 264–7.

kept on better terms with the Venetians than with any of the other major trading communities. Immediately after Hugh IV's accession there were problems over the republic's commercial franchises in the island, and at one point Venice instructed her merchants to boycott Cyprus. But in 1328 the king confirmed the privileges originally granted by Amaury of Tyre in 1306, and from then onwards relations were much better.[45] As will be seen, Hugh co-operated with the republic in the anti-Turkish leagues which began in the 1330s, and from time to time Venice showed her appreciation by conferring citizenship on leading Cypriots or on westerners prominent in royal service.[46] In 1349, however, a dispute in Famagusta involving a Venetian merchant and a Sicilian escalated into a major riot in which, according to the Venetian report, the local populace and several royal officials forced their way into the republic's *loggia*, broke open boxes of legal records, wounded at least thirty Venetians and struck the consul. At first the Venetians demanded vengence and reparations as well as greater security for their community, but they added – and this is perhaps a significant concession on their part – that if any of their people were guilty they were to be punished to the king's satisfaction. Then, on learning that the king had imposed adequate penalties on the perpetrators of the riot, they apparently dropped their demands for further restitution. Tension undoubtedly existed between the merchants and the local inhabitants, but at governmental level there was no desire to allow a quarrel of this type to lead to a major breach.[47]

Early in his reign, in 1360, Peter I renewed Venice's privileges and at the same time clarified various issues concerned with jurisdiction over Venetian nationals. But it was probably inevitable that their franchises would still give rise to disputes. In 1361 the Cypriots complained of people falsely claiming to be Venetians, of merchants importing merchandise belonging to non-Venetians and fraudulently claiming customs exemptions, and of Venetian ships taking Cypriot passengers on board who lacked the requisite exit papers.[48] But these complaints were of little consequence. In December 1362 and again from late 1364 until June 1365 Peter stayed in Venice itself. The Venetians were clearly appreciative of his gestures on their behalf at the time of the Cretan revolt of 1363–4, and they agreed generous terms for transporting his crusading forces to the East.[49] But when in 1365 Peter and his crusaders destroyed Alexandria, this long tradition of harmony and co-operation came to an abrupt end.

[45] Mas Latrie, *Histoire*, II, 135, 137–40, 142–4; *Duca di Candia Bandi (1313–1329)*, ed. P. R. Vidulich (Venice, 1965), no. 403.

[46] Thomas of Montolif, the marshal of Cyprus, in 1328; Guy Babin, a prominent vassal, in 1332; Thomas Picquigny, the *bailli* of the *secrète*, and Guy of Ibelin, the seneschal of Cyprus, both in 1334; Uomobuono (Ognibene), the king's physician, in 1358, and another royal physician, Guido da Bagnolo, in 1360. *I libri commemoriali*, II, 44, 54, 57, 281, 312.

[47] 'Nouvelles preuves' (1874), pp. 102–3.

[48] Mas Latrie, *Histoire*, II, 229–32, 233–5; D. Jacoby, 'Citoyens, sujets and protégés de Venise et de Gênes en Chypre du XIIIe au XVe siècle', *BF*, V (1977), 181.

[49] Setton, *PL*, I, 252–3.

In marked contrast, relations between Cyprus and Genoa had been consistently poor ever since the thirteenth century. As has been seen, Henry II's reign had been punctuated by violent incidents, and, although in 1329 and 1338 there were treaties intended to settle outstanding differences, the violence continued. There is evidence for disorder involving the Genoese in 1331 and for fighting between Genoese and Venetians in Famagusta in about 1344 and in 1368.[50] In 1343–4 and again in 1364–5 the government in Genoa was preparing for war with Cyprus. What prompted the threatened hostilities in the 1340s is not entirely clear, although the peace terms proposed in 1344 were largely concerned with redefining the terms of Henry I's 1232 trading privilege and reveal something of the perennial disputes beteeen the royal officers and the Genoese merchants.[51] In 1364 Cyprus and Genoa were again in danger of a full-scale conflict, this time following a violent affray in Famagusta. According to Leontios Makhairas, it began when two deserters from a Cypriot ship were each sentenced to having an ear cut off. They claimed to be Genoese nationals and hence outside the jurisdiction of the court, whereupon the Genoese crew of a galley that was about to take provisions to Satalia mutinied and absconded with their ship to Chios. The Genoese *podestà* arranged for the galley's return, but as it drew near to Cyprus some Sicilian mercenaries from another Cypriot vessel boarded it and killed some of the seamen. There then followed a serious altercation between the *podestà* and two senior royal officials in Famagusta, the *bailli*, John of Soissons, and the admiral, John of Tyre, and yet more blood was shed. The *podestà* instructed all Genoese subjects to leave Cyprus and his order was confirmed later in the year when another Genoese came from Europe to investigate. Peter was then in the West preparing for his crusade, and the pope, afraid that a war with Genoa would put paid to the chances of the expedition taking place, took urgent steps to restore peace. In April 1365 an agreement was reached in Genoa with the king's envoys giving way to all the Genoese demands. The Cypriots were obliged to extend the commercial franchises enjoyed by Genoese merchants, and among the more humiliating provisions they had to accept was the stipulation that the two royal officers involved in the affair should go into exile.[52]

It is clear that throughout these years the Genoese authorities were engaged in a series of long-running conflicts with the Cypriot government over the ill-defined rights their merchants supposedly enjoyed. Who precisely counted as Genoese and how cases of disputed Genoese nationality were to be resolved were contentious issues, especially as Genoa numbered among her subjects the inhabitants of her colonies in the Aegean and Black Sea regions as well as people descended from the

---

[50] Mas Latrie, *Histoire*, II, 150–8, 166–79 (for 1331 see p. 177); *DVL*, I, 287–9; Leontios Makhairas, §250.   [51] Clement VI, *Lettres closes . . . France*, no. 833, cf. nos. 360, 575.

[52] Mas Latrie, *Histoire*, II, 254–66; Urban V, *Lettres secrètes*, nos. 1027, 1034–5, 1102, 1602, 1609, 1619, 1649–50, 1681, 1700, 1724; Leontios Makhairas, §§145–9, 153–6; Hill, II, 312–16. Leontios Makhairas states (§155) that Peter refused to agree to the exiling of his officers, but he then indicates (§§173–4, 209) that he complied.

population of the Genoese quarters in the ports of Latin Syria. Most of these people, the so-called 'White Genoese', would have had only the most tenuous connections with Genoa itself, but, except when charged with theft, kidnapping or homicide, they nevertheless came under the jurisdiction of the *podestà* and not that of the royal judicial officers. Included among them were some prominent burgess families, and their legal exemptions must have been the occasion of considerable resentment. Since the thirteenth century the Genoese had enjoyed freedom to trade and freedom from tariffs, but the degree to which the Cypriot officials could nevertheless supervise their activities and check that they were not abusing their rights was another long-running source of dispute. In all probability the Cypriots were trying to curtail the freedom they had given the Genoese, and the Genoese for their part reacted strongly against any attempts to constrict their commerce and impede its profitability.[53]

Catalan merchants evidently traded regularly in Cyprus as well as in Alexandria. Their compatriots who engaged in piracy were a source of annoyance, but there is nothing to suggest that legitimate merchants had any major complaints or that they themselves caused trouble.[54] On the other hand, the southern French merchants who traded through Montpellier were involved in a protracted dispute over the tariffs they should pay. The rights and wrongs of the issue, which was first raised in 1352, are obscure, but in 1362 the Montpellerins had the pope write to Peter I on the subject, and it emerges from this correspondence that the royal officials had been charging twice as much as the merchants claimed they should. In 1363 Peter gave instructions that tariffs were to be charged at the same rate as in his father's reign, and then in 1365 he granted a new privilege, apparently conceding the Montpellerins' requests. Their original grant dated from as far back as 1236, and from the scattered references to their activities it seems that men from Montpellier and the other ports of southern France had a significant role in the island's commerce, although not on the same scale as those from Venice and Genoa.[55]

The early part of Hugh IV's reign coincided with the end of the illusion that the French royal dynasty would provide the leadership and the resources needed to recover the Holy Land. The idea that France could and would re-establish Christian rule in the East had been avidly fostered by Philip IV and his sons in the first quarter of the century. But, as has been seen, nothing was achieved. Periodic bouts of administrative, diplomatic and propagandist activity had failed to

[53] Edbury, 'Cyprus and Genoa', pp. 121–5.
[54] Hill, II, 291, 310; Ashtor, *Levant Trade*, pp. 46, 50, 87.
[55] Mas Latrie, *Histoire*, II, 219–20, 250, 268–72; A. C. Germain, *Histoire du commerce de Montpellier* (Montpellier, 1861), II, 259–61; Urban V, *Lettres secrètes*, nos. 115, 1895.

produce a crusade: the practical difficulties were too large, and despite the sincerity of French intentions, the price of failure too great.[56] Charles IV's projects had ground to a halt in 1323, and it was not until 1331 that the new king, Philip VI, came forward with a fresh scheme for the liberation of Jerusalem. This new initiative derived part of its impetus from the patriarch of Jerusalem, who was now back in France after conducting Maria of Bourbon to Cyprus for her marriage to Guy of Lusignan and who had taken the opportunity of being in the East to visit Palestine and Cairo. At the end of 1331 the pope authorized crusade preaching in France, but it was only in 1333 that he came to an agreement with the king over the financial arrangements and preparations could begin in earnest. But once again the plans foundered. Philip could not raise enough money sufficiently quickly; the threat of war with England as well as the pope's own lack of enthusiasm for the venture undermined its chances of success. In 1335 the Mamlūks invaded the kingdom of Armenia, and the following January the pope ordered the suspension of crusade preaching in Cyprus on the grounds that it was dangerously provocative. Then in March he formally cancelled the whole project. The moneys raised in France and the French fleet that was being assembled were subsequently deployed against the English in the opening phase of the Hundred Years War.[57]

While plans for this abortive crusade were still in train, Cyprus had become involved in a different sphere of activity. The kings of France may have been thinking in terms of the restoration of Christian rule in the Holy Land, but the Venetians and the Knights of St John in Rhodes were more concerned at the growth of Turkish piracy and at the threat to Christian possessions and to Christian shipping posed by the *ghazi* emirates of western Anatolia. The idea of concerted action against the Turks had its origins in the mid-1320s, but the diplomatic manoeuvrings required to bring the interested parties together took time. At first the Venetians concentrated on forming a Christian naval league in conjunction with Rhodes and Byzantium. Philip VI and Pope John XXII were then induced to participate. In their eyes the proposed expedition was to serve as a *primum passagium* to prepare the way for Philip's projected crusade to Jerusalem. Another party to the alliance was Hugh IV. The Venetian Senate agreed to invite him to participate in November 1333, and the following March the league, now comprising Venice, Rhodes, France, the Papacy, Byzantium and Cyprus, was finalized. The Cypriots were to contribute six galleys out of a total of forty. In the late summer of 1334 the combined Christian fleet made a series of assaults on Turkish shipping in the Aegean, culminating in a victory in the Gulf

---

[56] Housley, 'Franco-Papal Crusade Negotiations', pp. 182–4; Tyerman, 'Sed nihil fecit?', *passim*.
[57] Tyerman, 'Philip VI and the Recovery of the Holy Land', pp. 25–52; Housley, *Avignon Papacy*, pp. 23–4, 28–9.

of Adramyttion.[58] The alliance and the campaign that followed from it mark a significant new departure, and, although papal efforts to organize a similar league for 1335 failed to make any progress,[59] the idea of joint naval operations, especially once French schemes for a full-scale crusade to Palestine had collapsed, was to remain prominent.

From this point onwards Hugh seems to have become increasingly involved in conflict with the Turks. In 1337 Christian interests in the East suffered a major setback when the Mamlūks seized the Armenian port of Ayas,[60] but the same year the king won what would seem to have been an important victory over the Turks, and a few years later a visitor to Cyprus, Ludolf of Sudheim, noted that Alaya, Anamur, Siq and Satalia – in other words of a large portion of the Turkish-controlled southern coastlands of Asia Minor – paid the Cypriots tribute.[61] Perhaps emboldened by these successes, perhaps worried by continued raids on Christian territory and Christian shipping, Hugh took the initiative in 1341 by dispatching Lambertino della Cecca, bishop of Limassol, on a mission to Rhodes, Venice and Avignon to propose a new Christian alliance. Lambertino was a Bolognese and a papal chaplain who had previously served as a member of the embassy that had negotiated the marriage of Guy of Lusignan and Maria of Bourbon and had then acted as a royal procurator at the papal court in the time of Benedict XII. His past diplomatic experiences and the fact, attested by his appointment in 1344 to the bishopric of Brescia, that he was held in high regard at Avignon meant that he was well qualified to conduct these negotiations.[62] The response at Venice was sympathetic but lacking in substance, and it was not until the beginning of 1343 that the Venetians, pressed by the new pope, Clement VI, formally acceded to the league which now consisted of themselves, Cyprus, the Hospitallers and the papacy. It proved to be a cumbersome process to bring the league into being – another Cypriot embassy was at the curia in the summer of 1343[63] – but eventually, in the spring of 1344, the allied powers assembled their

---

[58] P. Lemerle, *L'émirat d'Aydin, Byzance et l'Occident. Recherches sur 'La geste d'Umur Pacha'* (Paris, 1957), pp. 90–100; E. A. Zachariadou, *Trade and Crusade. Venetian Crete and the Emirates of Menteshe and Aydin (1300–1415)* (Venice, 1983), pp. 29–33; Housley, *Avignon Papacy*, pp. 25–6.

[59] Benedict XII, *Lettres closes, patentes et curiales se rapportant à la France*, ed. G. Daumet (Paris, 1899–1920), nos. 28, 40, 54; Zachariadou, *Trade and Crusade*, p. 34; Housley, *Avignon Papacy*, pp. 25, 28.

[60] Luttrell, 'The Hospitallers in Cilician Armenia', pp. 137–43 (correcting the previous confusion over the date of the fall of Ayas).

[61] Benedict XII, *Lettres closes . . . les pays autres*, no. 1673; Mas Latrie, *Histoire*, II, 216.

[62] Mas Latrie, *Histoire*, II, 180–1; Zachariadou, *Trade and Crusade*, pp. 41–3. For Lambertino's career, Mas Latrie, *Histoire*, II, 140, 144–5; Benedict XII, *Lettres closes . . . les pays autres*, nos. 732, 3020; *idem, Lettres communes*, nos. 867, 2696, 3392, 4078, 8766, 8787, 8947; W. H. Rudt de Collenberg, 'Etat et origine du haut clergé de Chypre avant le Grand Schisme d'après les registres des papes du XIIIe et du XIVe siècle', *MEFR*, XCI (1979), 278–9.

[63] Clement VI, *Lettres closes . . . France*, no. 311.

naval forces. They were under the overall command of Henry of Asti, the Latin patriarch of Constantinople, and Cyprus contributed four galleys out of a total of twenty.[64]

The Christian forces mustered at Negroponte and in May destroyed a substantial Turkish fleet at Pallena, the western prong of the Chalkidike peninsula. Then at the end of the October they overran the port of Smyrna, hitherto a major centre for Turkish seaborne depredations.[65] The capture of Smyrna has deservedly been described as 'the most positive and lasting success achieved by Latin co-operation in the Levant during the fourteenth century'[66] – the Christians hung on there until 1402 – but only the harbour area was secured, and it soon became apparent that no further advance was possible. In January 1345 a number of the leaders, including Henry of Asti and, according to one writer, the marshal of Cyprus, were killed in a surprise attack.[67] Henceforth attempts to sustain the Christian naval union were subsumed under the need to defend this precarious toe-hold on the Aegean coast of Asia Minor. Although credit for the league of 1344 belongs primarily to Pope Clement VI, the fact that King Hugh had actively promoted it is clear evidence of his determination to resist Turkish advance and of his realization that the security of his kingdom was best served by alliances with those western powers with whom he had a common interest in defending the sea lanes to Europe.

Hugh's commitment persisted. In 1346, at the time of the crusade of Humbert of Viennois, he made it clear that the Christian alliance should be extended, provided that the other participants agreed,[68] and although there seems to be no definite evidence for Cypriot involvement in the naval victory over the Turks at Imbros in 1347, it would appear that he continued to provide ships for action in the Aegean until 1348 when a truce was made with the Turkish ruler of Ephesus.[69] However, after the acquisition of Smyrna the Christian effort lost momentum. The failure of Humbert's crusade, ill-feeling between the Hospitallers and the Venetians, and the onset of the Black Death of 1347–8, together with Hospitaller reluctance to assume overall responsibility for Smyrna's defence, combined to sap resolve. Nevertheless in August 1350, after Turkish assaults had been resumed, the league was revived. Cyprus was to supply two galleys and Venice and Rhodes three each to police the coast of Asia Minor for

[64] Lemerle, *Aydin*, pp. 181–4; Setton, *PL*, I, 183–90.

[65] Lemerle, *Aydin*, pp. 187–90; Setton, *PL*, I, 190–1.

[66] A. T. Luttrell, 'Venice and the Knights Hospitallers of Rhodes in the Fourteenth Century', *PBSR*, XXVI (1958), 203.

[67] Lemerle, *Aydin*, pp. 191–3; Setton, *PL*, I, 192–3; Zachariadou, *Trade and Crusade*, pp. 50–1. Cf. Mas Latrie, *Histoire*, II, 184 note 1.

[68] Clement VI, *Lettres closes . . . France*, nos. 2580, 2591, cf. nos. 2748, 2957; *idem, Lettres closes . . . les pays autres*, no. 1079.

[69] Setton, *PL*, I, 212, 216–18; Zachariadou, *Trade and Crusade*, pp. 53–5. Cf. Clement VI, *Lettres closes . . . France*, no. 4130.

the next ten years, and the parties also agreed that, together with the pope, they would share the costs of garrisoning Smyrna.[70]

But before these new measures could become operative, war broke out between Venice and Genoa, and in September 1351 Pope Clement was obliged to admit that the alliance had foundered and that the allies were no longer bound by their undertakings to supply ships and money. At the same time he told the Cypriot clergy to stop preaching the crusade in the island on account of the plague.[71] Even so, he still expected Hugh to do his utmost to help defend Smyrna, and his successor, Innocent VI (1352–62), showed himself equally determined to maintain the Christian occupation and keep the league in being. In November 1353 the new pope told King Hugh, the doge of Venice and the master of the Hospital to pay the 3,000 florins each owed as their contribution to Smyrna's defence, and there is evidence to show that he did indeed use this money to organize supplies for the garrison.[72] In 1355 the pope was again chivvying the powers for their annual payment of 3,000 florins, and from papal letters of that year it would appear that Hugh regarded himself as bound to provide either this sum in cash or the two galleys he had promised in 1350. It also emerges that the pope was assigning 3,000 florins from the clerical taxes raised in Cyprus as his share of the money required to maintain the Christian foothold in Smyrna.[73] In 1356, their war with Genoa over, the Venetians approached Innocent with an eye to reactivating the 1350 league. The pope thereupon wrote to the authorities in Venice, Cyprus and Rhodes, ordering them to furnish galleys as stipulated in 1350 and dispatch embassies to Avignon to renegotiate the treaty. Eventually, on 20 March 1357, the league was renewed for five years: the Venetians, Hospitallers and Cypriots each undertook to provide two galleys to police the seas, and in addition the pope expected each of the parties to provide 3,000 florins annually for Smyrna's defence.[74]

In piecing together this history of Cypriot participation in the naval leagues of the 1340s and 1350s we are heavily dependent on the surviving papal correspondence which has much to say about what the popes expected, less about what was actually being done. In any case the effectiveness of a patrol of, at most, six to eight galleys operating in the Aegean to curb Turkish raids and piracy is open to doubt. Nevertheless, the king did take his responsibilities seriously. Although the popes had to remind all the participants of their obligations, the impression is left that Hugh was reasonably conscientious in

[70] Luttrell, 'Venice and the Knights', pp. 203–4; Setton, *PL*, I, 218–22. Cf. Clement VI, *Lettres closes . . . France*, no. 4661.
[71] Clement VI, *Lettres closes France*, nos. 5052, 5056; *idem, Lettres closes . . . les pays autres*, no. 2496; Setton, *PL*, I, 222–3.
[72] Clement VI, *Lettres closes . . . les pays autres*, no. 2377; Innocent VI, *Lettres secrètes*, no. 618, cf. nos. 642, 645–6, 689, 693.
[73] Innocent VI, *Lettres secrètes*, nos. 80, 1630–2, 1788, 1791.
[74] *DVL*, II, 26–8, 35–9; *I libri commemoriali*, II, 264; Innocent VI, *Lettres secrètes*, no. 2006; Luttrell, 'Venice and the Knights', pp. 205–6; Setton, *PL*, I, 230–1; Housley, *Avignon Papacy*, pp. 37–8.

keeping to his undertaking to provide money and ships. When in 1360 Leontios Makhairas mentions the Smyrna galleys, he was evidently referring to a well-established element in the naval resources of the kingdom, and in this connection it is probably worth noting that in the mid-1350s Angelo of Arezzo, the captain of Hugh's galleys, made what would seem to have been a substantial bequest to support the defence of Smyrna.[75] On the other hand, there is no way of knowing whether Hugh did anything to assist the Byzantine emperors John VI Cantacuzenus and John V Palaeologus in response to papal requests made in 1353 and 1356, although it would seem that he had sent aid to the Armenians in the mid-1340s.[76] But the evidence clearly demonstrates that for most of his reign Hugh was active in seeking to curb Turkish depredations. In view of Cyprus' dependence for its prosperity on trade with the West, it was essential to keep the seas free for merchant ships to operate. Even though Smyrna was distant, Turkish piracy in the waters around Rhodes and Crete posed a direct threat to the shipping lanes and to Cypriot commerce, and so it was as much to Hugh's advantage as it was to the Hospitallers' or the Venetians' to take action against them.

What Hugh did not do was antagonize the Mamlūks of Egypt and Syria. It was not simply that he dared not come into conflict with them unaided. Cypriot commerce with the West, especially after the Mamlūk conquest of Ayas in 1337, depended extensively on the availability in the island of goods that had been shipped through Mamlūk-controlled ports,[77] and so war was not only dangerous, it would have been economically disastrous. It seems to have been to avoid antagonizing the sultan that Hugh had had Pope Benedict XII order the cessation of crusade preaching in Cyprus in 1336, and the same reasoning may have been partially responsible for similar instruction from Clement VI in 1346 and again in 1351.[78] Those who fought in the leagues directed against the Turks enjoyed the status and privileges of crusaders, but what motivated the powers that constituted those leagues was self-interest and security rather than Christian idealism. It was important for the mutual political and economic well-being of Cyprus, Venice and Rhodes to make war on Turkish corsairs; there was no advantage in attacking the Mamlūk sultanate, even if it did have control over the Christian Holy Places.

With the accession of King Peter I (1359–69), we come to the most famous period of Cypriot involvement in the crusading movement.[79] In October 1365 Peter led

---

[75] Leontios Makhairas, §§114, 119; Innocent VI, *Lettres secrètes* nos. 2019, 2087.

[76] Innocent VI, *Lettres secrètes*, nos. 215, 2270. For Armenia, Clement VI, *Lettres closes . . . les pays autres*, no. 1490, cf. nos. 2502–3; Luttrell, 'The Hospitallers in Cilician Armenia', p. 130.

[77] Ashtor, *Levant Trade*, pp. 38, 54, 80–1.

[78] Benedict XII, *Lettres closes . . . les pays autres*, nos. 732–3; Clement VI, *Lettres closes . . . les pays autres*, nos. 1081, 2496.

[79] For modern accounts, Hill, II, 318–60; Setton, *PL*, I, chapters 11–12. Jorga, *Philippe de Mézières*, remains useful.

the expedition which sacked Alexandria and so delivered the most notable blow struck by a Christian army against the Mamlūk sultanate at any point in its history. From 1362 until 1365 he had been in the West recruiting support for his crusade, and the war that followed lasted until 1370. This burst of military activity stands in marked contrast to the more cautious policy pursued by Hugh IV, so much so that Hugh has often, mistakenly, been thought of as a peace-loving monarch. It is generally said that Peter was obsessed with the idea of winning back the Holy Land: he sought to re-live the heroic and, by the mid-fourteenth century, almost legendary events of the First Crusade; he wanted to gain for himself his ancestral kingdom of Jerusalem and restore the places associated with the life and passion of Jesus to Christendom. There can be little doubt that these aspirations were indeed entertained by Peter Thomas, the papal legate who had crowned Peter as king of Jerusalem in 1360 and who was to represent the pope on the 1365 expedition, and by Philip of Mézières, a Frenchman who was Peter's chancellor and who devoted the remainder of his life – he survived until 1405 – to trying to organize his own military order, the Order of the Passion, and re-kindle crusading enthusiasm in the West. Propaganda close to the event presented Peter's crusade as having traditional goals: Pope Urban V's bulls described the expedition as being 'for the recovery of the Holy Land', and Philip of Mézières' contemporary hagiographical *vita* of Peter Thomas took it for granted that what was envisaged was the reconquest of the Holy Land by a Christian army fighting with the aid of God.[80]

The chief objection to this interpretation of Peter's intentions and motivation is that it is hard to believe that the king could really have believed that his army could take Jerusalem from the Mamlūks and then defend it against the might of the Muslim world. The difficulties and expenses involved in protecting such island or coastal strongholds as Rhodes and Smyrna against appreciably less formidable opponents must have argued against so ambitious an undertaking. So when Peter launched his attack on Alexandria, it may well be that his expectations were quite different from those expressed in the contemporary crusading *excitatoriae* which were designed primarily to elicit alms and whip up support in Europe. When in 1363 the crusade was proclaimed, the leader was to be not Peter but the king of France. Peace with England had been restored in 1360, and Pope Urban V and others in the West then set about reviving the idea of a French-led crusade such as had dominated thinking until the mid-1330s. A royal crusade might restore the battered reputation of the French monarchy, and, although conditions in France – war-torn and impoverished after years of conflict with the English – meant that the whole idea was far-fetched, it may well be that King John II was desperate for such kudos and perhaps such finance as

---

[80] *Annales ecclesiasatici*, 1363, §§15–19; Urban V, *Lettres secrètes*, nos. 476–89; Philip of Mézières, *St Peter Thomas*, pp. 102, 103, 128, 131, 134. Cf. Peter I's letter to the Florentines, almost certainly drafted by Philip of Mézières. Mas Latrie, *Histoire*, II, 236–7.

his status as a crusader might bring. Papal crusade propaganda thus harked back to an earlier tradition which demanded that Jerusalem should be the goal for a *passagium generale* led by the heir of St Louis. As Frenchmen, Philip of Mézières and Peter Thomas would have been familiar with this tradition, even though the war with England had lost it the prominence it had had earlier in the century. So when King John died in 1364 and Peter assumed his role as the leader of the crusade, it was as leader of a crusade for which the formal terms of reference had already been set.

Had the history of the previous half century been one of raid and counter-raid by Cypriots and Mamlūks on each other's territory, the Alexandria crusade could be explained as simply an aggravation of hostilities, but in fact there is no evidence whatever for Cyprus-based attacks on the sultanate since the beginning of the century. In certain respects, however, Peter did continue earlier policies. Hugh IV had helped contain Turkish aggression by participating in the capture of Smyrna, by seeking to curb piracy and by placing the emirates of southern Anatolia under tribute. Peter's first military and naval exploits clearly show him following in his father's footsteps. In August 1361 he led his fleet against Satalia on the coast of Asia Minor. Although he had Genoese and Hospitaller support, he seems to have relied primarily on his own Cypriot resources. The town was stormed, the Muslim ruler expelled, and a Christian garrison installed. Satalia had in effect become a second Smyrna, except that here the Cypriots could claim sole credit for its capture and took sole responsibility for defence. Turkish counter-attacks in 1361, 1362 and 1370 were beaten off, but in 1373, with the Genoese invasion of Cyprus imminent, it was handed back.[81] The acquisition of Satalia was accompanied by raids on other places along the coast of Anatolia including Myra, Anamur, Siq and Alaya and by the re-imposition of tribute on the local emirates. There were also naval skirmishes. John prince of Antioch continued to take firm action while Peter was in Europe, and after 1364 we hear of no more Turkish piratical attacks on Cyprus itself for the remainder of the reign.[82] Satalia was probably the most important trading centre on the southern coast of Asia Minor and a useful port of call for ships sailing between Cyprus and the West. There had been attempts to capture it early in the thirteenth century. In Turkish hands it posed a threat to communications with Europe; in Cypriot hands it had considerable strategic and commercial potential.[83]

Earlier, in 1360, Peter had taken another mainland port, Gorhigos (the ancient Corycus), under his protection. Gorhigos had previously been under Christian rule, but its Armenian inhabitants had despaired of their own king's ability to

[81] Leontios Makhairas, §§117–28, 132–4, 317, 366–8. For other references, Hill, II, 320–3.

[82] Leontios Makhairas, §§116, 137–44, 150–2, 208, 318.

[83] J. H. Pryor, *Geography, Technology and War: Studies in the Maritime History of the Mediterranean 649–1571* (Cambridge, 1988), pp. 95–7, 158, 165–73 *passim*. For the thirteenth-century attempt to gain Satalia, above, p. 43.

defend them and were begging Peter to assume control. It was to remain under Cypriot jurisdiction until 1448, and Peter showed that the townspeople's confidence was well placed when in 1367 he fought off a major attack by the Turks of the nearby emirate of Karamania.[84]

In October 1362 Peter left his brother John in charge in Cyprus and set sail for the West. He took with him the papal legate, Peter Thomas, the chancellor, Philip of Mézières, and an appropriate retinue of nobles and servants. The royal party arrived in Venice early in December. There the king was honourably received, and he and the doge were able to discuss the dangers threatening Christian interests in the East. Moving on from Venice at the beginning of January, Peter travelled via Milan to Genoa where on 5 March he reissued the commercial privileges granted by Henry I in 1232.[85] Finally, having spent about a month in each of the two great maritime cities of northern Italy, he arrived at the papal court at Avignon on 29 March 1363. Two days later, on Good Friday, King John, who had been residing near by since the previous November, and a host of barons and nobles took the Cross. So too did Peter himself. That same day the crusade was formally proclaimed. It was to be led by the French king and would start on 1 May 1365.[86] Never before had a crowned king of Cyprus visited western Europe. How far his voyage was motivated by the need to settle Hugh of Lusignan's claim to the throne and how far by a premeditated desire to pose as a leader of Christendom in its conflict with the Muslim remains unclear. The principal Cypriot chronicler of these events, Leontios Makhairas, made only a single passing reference to the idea of recovering Jerusalem and explained Peter's voyage as being his response to the nephew's challenge and the need to justify his accession to the pope.[87] But Leontios was mistaken in his belief that the pope had summoned Peter to appear in person to answer Hugh's claim. Nor is there any hint in earlier papal correspondence that the pope had been anticipating that the king would join the crusade, although two surviving letters from Peter – one to the rulers of Florence, the other to the seneschal of the kingdom of Naples – written before his departure from Cyprus make it plain that further warfare was at the forefront of his mind.[88]

Although the crusade was for 'the recovery of the Holy Land', the precise

[84] Leontios Makhairas, §§112–16; Hill, II, 348–9.
[85] Hill, II, 324–5; Setton, PL, I, 242–3. For Peter in Venice, see the account by Gian Giacomo Caroldo in 'Nouvelles preuves' (1873), p. 68. For the Genoese privilege, Mas Latrie, Histoire, II, 248–9. [86] Setton, PL, I, 244–5.
[87] Leontios Makhairas, §129. Cf. §131 for the reference (and that only in one ms.) to Jerusalem as Peter's goal.
[88] Above, p. 149. Mas Latrie, Histoire, II, 236–7; J. A. C. Buchon, Nouvelles recherches historiques sur la principauté française de Morée et ses hautes baronnies (Paris, 1843) II, 134–5. In his letter to the Florentines Peter spoke of the recovery of the Holy Land and an expedition to be ready on 1 March 1364. Perhaps he was hoping to recruit Italian mercenaries as he had done previously. Leontios Makhairas, §109.

strategy as conceived by the pope and the king of France in 1363 is by no means certain. Urban's bulls show a degree of ambiguity as to whether the immediate goal was the Mamlūk sultanate or the areas in the Aegean and the Balkans under pressure from the Turks. However, he was evidently impressed by Peter, whose capture of Satalia must have stood him in good stead, and in May 1363 he announced that the Cypriot king would lead a preliminary expedition ahead of the main crusading army. It was laid down that he could recruit no more than 200 nobles, 2,000 horse and 6,000 foot in the West, but exactly what they should do was not specified.[89]

Peter stayed at the papal court until the end of May and then set off on an extended tour of Europe to publicize the crusade and seek recruits. His travels took him through France and thence to England where in November he was entertained by King Edward III. Christmas he spent in Paris, and then, in the opening months of 1364, he visited Plantagenet-controlled areas in western France.[90] For the crusade to be a success there had to be peace in Europe, but since the cessation of hostilities between France and England in 1360 bands of unemployed mercenaries, the so-called 'Free-Companies', were terrorizing the countryside and even threatening the security of Avignon. Urban hoped that this problem could be solved by recruiting these *routiers* for the crusade, and it may be that it was thought that Peter would stand a better chance of enlisting them than the pope's own agents. But attempts to involve the Free Companies were to little avail, and by February Urban had stopped trying and was issuing indulgences for anyone willing to wage war to suppress them. With the *routiers* still at large, it was difficult attracting volunteers for the crusade.[91] In April 1364 King John died. His death meant that recruitment among the French nobility would now be even harder, and it also meant that the headship of the crusade in effect devolved upon Peter. Peter himself attended John's funeral and the consecration of his successor. He then set off on a second stage of his tour which took him through Germany, Bohemia and Poland, and he eventually arrived back in Venice on 11 November.[92]

Quite apart from the political and military troubles in Europe, two episodes in the East threatened the crusade's prospects. In the summer of 1363 the Venetian settlers in Crete rose in rebellion against their home-government. Peter was expecting to rely heavily on Venetian shipping to transport his army to the East, but, with the republic's naval and military resources tied up in suppressing the revolt, the future of the whole expedition was now in doubt. In November Peter

[89] Housley, *Avignon Papacy*, pp. 41–3, 125, 248.

[90] Jorga, *Philippe de Mézières*, pp. 173–85; Hill, II, 325–7. Evidently Peter spent longer in the West than Urban intended. In November 1363 the pope wrote telling him to return to the East: Setton, *PL*, I, 246 note 108.

[91] Urban V, *Lettres secrètes*, no. 487; Setton, *PL*, I, 248; N. Housley, 'The Mercenary Companies, the Papacy and the Crusades, 1356–1378', *Traditio*, XXXVIII (1982), 271–2; idem, *Avignon Papacy*, pp. 42, 249.   [92] Jorga, *Philippe de Mézières*, pp. 186–99.

offered to go in person with some of his crusade recruits to help crush the rebels, and the following January the Venetian government undertook to convey 1,000 horsemen and 2,000 foot wherever they wished in the East to continue their crusade on the understanding they would first assist in bringing the rebellion to an end. In the end the authorities managed without the crusaders' aid and broke the backbone of the rebellion before it could seriously interfere with Peter's plans.[93] The other incident which placed the crusade in jeopardy has been outlined already. In 1364 a dispute in Famagusta over punishments inflicted on two Genoese mariners who had deserted from a Cypriot ship escalated into a violent affray which in turn threatened to plunge Cyprus and Genoa into a major war. It was only in April 1365 when Peter's representatives conceded all the Genoese demands in what must have been regarded as a most abject climb-down that this danger was averted.[94]

Peter's fleet sailed from Venice in June and rendezvoused at Rhodes with the forces from Cyprus under the prince of Antioch in August. The king had spent just over two and a half years in the West. He had enjoyed lavish hospitality throughout his stay, but in practical terms his success in persuading western nobles, knights and footmen to join his expedition had been limited. Indeed, Philip of Mézières tells of Peter Thomas comforting the king, downcast at the meagre result of his labours. Philip mentions figures of 600 armed men paid for by the king and almost 500 horses in the fleet sailing from Venice, and tells of the master of the Hospitallers providing about 100 knights from Rhodes. But he puts the total under Peter's command at about 10,000 armed men (with 1,400 horses) and including about 1,000 'nobiles armati'.[95] The impression left by these statistics is reinforced by the various figures given for the size of the fleet. Philip of Mézières says that the prince of Antioch brought almost 60 ships from Cyprus to Rhodes and that the total for the fleet was almost 100 ships of different types, not counting those provided by the Hospitallers. Leontios Makhairas believed that there were 165 ships at Rhodes, of which 108 were from Cyprus. According to Leontios, Peter and the westerners had been transported in sixteen galleys from Venice and the Knights of St John provided a further four. Even allowing for the discrepancies in the arithmetic and the widely differing capacity of the vessels in the Christian fleet, it would seem that, for all Peter's efforts to find recruits in the West, the force which attacked Alexandria in October 1365 consisted in the main of his own Cypriot vassals and men-at-arms together with foreigners already present in the East.[96]

[93] Hill, II, 327 note 2; Setton, PL, I, 249–57.   [94] Above, p. 155.

[95] Philip of Mézières, Saint Peter Thomas, pp. 120–1, 125, 127–8.

[96] Ibid., pp. 125, 127; Leontios Makhairas, §§162, 167. Cf. 'Amadi', p. 414 (92 Cypriot ships, including 33 galleys, out of a total of 165). Arab estimates put the fleet at 70–100 ships. Ashtor, Levant Trade, p. 89. See also A. T. Luttrell, 'English Levantine Crusaders, 1363–1367', Renaissance Studies, II (1988), 148–50.

The fleet set sail from Rhodes on 4 October. Only then did the king make known publicly his decision to attack Alexandria. Partly the secrecy which had hitherto surrounded the crusade's destination would have been to keep the Muslims guessing; partly to prevent those European merchants with business interests there from trying to stop the expedition taking place or alerting the Mamlūks. Certainly the secret had been well kept: the Venetian authorities were in the dark as letters written at the time of Peter's departure the previous June make clear.[97] The fleet made speedy progress, arriving off Alexandria on 9 October. Next day the Christian ships came close inshore, and the forces disembarked, routing the troops that attempted to prevent their landing. The garrison seems to have been taken wholly by surprise and was evidently insufficient and inadequately commanded to make much resistance. Peter's men were able to force an entry into the city by setting fire to the custom-house gate, and, once they were inside, the Muslim defenders fled. The crusaders then indulged in a fury of indiscriminate massacre and destruction. The property of the western merchants was seized along with anything else of value. Also destroyed were two of the three landward gates, but for which, according to an-Nuwairī, the author of the fullest Arabic account of the sack, the Christians would have been able to retain the city.[98]

The problem now was what to do next. The main Mamlūk forces were billeted in Cairo and would doubtless make for Alexandria as quickly as possible. But with the city gates in ruins and after the failure of an attempt to destroy a key bridge over the Nile canal at Fūwah and so impede the Egyptian army's progress, it was realized that Alexandria was untenable. Peter had been unable to keep his forces under control, the city could not be defended, and the crusaders were anxious to make off with their loot. The Christian sources agree that Peter himself was all for holding Alexandria, but although he had the support of Philip of Mézières and Peter Thomas, the two most ardent exponents of the crusade ideal, the westerners and, if Philip is to be believed, the Hospitallers and Peter's own brothers insisted on withdrawing. And so, on 16 October, as the Mamlūk troops entered Alexandria from the direction of Cairo, Peter and the last of his men made off for Cyprus.[99]

[97] Mas Latrie, *Histoire*, III, 751–3. There is later evidence to suggest that the Venetians did know of the intention to attack Egypt. 'Nouvelles preuves' (1873), p. 79 note 1. For a discussion of whether the pope knew, Housley, *Avignon Papacy*, pp. 249–50.

[98] For the sack of Alexandria, with reference to the sources and earlier literature, Setton, *PL*, I, 266–71.

[99] Philip of Mézières, *Saint Peter Thomas*, pp. 133–4, 138; William of Machaut, pp. 100–9; Leontios Makhairas, §§172–3. For the Hospitallers and Peter's brothers, Joga, *Philippe de Mézières*, pp. 301–2, citing Mézières' unpublished 'Oratio tragedica' of 1389/90; the near contemporary life of St Peter Thomas mentions only westerners. For the army's departure, see Setton, *PL*, I, 272.

Spectacular though the events of October 1365 might seem, the positive achievement had been slight, and on the debit side Cyprus was now plunged into war with the sultanate. From the Christian point of view it was just as well that the ingrained antipathy to naval activity and seaborne military campaigns which characterized the regime for much of its history meant that the Mamlūks were in no position to launch a retaliatory attack. After the sack of Alexandria they did set about building a fleet, but it was never completed and so Cyprus itself escaped unscathed.[100] Not all western Europe applauded what had been done. In particular, the Venetians and the other western merchants were incensed by the disruption of their trade. Merchandise had been lost in the pillage or confiscated by way of reprisal; merchants and other westerners who had been in the sultan's lands at the time were held captive. For Peter to have capitalized on the destruction of Alexandria, further large-scale assaults on the coasts of Egypt and Syria were required. Once news of the events of October reached the West there was a chance that prospects of further military glory and booty would add fresh recruits to Peter's forces, and, indeed, during 1366 some adventure-seeking nobles such as the Gascon Florimond of Lesparre did come to Cyprus. But hopes that the count of Savoy, the king of France or the ablest of the French commanders, Bertrand du Guesclin, would come east proved vain. Rumours of peace were in the air – Leontios Makhairas accused the Venetians of falsely spreading them – and few western leaders were prepared to go to the trouble and expense of equipping a force of men-at-arms for service with the Cypriots only to risk finding on their arrival that hostilities had ceased.[101]

For their part, the Mamlūks expected further attacks, and almost at once they began pressing the trading cities, themselves anxious for a return to normality, to work for peace. It seems that by the beginning of 1366 they had sent embassies to Venice and Genoa, and in January the Venetians in their turn dispatched ambassadors to the sultan to secure the release of the imprisoned merchants and restore normal relations. The Mamlūks, however, insisted that there could be no treaty with Venice until a settlement was also reached with Cyprus. The Venetians now had every reason to put pressure on Peter to open negotiations. They had a measure of success: Peter was persuaded to divert his fleet from a projected assault on Beirut, the most important port on the coast of Syria, to Asia Minor, and to invite a Muslim embassy to Cyprus. The envoys met the king in Nicosia early in June, but Peter made unrealistic demands as the price of peace – the cession of the former territories of the kingdom of Jerusalem coupled with the release of the captives and customs exemptions for Cypriot traders – and he

---

[100] D. Ayalon, 'The Mamluks and Naval Power – a Phase of the Struggle between Islam and Christian Europe', *Proceedings of the Israel Academy of Sciences and Humanities*, 1 (1965), 1-12 (see p. 6 for the fleet begun after 1365).

[101] Leontios Makhairas, §§175, 186-7; Hill, II, 335-6.

then sent his own ambassadors back to the sultan for further discussions. In effect he was playing for time while he built up his forces for a fresh assault. The Venetians, on the other hand, seem to have believed, or at least they pretended to believe, that peace was imminent, and they even persuaded the pope to issue new licences for them to trade with Egypt. But towards the end of June Peter sent Philip of Mézières to the West to make it clear that he was planning a new invasion of the sultanate for that August and to seek military and diplomatic support. Pope Urban rescinded the Venetian trading licences, and the Venetians responded by forbidding their subjects to participate in Peter's expedition and by placing an embargo on the export of arms and horses to Cyprus. They also arranged for a gift of falcons to be sent to the emir Yalbughā, who as atabak al-'asakir was the dominant figure in Cairo.[102]

The new campaign took longer than expected to muster. It was not until October that Peter's diplomatic contacts with the sultan came to an end with the imprisonment of his envoy and the Mamlūk seizure of those westerners who had been unwise enough to resume trading. By November the fleet was ready. It consisted of 56 galleys and 60 other vessels and included a contingent from Rhodes. It was thus comparable in size to the fleet which had destroyed Alexandria the previous year. Its departure, however, was delayed by the king's illness, and, so Peter alleged in a letter in which he remonstrated with the Venetians over their obstructive behaviour, by his desire to give Venetian merchants in the Mamlūk ports the chance to get away. It was not until the beginning of January that the armada could set sail, and when at last it did it was dispersed in a storm. Fifteen galleys, including the one commanded by Florimond of Lesparre, sacked the Syrian port of Tripoli. The other ships retired to Cypriot waters without, so it would seem, striking a blow.[103]

This fiasco would appear to have marked a turning-point. Peter would have known that military failure or inaction would in itself deter further support from the West. He was also coming under increased pressure from the Catalans and Genoese as well as from the Venetians to make peace. The sultanate had far greater resources than he had, and warfare was expensive. As early as October 1366 the pope had made it clear that Peter could expect no major financial support from papal taxation revenues and had begun advising him to put an end to hostilities. So when fresh Mamlūk envoys arrived in Cyprus in February, Peter was disposed to engage in serious negotiations. A draft peace treaty was prepared, and in March an embassy headed by James of Nores, the turcopolier of Cyprus, was sent to Cairo to secure its ratification. But the sultan refused.[104]

---

[102] *Ibid.* 335–43; Setton, *PL*, I, 274–8.

[103] Leontios Makhairas, §§190–1, cf. II, 119–20; William of Machaut, pp. 130–2. For Peter's letter to Venice, Mas Latrie, *Histoire*, II, 286–8.

[104] *Annales ecclesiastici*, 1366, §13; Leontios Makhairas, §§189, 192–3, 197–8. For the draft treaty, Mas Latrie, *Histoire*, II, 291–302. Cf. William of Machaut, pp. 132–5, 172–9.

Peter's attention had been diverted by a Turkish attack on Gorhigos in February and March, and then in May his own garrison at Satalia mutinied. Both necessitated decisive military action, and in all probability these events encouraged the Mamlūks to drive a harder bargain.[105] In June James returned from Egypt accompanied by Muslim envoys who were to negotiate a new, less favourable, treaty. They found the king in Rhodes, whence he had gone after suppressing the Satalia mutiny, but he was in no mood to accept peace at any price. He imprisoned the envoys and set about organizing his forces for yet another assault on the ports of northern Syria. The fleet sailed in late September and attacked Tripoli. It then moved northwards, ravaging Tortosa and Valania. Unable to force a landing at Lattakia, it pressed on to the Cilician ports of Malo and Ayas where the Christians broke into the town but met strong resistance at the landward castle. By early October the raid was over. Peter decreed that any Christian captain who would engage in privateering against the Mamlūks could use Famagusta as a base.[106]

This raid was the last that Peter was to lead. Soon after his return to Cyprus he set off on a second visit to Europe. The chroniclers explain his going in terms of his need to satisfy his honour in a dispute with the Gascon lord, Florimond of Lesparre: in the summer of 1367 while at Rhodes, Peter and Florimond had become involved in a heated argument which ended with an undertaking between them to fight a duel at the court of the king of France.[107] But Peter must also have been anxious to revive the flagging western interest in his war. He sailed to Naples and in March 1368 reached Rome where Pope Urban had been residing since the previous October. At Easter the pope effected a reconciliation between the king and his adversary, apparently on Peter's terms.[108] But the king had lost the papal backing he had hitherto enjoyed. The pope had already resumed issuing permits for the Venetians to trade in Mamlūk ports, and now, with Peter in Rome, he insisted that the king allow Venetian and Genoese ambassadors to negotiate peace on his behalf. In May Peter yielded to papal pressure and gave instructions that the embassy was to ask for the same terms as had been set out in the draft treaty of 1367. He then travelled to Venice and sailed for Cyprus in late September. Any hopes he may have had of gaining further military or financial aid had been in vain.[109]

The closing phase of the war can be briefly told. The joint Venetian and Genoese embassy to the sultan was unsuccessful. Then in January 1369 Peter was murdered. Later that year the regent, John prince of Antioch, who had

[105] Leontios Makhairas, §§194–5, 200–1; William of Machaut, pp. 135–72.
[106] Leontios Makhairas, §§202–5, 209–13; William of Machaut, pp. 179–217 *passim*; *Chronique des Quatre Premiers Valois*, pp. 188–91 (recording an otherwise unknown attack on Jaffa); Hill, II, 352–4. For privateering, Leontios Makhairas, §§213, 219–22.
[107] Leontios Makhairas, §§206, 214; William of Machaut, pp. 224–45.
[108] Jorga, *Philippe de Mézières*, pp. 369–72.
[109] DVL, II, 123–6; Mas Latrie, *Histoire*, II, 291–308; Hill, II, 356–8.

repeated Peter's decree encouraging privateering at Muslim expense, sent out a small raiding party which attacked various ports along the coasts of Syria, Cilicia and Egypt. Eventually negotiations involving Cyprus, Rhodes, Genoa, Venice and the Mamlūk sultanate were resumed, and after a long and difficult round of diplomatic activity peace was finally ratified in October 1370.[110]

The story of Peter's war is thus one of high hopes and a spectacular start followed by loss of momentum, military and diplomatic stalemate, increasing frustration and finally a peace agreement which, so far as can be ascertained since the actual text has not survived, brought Cyprus nothing.[111] But the question remains: what was Peter hoping to achieve? It was suggested earlier that the idea of winning back the Holy Land was merely propaganda designed for consumption in the West. Jerusalem as the goal of the venture was all very well as an element in the *excitatoriae* for the crusade or in the subsequent *apologiae* for Peter's actions, but it was never a practicable proposition and Peter must have known it. However, if the occupation of Satelia can be seen as a development of earlier policies, is it not possible that the attempted occupation of Alexandria or its destruction, can also be explained in such terms? So far as the negotiations of 1367 and 1368 are concerned, the surviving draft treaty from 1367 makes it clear that at that time Peter's foremost aim was to get the sultan to concede preferential commercial facilities, tariff reductions, and legal franchises and guarantees for Cypriot merchants trading in his lands. He was thus using aggression and the threat of aggression not to make territorial gains in areas once under Christian rule, but to derive commercial advantages for his subjects at the expense of the Mamlūk regime and, by implication, at the expense of the Cypriots' competitors in Egypt and Syria, the merchants from the West. And herein perhaps lies the clue to the entire strategy. As has been seen, Cyprus' own prosperity was in decline; increasingly western merchants were bypassing the island and dealing direct with the Muslims. Had Peter been able to hold Alexandria, he could have exploited its commerce for his own advantage and so once again obtained control over a substantial portion of east–west trade. But having failed to hold Alexandria, he could still hope to restore Famagusta to something of its former prosperity by disrupting the existing commercial patterns and by obtaining favourable terms for his own merchants who might then be better placed to act as middlemen, re-selling eastern goods to westerners. If the war waged against Turkish corsairs and the acquisition of Satalia were intended to safeguard and extend Cypriot commercial interests, why not the war waged against the sultan and the attempted acquisition of Alexandria?

After its glorious start, the final episode in Peter's reign comes as a sad anticlimax. By the time he returned empty-handed from his second visit to the

---

[110] *Ibid.*, pp. 359–60, 372–6. Cf. Urban V, *Lettres communes*, ed. M.-H. Laurent *et al.* (Paris, 1954–86), nos. 26767, 26795.   [111] For the 1370 treaty, Hill, II, 376.

West, the prospects for any lasting advantage to Cyprus from the hostilities were fast ebbing away. A sense of failure must have been all-pervasive, and, as stories preserved by the various chroniclers imply, the effect on Peter seems to have been to weaken his judgement. Several instances can illustrate this point. They range from the quarrel with Florimond of Lesparre and the king's acceptance of his challenge to a duel to the scarcely credible incident in which on the day before his death Peter had imprisoned and threatened to execute John Gorap, the steward of his household, for failing to provide oil for the asparagus.[112] Even in the context of the exaggerated chivalric ideals of the fourteenth century, for a king to travel far from his kingdom with the intention of fighting a duel with a foreign nobleman indicates a complete lack of any sense of proportion. Yet the narrative accounts of the reign present this duel as the principal reason for the king's journey to Europe in 1367, and, although they may be accused of highlighting only the most sensational aspect of his visit, their perspective on this episode finds support in a contemporary papal letter in which the king was ordered to desist and told that the engagement would be a derogation of his royal dignity.[113]

Eleanor of Aragon had borne Peter two children: a son, who was to succeed him as king, and a daughter.[114] According to Leontios Makhairas, whenever Peter was away from home he would have his servant put one of Eleanor's shifts by his bed, '. . . and when the king lay down to sleep he would take the shift in his arms (because of the love which he had for the queen) and thus he would sleep'.[115] Nevertheless, he took mistresses, and by 1367 his behaviour had become sufficiently notorious for the pope to issue a rebuke. The sources mention two women, both members of the lesser nobility: Joanna L'Aleman, concerning whom Leontios gave a lurid account of the queen's attempts to induce a miscarriage, and Eschiva of Scandelion.[116] While Peter was in the West in 1367–8 rumours began to circulate that the queen in her turn had taken a lover, John of Morphou, the marshal of Cyprus and since 1365 titular count of Edessa. It is difficult to know whether there was any substance to them, although there is no indication that the pair had any association after Peter's death when presumably there would have been less cause for discretion. The controller of the royal household in the king's absence was a knight named John Viscount, and he was foolhardy enough to write to the king to inform him of the rumours, adding that he himself did not believe them. On his return Peter tried to find out the truth but was confronted by a wall of silence. He summoned his vassals, who, fearful of the likely repercussions if they corroborated the controller's report, preferred to perjure themselves and told the king that Viscount had

---

[112] Leontios Makhairas, §279. Richard, 'La révolution', p. 109.
[113] Urban V, *Lettres secrètes*, no. 2567; William of Machaut, pp. 224–45; Leontios Makhairas, §214.   [114] For a possible second daughter, Rudt de Collenberg, 'Les Lusignan', p. 147.
[115] Leontios Makhairas, §130; cf. §§216, 242.
[116] *Annales ecclesiastici*, 1367, §13; Leontios Makhairas, §§234–8, 245, 248–9, 280.

concocted the story himself out of spite for the queen. He was thereupon thrown into prison and died soon afterwards. The effect of this episode was to foster an atmosphere of fear and suspicion. The nobles were ashamed, and Peter, who had a shrewd idea of what had been going on, gave vent to his feelings by adopting a truculent attitude towards them and by going out of his way to be offensive to their womenfolk.[117]

The stage was set for the final drama. Peter, the king's son who would have been aged about twelve at the time, coveted a pair of greyhounds belonging to James of Jubail and was furious when James refused to give them to him. When the king came to hear of the matter, he made overtures to buy the dogs, but James and his father, Henry of Jubail, refused to sell. The king was not prepared to countenance this rebuff; he stripped Henry of his office of viscount of Nicosia and had both him and his son locked up; at the same time he made preparations to marry Henry's daughter to an artisan and then had her tortured when she tried to hide. The other nobles learnt of these developments with consternation. The king had set about destroying an old and distinguished family on the most trivial of pretexts and had acted illegally by imprisoning a liegeman without due legal process and by attempting to disparage his daughter. There was no knowing whom he might turn on next. They persuaded the king's two brothers, John prince of Antioch and James, the later King James I, to intervene, but when they broached the subject Peter grew angry and refused to make amends. John and James then conferred with the nobles, and they decided to go in a body to demand that the king renew the oaths concening good government and the maintenance of law that he had sworn at his accession. But some of the vassals decided that he would only go back on his promises, and so they resolved to kill him. In the early hours of the morning of Tuesday 16 January the party consisting of the royal princes, the knights who were set on murder and some others who were apparently unaware of their intent set off, on their way releasing the Jubails and also John Gorap from prison. They gained admission to the king's private apartments. There three of their number, Philip of Ibelin lord of Arsur, Henry of Jubail and John of Gaurelle, struck Peter down with their swords; others, including John Gorap and also James of Nores the turcopolier, who had not been privy to the plot but who wanted to identify himself with the conspirators, further mutilated his body.[118]

That at least is a summary of the tale as told by the Cypriot chroniclers. The murder is portrayed as the outcome of a quarrel arising from a petty dispute in the course of which the king, whose behaviour had already cost him the trust and

---

[117] Leontios Makhairas (§§239–49, 251–9) gives a detailed account vitiated by some chronological impossibilities. Richard, 'La révolution', p. 108. Machaut (pp. 248–54) has a similar story although with differing nuances.

[118] Leontios Makhairas, §§261–81; William of Machaut, pp. 254–71; 'Amadi', pp. 422–6. For the date and further comment, P. W. Edbury, 'The Murder of King Peter I of Cyprus (1359–1369)', *Journal of Medieval History*, VI (1980), 222–4.

goodwill of many of his men, had victimized a noble family. It is a story of passion, fear, intrigue and violence, and as such may well have grown in the telling. In one important respect, however, the testimony of Leontios Makhairas and the later sources dependent on him or on the sources he himself had used should be called into question. The Cypriot writers were careful to disassociate Peter's brothers from the plan to murder the king. Allegedly they had agreed to get him to renew his coronation oaths and had gone with the murderers thinking that this was what they were going to do. Once in the royal apartments the actual murderers rushed at the king and stabbed him to death before the two princes of the blood-royal realized what was happening. So although they were present at the murder, they were innocent of the king's blood. But to writers in the West there was no doubt that they were guilty men: they were either in the conspiracy, urging the murderers on, or, according to some accounts, struck the fatal blows themselves. William of Machaut, whose *Prise d'Alexandrie* is a full-length biography of King Peter, Philip of Mézières, Froissart, Christine of Pisan, and the anonymous author of the *Chronographia regum Francorum* – to mention only a few of the better known writers and sources – are agreed on their complicity.[119] When we take into consideration circumstantial evidence provided by the Cypriot chroniclers – the brothers' presence at the murder, the time of day that the incident occurred, the fact that the actual murderers went unpunished during the prince of Antioch's regency (1369–72), and the fact that the queen held Prince John personally responsible – it is difficult to accept that James and John were indeed free from guilt.[120] In all probability Leontios Makhairas and later writers either drew on an 'official' account of Peter's death, put out by the regime headed by the prince of Antioch which came to power immediately after the murder, or repeated historical traditions current at the court of James I (1382–98) or his son Janus (1398–1432) which would naturally have avoided accusing the then king or his father of regicide and fratricide.

There is, however, no evidence for long-term personal ill-feeling between the king and his brothers. John of Antioch had a fine record as the regent while Peter was in the West in 1362–5 and 1367–8 and as a military commander. According to Leontios Makhairas, Peter intended to imprison John and James together with those knights he knew hated him, but this section of his account has the air of a piece of literary fantasy and presents chronological difficulties which make it impossible to accept as it stands.[121] On the eve of the murder there occurred the stormy scene at which the brothers tried to remonstrate with the king on behalf of the Jubails, and perhaps it was only then that the vassals convinced them that

---

[119] Jorga, *Philippe de Mézières*, p. 394 note 5; Edbury, 'Murder of Peter I', pp. 224–5 and note 5 (p. 231).

[120] Leontios Makhairas (§§290, 325) shows that John Gorap and Philip of Arsur continued to enjoy favour. For Eleanor and John of Antioch, see §§553–4.   [121] Leontios Makhairas, §260.

Peter meant them harm.[122] On the other hand, of the knights mentioned as being party to the murder Henry of Jubail and John Gorap were victims of the king's wrath and, especially in view of the fate of John Viscount, would have had good cause for wanting to see Peter dead. Philip of Arsur had quarrelled with the king much earlier in his reign and had gone to the length of having the pope intercede on his behalf. By late 1366 he was back in royal service, and in 1367 he accompanied Peter on his journey to the West.[123] But evidently the reconciliation was only temporary. Otherwise the knights named in our sources had good records of service. James of Nores had been turcopolier since before 1344 and had an outstanding military and diplomatic career. Raymond Babin, in whose house the conspirators were said to have met prior to the murder, had also been a prominent counsellor from the time of Hugh IV. Henry of Jubail was a regular participant in Peter's campaigns, while John of Gaurelle had gone with the king on his first visit to the West. With the exception of John Gorap, whose family is not known before 1350, all these men were descended from Cypriot vassals who were present in the island by the opening decades of the thirteenth century and who could trace their ancestry in the East back to the twelfth.[124]

Although the narrative sources explain the murder primarily in terms of personalities and the breakdown of mutual confidence and respect, there can be no doubt that there were other factors lying just below the surface which had prompted disaffection. Later on the day of the murder the High Court was convened to make provision for the regency occasioned by the minority of the heir to the throne, and the assembled vassals took the opportunity to issue an *ordonnance* designed to remedy a number of abuses. This enactment thus provides an invaluable guide to their grievances at the time.[125] Two clauses would seem to derive directly from the treatment of the Jubail family: the necessity for a judgement in the High Court before the king could lay hands on the person or fief of a vassal was re-affirmed, and the rights that a lord had over the marriage of heiresses or widows were summarized with emphasis on the point that the woman had to be married to a man of comparable social standing. Other clauses sought to defend the vassals' legal position in more general terms: they were to be able to swear to defend one another in the face of unjust legal actions by their lord; they were to have their rights and fiefs and not be made to perform services over and above what was due; the High Court was to meet regularly, at least once a month; and, to obviate doubt as to the customs to be employed, a copy of the legal treatise by the thirteenth-century count of Jaffa, John of Ibelin, was to be deposited in safe keeping for use as a work of reference.

[122] *Ibid.* §§269-71.
[123] Edbury, 'Murder of Peter I', p. 226 and note 9 (p. 231).   [124] *Ibid.*, pp. 225-7.
[125] For the text, 'Bans et Ordonnances', pp. 378-9. For the date (given incorrectly in the printed edition), Edbury, 'Murder of Peter I', p. 231 note 10.

Almost all the other clauses can be linked directly to the effects of Peter's wars on Cyprus. Henceforth the king was not to declare war, make peace or recruit more than a hundred men-at-arms without the vassals' consent. Evidently they took the view that they had been insufficiently consulted in the past. Another clause sought to restrict the right of mercenaries to discharge themselves at will. The number of men employed in the armed forces was a matter of some delicacy: the authorities were still trying to exert military pressure on the Mamlūks in the hope of getting favourable terms for peace, and unless they could hold their armies together they would be unable to do so. The problem was that, while no satisfactory conclusion to the fighting was in prospect, Cypriot resources were insufficient to maintain the war-effort. Indeed, the opening clauses of the *ordonnance* have much to say about the strains on royal finances due to the war. It would appear that special taxes for military purposes had been extended beyond the agreed terminal dates and the revenues put to other uses. Furthermore, in making his financial demands the king had managed to bypass the High Court and so had avoided consulting the vassals over taxation. He had also been alienating crown assets – the royal salt works are singled out for special mention – again without proper consultation.[126]

Clearly the war had been costing far more than the ordinary revenues of the Cypriot crown could sustain, and the king had been resorting to various expedients, some of which were of questionable legality or wisdom, to support his military endeavours. Leontios Makhairas has other information to illustrate this state of affairs: the wealth accumulated by Hugh IV had been used up in the expeditions against the Turks at the beginning of the reign; before each of the king's visits to the West revenue had been raised by allowing individuals to purchase immunity from the poll tax; as early as 1366 the king's counsellors had been showing concern at the cost of the military expeditions.[127] Other evidence shows that at the time of his death Peter was heavily in debt.[128] Royal insolvency, unsanctioned exactions and the dissipation of the sources of royal income were matters of concern to the king's leading subjects and were precisely the sort of issues that would generate ill-will.

But if the vassals resented the king's arbitrary behaviour, his failure to consult them on important questions of military or fiscal policy, and the consequences of the cost of warfare, they also felt threatened by his patronage of the foreign nobles he had welcomed into his service. Foreigners had received military commands;[129] Peter's chivalric order, the Order of the Sword, had been explicitly designed to appeal to them,[130] and he had rewarded them generously.

[126] Richard, 'La révolution', pp. 111–15.   [127] Leontios Makhairas, §§157, 182, 215.
[128] Gregory XI, *Lettres secrètes et curiales intéressant les pays autres que la France*, ed. G. Mollat (Paris, 1962–5), nos. 13, 20, 128, 134, 291, 718.
[129] See, for example, Leontios Makhairas, §§167, 190, 200; William of Machaut, pp. 138–45.
[130] M. H. Keen, *Chivalry* (New Haven/London, 1984), pp. 183, 185, 194–5.

Brémond of La Voulte, for example, had received the valuable estates of Polemidhia and Ayios Reginos near Limassol, and among other recipients of fiefs or annuities were the Greek John Lascaris Calopheros, the Frenchman Geoffrey of Ligier Luc, and the Genoese Ottobuono of Cathania.[131] The desire to avoid losing face in front of his western knights was probably the primary reason for Peter's acceptance of Florimond of Lesparre's challenge. Writing about twenty years after the murder, Philip of Mézières (another of the king's westerners) commented on the Cypriots' jealousy of the foreigners in royal service, and it is certainly true that after Peter's death there was a reaction against them as well as against other favourites such as John Moustry and the king's mistress, Eschiva of Scandelion.[132]

Indeed, the presence of foreign troops and nobles on Cypriot soil may have been an important consideration in persuading the Cypriots that the king would have to be killed. Because Peter had a significant force of men-at-arms at his disposal which he could call on independently of the traditional royal army officered by his vassals, he was in a position to threaten his own nobles should they try to concert action against him. The nobles feared that if they tried to restrain the king by getting him to renew his coronation oaths he would no more abide by them in the future than he had in the past and would simply wait for a convenient moment to strike back. Similarly, they would have known that suspending him from the exercise of royal authority as had happened to Henry II in 1306 would not work, since Peter could look elsewhere – in particular to the foreigners in his service – for support. The vassals were not the only element in the power-structure in Cyprus, and so to ensure that their action would be effective they had to pre-empt the possibility of a royal counter-coup. Nothing short of removing the king permanently would suffice.

Peter's murder highlights the effects the war had been having on Cypriot society. The strains and disappointments had clearly taken their toll on the king himself and must go some way at least to explaining his erratic and provocative behaviour. To pay for the war he had borrowed heavily and had disposed of crown assets, thereby leaving a legacy of insolvency for his successors. The nobles too were under pressure. They seem to have been happy to play their part in the campaigns but were worried by the costs involved and by the threat to their own position posed by the introduction of new men from outside. Another group who must have been concerned at the financial implications of the conflict and who could well have been apprehensive about the likely long-term commercial consequences if no satisfactory conclusion could be achieved were the Cypriot merchants. Many of them came from the non-Latin population of Famagusta, and they would already have suffered from the disruption of trade

---

[131] Mas Latrie, *Histoire*, II, 358–9; Richard, *Chypre sous les Lusignan*, pp. 80, 84, 91; Gregory XI, *Lettres secrètes . . . les pays autres*, nos. 1540, 2290.

[132] Jorga, *Philippe de Mézières*, pp. 386–7; Edbury, 'Murder of Peter I', p. 229.

between Famagusta and the ports under Mamlūk control. Some, such as Joseph Zaphet, who in the mid-1360s had transferred his activities to Montpellier, or the Nestorian Lakha brothers, whose fabulous riches were described by Leontios Makhairas, were clearly the equals of western merchants in terms of wealth and business acumen.[133] It was for this class's benefit that Peter had pressed for commercial privileges in his abortive negotiations with the sultanate in 1367 and 1368. These were the people who should have been the first to be able to profit from the capture of Alexandria or from the revival of trade through Cyprus following a Mamlūk defeat, and it is scarcely surprising that when in 1368 the peace negotiations were entrusted to members of the Genoese and Venetian mercantile communities – their rivals – they failed.

The sack of Alexandria and the raids that followed greatly damaged the interests of the western merchants. As mentioned previously, in 1366 the Venetians forbade their ships to carry men and war materials to Cyprus, and they were accused of spreading rumours of an armistice so as to deflect further recruitment in the West. Their object was to make peace with the sultan, get their own merchants and merchandise released, and, furnished with fresh papal licences, resume trading as soon as possible. The Catalans pursued a similar policy. In the spring of 1366 their king, Peter IV of Aragon, sent ambassadors to the sultan disassociating himself from the 1365 expedition and requesting the release of the Catalan merchants who had been interned by way of reprisal. At the same time he took action against those of his subjects who were known to have joined in the pillage at Alexandria, and, when early in 1367 Philip of Mézières came to Aragon in search of military assistance for Peter's war, he declined the help. After 1365 trade between Europe and the sultanate resumed remarkably quickly, although subsequent Cypriot raids and privateering and the uncertain temper of the Mamlūk government meant that the merchants' security remained precarious.[134]

The war had soured relations between Cyprus and the western mercantile communities as well as severely jeopardizing the Cypriots' own trade in the ports of the sultanate. But from 1366 an additional threat to the island's commerce loomed: the Venetian government began sponsoring galleys and cogs on a new route to Beirut.[135] If changing trade routes in Asia had encouraged the growth of Alexandria as an emporium for Far Eastern and Indian spices while routes through Cilicia and northern Syria and thence via Cyprus declined, any development of direct trade between Syria and the West – and Beirut, as the

[133] J. Combes, 'Un marchand de Chypre, bourgeois de Montpellier' in *Etudes médiévales offertes à M. le doyen Augustin Fliche* (Montpellier, 1952), pp. 33–9; Leontios Makhairas, §§91–6.

[134] M. Sáez Pomés, 'Un viaje del literato Felipe de Mézières a Catalunya en 1367', *Estudios de Edad Media de la Corona de Aragón*, IV (1951), 434–5; *idem*, 'Los Aragoneses en la conquista saqueo de Alejandría por Pedro I de Chipre', *ibid.*, V (1952), 385–91; Ashtor. *Levant Trade*, pp. 91–102.

[135] Ashtor, *Levant Trade*, pp. 96, 100.

principal outlet for Damascus, was the most important port on the Syrian coast – would strike another blow at Cyprus. It would mean that the western merchants would be bypassing Famagusta and, by dealing direct with the Muslims, would be cutting out the Cypriot middlemen. Up to a point western merchants had always traded in Syrian ports, but now that the Venetian government was actively promoting this route, it was likely that the proportion of trade flowing directly between Syria and the West would increase to the further detriment of Cyprus. Indeed, changing trade routes and the effects of the Black Death coupled with the loss of goodwill as a result of the sack of Alexandria spelled the end of Cyprus' prosperity through long-distance trade. Peter's war, which arguably had been intended to enable the island to recover something of its share of international commerce, probably succeeded in aggravating its decline. It had been a gamble that had failed. The Genoese capture of Famagusta in 1373 and the pillaging which accompanied it were to be the final disaster.

From the point of view of western Christendom and with the benefit of hindsight, the crusade can be seen as a great mistake. The campaigns of the 1360s against Egypt and Syria diverted attention to the eastern Mediterranean and away from the Aegean at precisely the time the Ottoman Turks were consolidating their position on the European side of the Bosphorus. Within a generation they had overrun much of the Balkans. So far as Europe was concerned, the theatre of conflict with the Muslims had now shifted decisively, and Cyprus was left as a distant and irrelevant outpost. With the minor exception of Marshal Boucicault's raid on Syria in 1403 and apart from occasional acts of piracy, there were to be no more Christian assaults on the Mamlūk sultanate. To that extent, the Alexandria expedition was the final chapter in a saga which had begun with the First Crusade and the capture of Jerusalem in 1099, although whether Peter also expected to be able to recover the Holy City as his apologists claimed is by no means certain.

8

KINGSHIP AND GOVERNMENT

THE SOCIAL and political system which operated in Lusignan Cyprus derived both from the island's Byzantine past and also from the concepts and institutions introduced by the new rulers after 1192. The monarchy remained essentially western in its outlook and attributes. What is known of the coronation ritual shows that the dynasty subscribed to ideas of kingship which belonged firmly within the European tradition.[1] At its inception, and theoretically until 1247, the kingdom existed as a dependency of the western empire, and Aimery, the first of the kings, was invested with a sceptre and diadem supplied by his suzerain, the Hohenstaufen Henry VI.[2] It is unfortunate that no crown jewels or insignia survive, but the royal seals and, from the early fourteenth century, the depiction of the monarch on the silver *gros* underline the distinctively European ethos of authority.[3] It is true that until the late thirteenth century the kings were represented on their bezants in Greek fashion wearing the chlamys or loros, although this is probably more a sign of their conservatism in maintaining an imitative coinage based on a Byzantine type familiar at the time of the conquest than a symbol of their concept of royalty. In any case the garments shown on these coins are not so very different from those seemingly being worn by some twelfth-century kings of Jerusalem on their seals.[4] The kings used the title 'rex', even when writing in Greek to the emperor at Nicaea, and made no attempt to adopt Byzantine formularies in their diplomatic correspondence. Their diplomas too conformed to the sub-Carolingian, western tradition of the private charter current in Latin Syria: unlike the kings Cilician Armenia, whose royal title had also been conferred by the western emperor in the 1190s, the Lusignans did not issue Byzantine-style chrysobulls.[5] There is thus no suggestion that they

---

[1] There is no pontifical from Cyprus giving a coronation *ordo*, but see H. E. Mayer, 'Das Pontifikale von Tyrus und die Krönung der lateinischen Könige von Jerusalem', *DOP*, XXI (1967), 222–4; Florio Bustron, pp. 282–7.   [2] Mas Latrie, *Histoire*, I, 127; II, 31.

[3] G. Schlumberger *et al.*, *Sigillographie de l'Orient latin* (Paris, 1943), pp. 143–52; Richard, *Chypre sous les Lusignans*, plate IV; Metcalf, *Coinage of the Crusades*, plates 19–27.

[4] Metcalf, *Coinage of the Crusades*, pp. 51–3; cf. Mayer, 'Pontifikale', plates 3–4.

[5] J. Richard, 'La diplomatique royale dans les royaumes d'Armenie et de Chypre (XIIe–XVe siècles)', *BEC*, CXLIV (1986), 73–4, 76, 83 (citing a letter to John Vatatzes in which Henry I used the title ῥήξ).

projected themselves as the successors to the rebel emperor Isaac Comnenus, and, although they exercised various rights which they had inherited from the Greeks, they did not see their authority primarily in Byzantine terms.

The dynasty's insistence on western as opposed to Byzantine ceremonial is further illustrated by the appointment of the traditional grand sergeants: the seneschal, constable, marshal, chamberlain and butler. In the twelfth century these offices had been introduced from Europe into the Latin East, and a Cypriot seneschal, constable and marshal all made their appearance as early as the 1190s.[6] The first known chamberlain of Cyprus is recorded in 1218, but there is no evidence for the presence of a butler until 1328.[7] In the fourteenth century Hugh IV revived the posts of seneschal, constable, marshal and butler of Jerusalem; a chamberlain of Jerusalem appeared in 1360, and when in 1394 James I was crowned king of the now defunct Armenian kingdom on the death of his distant kinsman, Leo VI, he appointed Cypriot knights as marshal and chamberlain of Armenia. From the early thirteenth century the seneschals and constables came from the higher nobility or from the royal house itself, while the holders of the other sergeanties were almost always knights from well-established families.[8] But whereas in certain instances in Latin Syria and commonly in the West these posts became hereditary, in no case in Cyprus was their tenure heritable until the late fifteenth century.[9]

There is no doubt that prestige and honour accrued to the occupants of these positions and that the grand sergeants had a major part to play in the pageantry and solemnities of royal government. But it is worth asking whether their offices only carried with them duties on formal occasions or if they also involved vital tasks in the day-to-day running of the kingdom. Writing in the 1260s about the kingdom of Jerusalem, John of Ibelin count of Jaffa described in detail the ceremonial role of the seneschal, constable, marshal and chamberlain on the day of the king's coronation and, in the case of the seneschal and the chamberlain, at other formal crown wearings, before giving an account of their administrative and military functions.[10] Most interesting is his account of the duties of the seneschal. According to John the seneschal was responsible for overseeing all royal *baillis* and *escrivains*, except those of the royal household, and for supervising their financial returns; for letting at farm the sources of royal

---

[6] Mas Latrie, *Histoire*, III, 599, 607.

[7] *Liber Iurium*, I, 625; Mas Latrie, *Histoire*, II, 140, 144.

[8] For the Cypriot grand sergeants and the fourteenth-century grand sergeants of Jerusalem and Armenia, P. W. Edbury, 'The Feudal Nobility of Cyprus, 1192–1400' (unpublished PhD thesis, St Andrews University, 1974), pp. 414–48.

[9] For the hereditary chamberlains of Jerusalem and constables of Tripoli, L. de Mas Latrie, 'Le fief de la Chamberlaine et les chambellans de Jérusalem', *BEC*, XLIII (1882), 651–2; J. Richard, *Le comté de Tripoli sous la dynastie toulousaine* (1102–1187) (Paris, 1945), pp. 49–50. For hereditary constables and marshals of Cyprus from the 1470s, C. du Fresne du Cange, *Les familles d'Outremer*, ed. E. G. Rey (Paris, 1869) pp. 682–3, 688–9.

[10] John of Ibelin, pp. 407–14, cf. p. 31.

income; for provisioning castles and appointing officers below the rank of
castellan; for presiding at the High Court in the absence of the king or his
deputy; normally he would be at the king's side in battle, and he took charge of
the king's share of the spoils of war. Perhaps as an afterthought John concluded
by mentioning that the seneschal's responsibilities included authorizing the
payment of assignations and other disbursements from the *secrète*. But Cypriot
evidence offers no corroboration for the seneschal exercising the major
administrative role that John had described. For example, in the fourteenth
century it was the *bailli* of the *secrète* to whom the *escrivains* of the *cour des
bourgeois* rendered account and who transmitted royal instructions to royal
baillis throughout the island,[11] and there is nothing to suggest that the *bailli* of
the *secrète* was himself held answerable to the seneschal. On the other hand, the
seneschal did preside at the High Court in the absence of the monarch, although
the evidence does not say much for his effectiveness in this role: in 1324 on the
death of Henry II and in 1369 on the death of Peter I the High Court met to give
its formal recognition to the new king, but on neither occasion could the
seneschal be present and the vassals had to choose one of their own number who,
as acting-seneschal, could conduct the business before them.[12]

The duties of the constable as described by John of Jaffa were basically those
of commander-in-chief: when the king went on campaign the constable was
under his direction, but otherwise he could be called upon to lead the army
himself. He had power to decide who should be summoned to perform military
service, and he had a court which took cognizance of military discipline and
matters such as disputed claims over pay. There are a number of instances on
which the constable can be seen acting as a commander: for example, Walter of
Caesarea led the Cypriots at Damietta during the Fifth Crusade, and Guy of
Ibelin shared the command with his brother during St Louis' expedition to
Egypt.[13] But our sources, other than the legal treatises, tell little about the
constable's military jurisdiction, although his control over the hiring of
mercenaries is attested in 1369.[14] The marshal's functions consisted in the main
of assisting the constable and acting as his deputy; he had jurisdiction over
squires and special responsibilities for horses, and he held his office from the
constable by feudal tenure. Here too evidence to illustrate the routine exercise
of his duties is lacking, although there is no doubt that the marshals regularly

[11] 'Abrégé des Assises', p. 243; *DVL*, I, 199.
[12] 'Documents relatifs à la successibilité', pp. 419–20; John of Ibelin, p. 3 (where the printed text at
line 6 should read, '. . . dou seneschau dou royaume de chipre'; Cod. Vat. lat. 4789 fo. 19 col. 1).
In 1324 the office may have been vacant. In 1369 the seneschal, James of Lusignan, was in
Famagusta. Leontios Makhairas, §283.
[13] 'Eracles', pp. 339–40; Joinville, pp. 95, 119, 121, 125–6.
[14] 'Le Livre au Roi', *RHC Lois*, I, 615–16; John of Ibelin, pp. 209–11, 212; 'Bans et Ordonnances',
p. 379. For evidence from 1367 that the constable was empowered to take purveyances for
supplying the army, Richard, 'Un évêque', pp. 118, 131–3.

participated in military expeditions: Simon of Montolif, for example, is known to have been killed at the siege of Acre in 1291, and John of Morphou served with distinction at Alexandria in 1365.[15]

The chamberlain administered the act of homage owed to the king by his vassals. He was entitled to a fee for this service, which at the beginning of Peter II's reign amounted to ten bezants.[16] However, it is not altogether clear whether this duty had always been his exclusive prerogative: two thirteenth-century writers, Geoffrey Le Tor and James of Ibelin, seem to indicate that the ceremony could be conducted by any liege man.[17] None of the legal treatises mentioned the duties of the fifth grand sergeant, the butler. It would appear that in Jerusalem, where the office-holder normally took the title of *pincerna*, the post had fallen into disuse by the end of the twelfth century.[18] In Cyprus *boutelerii* of both Cyprus and Jerusalem first appear in the fourteenth century, early in the reign of Hugh IV, and it is likely that the king had revived these posts at the time of his accession.[19] There is no reason to suppose that their holders ever had anything more than a ceremonial role.

One way of gauging the extent to which these offices played an essential part in the kingdom's routine administration is to see whether they were allowed to remain vacant for any appreciable periods. In the case of the fourteenth-century grand sergeants of Jerusalem a clear pattern is discernible. Henry II seems not to have made any appointments between 1291 and his death in 1324; Hugh IV, Peter I, Peter II, and also James I appointed men to fill these positions at their accession, and then, as one by one their appointees died, they left the offices unfilled.[20] The implication is clear: the grand sergeants performed their ceremonial function at the coronation and otherwise did nothing. On the other hand, the start of a new reign was not the only occasion on which kings filled vacant Cypriot grand sergeanties. For example, Henry I replaced Balian lord of Beirut as constable of Cyprus with Balian's brother Guy after his death in 1246,

---

[15] 'Livre au Roi', pp. 613–14, 615–16; John of Ibelin, pp. 212, 410–14. For 1291, 'Lignages', p. 463. For 1365, William of Machaut, p. 74; cf. Leontios Makhairas, §§119, 163, 190, 200, 285. For the constable and marshal's military jurisdiction in the West, M. H. Keen, *The Laws of War in the Late Middle Ages* (London, 1965), pp. 26–8.

[16] Mas Latrie, *Histoire*, II, 425; John of Ibelin, p. 414, cf. p. 400.

[17] Geoffrey Le Tor, 'Livre de Geoffrey le Tort', *RHC Lois*, I, 445; James of Ibelin, p. 454 (but note the variant reading specifying the role of the chamberlain).

[18] The last reference is dated 1186. *RRH*, no. 657.

[19] Mas Latrie, *Histoire*, II, 140, 144; *DVL*, I, 210, 214.

[20] The only possible exceptions date from Peter I's reign. According to Leontios Makhairas, Peter appointed his brother James constable of Jerusalem in succession to James of Ibelin (§119). Leontios (§104) also states that Peter appointed John Viscount marshal of Jerusalem in 1360, although later in the reign Simon Tenoury is found with this office. Mas Latrie, *Histoire*, II, 254; John of Ibelin, p. 6. But Leontios is frequently mistaken about these appointments, and it is possible that James of Lusignan was appointed at the time of Peter II's coronation and that neither James of Ibelin nor John Viscount held office.

and on Balian of Ibelin's death in 1302 Henry II appointed his brother Philip of Ibelin to be seneschal.[21] Henry II had at least four constables during his reign and Hugh IV at least two.[22] The chief problem is that the evidence is so patchy. Thus although the documentary materials for the period are relatively plentiful and the post of constable remained filled, there is no evidence for there being a seneschal, marshal or chamberlain of Cyprus between Henry I's majority in 1232 and the year 1247. It is therefore by no means certain that kings always replaced vacated Cypriot sergeanties, and the picture is obscured still further by the dearth of sources for the third quarter of the thirteenth century and the likelihood that no appointments could be made during the long royal minorities which occupied so much of the island's history between 1205 and the accession of Hugh III in 1267. The eminence of many of the appointees and the absence of concrete evidence to illustrate the routine duties of their office raise further difficulties in assessing their role. Did Philip of Ibelin acquire his dominance in the reign of Henry II because he held the post of seneschal or because he was the king's uncle? Did John prince of Antioch play a major part in the campaigns of the 1360s because he was constable or because as brother of the king he naturally had a place as one of the greatest lords in the kingdom?

At best therefore we have to be content with a hypothesis. It is possible that under Guy of Lusignan, Aimery, and Hugh I the grand sergeanties carried onerous responsibilities and that the constable continued to fulfil his military duties long afterwards, but later in the thirteenth century and more definitely in the fourteenth appointments to these offices became more a matter of honouring men who were either members of the royal family, leading magnates or already prominent as royal counsellors. The existence of grand sergeants is not therefore a pointer to the structure of royal administration; their significance lies rather in what they have to say about contemporary notions of monarchy. The kings needed the traditional officers of state for the same reason that they used conventional iconography and maintained the long-established rituals on great occasions: they wanted to be seen as monarchs in a time-honoured mould that placed them firmly in the European tradition of kingship and gave them the right to be treated as equals by the other kings in Latin Christendom. In surrounding themselves with specially selected vassals who would perform the ritual acts of service that belonged with their offices they were not just conferring distinction on the individuals concerned but were basking in the reflected glory of men who by blood, prowess or service would in their turn add lustre to the crown.

---

[21] For Balian of Beirut, RRH, nos. 1071, 1078, 1092. For Guy of Ibelin, Layettes du Trésor des Chartes, ed. A. Teulet et al. (Paris, 1863–1909), no. 3648. For Balian and Philip of Ibelin, 'Gestes', p. 857; 'Amadi', 238.

[22] Baldwin of Ibelin, Guy of Lusignan, Aimery of Lusignan, and Hugh, later Hugh IV; Humphrey of Montfort, Guy of Lusignan, and probably John prince of Antioch.

As kings of Cyprus the Lusignans took the lead in both peace and war, acted as the guardians of justice and equity, accepted their duty as the protectors of their people, possessed a wide range of prerogatives and, in consequence of their wealth and pre-eminence, controlled the most extensive network of patronage in their island realm. As *chef seigneurs* they took homage and fealty from their vassals and so stood in a special relationship to all the major secular landholders from whose ranks they drew many of their counsellors, military commanders and officials. They were careful to retain the major towns as part of their domain, and at no point did they grant any significant fortification in the island to a vassal to be held as a part of his fief. Commercial taxation and defence thus remained royal monopolies, and the financial and military advantages that resulted meant that, except under extraordinary circumstances as in 1310, armed insurrection could never be a serious proposition. Hand in hand with royal control of towns and fortifications went royal control over the administration of justice. In striking contrast to the situation in both the kingdom of Jerusalem and in Frankish Greece, there was no privatization of judicial authority with the result that no Cypriot vassal ever acquired legal franchises such as the right to try criminal cases for which the penalty would be death or mutilation. The only inroads into the kings' control of justice came about as a result of the privileges granted to the Genoese and Venetian communities and meant that their nationals were justiciable by their own officers. The kings also seem to have retained rights over public roads – what Philip of Novara referred to as 'vaselico', a term which is to be understood as his rendering of the Byzantine $\beta\alpha\sigma\iota\lambda\iota\kappa\dot{\eta}$ $\gamma\hat{\eta}$ and which another legal writer translated as 'chemin reau' – and one implication of this would presumably have been that landowners could not levy tolls on the traffic on major highways crossing their estates.[23] The production of salt, notably at the salines near the modern town of Larnaca, remained a royal monopoly, as did the minting of coins. In contrast to the situation in Latin Syria where in the thirteenth century an array of western coinage circulated alongside the local issues, in Cyprus the authorities ensured that the silver currency in daily use came from their own mints.[24] Taken together these royal prerogatives clearly point to the Lusignans inheriting and adapting much of the substance and concept of Byzantine public authority.

But like all western monarchs the kings remained limited by convention and precedent as well as by practical considerations, and their capacity to act depended to a considerable extent on the advice and co-operation of their leading men. Peter I's violation of feudal custom was a principal element in the

[23] Philip of Novara, p. 533; J. Prawer, *Crusader Institutions* (Oxford, 1980), p. 166.
[24] For salt, Richard, 'La révolution', p. 113. For the absence of foreign coins, Metcalf, 'A Decline', pp. 264–5; cf. *idem*, *Coinage of the Crusades*, pp. 91–3.

events leading to his assassination in 1369, and it is noteworthy that on that occasion the vassals considered making him renew his coronation oaths; they were no doubt thinking primarily of the promise to abide by the law and customs of the kingdom that he would have made at the start of his reign. The *ordonnance* issued directly after Peter's death laid down that in future the king could not declare war, make peace or recruit more than a hundred men-at-arms without 'the assent of all the vassals or the greater part of them', but although kings doubtless discussed military policy with their chosen counsellors there is nothing to suggest that hitherto they had been under any obligation to gain the approval of their liegemen as a whole. At the same time it was asserted that there could be no taxation or financial impositions without the vassals' agreement, and here, by contrast, the document's wording clearly implies that their consent to extraordinary taxation had hitherto been normal.[25] It is worth noting, however, that in 1369 there was no suggestion that consent to military policy or taxation should be sought beyond the comparatively restricted circle of the royal vassals: participation from the 'Third Estate' had no place in the system of governance. Although the urban population could be called together at times of particular gravity, such meetings seem to have been organized on a purely *ad hoc* basis and showed no sign of developing the characteristics of communal government or of providing the framework for the regular involvement of the populace in representative institutions.[26]

All royal vassals had access to the High Court. This remained the king's court *par excellence*, the highest tribunal in the realm, and it was here that a wide variety of his judicial and governmental business was transacted and received its validation. The law, customs and procedures of the court had been imported from Jerusalem at the time of the Latin settlement of Cyprus. The king, advised by his men, who were thereby fulfilling their formal obligation to provide *consilium*, normally presided in person. Questions of royal succession and regency were determined in the High Court; all matters concerning fiefs and fiefholders came within its competence; it was the forum in which the feudatories could engage in litigation, and it was there that they gave assent to the alienation of royal lands and to diplomatic treaties. It also had legislative powers: in 1311, for example, the High Court gave its approval to a measure which sought to resolve the legal difficulties arising from the interruption of normal royal government caused by the usurpation of Amaury of Tyre, and in 1312 it passed an *assise* (apparently re-enacted in 1355) which dealt with an assortment of matters including ownership of strayed falcons, dogs and horses.[27]

[25] 'Bans et Ordonnances', pp. 378–9.
[26] B. Arbel, 'Urban Assembles and Town Councils in Frankish and Venetian Cyprus', Πρακτικα του Δευτέρου Διεθνοῦς Κυπριολογικοῦ Συνεδρίου, II, (Nicosia, 1986), 204–5.
[27] Perrat, 'Un diplomate gascon', pp. 82–3; Mas Latrie, *Histoire*, II, 423; 'Ban et ordonnances', pp. 368–70, 373–7.

The line between enactments agreed in the High Court which had the effect of changing the law and administrative instructions which the king could issue to his officials on his own authority could be a fine one. In 1300 Henry II empowered the viscount of Nicosia to change the procedures for arraigning criminals before the *cour des bourgeois*, but the viscount and the jurats of his court refused to accept the new measures on the grounds that they contravened the *assises* and *usages* which they had sworn to apply. Eventually there was a showdown: the viscount was dismissed and the oath to be taken by his successors and the jurats amended to include an undertaking to accept the king's 'special commandment' even if it seemed at variance with the customs and usages of the kingdom. Had the viscount been required to enforce a new *assise* issued in the High Court with the consent of the liegemen there would have been no argument; his objection was to Henry in effect changing the law by decree. This episode is a useful reminder that the king could and did act independently of the High Court in his dealings with his own administrators. What seems extraordinary was that the viscount should have risked his own position by turning the matter into an issue of principle.[28]

Although there is a wealth of information on the judicial procedures applicable in the High Court, not much is known about the overall structure of its workings. How far litigation was separated from what might be loosely described as government business is unclear. Nor do we know how well attended the court was, although it is probably safe to assume that the greatest lords and those closest to the king took a dominant role and that kings normally met little opposition. On one occasion in the 1230s, however, a large number of vassals complaining about the arrears in paying their fief-rents confronted King Henry I.[29] In the fifteenth century just two vassals, who together with the king as president constituted a quorum, witnessed the High Court's written *acta*; how many others would have been present when the business itself was transacted is unrecorded.[30] There is also a question mark over the frequency of its meetings and its adequacy as a court where the vassals could gain redress. In 1306 there were complaints about delays of up to twenty years, and in 1369 it was laid down that the court should meet at least once a month so that people could be given a hearing. But at the end of the fourteenth century the celebrated Lusignan apologist, Philip of Mézières, could nevertheless hold up the Cypriot judicial system as a model of equitable and speedy justice.[31]

---

[28] 'Abrégé des Assises', pp. 320–3; cf. 'Bans et Ordonnances', pp. 370–1.
[29] Philip of Novara, pp. 515–16; John of Ibelin, pp. 383–4.
[30] See, for example, Richard, *Chypre sous les Lusignan*, pp. 139–57 *passim*; *Le Livre des remembrances de la secrète du royaume de Chypre (1468–1469)* ed. J. Richard and T. Papadopoullos (Nicosia, 1983), nos. 145–85.
[31] 'Texte officiel', p. 536; 'Bans et Ordonnances', p. 379; Philip of Mézières, *Le Songe du Vieil Pelerin*, I, 487.

The High Court provided a formal setting for kings to speak with their liegemen, but kings also took advice less formally from whomever they might choose to consult. For their part the leading men in the kingdom expected to gain their monarch's ear. A major complaint against Henry II was that he relied exclusively on the counsel of his uncle, Philip of Ibelin, and his disregard of his other vassals prompted the charge in 1306 that he had allowed various abuses to continue 'sans nul conseil, sauve le conseil de volonté'. Taking proper advice was sensible; royal wilfulness was not.[32] Out of the practice of informal consultation grew the royal Council. Its origins are necessarily obscure. Speaking in 1271 James of Ibelin provided an early reference to royal counsellors: in 1248 Henry I had summoned his vassals to serve on St Louis' crusade to Damietta; they, however, refused to answer the summons on the grounds that it went beyond their feudal obligations, but the king and those who were counselling him, so James alleged, prevented the court from taking the opportunity to make a ruling on the issue.[33] In his legal treatise, written in 1276, James made a more specific allusion to the Council: it was treasonable to betray its secrets.[34] However, it is not until the fourteenth century that references to the Council or to royal counsellors become frequent. In 1311 the king and his Council discussed a memorandum to be sent to the pope on the subject of the recovery of the Holy Land, and in the reigns of Peter I and Peter II the 'lords of the Council' are regularly mentioned advising the monarch on military and diplomatic matters.[35] Only a scattering of individuals are specifically described as counsellors in the surviving sources: among them members of the royal family such as John of Lusignan lord of Beirut in 1395; knights such as Hugh Beduin, Thomas of Picquigny and Simon of Montolif in 1328, John Beduin in 1344 and Peter of Caffran in 1390; clergy such as the Franciscan Aimery, later bishop of Paphos, in 1315; and foreigners such as Giustino dei Giustini in 1328 or the physician Guido da Bagnolo in 1365.[36] It has to be assumed that the Council met behind closed doors, that its composition varied according to circumstances, and that no one had a place there as of right. Those members of the Council who were liegemen would probably have taken a prominent role in expediting royal business in the High Court, but there is nothing to suggest that the Council came to acquire any of the High Court's juridical functions.

For the thirteenth century information is sparse on the subject of the royal central administration and its personnel. On the one hand it is possible to piece

---

[32] 'Texte officiel', p. 536; 'Gestes', p. 857.

[33] 'Document relatif au service militaire', p. 432.

[34] James of Ibelin, p. 459. Cf. Philip of Novara, p. 487. For the confidentiality of Council business, see also 'Bans et Ordonnances', p. 371.

[35] Mas Latrie, *Histoire*, II, 119; John Dardel, p. 44; Leontios Makhairas, §§123, 182, 192, 411 (ἄρχοντες τῆς βουλῆς του), cf. §§373, 390.

[36] Mas Latrie, *Histoire*, II, 266, 420, 428; III, 705; *DVL*, I, 210; Clement VI, *Lettres closes . . . France*, no. 833.

together a partial sequence of chancellors of the kingdom, and on the other there is a single isolated reference to a *bailli* of the *secrète* – Arneis of Jubail, who is mentioned as holding that office in Philip of Novara's narrative of the events of 1231.[37] As earlier in the kingdom of Jerusalem, the chancellor's duties involved drafting the king's formal *acta* and diplomatic correspondence. It was a post which required that its holder should be able to express the king's wishes with legal precision. All the known chancellors before 1300 were Latin clergy, beneficed in one or other of the cathedrals on the island: in the 1190s Alan, archdeacon of Lydda and first archbishop of Nicosia; in the time of Hugh I Ralph, archdeacon of Nicosia; under Henry I a canon of Nicosia named Bonvassal of Aude; Peter bishop of Paphos under Hugh III, and then Henry of Jubail, archdeacon of Nicosia, who had already taken office by 1289 and is last found in 1330.[38] But in the fourteenth century the pattern changed. After Henry of Jubail no chancellors are known until the appointment of Uomobuono of Mantua, a royal physician, at the beginning of Peter I's reign. Another layman, Philip of Mézières who had taken office by March 1363, soon followed.[39] After Peter's murder Philip lived in the West while remaining nominally chancellor of Cyprus, and, although a vice-chancellor is mentioned in documents from the mid-1370s,[40] no other chancellor of the kingdom is known until after the middle of the fifteenth century. Henry of Jubail too stayed away from the island for several years, and his chequered career must have prevented him from performing his functions as chancellor regularly. At the end of his life he was definitely delegating his duties.[41]

The fact that royal business could proceed without the presence of a chancellor for years at a time would suggest that the office had become something of a sinecure, and it is clear that in practice the task of drawing up the king's legal documents passed at some point, probably during the reign of Henry II, into the hands of laymen whom the kings employed because they were qualified as notaries. In 1328 John *de Galiana*, 'publicus imperiali auctoritate notarius et nunc ipsius domini regis cancellarie scriba publicus', was drafting royal documents. The following year we find Stephen of Cyprus, 'publicus imperiali auctoritate notarius et judex ordinarius' – elsewhere he is described as

---

[37] 'Gestes', p. 710.

[38] Richard, 'La diplomatique royale', p. 77. For the earliest reference to Henry of Jubail as chancellor, Nicholas IV, no. 1013.

[39] Mas Latrie, *Histoire*, II, 230, 249. For Uomobuono, see also Leontios Makhairas, §§100 and note 233. Cf. *I libri commemoriali*, II, 281.

[40] Mas Latrie, *Histoire*, III, 781 note 1, cf. p. 778 note 2; Gregory XI, *Lettres secrètes . . . les pays autres*, no. 2073.

[41] Henry was at the papal court between 1308 and 1313 unsuccessfully seeking recognition as archbishop of Nicosia. *Reg. Clementis V*, nos. 8013, 9815; *I Testamenti di cardinali del ducento*, ed. A. Paravicini Bagliani (Rome, 1980), p. 445. Twice in the 1280s and 1290s he had been under sentence of excommunication, and on a previous visit to the papal curia in the mid-1300s he had been imprisoned. Nicholas IV, no. 1013; Boniface VIII, no. 1317; *Reg. Clementis V*, appendices pp. 353–4, cf. no. 9815. For his delegation of duties, Mas Latrie, *Histoire*, II, 164.

a 'notary of the lord king' – acting in the same capacity, and at the end of the fourteenth century king's chancellors as distinct from chancellors of the kingdom were preparing the king's legal *acta*: Odo Benedict, 'sacre majestatis Jerusalem et Cypri regie cancellarius', in 1389, and Manuel *de Valente*, 'imperiali auctoritate notarius et . . . domini regis cancellarius' in 1395.[42] Like the famous twelfth-century chancellor of Jerusalem, William of Tyre, the clerics who held office as chancellor in the thirteenth century had probably received some legal training. But the subsequent use of notaries who were laymen nevertheless suggests a greater professionalism in the royal secretariat. It may also imply that the kings had less opportunity to secure ecclesiastical benefices for their servants. The last fourteenth-century chancellor, Philip of Mézières, was a knight who is not known to have studied law.[43] Maybe he owed his position to the king's desire to have him in his service as a counsellor, diplomat and propagandist and had little part in the routine business of his office.

In the fourteenth century if not earlier, the chancery came to acquire a judicial function – that of scrutinizing petitions presented to the king. From 1324 there is a reference to a Venetian merchant being allowed to apply to the chancery and the *cour des bourgeois* for redress; the precise circumstances are unclear, but presumably as a foreigner he would not have had access to the High Court, and although he could sue in the *cour des bourgeois* it may be that his case raised questions which went beyond its competence; a petition to the king, or rather to the chancery, might thus provide the only prospect of satisfaction.[44] The employment of western-trained lawyers and the appearance of a 'protonotary of the royal chancery of Cyprus' in 1378 and then of a certain Thomas *de Zenariis* of Padua, 'legum doctor, judex cancellarie regni Cipri', who remained active in the island for several years after 1398, strongly suggests that petitioners may have had their cases considered in the light of Roman Law precepts rather than in line with Cypriot and Latin Syrian custom.[45]

The kings needed men like Thomas *de Zenariis* who had received a thorough training in civil law in western Europe. Their expertise was indispensable in the legal aspects of international diplomacy, and some rose high as royal counsellors. Although Cypriots such as Bartholomew of Conches, 'publicus apostolica auctoritate notarius', and Philip Chappe, 'utriusque juris professor', did go to the West to study law,[46] the kings frequently recruited foreigners. Although a 'Magister Petrus Vuasco' and a 'Magister Bernardus medicus' are found in the king's entourage as far back as 1195, the first of these European-trained lawyers whose career can be traced in any detail was Giustino dei

[42] *Ibid.*, II, 142, 158, 164, 418, 429; Richard, 'La diplomatique royale', pp. 78–9.
[43] Jorga, *Philippe de Mézières*, p. 27.   [44] *DVL*, I, 199.
[45] Mas Latrie, *Histoire*, II, 372, 441, 495; 'Nouvelles preuves' (1874), p. 120.
[46] For Bartholomew (1315), 'Nouvelles preuves' (1873), p. 64. For Philip (1319), John XXII, *Lettres communes*, no. 9950.

Giustini, a native of Città di Castello, who was acting as a secretary to Henry II in 1309. From then until about 1342 'Justinus de Justinis, jurisperitus, consiliarius regis' remained in regular attendance on both Henry and Hugh IV.[47] In the 1360s and 1370s the Lombard knight, James of St Michael, 'in legibus doctor' evidently occupied a similar role as a prominent royal servant and legal adviser, eventually becoming vice-chancellor of the kingdom.[48] Two other legal specialists, both of whom acquired the title of 'judex' of the lord king and so were perhaps precursors of Thomas de Zenariis as chancery judges, were Matteo dei Pasquali who served Hugh IV during the first half of his reign and Domenico Rodolfi of Bologna who appears in 1360.[49] But irrespective of whether they held a formal position in government or simply belonged in the king's entourage, these lawyers were obviously greatly valued. And not only lawyers. As has been seen, Peter I made his Italian physician, Uomobuono of Mantua, chancellor, and another physician, Guido da Bagnolo of Reggio, served him as a counsellor and diplomat.[50]

The secrète was the king's central financial office where the farmers of the royal estates and the viscounts and other royal officials rendered account. From its receipts were disbursed pensions and annuities and other items of government expenditure. It seems to have had an extensive archive, which included details of fief-rents, information about rights of restor and registers of title to property and royal debts.[51] Physical control of the personnel and records of the secrète was seen as essential: thus in 1306 Amaury of Tyre had it moved from the royal palace to his own residence, and on the king's restoration in 1310 it was transferred back again.[52] The name would seem to indicate that it was descended from the Byzantine σέκρετον but the paucity of materials for its workings during

---

[47] Mas Latrie, Histoire, II, 141–2, 150, 158, 162, 164, 167, 179, 202, III, 705; 'Nouvelles preuves' (1873), p. 64; DVL, I, 210–11, 214; I libri commemoriali, I, 111, II, 69; 'Amadi', p. 310. For the magistri of 1195, Mas Latrie, Histoire, III, 599.

[48] For his origin, 'Amadi', p. 479. For other references, Biblioteca bio-bibliografica della Terra Santa e dell'Oriente francescano, ed. G. Golubovich (Quarrachi, 1906–27), V, 165; Gregory XI, Lettres secrètes . . . les pays autres, nos. 2073, 3616, 3652; Philip of Mézières, St Peter Thomas, p. 169; Leontios Makhairas, §§147, 333–5, 500, 515, 524.

[49] Mas Latrie, Histoire, II, 158, 162, 164, 179, 230, III, 725; Richard, Chypre sous les Lusignans, p. 58 note 2.

[50] Mas Latrie, Histoire, II, 249, 254, 255, 265, 266, 302; R. Livi, 'Guido da Bagnolo, medico de re di Cipro', Atti e memorie della R. deputazione di Storia Patria per le provincie Modenesi, ser. 5, XI, (1918).

[51] Mas Latrie, Histoire, II, 148, 154, 163, 184, 423–5; 'Texte officiel', pp. 538–9; Gregory XI, Lettres secrètes . . . autres que la France, no. 128; Richard, Chypre sous les Lusignans, pp. 79, 103; Philip of Novara, pp. 511, 550; 'Bans et Ordonnances', pp. 369, 372; 'Abrégé des Assises', pp. 241, 243, 255, 287; Leontios Makhairas, §§157, 402, (Dawkins errs in translating σύγκριτον as 'chancery'); 'Amadi', p. 495. for the secrète in the fifteenth century Le Livre des remembrances, introduction passim1.

[52] 'Amadi', pp. 249, 252, 346, 348. By the 1370s it seems to have had its own premises. Leontios Makhairas, §454.

the first century of Lusignan rule means that it is impossible to be certain how far continuity from the previous regime had been maintained at the time of the Latin conquest.[53] There does, however, appear to have been a tradition for the office to be staffed by Greeks, although it is not until 1318 that an *escrivain*, George Capadoca, is actually mentioned by name. When in the fifteenth century evidence becomes more plentiful, it is found that all the *secrète* officials except the *bailli* had names that betray their Greek or Syrian origin.[54]

The head of the *secrète*, the *bailli*, was a Latin, and until well into the fifteenth century this office was normally held by a knight. The list of *baillis*, however, is fragmentary: after Arneis of Jubail, *bailli* in 1231, there is no recorded occupant of the post until Thomas of Picquigny in 1301. Hugh Beduin was *bailli* in 1314, and James of Fleury in 1315; Thomas of Picquigny had returned to office by 1318 and remained there until at least as late as 1338. Under Peter I the post was held by John Tenoury (1360) and then Nicholas *Catellus* (1362) and under Peter II by Thomas of Montolif (1372–83).[55] The title was sometimes embellished. Philip of Novara speaks of the 'grant bailli' of the *secrète*, and in the late fourteenth century Renier of Scolar is described as 'secrete regie Cipri capitaneus et ballivus'.[56] But although the chancery came to be staffed by western-trained lawyers, many of them from Europe, it would seem that the *secrète* remained the preserve of Cypriots. The *escrivains* were recruited from a group of families who can be thought of as forming a professional civil service. On one occasion Leontios Makhairas mentions a grand chancellor (καντζιλιέρης μέγας) of the *secrète* who was a notary (1370) and on another a judge (νομόκριτος) of the *secrète* (1432), but except for these two stray references there is no sign that professional lawyers featured among its personnel.[57]

Although it is clear that the organs of central government did not remain static during the centuries of Lusignan rule, the surviving evidence allows at best a partial insight into how the system worked. Philip of Novara and the other legal writers of the mid-thirteenth century describe the High Court at length and refer to the *cour des bourgeois*, but they make no reference to what were presumably

[53] Note, however, that Leontios Makhairas uses the form σύγκριτον rather than σέκρετον.

[54] Richard, 'Psimolofo', pp. 124, 140; *idem*, *Chypre sous les Lusignans*, p. 12; *Le Livre des remembrances*, pp. xiii–xiv.

[55] Thomas of Picquigny: 'Bans et Ordonnances', p. 365. Hugh: Martínez Ferrando, *Jaime II*, II, 101, 107. James: 'Nouvelles preuves' (1873), p. 64. Thomas of Picquigny again: Mas Latrie, *Histoire*, II, 150, 158, 162, 167, 178; *DVL*, I, 210, 214; *I libri commemoriali*, II, 54, 69; John XXII, *Lettres secrètes*, no. 2003; John XXII, *Lettres communes*, no. 43150; Richard, 'Psimolofo', p. 140; 'Amadi', p. 401. John: *DVL*, II, 64. Nicholas: Livi, 'Guido da Bagnolo', p. 54. Thomas of Montolif: Mas Latrie, *Histoire*, II, 396; Gregory XI, *Lettres secrètes . . . les pays autres*, no. 849.

[56] Philip of Novara, p. 511; Mas Latrie, *Histoire*, II, 420. Cf. Leontios Makhairas, §599; 'Amadi', p. 490 ('capitanio de la secreta').

[57] Leontios Makhairas, §§311, 704; *Le Livre des remembrances*, p. xii.

later developments: the hearing of petitions in the chancery and the operation of the court or office of the auditor. The earliest references to the auditor date to the early fourteenth century and suggest that he was a judicial officer who among other things kept records of debts.[58] It may be that his primary responsibilities lay in examining petitions presented to the king in the light of traditional Cypriot customary law. If so, his function would have paralleled that of the chancery judges who took cognizance of petitions to the king and applied Roman Law principles. The first auditor who can be identified was a knight named Thomas of Montolif whose earliest appearance is in a document of 1355. He remained in office until at least 1373 when the pope addressed him as 'auditor generalis causarum regni Cipri'.[59] Thomas had a distinguished career as a royal servant and diplomat; in 1372 he was rewarded with the post of butler of Jerusalem and at about the same time became *bailli* of the *secrète*.[60] He was clearly an expert in the law and procedures of the High Court. In 1369 he acted as John prince of Antioch's procurator at the hearing at which John received recognition as regent, and then in 1372 he performed a similar duty when he made the formal request for Peter II to be deemed to have come of age. He also became a member of the commission set up in 1369 to prepare an official version of John of Jaffa's legal treatise.[61] Later auditors similarly were prominent vassals: John Gorap and then Alnard of Soissons held office in the closing years of the fourteenth century and among other occupants of the office in the fifteenth were James of Fleury and Janus of Montolif.[62]

Pleas concerning liegemen would have been heard in the High Court and petitions to the crown might have been examined by the chancery judges or by the auditor, but normally the tribunal in which civil and criminal proceedings were conducted was the *cour des bourgeois*. The court comprised a body of assessors or jurats drawn from the local Latin burgess population presided over by a knight who held the title of viscount or *bailli*.[63] At the close of the thirteenth century there were viscounts at Nicosia and Famagusta and *baillis* elsewhere as at Limassol,[64] but from early in the fourteenth century a pattern emerged in

---

[58] *Notai Genovesi* (CFFS 43), p. 195 (1307); 'Bans et Ordonnances', p. 369 (1311).

[59] 'Bans et Ordonnances', p. 377; Gregory XI, *Lettres secrètes . . . les pays autres*, no. 2073, cf. no. 849.

[60] Mas Latrie, *Histoire*, II, 233; Leontios Makhairas, §§108, 147, 326. For Thomas as *bailli* of the *secrète* above note 55. It is often difficult to distinguish him from a namesake who was also prominent at this time.

[61] John of Ibelin, pp. 5–6; Leontios Makhairas, §320.

[62] Mas Latrie, *Histoire*, II, 420, 428; *DVL*, II, 181, 219; Leontios Makhairas, §620; Richard, *Chypre sous les Lusignans*, pp. 128–9.

[63] For a fourteenth-century description, 'Abrégé des Assises', pp. 236–44 *et passim*.

[64] For the viscount of Famagusta, 'Actes passés à Famagouste de 1299 à 1301 par devant le notaire génois Lamberto di Sambuceto', ed. C. Desimoni, *AOL*, II, (1884), no. 114 (1300); 'Gestes', p. 866. For a *bailli* of Limassol in the 1290s, *Procès des Templiers*, ed. M. Michelet (Paris, 1841–51), II, 223.

which a viscount held office at Nicosia and *baillis* functioned in Famagusta, Limassol, Paphos and Karpasia.[65] The business before the *cour des bourgeois* ranged from witnessing property transactions to administering criminal justice. The court's procedures and the functions of its officers clearly derived from those of Latin Syria, so much so that the mid-thirteenth-century *Livre des assises de la cour des bourgeois* which described the law as it had operated in Acre was still being copied in Cyprus in the fourteenth century. The responsibilities of the viscounts or *baillis* included collecting urban rents owed to the crown and maintaining public order. In their police duties they were assisted by a *muhtasib* who had under him a force of sergeants.[66] Their competence, however, was not all-embracing: jurisdiction over commercial matters, in particular in connection with foreign trade, belonged in the hands of the *bailli* of the *commerchium*,[67] and for disputes involving members of the Syrian population there was also the *cour des Suriens* presided over, as in the kingdom of Jerusalem, by a *raïs* who was a knight.[68] The provincial *baillis* are also found with responsibilities for defence. At Famagusta the posts of viscount or *bailli* on the one hand and of captain or castellan on the other seem to have been differentiated at the start of the fourteenth century but had evidently been merged by the early 1370s.[69] At Kyrenia early fifteenth-century evidence shows that by then the castellan also acted as the president of the *cour des bourgeois*.[70]

Towards the end of the fourteenth century there appears to have been a considerable reorganization of local government with the division of the island into twelve districts each under a royal officer known as a captain or *chevetaine*, but it is not possible to pin-point the precise date for this reform. The *chevetaines* were much concerned with collecting taxes and other royal revenues, and Professor Richard has suggested that their introduction may be linked with the switch from a policy of letting the royal estates at farm to direct exploitation by the crown which he dates to the reign of Peter II.[71] Until then it would appear that kings had normally farmed the revenues of the lands which comprised the royal domain and so, at least in the countryside, they did not possess a large revenue-gathering bureaucracy. There is evidence too that initially they farmed their urban revenues. In 1199 King Aimery accepted a proffer of 28,050 white bezants in return for the right to levy commercial

[65] 'Bans et Ordonnances', pp. 377–8. Cf. Mas Latrie, *Histoire*, II, 170.
[66] Prawer, *Crusader Institutions*, pp. 290–1, 369.
[67] *Documenti sulle relazioni delle città toscane*, pp. 123–4; Francesco Balducci Pegolotti, *La pratica della mercatura*, ed. A. Evans (Cambridge, Mass., 1936), p. 89.
[68] J. Richard, 'La cour des Syriens de Famagouste d'après un texte de 1448', *BF*, XII, (1987), 383–8. Cf. Riley-Smith, *Feudal Nobility*, pp. 89–91.
[69] Richard, 'La cour des Syriens', p. 389; cf. 'Amadi', p. 250. Leontios Makhairas, §361.
[70] 'Nouvelles preuves' (1874), pp. 120–1.   [71] *Le Livre des remembrances*, pp. xxi–xxiii.

taxation in Limassol for two years; in the 1360s, however, these revenues were being collected by *secrète* officials.[72]

Peter I's warfare in the 1360s and then the crippling financial burdens which resulted from the Genoese War in the 1370s resulted in various measures being taken to increase royal income, and the introduction of the twelve *chevetaines* has to be seen as an administrative change designed to make the collection of dues demanded by the crown more efficient. But exactly how the new forms of taxation were organized is not made clear, nor is there any information as to how the *testagium* or poll tax, introduced or at least extended at the end of the thirteenth century, had been administered. Leontios Makhairas relates that early in the 1360s Peters I had entrusted a burgess named John of Stathia (or Castia) with responsibilities for collecting the revenues from irregular taxes and undischarged crown debts. It would seem that John held office as the king's *camerarius*, the head of the chamber or financial section of the royal household, and that what was happening was that the king was channelling extraordinary revenues through there and so bypassing the *secrète*.[73] Peter also created or expanded a department known as the *office des enquestes* whose duties evidently included ferreting out moneys owed to the crown. As the protests made directly after his murder make clear, the activities of its officers were deeply resented.[74] After 1369 it is likely that the administration of extraordinary taxation came under the aegis of a financial officer known as the collector or πράχτορας. A Greek, Nicholas Bili, who appears in the mid-1370s is the only named occupant of this post before 1400, although a precursor may have been John of Plessia, described as 'bailivus talie' in a document of 1329.[75] By the mid-fifteenth century the collector's duties seem to have been merged with those of the *bailli* of the *secrète*, and from then on the occupants of the combined post came from the non-Frankish, civil-service families.[76]

Royal government in Cyprus owed much to its Greek inheritance. The kings' continued control of the organs of justice is commensurate with the Byzantine concept of the state, while the farming of sources of royal revenue could well have been a feature of Cypriot administration before the Latin conquest. But it is equally clear that the Byzantine features of government were adapted to suit the needs and traditions of the new ruling class, and that, at least in the fourteenth

---

[72] *RRH*, no. 755a; Richard, *Chypre sous les Lusignans*, p. 78, cf. pp. 64–5.

[73] Leontios Makhairas, §§157, 215. Leontios errs in stating that John was made chamberlain of the kingdom, a post then held by Peter Malocello.   [74] Richard, 'La révolution', pp. 111–15.

[75] Leontios Makhairas, §§88, 445, 563 and note, 693; Mas Latrie, *Histoire*, II, 158.

[76] Philip Salah, *bailli* of the *secrète* from about 1448, is described on one occasion as 'pretoris nostre secrete regalis', and Philip Ceba, *bailli* in 1468 is referred by as πράκτορις (a variant on πράχτορας, the form preferred by Leontios). Richard, *Chypre sous les Lusignans*, p. 141 note 1; *Le Livre des remembrances*, p. xii.

century when the evidence becomes relatively plentiful, innovations and reforms in response to changing circumstances and external influences were being carried through. The Lusignans' ability to adapt the administrative infrastructure of their kingdom must have counted much towards their survival in the face of growing difficulties after the mid-fourteenth century. On the other hand, the kings were of necessity conservative in their concept of regality, and they were ably served and supported by an equally conservative nobility. Vassals played an indispensable role in government, as counsellors, administrators, military commanders and envoys, and there can be no doubt that the successful interdependence of the king and his nobles contributed much to the stability of the regime. The presence of sound administrative traditions and the existence of an articulate and co-operative nobility meant that the royal house could and did survive the minorities of the thirteenth century and the dangerous dynastic crises of the fourteenth.

9

CLIMACTERIC

PETER I was murdered on 16 January 1369. Later that same day his thirteen-year-old son was proclaimed king as Peter II. As the new monarch was too young to rule in his own right, it was necessary to appoint a regent, and the High Court immediately ratified the candidature of his uncle, John prince of Antioch.[1] On the basis of thirteenth-century precedents it could have been argued that the widowed queen-mother should have been chosen instead: in 1218 Alice of Champagne had become regent for the infant Henry I, and in 1253 it was Plaisance of Antioch who nominally at least held the reins of government for Hugh II. But in 1369 Eleanor of Aragon was passed over. What in effect had happened was that the regicides themselves had seized power. The prince evidently enjoyed the support of the overwhelming majority of the nobility and was to remain the dominant figure in the kingdom until 1373. For her part, Eleanor became the focus for opposition to the new regime, increasingly determined to seek vengeance on her husband's killers.

The chief problems facing the regent were how to end the war with the Muslims and the related question of how to get the royal finances back on an even keel. As we have seen, since 1367 the Cypriots had been keeping up their attacks on the Mamlūk coastline in the hope of extracting advantageous terms in a negotiated settlement. John continued this approach, sending raiding expeditions against Syrian and Egyptian ports in the summer of 1369 and then co-operating with the Venetians and Genoese in the initiative which eventually led to the treaty of 1370.[2] The return to peace would have led directly to a reduction in royal expenditure and at the same time facilitated the resumption of normal commercial activity and hence a revival in royal revenues from trade. John also adopted draconian measures to restore the royal domain. In the words of John Dardel,

> After the death of King Peter . . . the prince who held the government of the realm repossessed all the fiefs which King Peter, his brother, had given to foreigners and seized them and took their revenues . . . [3]

---

[1] John of Ibelin, pp. 3–6.   [2] Above, pp. 170–1.   [3] John Dardel, pp. 39–40.

The assertion that all the fiefs were taken back is an exaggeration – the Cornaro family, for example, retained their estate at Episkopi – but there is no doubt that the prince and his followers pursued a rigorous policy. Non-resident fief-holders were particularly vulnerable since failure to perform homage to the new king or his regent within a year and a day was grounds for forfeiture. Peter's favourite, Brémond of La Voulte, evidently lost his fiefs for this reason. In March 1371 and again in May he had the pope write to the prince asking for him to be permitted to defer the homage due to the young king for five years; in August the pope wrote once more, this time reporting Brémond's death and requesting that his son be allowed to inherit his fiefs and postpone homage. But to no avail: when we next hear of Brémond's estates, Polemidhia and Ayios Reginos, they were in the hands of the prince of Antioch's own sons.[4] Nor was Brémond alone in seeking papal help: other westerners with fiefs in Cyprus tried a similar course of action. The authorities also seized upon the failure to perform the service owed for fiefs or the absence of adequate legal title as pretexts for rescinding Peter I's alienations and so hounding the foreigners who had benefited from his largesse.[5]

But although the new rulers of Cyprus were able to repair some of the damage caused by Peter's extravagance, the murder gave rise to serious diplomatic problems. In particular, John was anxious to avoid papal displeasure and sent a canon of Nicosia cathedral named Bartholomew Escaface to report the late king's death to the pope. News of the erstwhile crusader's fate, however, had already reached Pope Urban, and the prince had to dispatch a second embassy, this time headed by the bishop of New Phocea, to turn aside his anger. The ambassadors arrived at the curia around the beginning of 1370. In a move reminiscent of the ploy tried by Amaury of Tyre in the first decade of the century, they apparently used the prospect of a Muslim invasion of Cyprus as a lever to gain grudging recognition for the prince's regime. The pope then wrote to John encouraging him to safeguard the kingdom and also telling him to proceed with the young king's coronation.[6]

It was not until the summer of 1370 that Queen Eleanor is reported to have taken steps to seek revenge on her husband's murderers and undermine the prince of Antioch's hold on the government. According to Leontios Makhairas, in the August of that year a notary and royal official named Nicholas of Naoun

[4] Gregory XI, *Lettres secrètes et curiales relatives à la France*, ed. L. Mirot et al. (Paris, 1935–57), no. 225; *idem, Lettres secrètes . . . les pays autres*, nos. 69, 265; Leontios Makhairas, §620. Cf. Richard, *Chypre sous les Lusignans*, p. 80. For the Cornaro, G. Luzzatto, 'Capitalismo coloniale nel trecento' in *Studi di storia economica veneziana* (Padua, 1954).

[5] Gregory XI, *Lettres secrètes . . . les pays autres*, nos. 352, 802–3, 897–8, 1004–5 (a fief granted by Hugh IV); John Dardel, pp. 37–41.

[6] For Bartholomew, Leontios Makhairas, §310. Leontios errs in stating that he received his canonry from the pope at this time: he had received it in 1365. Rudt de Collenberg, 'Etat et origine', p. 298 no. 120. For the bishop of New Phocea, *Annales ecclesiastici*, 1370, §13; Urban V, *Lettres secrètes*, nos. 3026, 3032; Jorga, *Philippe de Mézières*, pp. 400–1.

was denounced for writing letters on her behalf intended for the pope, the king of France and other western rulers demanding justice to be meted out on the regicides and calling on Genoa to send galleys to take Eleanor herself and her son to the West so that they could make their accusations at the papal court. The letters were intercepted; Nicholas was tortured and then executed, and a Genoese who was to have acted as courier was only saved thanks to the intervention of the *podestà*.[7] But although the prince may have prevented Eleanor appealing to the West in 1370, a series of letters from the new pope, Gregory XI, prove that information from sources hostile to his rule was nevertheless reaching the curia. In March 1371 Gregory wrote admonishing the young king and the prince to rule well, and telling the queen to care for her son.[8] But at the beginning of May he showed a much deeper concern for the political situation on the island by announcing that he was sending Bertrand Flote, a brother of the Hospital, and a second, unnamed knight to act as guardians for the king. At the same time he ordered the regent to arrange for Peter's coronation ceremony to go ahead and gave instructions for the castle at either Famagusta or Kyrenia to be assigned to the king for his safe keeping.[9] In June Gregory sent another batch of letters: Eleanor's father, Peter formerly count of Ribargoza and now a Franciscan friar, was on his way to Cyprus and the prince was to provide for expenses from the royal revenues; the Hospitallers of Rhodes were to assist Peter on his journey; the master of the Hospital, Raymond Berenger, was appointed papal nuncio and, together with Eleanor, her father, John of Antioch and John's brother James, was to work for the peaceful ordering of the kingdom.[10] Our sources provide no confirmation that Bertrand Flote, Raymond Berenger or Peter of Ribargoza actually visited Cyprus or played any part in the government, but the papal correspondence would make it seem that Eleanor or someone sympathetic towards her had been trying to get the pope to dismantle the prince's authority and had managed to give the impression that John might do away with his nephew and seize power for himself.

In December 1371 Peter II was declared to be of age, and the prince of Antioch formally surrendered the regency. Peter's coronation as king of Cyprus followed early in January in Nicosia.[11] Then on 10 October 1372, in keeping with the precedent set by his father and grandfather, he was crowned king of Jerusalem at Famagusta. It was this second coronation that occasioned the riot which was to have such devastating consequences. As Peter emerged from the cathedral for the start of the state procession back to the palace, representatives of the Venetian and Genoese communities stepped forward to perform their

---

[7] Leontios Makhairas, §§311–16.
[8] Gregory XI, *Lettres secrètes . . . les pays autres*, nos. 61–2, 66, cf. no. 63.
[9] *Ibid.*, nos. 133, 135, cf. nos. 128, 130, 132 bis, 132 ter, 134, 136.
[10] *Ibid.*, nos. 182, 184–6.
[11] Leontios Makhairas, §§319–24. For the date, Jorga, *Philippe de Mézières*, p. 406 note 5.

ceremonial service of leading the king's horse. There then followed a tussle for the privilege of taking hold of the right-hand side of the bridle, and the sight of this dispute led to a tumult in the crowd. The disorder was suppressed, and the king, his horse led by the prince of Antioch and the lord of Arsur, returned to the palace by a shortened route. There were fresh disturbances at the coronation banquet afterwards, and the violence spread throughout the city with the local inhabitants and the Venetians pursuing and killing many Genoese and destroying their property. Once order was restored, there were heated exchanges between the Genoese *podestà* who now demanded retribution and compensation and the royal officers. Peter was angered by the fact that the celebrations had been marred by rioting; he held the Genoese responsible, and he was not prepared to be conciliatory.[12]

The refusal of the Cypriots to give the Genoese demands a sympathetic hearing led directly to a section of the Genoese community evacuating the island and to the decision to exact reparations by force. Under Doge Dominic of Campofregoso, Genoa was taking a generally aggressive stance towards her neighbours, rivals and trading partners, and a few years later, in 1379–80 this assertiveness was to culminate in spectacular fashion in the naval blockade of her greatest competitor, Venice. Once news of the events in Famagusta reached the West, it was decided to raise a fleet to be commanded by the doge's brother, Peter, and paid for by a *maona*, a joint stock enterprise whose shareholders would be entitled to a proportion of the indemnity they hoped to impose.[13] According to Leontios Makhairas, in 1373, just before hostilities began in earnest, the Genoese were demanding the punishment of those responsible for killing their merchants or 50,000 florins instead; 100,000 florins as prescribed in the 1365 treaty for failing to maintain the security and privileges of their citizens in Cyprus; 100,000 florins compensation for loss or damage to property, and a further 100,000 for the expenses of the naval expedition under Damian Cattaneo which had sailed earlier that year ahead of the main fleet. In addition, they demanded a stronghold or castle where their merchants would live and do business since they no longer had any faith in the promises of security they had received in the past. This desire for a sovereign defensible enclave has been described as a manifestation of their 'fortress mentality'; they had just such fortresses at Caffa and Tana in the Black Sea, and in 1379 they even asked the English government to give them Southampton. From 1373 they had Famagusta.[14]

---

[12] For the fullest account, Leontios Makhairas, §§324–5, 328–40. Cf. Hill, II, 382–4.

[13] G. Petti Balbi, 'La maona di Cipro del 1373', *Rassegna storica della Liguria*, I (1974). Cf. Leontios Makhairas, §358.

[14] Leontios Makhairas, §§370, 372. For the 1365 penalty clause, Mas Latrie, *Histoire*, II, 265. For the 'fortress mentality', B. Z. Kedar, *Merchants in Crisis: Genoese and Venetian Men of Affairs and the Fourteenth-Century Depression* (New Haven/London, 1976), p. 125.

Although Peter was now legally of age and had been crowned and anointed as king of Cyprus and Jerusalem, the prince of Antioch continued to dominate affairs. After the first coronation, a cleric named Guy of Nephin was sent on an embassy to the pope, and in June 1372 Gregory responded by congratulating Peter and once again encouraging him to rule well. At the same time he granted a series of indults to John and his wife at Guy's request – a clear sign that it was the former regent who had briefed Guy before his departure. This embassy seems to have reassured the pope that the government of Cyprus was in safe hands. In November the pope invited Peter to send ambassadors to Thebes to discuss a proposed Christian alliance against the Turks. The prince was told to make sure that Peter complied – further evidence that he was regarded as the power behind the throne.[15] Again, after the Famagusta riot it was John who took the lead in restoring order and upbraiding the Genoese *podestà*. His role in the affair was apparently echoed by the pope who in a letter written the following January to the patriarch of Grado voiced the opinion that the impending conflict was not the fault of the king but of the prince. A contemporary Genoese document adds currency to this contention, describing the war as being 'against the prince of Antioch and his followers'.[16]

Peter's coronation as king of Jerusalem seems also to have been the occasion for heightened ill-feeling between the prince and Queen Eleanor. According to Leontios Makhairas, Peter, at his mother's bidding, started granting fiefs to her supporters in the island, and the prince and the other vassals responded by getting him to issue a decree to the effect that no grant made before his twenty-fifth birthday would be valid. Needless to say, Eleanor was much chagrined by this turn of events which plainly illustrates the problem inherent in having a king who was legally of age but not old enough to adopt a sensible policy of his own and stand up to the blandishments of the relatives. Leontios subsequently accused the queen of encouraging the Genoese to invade Cyprus and avenge her husband's murderers. Allegedly she had her father, Peter of Ribargoza, go to the pope with letters calling for justice to be done on the late king's killers and seeking papal support for the planned invasion; she was also claiming that the prince of Antioch was still in control of the royal revenues and was keeping the king in penury.[17] It is difficult to know how much credence Leontios deserves – he was distinctly hostile to Eleanor – but there is independent evidence for Eleanor making contact with her father and the pope at this time. In February

---

[15] Gregory XI, *Lettres secrètes . . . les pays autres*, nos. 787–91, 1170, 1174; Rudt de Collenberg, 'Les grâces papales', pp. 236, 237, 243. For the proposed alliance, A. T. Luttrell, 'Gregory XI and the Turks, 1370–1378', *Orientalia Christiana Periodica*, XLVI (1980), 394–5.

[16] Leontios Makhairas, §§331, 332; Gregory XI, *Lettres secrètes . . . les pays autres*, no. 1408; P. Argenti, *The Occupation of Chios by the Genoese and their Administration of the Island, 1346–1566* (Cambridge, 1958), II, 104.

[17] Leontios Makhairas, §§327, 354–7. Eleanor is also said to have written to the king of Aragon and the queen of Naples.

1373 she sent John Lascaris Calopheros, an erstwhile favourite of Peter I who had suffered at the hands of the prince's regime, to the papal court with an oral message for her father; in August another of her emissaries, Alphonso Ferrand, was at the papal court with instructions to make contact with Peter of Ribargoza.[18]

The story of the four and a half years between the death of Peter I and the arrival of the Genoese invasion-fleet is thus one of political uncertainty with the prince of Antioch and the queen-mother contending for control. John of Antioch had much to fear if power passed to Eleanor; on the other hand, anxieties about the Aragonese crown and Catalan naval might probably prevented him from imprisoning her or sending her into exile.[19] John had seized power in a *coup d'état*, and in common with most usurpers he could not safely relinquish control and go into retirement. But the conflicts around the Cypriot throne had more than just a disruptive effect on internal politics: they also provided the Genoese with the opportunity to give what was essentially a punitive invasion some higher moral justification.

As soon as news of the events of October 1372 and Genoa's plans for reprisals became known, Pope Gregory began a series of attempts to head off the impending confrontation. In December he called on the Genoese to stop their preparations, and in the course of the next two months he tried unsuccessfully to arrange talks. A further initiative began at the end of May with the pope proposing the archbishop of Nicosia and the bishop of Famagusta as mediators, but this plan too seems to have come to nothing. In June Gregory told the queen of Sicily and the Hospitallers in Rhodes not to help the Genoese expedition by furnishing it with provisions, and at the end of that month he sent John Lascaris Calopheros to Genoa in a further effort at conciliation. At the same time he wrote to Peter II urging him to make peace.[20]

By then, however, events in the East had brought all-out war inexorably nearer. In February Peter ordered the arrest of Genoese shipping in Cypriot ports. At around the same time he and the prince of Antioch had sent the archbishop of Tarsus to Venice, but although the Venetians were sympathetic and were prepared to help seek a negotiated peace they were not prepared to offer Cyprus any military assistance.[21] Then in March the Genoese government dispatched seven galleys under the command of Damian Cattaneo with instructions to get the Cypriots to concede their demands or, failing that, to

---

[18] For John Lascaris, Gregory XI, *Lettres secrètes . . . les pays autres*, no. 1487; D. Jacoby, 'Jean Lascaris Calophéros, Chypre et la Morée, *Revue des études byzantines*, XXVI (1968), 193–5. For Alphonso, Rudt de Collenberg, 'Les grâces papales', p. 234; cf. Leontios Makhairas, §342.

[19] Cf. Leontios Makhairas, §255.

[20] Gregory XI, *Lettres secrètes . . . les pays autres*, nos. 1327–8, 1408, 1486, 1489, 1491, 1838, 1884, 1888–9, 1896–7, 1946–7, 1960.   [21] Mas Latrie, *Histoire*, II, 359–60; 'Amadi', p. 439.

assess the island's military preparedness and send word back to Genoa so that the main fleet could be sent. Damian arrived off Famagusta at the end of April and opened negotiations. According to a Genoese source these broke down because the king's uncles and the other magnates, who, rather than the king, were governing the island, refused to accept Damian's terms. But Leontios Makhairas, who gives the fullest account of the war from a Cypriot perspective, reported that the Genoese had no serious intention of making peace and instead devoted most of their energies to creating difficulties about the hostages they required to guarantee the safety of their negotiators. On 12 May the Genoese began pillaging the gardens around Famagusta; they were fought off, and the Cypriots responded by interning all Genoese nationals still in the island.[22]

These events were quickly followed by the evacuation of the Anatolian port of Satalia, which had been captured by Peter I in 1361 and occupied ever since. Rather than risk letting it fall into the hands of Genoa, it was decided to return it to the Turks, especially since the garrison and the resources required for its upkeep could now be deployed in the defence of Cyprus itself. The transfer took place in mid-May, and the garrison, bringing away various icons and relics including a portrait of the Virgin Mary believed to have been painted by St Luke, managed to avoid two of Damian Cattaneo's galleys which had been sent to intercept it and landed at Kyrenia.[23]

In June the Hospitallers tried to mediate. The marshal of the Order came to Cyprus and succeeded in restarting talks between Damian Cattaneo and the government. But the Cypriots showed no inclination to pay the 350,000 ducats the Genoese were now demanding, still less agree to the cession of a fortress for the protection of their merchants; they did, however, indicate a willingness to accept papal arbitration.[24] The failure of these discussions marked the end of any possibility of a negotiated settlement. Nevertheless the pope, hamstrung by his distance from events which meant that he was out of touch with the pace of developments, continued in his hope that the Hospitallers might yet achieve a settlement, and as late as October he was trying to get the doge of Venice to arrange talks. During the summer of 1373 there were two Cypriot embassies in the West. Queen Eleanor's representative, Alphonso Ferrand, was with the pope in August; according to Leontios Makhairas, he bore letters to her father calling for retribution on the murderers of her husband. Shortly after the Famagusta affray the king had sent two knights, Renier Le Petit and William of Charny, to the pope to put the Cypriot version of events and persuade him to intervene as necessary on his behalf. Renier was still at the papal court in September and only set out to return to Cyprus at the beginning of October. In his response to

---

[22] Giorgio and Giovanni Stella, 'Annales Genuenses', ed. G. Petti Balbi, *Rerum Italicarum Scriptores*, n. s. XVII, 2 (Bologna, 1975), 166; Leontios Makhairas, §§358–65, cf. §375.
[23] Leontios Makhairas, §§366–9.   [24] *Ibid.*, §§370–4, 376.

Renier's embassy Gregory expressed his horror at the proposal to return Satalia to the Turks, explained how he had gone to considerable lengths to reach a settlement with Genoa and noted with apparent regret that Renier himself had no authority to treat for peace; his injunction that Peter should rely on the counsel of both his mother and the prince of Antioch demonstrates his failure to appreciate the political set-up in the island.[25]

With the breakdown of talks, Damian Cattaneo's galleys began depredations in earnest. They sailed from Famagusta along the south coast and round as far as the Bay of Morphou before returning to Limassol which they burnt. They then doubled back to Paphos where they captured the castle. There, assembling a motley force of foreigners – Bulgarians, non-Cypriot Greeks and Tartars – they dug themselves in. At the beginning of July the prince of Antioch brought up a force said to number a thousand men but was unable to dislodge them. Later his brother James tried to do the same, but withdrew on learning that the arrival of the main Genoese fleet was imminent.[26]

Peter of Campofregoso had thirty-six galleys under his command, not counting Damian Cattaneo's seven. According to the principal Genoese account of these events, he also had transport vessels and his army totalled over 14,000 men.[27] The fleet appeared off Famagusta at the beginning of October, and at once the Genoese set about trying to land their men and place the city under siege. The king immediately brought 2,000 levies from Nicosia to reinforce the garrison and engage the besiegers. On 3 October this relief column came into conflict with the Genoese who had already come ashore and was able to drive them back temporarily to their ships. Two days later James of Lusignan led a successful sortie and then, after rounding up some of the marauders, retired to Nicosia where he took charge.[28]

Despite these early successes, opinion seems to have gained ground among the Cypriot leadership that there would have to be a negotiated peace. Presumably it was realized that the Genoese were too powerful, and in any case their raiders were already at work destroying the countryside. But first adequate guarantees for the personal safety of the negotiators had to be agreed. The Genoese began by suggesting that the discussions could be held on board one of their galleys. They then proposed that the castle at Famagusta should be evacuated by its garrison and that the talks might take place there with only five negotiators and twelve men-at-arms present from each side. The castle, then as now, stood at the harbour entrance, and the Genoese could enter by the sea gate without having to pass through the city. This suggestion met with general assent. Leontios Makhairas mentioned that there were just four Cypriot nobles who were opposed on the grounds that the Genoese were not to be trusted. The king

[25] Gregory XI, *Lettres secrètesFrance*, no. 3089; *idem*, *Lettres secrètes . . . les pays autres*, nos. 2072–5, 2198–9, 2214–18, 2266. Leontios Makhairas, §§342, 352. For references to Alphonso's mission, see note 18.   [26] Leontios Makhairas, §§377–82.

[27] Giorgio Stella, p. 167. Cf. Hill, II, 392 note 2.   [28] Leontios Makhairas, §§383–9.

thereupon ordered James to join him at Famagusta, but he refused either to come – he pleaded illness – or to give his approval to the scheme to hold the talks in the castle. When the king repeated his order, James found himself forcibly prevented from leaving Nicosia by the local populace. Fear of the Genoese and fear of being left leaderless in the emergency had convinced the people that the continued presence of the king's uncle was essential for their own well-being.[29]

The preliminaries to the talks therefore went ahead in James' absence. John of Morphou, the man who at one time had been reputed to be the lover of Queen Eleanor, seems to have been the chief negotiator on the Cypriot side. According to Leontios Makhairas, he was corrupted by the Genoese by an offer to help his son-in-law, Hugh of Lusignan prince of Galilee, take over the kingdom. Hugh had been the rival claimant to the throne in 1359, and the Genoese now put it about that they had brought him with them in their fleet. John's task was to see to it that the negotiations could take place in Famagusta castle as proposed. So, aided by Raymond Babin, whom he won over by the prospect of a marriage alliance between their families, he persuaded the king's council to go ahead with the plan. The story as related by Leontios Makhairas then acquires an air of seeming inevitability: the castle was evacuated; the embassies arrived; the Genoese soldiers overpowered the Cypriots; their forces swarmed ashore and into the fortress, and John of Morphou and Raymond Babin were left 'sorry, just as Judas was sorry about Christ'.[30]

The next day Peter of Campofregoso and the other captains swore on the consecrated host at mass to guarantee the safety of the king and his lords as they negotiated a peace agreement. The king, his mother and the prince of Antioch then entered the castle, but in blatant violation of the oaths were taken prisoner. When Eleanor remonstrated she was told that she was being held in protective custody while the Genoese avenged the murder of Peter I as she had wished. Peter and Eleanor were put under house arrest, and the prince was kept in irons. The king, evidently at the bidding of the Genoese, then sent for his uncle James and his knights. Those of his vassals who answered his summons were likewise taken into custody. An attempt to prevent the invaders from occupying the whole of Famagusta proved futile. The citizens were plundered; many were killed. By way of giving colour to the assertion that they were in the island to take vengeance on the late king's murderers, the Genoese proceeded to have Philip of Ibelin lord of Arsur, Henry of Jubail and John of Gaurelle executed.[31]

[29] *Ibid.*, §§390–5. Leontios goes on to record events in Nicosia before relating the capture of Famagusta; almost certainly there is a considerable chronological overlap with §§397–409 referring to events subsequent to those described in §§410–22.

[30] *Ibid.*, §§410–15; 'Amadi', pp. 450–1 (filling a lacuna in Leontios' text). Hugh had been in the West since 1367, and there is no reason to believe that he was involved in the Genoese expedition. The idea that the Genoese were planning to put him on the throne may have been widely believed. Leontios Makhairas, §409.

[31] Giorgio Stella, p. 167; Leontios Makhairas, §§415–18, 420–23. For the date of the executions, Hill, II, 397 note 2.

From here on it is James of Lusignan, the future King James I, who holds centre-stage in the Cypriot accounts of the war, and there can be no doubt that Leontios Makhairas and later Cypriot writers preserve a version of events that was written up expressly to celebrate his exploits. It is hard to tell how far their narratives exaggerate his prowess, but the circumstantial details they contain would indicate that they were well-informed even if distinctly partisan, and, although they may have embellished particular episodes, there seems no reason to doubt their general accuracy.

These latest developments placed James in a dilemma. If he obeyed the king and came to Famagusta, he was likely to be imprisoned; if on the other hand he refused, he laid himself open to the charge that his continued absence was prolonging the hostilities, and sooner or later he might have to face the king's wrath. Nicosia itself, with its sprawling fortifications, could not hold out against a full-scale Genoese assault. James' quandary increased when he learnt that the Genoese, using royal letters, had tried to install a new castellan in Kyrenia. Eventually, on 18 November, the king managed to get a secret message to James to the effect that he should go to Kyrenia and take charge of its defence against the enemy. James gave orders for supplies to be sent to the garrison, and then at midnight on 21 November together with his wife, daughter and servants he slipped out of Nicosia and made for Kyrenia.[32] At some point around this time the prince of Antioch made good his escape from Famagusta thanks to the daring of one of his servants and managed to reach Kantara. He then went on to St Hilarion.[33]

These developments put an end to any Genoese hopes that they could simply dictate terms. The king's uncles now controlled the best defended points in the whole island, and, as the king reportedly told Peter of Campofregoso, they were every bit as powerful in the kingdom as he was. No settlement was possible while they were still in arms. The king was forced to order James to surrender Kyrenia. So that the garrison would comply, they decided to send Queen Eleanor with their forces to take charge for them. The queen's co-operation was secured by pointing out that James had been in the plot to kill her husband, but from Leontios Makhairas' narrative it would seem that by this stage in the war her thirst for vengeance was outweighed by the wish to thwart the Genoese and so preserve at least something of the kingdom for her son. So while Eleanor was setting off for Nicosia with the Genoese troops ostensibly with the intention of taking Kyrenia on their behalf, she and the king succeeded in getting instructions to James to take all necessary measures to guard his stronghold and the defile through the mountains below St Hilarion.[34]

[32] Leontios Makhairas, §§399–409.

[33] Ibid., §§419, 425. The narrative seems to indicate that the escape took place soon after the capture of Famagusta castle, but the remark at the end of §419 linking the prince's presence at Kantara with James' presence in Kyrenia might suggest that it was later.   [34] Ibid., §§425–30.

On 4 December the queen and the Genoese forces, which were said to number 300 horse and 400 foot, entered Nicosia. The royal officers made no attempt to resist their occupation, but there was considerable fighting two days later when the Genoese tried to disarm the local population. The next day James brought his troops up in a show of strength and was joined by a section of the Cypriot forces still in the city. There was fighting in the suburbs, and then James' men withdrew at Eleanor's insistence. Disorder ensued with the Cypriots pillaging Genoese property and the property of people accused of being Genoese sympathizers. The invaders thereupon called in reinforcements and ruthlessly crushed pockets of resistance. The capital was then given over to indiscriminate looting and slaughter. After that nothing much happened for several weeks. It would seem that the bulk of the population in the countryside remained strongly opposed to the Genoese, and that James was able to rely on popular support in his efforts to provision Kyrenia. If Leontios Makhairas is to be believed, there were various skirmishes in which the invaders generally came off worse, although when a knight named Peter of Cassi made an enterprising attempt to cut the Genoese supply-lines into Famagusta he and his men were betrayed by a peasant. More spectacular was James of Lusignan's attack on a wagon convoy taking valuables looted from Nicosia to the coast; the Cypriots recovered the spoils and killed almost all the escort.[35]

It was not until the early part of January that the Genoese were ready to complete their scheme of using Queen Eleanor to get James of Lusignan and Kyrenia castle into their power. The plan, however, seriously backfired. As their forces approached the top of the pass below St Hilarion, the queen spurred her mule forward and, breaking away from the main party, escaped to join her brother-in-law's men. The Genoese were then easily driven off.[36] They now concentrated their efforts on taking Kyrenia by siege. But things did not go at all as they would have hoped. It was only after a week of repeated attempts to force their way over the pass that they discovered an alternative route from Nicosia through the mountains. When they reached Kyrenia they found that the defenders were well supplied with Greek fire and were more than able to put up a spirited defence. Successive assaults were repulsed, and Leontios Makhairas, whose account is admittedly highly coloured – a relative of his served with distinction in the beleaguered garrison – claims that the Genoese suffered heavy losses. The prince's men in St Hilarion played their part by disrupting the enemy supply-lines. Towards the end of February there was an attempt to open negotiations, but at the beginning of March the siege was resumed once more with renewed ferocity.[37]

By then, however, both sides were ready for peace. It may be that tensions among his commanders coupled with the losses his forces had sustained helped

---

[35] Ibid., §§432–58.   [36] Ibid., §§459–60.   [37] Ibid., §§464–99.

convince Peter of Campofregoso that the reduction of Kyrenia was not feasible. Despite the failure of an attempt at the recovery of Nicosia promoted by the queen, an armistice was agreed. The siege of Kyrenia was lifted on 15 March on the understanding that James of Lusignan would hand the fortress over to its former castellan, a Cypriot knight named Luke of Antiaume, and go into exile.[38] The Genoese admiral was nevertheless able to impose heavy terms. Cyprus was placed under an annual tribute of 40,000 florins and had to pay an indemnity to the *maona* of just over two million florins within twelve years. In addition 90,000 florins were to be paid to cover the expenses of the Genoese galleys, and all those Genoese who had suffered at the hands of the Cypriots between the day of Peter II's coronation as king of Jerusalem and the Genoese capture of Famagusta were to be compensated. As security for the payment of the indemnity, the Genoese were to occupy Famagusta and hold a number of prominent Cypriots hostage in Genoa.[39] The financial penalties were harsh to say the least. As for the hostages, it would seem that only the prince of Antioch's two sons were actually surrendered to the Genoese after the negotiations had commenced; the others were the prisoners of war captured earlier in the campaign. Altogether over seventy knights were taken into captivity, either to Genoa or to Chios, although not all were regarded as security for the money demanded from the crown: a number were simply held to ransom, while others were exiled for their complicity in the murder of Peter I; a few were taken to be married off to the daughters of high-ranking Genoese commanders.[40]

At the end of April the invasion fleet left for home. According to Leontios Makhairas, so great had been their losses that only twelve galleys were needed to bear away the Genoese and their prisoners as compared with the total of between forty and fifty that had come to the island the previous year. Admittedly the Genoese had left a garrison in Famagusta, and, as Leontios himself noted, some galleys had sailed for Genoa in December, but it is nonetheless clear that their casualties had been considerable.[41] At Rhodes they caught up with James of Lusignan. He had departed about a fortnight earlier to go into exile. His ship had

---

[38] *Ibid.*, §§500–24. For strife among the Genoese, §§519, 520.

[39] The treaty, dated 21 October 1374, is in *Liber Iurium*, II, 806–15. The terms were evidently agreed in March or April, and the delay in completing it is probably due to the need to refer to Genoa for approval. Other clauses specified that Peter of Cassi and Montolif of Verny, a knight who had been James of Lusignan's right-hand man at Kyrenia, should go into exile, and that the Hospitallers should occupy Buffavento. There is no evidence for this last stipulation being put into effect.

[40] For the prince's sons, Leontios Makhairas, §529. Two lists of hostages and exiles survive. Mas Latrie, 'Nouvelles preuves' (1873), pp. 80–4; Leontios Makhairas, §542. Most names appear on both lists, but Leontios' is clearly incomplete since in describing a subsequent escape-attempt from Genoa (§548) he mentioned additional knights, two of whom, Guy of Mimars and Raymond Viscount, appear on the other. For the ransoming of Leo of Lusignan, who had been taken captive at Famagusta, John Dardel, pp. 49–51.   [41] Leontios Makhairas, §§484, 549.

been escorted into Rhodes harbour by two Genoese galleys which had made out that they were acting as a guard of honour. In fact it would seem that, notwithstanding the assurances that James would have a safe passage to go wherever he wished, the Genoese were determined to take him into their custody. At Rhodes he was received by the Hospitallers, but his departure was delayed owing to the death of his infant daughter. When the main Genoese fleet arrived, he tried to persuade the Order to give him sanctuary, but it refused, fearing retaliation. So it was that the future king of Cyprus who had led his people's resistance once King Peter had been captured and who had defied the Genoese from Kyrenia for more than three months, fell into the hands of his enemies to be carried off to Genoa and years of imprisonment.[42]

The war can be thought of either as the consummation of almost a century of bad relations between Genoa and the Lusignans or, more immediately, as retaliation for a particularly brutal attack on Genoese citizens and their property.[43] But however it is viewed, so far as Cyprus was concerned it had been a calamity. There is no way of knowing how many Cypriots had died or precisely how widespread the destruction and looting had been, but the island had been exposed to the horrors of foreign invasion for several months. Paphos and Limassol as well as Famagusta and Nicosia had been severely damaged. Some coastal areas and the rural communities along the main routes from Famagusta to the capital and in the vicinity of Kyrenia had evidently suffered badly.[44] The Genoese had employed several thousand troops, many of whom would have been hardened mercenaries with long experience of warfare elsewhere. The Cypriots also used foreign soldiers – Leontios Makhairas makes frequent reference to a force of Bulgars in their service – and it is highly likely that these men too would have had little regard for the property or sensibilities of the local population.[45] The invaders destroyed the personal wealth of nobles and merchants alike. Famagusta in particular seems to have been thoroughly ransacked, and it could well be that many of the local merchants lost their working capital and so were forced out of business for good.[46] There can be little doubt that the invasion served to aggravate Famagusta's economic decline. The Genoese occupation – they held the city notionally as security for the payment of the indemnity until 1383 and in outright sovereignty thereafter – in itself had the effect of deterring other merchants from the West from trading there. For

---

[42] *Ibid.*, §§512–13, 515, 518, 522–6, 528, 530, 533–41, 544–7.
[43] For the long-term hostility, Edbury, 'Cyprus and Genoa', pp. 109–26.
[44] For references to pillaging in rural areas, Leontios Makhairas, §§362, 377, 381.
[45] For the Bulgars, Leontios Makhairas, §§434, 446, 456, 460, 466, 468–9, 471, 483, 503–4, 552. Apparently they had been recruited by the Genoese and had then deserted. *Ibid.*, §427, cf. §§377–8. The prince of Antioch is said to have had mainland Greeks and Tartars as well as Bulgars in his service. *Ibid.* §509, cf. §377 where the Genoese are said to have troops from these same nations. [46] *Ibid.*, §§96, 349, 422, 451–3.

example, in the spring of 1374 the Venetian authorities forbade their subjects to go there – an order not rescinded until 1378 – and their trade with Cyprus seems generally to have been slow to recover. In the 1390s a western traveller, Nicolo da Martoni, could give a vivid description of Famagusta in ruinous decay.[47]

King Peter was left with the task of trying to salvage what he could. Most of the knights who had given their backing to the prince of Antioch before the war were now dead or in prison in the West, and Queen Eleanor could now dominate the government. It was not long before she was able to bring about the prince's murder. Peter, however, gradually managed to free himself from his mother's tutelage, and eventually, in 1380, he had her shipped back to Aragon. He himself chose to rely on the counsel of the few remaining veterans of his father's reign, and from the end of 1375, in flagrant disregard of the terms of the 1374 treaty, he set about trying to dislodge the Genoese from Famagusta. Master at last in his own house, he showed greater ability and determination than he is usually credited with, but his efforts to recover the principal port of his kingdom by force were abandoned after his death in 1382.[48]

The truth was that the Lusignan kingdom could never be the same again. The royal dynasty survived for a further century, but its image was tarnished, its power weakened. The old nobility, many of whose members could trace their ancestry to the twelfth-century Latin states in Syria and the Holy Land, had also lost much of their pre-eminence. Some families survived to play a significant role in the fifteenth century, but they had to share their position as counsellors and servants of successive kings with newcomers to the aristocracy whose backgrounds differed widely from theirs. The events of 1373–4 and the taking of hostages contributed to the disappearance of a number of noble houses. It has been calculated that out of the forty-four families whose members were taken away, eighteen are not found in the island again. The most famous family whose demise was hastened by the war was the house of Ibelin. Since the thirteenth century the Ibelins had outstripped all others in power and influence, but the Genoese beheaded the last Ibelin lord of Arsur, and, with a certain Nicholas of Ibelin going as a hostage to Genoa in 1374 never to be heard of again, the last known male bearer of the family name passes from sight.[49]

The Genoese war spelled the end of prosperity. For the next fifty years the kings alternated between setting out deliberately to seize Famagusta by force and trying to appease Genoa by seeking to pay the tribute. In neither policy were they successful. The loss of trade and the drain of bullion attendant on this state

[47] Mas Latrie, *Histoire*, II, 363–4; Racine, 'Note sur le trafic', pp. 318–19; Ashtor, *Levant Trade*, pp. 115, 120. For Martoni 'Relation de pèlerinage à Jérusalem de Nicolas de Martoni, notaire Italien', ed. L. Le Grand, *ROL*, III (1895), 628–32.

[48] For Peter's reign after the Genoese war, Hill, II, 413–30.

[49] W. H. Rudt de Collenberg, 'The Fate of Frankish Noble Families Settled in Cyprus', *CS*, p. 270. For Nicholas, *idem*, 'Les Ibelin', pp. 228–9.

of affairs were serious enough in themselves and were compounded by locusts and by outbreaks of plague which must have had the effect of lowering the resources of man-power in the island still further. Under these circumstances there was no way that Cyprus could play any positive role in the continuing conflict between Christianity and Islam, and in any case the main theatres of this struggle had by now moved away from the eastern end of the Mediterranean. Somehow the royal dynasty survived the Egyptian invasions of the 1420s and a civil war in the 1460s only to fall victim to Venetian colonial expansionism in the course of a dynastic crisis precipitated by the death of King James II in 1473. But although the last century of royal government was marked by political crisis and economic and military frailty, the period of almost 200 years before 1373 witnessed a remarkable degree of stability and prosperity, sufficient to make the kingdom of Cyprus stand out as one of the most successful western regimes established by the crusaders either in the Levant or in the former Byzantine lands around the Aegean. The settlement begun in the last decade of the twelfth century had proved durable, and the Lusignan dynasty had governed Cyprus during one of the most striking epochs in its history.

BIBLIOGRAPHY

I ORIGINAL SOURCES

(A)   Documents and collections of materials

'Actes passés à Famagouste de 1299 à 1301 par devant le notaire génois Lamberto di Sambuceto' ed. C. Desimoni, *AOL*, II (1884), 3–120. Continued in *ROL*, III (1893), 58–139, 275–312, 321–53.

Pope Alexander IV. *Registres*, ed. C. Bourel de la Roncière *et al.* BEFAR. 3 vols. Paris, 1895–1959.

Annales Ecclesiastici, ed. C. Baronius and O. Raynaldus. New edn by A. Theiner. 37 vols. Bar-le-Duc/Paris, 1864–82.

'Bans et Ordonnances des rois de Chypre', *RHC Lois*, II.

Pope Benedict XII. *Lettres closes, patentes et curiales se rapportant à la France*, ed. G. Daumet. BEFAR. Paris, 1899–1920.

Lettres closes et patentes intéressant les pays autres que la France, ed. J.-M. Vidal and G. Mollat. BEFAR. Paris, 1913–50.

Lettres communes, ed. J.-M. Vidal. BEFAR. 3 vols. Paris, 1903–11.

Biblioteca bio-bibliografica della Terra Santa e dell'Oriente francescano, ed. G. Golubovich. 5 vols. Quarrachi, 1906–27.

Pope Boniface VIII. *Registres*, ed. G. Digard *et al.* BEFAR. 4 vols. Paris, 1884–1939.

Calendar of Liberate Rolls Preserved in the Public Record Office, 1251–60. London, 1959.

'Carte et chronica de obedentia Mairomno' in *Chroniques des églises d'Anjou*, ed. P. Marchegay and E. Mabille. Paris, 1869.

Le cartulaire du chapitre du Saint-Sépulcre de Jérusalem, ed. G. Bresc-Bautier. Paris, 1984.

Cartulaire général de l'Ordre des Hospitaliers de St-Jean de Jérusalem, ed. J. Delaville Le Roulx. 4 vols. Paris, 1894–1906.

Cartulaires et chartes de l'abbaye de l'Absie, ed. B. Ledain. Poitiers, 1895.

Pope Clement V. *Regesti Clementis papae V*, ed. cura et studio monachorum Ordinis S. Benedicti. 8 vols. Rome, 1885–92.

Pope Clement VI. *Lettres closes, patents et curiales se rapportant à la France*, ed. E. Déprez *et al.* BEFAR. 3 vols. Paris, 1901–61.

Lettres closes, patents et curiales intéressant les pays autres que la France, ed. E. Déprez and G. Mollat. BEFAR. Paris, 1960–1.

Close Rolls of Henry III Preserved in the Public Record Office (1254–6). London, 1931.

'Compte du domaine de Gautier de Brienne au royaume de Chypre', ed. E. Poncellet, *Bulletin de la commission royale d'histoire*, XCVIII (1934), 14–28.

Délibérations des assemblées vénitiennes concernant la Romanie, ed. F. Thiriet. 2 vols. Paris/The Hague, 1966–71.

Diplomatarium Veneto-Levantinum, sive acta et diplomata res Venetas, Graecas atque Levantiis illustrantia a. 1300–1454, ed. G. M. Thomas and R. Predelli. 2 vols. Venice, 1880–99.

Documenti del commercio veneziano nei secoli XI–XIII, ed. R. Morozzo della Rocca and A. Lombardo. 2 vols. Rome/Turin, 1940.

Documenti sulle relazioni delle città toscane coll'Oriente cristiano e coi Turchi fino all'anno 1531, ed. G. Müller. Florence, 1879.

'Documents chypriotes du début du XIVe siècle', ed. C. Kohler, *ROL*, XI (1905–8), 440–52.

'Documents nouveaux servant de preuves à l'histoire de l'île de Chypre sous le règne des princes de la maison de Lusignan', ed. L. de Mas Latrie in *Collection des documents inédits: Mélanges historiques*, IV (1882).

'Documents relatifs à la successibilité au trône et à la régence', *RHC Lois*, II.

Duca di Candia Bandi (1313–1329), ed. P. R. Vidulich. Venice, 1965.

'Epistolae Cantuarienses', ed. W. Stubbs in *Chronicles and Memorials of the Reign of Richard I*. RS 38. 2 vols. London, 1864–5, II.

'Epistolarum Volumen . . . ad Ludovicum VII', *RHF*, XVI.

Pope Gregory IX. *Registres*, ed. L. Auvray. BEFAR. 3 vols. Paris, 1890–1955.

Popes Gregory X and John XXI. *Registres*, ed. J. Guiraud and L. Cadier. BEFAR. Paris, 1892–1960.

Pope Gregory XI. *Lettres secrètes et curiales relatives à la France*, ed. L. Mirot *et al.* BEFAR. Paris, 1935–57.

Lettres secrètes et curiales intéressant les pays autres que la France, ed. G. Mollat. BEFAR. Paris, 1962–5.

Historia diplomatica Frederici secundi, ed. J. L. A. Huillard-Bréholles. 6 vols. in 12 parts. Paris, 1852–61.

Pope Honorius III. *Regesta*, ed. P. Pressutti. 2 vols. Rome, 1888–95.

Pope Honorius IV. *Registres*, ed. M. Prou. BEFAR. Paris, 1886–8.

Pope Innocent III. *Opera Omnia*. 4 vols. *PL*, CCXIV–CCXVII.

Die Register Innocenz' III, ed. O. Hagender and A. Haidacher. 2 vols. so far. Graz/Cologne, 1964–.

Pope Innocent IV. *Registres*, ed. E. Berger. BEFAR. 4 vols. Paris, 1881–1921.

Pope Innocent VI. *Lettres secrètes et curiales*, ed. P. Gasnault *et al.* BEFAR. 4 vols. so far. Paris 1959–.

Pope John XXII. *Acta Ioannis XXII (1317–1334)*, ed. A. L. Tăutu. Città del Vaticano, 1952.

Lettres communes ed. G. Mollat. BEFAR. 16 vols. Paris, 1904–47.

Lettres secrètes et curiales relatives à la France, ed. A. Coulon and S. Clémencet. 4 vols. Paris, 1906–72.

Lacrimae Nicossienses. Recueil d'inscriptions funéraires la plupart françaises existant encore dans l'île de Chypre, ed. T. J. Chamberlayne. Paris, 1894.

Layettes du Trésor des Chartes, ed. A. Teulet *et al.* 5 vols. Paris, 1863–1909.

Lettres de Jacques de Vitry, ed. R. B. C. Huygens. Leiden, 1960.

Liber Iurium Reipublicae Genuensis. 2 vols. *Historiae Patriae Monumenta*, VII, XI.

I libri commemoriali della repubblica di Venezia regesti (1293–1778), ed. R. Predelli and P. Bosmin. 8 vols. Venice, 1876–1914.

Le Livre des remembrances de la secrète du royaume de Chypre (1468–1469), ed. J. Richard and T. Papadopoullos. Nicosia, 1983.

Memorias históricas sobre la marina, comercio y artes de la antigua ciudad de Barcelona, ed. A. de Capmany y de Montpalau. 4 vols. Madrid, 1779–92.

Pope Nicholas IV. *Registres*, ed. E. Langlois. BEFAR. 2 vols. Paris, 1886–1905.

Nicola de Boateriis, notaio in Famagosta e Venezia (1355–1365), ed. A. Lombardo. Venice, 1973.

Notai Genovesi in Oltremare: Atti rogati a Cipro da Lamberto di Sambuceto (3 Iuglio 1300–3 Agosto 1301), ed. V. Polonio. CSFS 31. Genoa, 1982.

Atti rogati a Cipro da Lamberto di Sambuceto (6 Iuglio–27 Ottobre 1301), ed. R. Pavoni. CSFS 32. Genoa, 1982.

Atti rogati a Cipro da Lamberto di Sambuceto (11 Ottobre 1296 – 23 Giugno 1299), ed. M. Balard. CSFS 39. Genoa, 1983.

Atti rogati a Cipro, ed. M. Balard. CSFS 43. Genoa, 1984.

'Nouvelles preuves de l'histoire de Chypre sous le règne des princes de la maison de Lusignan', ed. L. de Mas Latrie, *BEC*, XXXII (1871), 341–78, XXXIV (1873), 47–87, XXXV (1874), 99–158.

Papsturkunden für Kirchen im Heiligen Lande, ed. R. Hiestand. Vorarbeiten zum Oriens Pontificius 3. Göttingen, 1985.

Procès des Templiers, ed. M. Michelet. 2 vols. Paris, 1841–51.

'Processus Cypricus', ed. K. Schottmüller, *Der Untergang des Templer-Ordens* (Berlin, 1887), II.

Regesta pontificum Romanorum inde ab anno post Christo nato 1198 ad annum 1304, compiled by A. Potthast. 2 vols. Berlin, 1874–5.

Regesta Regni Hierosolymitani (1097–1291), compiled by R. Röhricht. 2 vols. Innsbruck, 1893–1904.

'A Register of the Cartulary of the Cathedral of Santa Sophia of Nicosia', ed. J. L. La Monte, *Byzantion*, V (1930), 439–522.

Tabulae ordinis Theutonici, ed. E. Strehlke. Berlin, 1869.

I Testamenti di cardinali del ducento, ed. A. Paravicini Bagliani. Rome, 1980.

Testimonia minora de Quinto Bello Sacro, ed. R. Röhricht. Geneva, 1882.

'Texte officiel de l'allocution adressée par les barons de Chypre au roi Henri II pour lui notifier sa déchéance', ed. L. de Mas Latrie, *Revue des questions historiques*, XLIII (1888), 524–41.

Thesaurus novus anecdotorum, ed. E. Martène and U. Durand. 5 vols. Paris, 1717.

Pope Urban IV. *Registres*, ed. L. Dorez and J. Guiraud. BEFAR. 4 vols. Paris, 1892–1929. Tables 1958.

Pope Urban V. *Lettres communes*, ed. M.-H. Laurent *et al.* BEFAR. 12 vols. Paris, 1954–86.

Lettres secrètes et curiales se rapportant à la France, ed. P. Lecacheux and G. Mollat. BEFAR. Paris, 1902–55.

Urkunden zur älteren Handels- und Staatsgeschichte der Republik Venedig, ed. G. L. F. Tafel and G. M. Thomas. 3 vols. Vienna, 1856–7.

Vetera Monumenta Slavorum Meridionalium Historiam Illustrantia, ed. A. Theiner. 2 vols. Rome/Zagreb, 1863–75.

Veterum Scriptorum et Monumentorum . . . Amplissima Collectio, ed. E. Martène and U. Durand. 9 vols. Paris, 1727–33.

Vitae Paparum Avenionensium hoc est historia pontificum Romanorum qui in Gallia sederunt ab anno Christi MCCCV usque annum MCCCXCIV, ed. S. Baluze. New edn by G. Mollat. 4 vols. Paris, 1914–27.

(B) Legal text and narrative sources

'Abrégé du Livre des Assises de la Cour des Bourgeois', *RHC Lois*, II.

Ambroise. *L'estoire de la guerre sainte*, ed. G. Paris. Paris, 1897.

'Annales de Terre Sainte', ed. R. Röhricht and G. Raynaud, *AOL*, II (1884), 429–61.

Annali Genovesi di Caffaro e de'suoi continuatori dal MXCIX al MCCXCIII, ed. L. T. Belgrano and C. Imperiale di Sant'Angelo. 5 vols. Rome, 1890–1929.

'Anonymi Continuatio appendicis Roberti de Monte ad Sigebertum', *RHF*, XVIII.

Arnold of Lübeck. 'Chronica', *MGHS*, XXI.

'Breve chronicon de rebus siculis' in *Historia diplomatica Frederici secundi*, ed. J. L. A. Huillard-Bréholles (Paris 1852–61). I.

Chronica Monasterii de Melsa, ed. E. A. Bond. RS 43. 3 vols. London, 1866–8.

'Chronique d'Amadi' in *Chroniques d'Amadi et de Strambaldi*, ed. R. de Mas Latrie. 2 vols. Paris, 1891–3, I.

Chronique d'Ernoul et de Bernard le Trésorier, ed. L. de Mas Latrie. Paris, 1871.

Chronique des quatre premiers Valois (1327–93), ed. S. Luce. Paris, 1862.

Chronographia Regum Francorum, ed. H. Moranvillé. 3 vols. Paris, 1891–7.

La continuation de Guillaume de Tyr (1184–1197), ed. M. R. Morgan. Paris, 1982.

'Continuation de Guillaume de Tyr, de 1229 à 1261, dite du manuscrit de Rothelin', *RHC Oc.*, II.

The Crusade and Death of Richard I, ed. R. C. Johnston. Oxford, 1961.

'Document relatif au service militaire', *RHC Lois*, II.

Domenico Malipiero. 'Annali Veneti dall'anno 1457 al 1500', ed. A. Sagredo, *Archivio Storico Italiano*, VII (1843–4), 3–720.

Estienne de Lusignan. *Description de toute l'isle de Cypre*. Paris, 1580.

'L'estoire de Eracles empereur et la conqueste de la Terre d'Outremer', *RHC Oc.*, II.

Felix Fabri. *The Book of Wanderings*, trans. A. Stewart. PPTS 7–10. 4 vols. London, 1892–3.

Florio Bustron. 'Chronique de l'île de Chypre', ed. R. de Mas Latrie in *Collection des documents inédits sur l'histoire de France: Mélanges historiques*, V (1886).

Francesco Balducci Pegolotti. *La pratica della mercatura*, ed. A. Evans. Cambridge, Mass., 1936.

Fulcher of Chartres. *Historia Hierosolymitana*, ed. H. Hagenmeyer. Heidelberg 1913.

Geoffrey de Villehardouin. *La Conquête de Constantinople*, ed. E. Faral. 2 vols. 5th edn Paris, 1973.

Geoffrey Le Tor. 'Livre de Geoffrey le Tort', *RHC Lois*, I.

Gesta Regis Henrici Secundi Benedicti Abbatis, ed. W. Stubbs. RS 49. 2 vols. London, 1869.

'Les Gestes des Chiprois', *RHC Arm.*, II.

Giorgio and Giovanni Stella. 'Annales Genuenses', ed. G. Petti Balbi. *Rerum Italicarum Scriptores*, n. s. XVII, II. Bologna, 1975.

Gislebert of Mons. 'Ex Gisleberti Montensis Praepositi Hannoniae Chronico', *RHF*, XVIII.

Hayton. 'La flor des estoires de la terre d'orient', *RHC Arm*, II.

Ibn al-Furāt. *Ayyubids, Mamlukes and Crusaders: Selections from the Tārīkh al-Duwal wa'l Mulūk*, ed. and trans. U. and M. C. Lyons with historical introduction and notes by J. Riley-Smith. 2 vols. Cambridge, 1971.

'Imād al-Dīn al-Iṣfahānī. *Conquête de la Syrie et de la Palestine par Saladin*, trans. H. Massé. Paris, 1972.

'Itinerarium Peregrinorum et Gesta Regis Ricardi' in *Chronicles and Memorials of the Reign of Richard I*, ed. W. Stubbs. RS 38. 2 vols. London, 1864–5. I.

Das Itinerarium peregrinorum, ed. H. E. Mayer. Stuttgart, 1962.

James of Ibelin. 'Livre de Jacques d'Ibelin', *RHC Lois*, I.

John Dardel. 'Chronique d'Arménie', *RHC Arm.*, II.

John of Ibelin. 'Livre de Jean d'Ibelin', *RHC Lois*, I.

John of Joinville. *Histoire de Saint Louis*, ed. N. de Wailly. Paris, 1868.

Leontios Makhairas. *Recital Concerning the Sweet Land of Cyprus entitled 'Chronicle'*, ed. R. M. Dawkins. 2 vols. Oxford, 1932.

'Les Lignages d'Outremer', *RHC Lois*, II.

'Le Livre au Roi', *RHC Lois*, I.

al-Maqrīzī. *A History of the Ayyūbid Sultans of Egypt*, trans. R. J. C. Broadhurst. Boston, 1980.

    Histoire des Sultans Mamlouks de l'Egypte, ed. and trans. M. Quatremère. 2 vols. in 4 parts. Paris, 1837–45.

Marino Sanudo. 'Liber Secretorum Fidelium Crucis' in *Gesta Dei per Francos*, ed. J. Bongars. Hanover, 1611.

Matthew Paris. *Chronica Majora*, ed. H. R. Luard. RS 57. 7 vols. London, 1872–83.

Muqqadasi. *Description of Syria including Palestine*, trans. G. Le Strange. PPTS 3. London, 1886.

Neophytus. Περὶ τῶν κατὰ χώπαν Κύπρου σκαιῶν in *Chronicles and Memorials of the Reign of Richard I*, ed. W. Stubbs. RS 38. 2 vols. London, 1864–5. I.

Nicholas of Martoni. 'Relation du pèlerinage à Jérusalem de Nicolas de Martoni, notaire italien', ed. L. Le Grand, *ROL*, III (1895), 566–669.

Oliver of Paderborn. 'Historia Damiatina' in *Die Schriften des Kölner Domscholasters, späteren Bischofs von Paderborn und Kardinal Bischofs von S. Sabina, Oliverus*, ed. H. Hoogeweg. Tübingen, 1894.

Peter Dubois. 'Opinio cujusdam suadentis regi Francie ut regnum Jerosolimitanum et Cipri acquireret pro altero filiorum suorum, ac de invasione regni Egipti' in *idem, De recuperatione Terre Sancte*, ed. C.–V. Langlois. Paris, 1891.

Philip of Mézières. 'Épistre lamentable et consolatoire sur le fait de la desconfiture lacrimable du noble et vaillant roy de Honguerie par les Turcs devant la ville de Nicopoli' in *Oeuvres de Froissart: Chroniques*, ed. J. M. B. C. Kervyn de Lettenhove. 25 vols. Brussels, 1867–77, XVI.

    The Life of St Peter Thomas, ed. J. Smet. Rome, 1954.

    Le Songe du Vieil Pelerin, ed. G. W. Coopland. 2 vols. Cambridge, 1969.

Philip of Novara. 'Livre de Philippe de Navarre', *RHC Lois*, I.

    The Wars of Frederick II against the Ibelins in Syria and Cyprus, trans. J. L. La Monte. New York, 1936.

Richard of Devizes. *Cronicon de Tempore Regis Richardi Primi*, ed. J. T. Appleby. London, 1963.

Robert of Torigny. 'Chronicle' in *Chronicles of the Reigns of Stephen, Henry II and Richard I*, ed. R. Howlett. RS 82. 4 vols. London, 1884–9, IV.

Roger of Howden. *Chronica*, ed. W. Stubbs. 4 vols. RS 51. London, 1868–71.

Saewulf. 'Relatio de peregrinatione ad Hierosolymam et Terram Sanctam' in *Itinera Hierosolymitana Crucesignatorum*, ed. S. de Sandoli. 4 vols. Jerusalem, 1978–84, II.

Thomas Wykes. 'Chronicon' in *Annales Monastici*, ed. H. R. Luard. 5 vols. RS 36. London, 1864–9, IV.

Walter of Guisborough. *Cronica*, ed. H. Rothwell. Camden Soc. 3rd ser., 89. London, 1957.

Wilbrand of Oldenburg. 'Itinerarium Terrae Sanctae' in *Itinera Hierosolymitana Crucesignatorum*, ed. S. de Sandoli. 4 vols. Jerusalem, 1978–84, III.

William of Machaut. *La prise d'Alexandrie ou chronique du roi Pierre Ier de Lusignan*, ed. L. de Mas Latrie. Geneva, 1877.

William of Tyre. *Chronicon*, ed. R. B. C. Huygens. 2 vols. Turnhout, 1986.

II SECONDARY WORKS

(Books and articles with asterisks contain printed documents to which reference has been made.)

Ahrweiler, H. *Byzance et la mer: la marine de guerre, la politique et les institutions maritimes de Byzance aux VIIe-XVe siècles*. Paris, 1966.

Arbel, B. 'Cypriot Population under Venetian Rule (1473–1571): A Demographic Study', Μελέται καί 'Υπομνήματα, I (1984), 181–215.

'Urban Assembles and Town Councils in Frankish and Venetian Cyprus' in Πρακτικα τοῦ Δευέρου Διεθνοῦς Κυπιολογικοῦ Συνεδρίου, II. Nicosia, 1986, pp. 203–13.

'Sauterelles et mentalités: le cas de la Chypre vénitienne', *Annales ESC* (1989), 1057–74.

* Argenti, P. *The Occupation of Chios by the Genoese and their Administration of the Island, 1346–1566*. 3 vols. Cambridge, 1958.

Ashtor, E. *Levant Trade in the Later Middle Ages*. Princeton, 1983.

Atiya, A. S. *The Crusade in the Later Middle Ages*. London, 1938.

Egypt and Aragon: Embassies and Diplomatic Correspondence between 1300 and 1330 A.D. Leipzig, 1938.

Ayalon, D. 'The Mamluks and Naval Power – A Phase of the Struggle between Islam and Christian Europe', *Proceedings of the Israel Academy of Sciences and Humanities*, I (1965), 1–12.

Balard, M. *La Romanie génoise (XIIe–début du XVe siècle)*. 2 vols. Genoa, 1978.

'L'activité commerciale en Chypre dans les années 1300' in *CS*, pp. 251–63.

Barag, D. 'A New Source Concerning the Ultimate Borders of the Latin Kingdom of Jerusalem', *Israel Exploration Journal*, XXIX (1979), 197–217.

Barber, M. 'James of Molay, the Last Grand Master of the Order of the Temple', *Studia Monastica*, XIV (1972), 91–124.

The Trial of the Templars. Cambridge, 1978.

Bertaux, E. 'Les Français d'outre-mer en Apulie et en Epire au temps des Hohenstaufen d'Italie', *Revue historique*, LXXXV (1904), 233–51.

Bertrand, R. O. 'Jean XXII et le mariage de Constance de Chypre avec l'infant Pierre d'Aragon', *Annales de Midi*, LXIII (1951), 5–31.

Boase, T. S. R. *Kingdoms and Strongholds of the Crusaders*. London, 1971.

'The History of the Kingdom' in his *The Cilician Kingdom of Armenia*. Edinburgh, 1978, pp. 1–33.

Bon, A. *La Morée franque: recherches historiques, topographiques et archéologiques sur la principauté d'Achaïe (1205–1430)*. 1 vol. with an album containing maps and plans. Paris, 1969.

Boulton, D'A. J. D. *The Knights of the Crown: The Monarchical Orders of Knighthood in Later Medieval Europe, 1325–1520*. Woodbridge, 1987.

Brand, C. M. 'The Byzantines and Saladin, 1185–1192: Opponents of the Third Crusade', *Speculum*, xxxvii (1962), 167–81.

Byzantium Confronts the West, 1180–1204. Cambridge, Mass., 1968.

Bromiley, J. 'Philip of Novara's Account of the War between Frederick II of Hohenstaufen and the Ibelins', *Journal of Medieval History*, iii (1977), 325–37.

Brundage, J. A. 'Richard the Lion-Heart and Byzantium', *Studies in Medieval Culture*, vi/vii (1976), 63–70.

* Buchon, J. A. C. *Nouvelles recherches historiques sur la principauté française de Morée et ses hautes baronnies*. 2 vols. Paris, 1843.

Buchthal, H. *Miniature Painting in the Latin Kingdom of Jerusalem*. Oxford, 1957.

Bulst-Thiele, M. L. *Sacrae Domus Militiae Templi Hierosolymitani Magistri*. Göttingen, 1974.

Cahen, C. *La Syrie du Nord à l'époque des croisades et la principauté franque d'Antioche*. Paris, 1940.

'Le commerce anatolien au début du xiiie siècle' in *Mélanges d'histoire du moyen âge dédiés à la mémoire de Louis Halphen*. Paris, 1951, pp. 91–101.

Chandon de Briailles, F. 'Lignages d'Outre-Mer, les seigneurs de Margat', *Syria*, xxv (1946–8), 231–58.

Clermont-Ganneau, C. 'Nouveaux monuments des croisés recueillis en Terre Sainte', *AOL*, ii (1884), part i, 457–61.

Combes, J. 'Un marchand de Chypre, bourgeois de Montpellier' in *Etudes médiévales offertes à M. le doyen Augustin Fliche* (Montpellier, 1952), pp. 33–9.

* Darrouzès, J. 'Un obituaire chypriote: le Parisinus graecus 1588', *Littérature et histoire des textes byzantins*. London, 1972.

* Delaville Le Roulx, J. *Les Hospitaliers à Rhodes jusqu'à la mort de Philibert de Naillac (1310–1421)*. Paris, 1913.

Der Nersessian, S. 'The Kingdom of Cilician Armenia' in *HC*, ii, 630–59.

Downs, N. *see* La Monte J. L. and Downs, N.

Du Fresne du Cange, C. *Les familles d'Outremer*, ed. E. G. Rey. Paris, 1869.

Edbury, P. W. 'The Feudal Nobility of Cyprus, 1192–1400'. Unpublished PhD thesis. St Andrews University, 1974.

* 'The Ibelin Counts of Jaffa: A Previously Unknown Passage from the "Lignages d'Outremer"', *EHR*, lxxxix (1974), 604–10.

'The Crusading Policy of King Peter I of Cyprus, 1359–1369' in *The Eastern Mediterranean Lands in the Period of the Crusades*, ed. P. M. Holt. Warminster, 1977, pp. 90–105.

'Feudal Obligations in the Latin East', *Byzantion*, xlvii (1977), 328–56.

* 'The "Cartulaire de Manosque": A Grant to the Templars in Latin Syria and a Charter of King Hugh I of Cyprus', *BIHR*, li (1978), 174–81.

'Latin Dioceses and Peristerona: A Contribution to the Topography of Lusignan Cyprus', *EEKE*, VIII (1978), 45–51.

* 'The Disputed Regency of the Kingdom of Jerusalem, 1264/6 and 1268' in *Camden Miscellany*, XXVII (= Camden 4th Ser., 22). London, 1979, pp. 1–47.

'The Murder of King Peter I of Cyprus (1359–1369)', *Journal of Medieval History*, VI (1980), 219–33.

'John of Ibelin's Title to the County of Jaffa and Ascalon', *EHR*, XCVIII (1983), 115–33.

'Cyprus and Genoa: The Origins of the War of 1373–1374' in Πρακτικα τοῦ Δευτέρου Διεθνοῦς Κυπριολογικοῦ Συνεδρίου, II. Nicosia, 1986, pp. 109–26.

'La classe des propriétaires terriens franco-chypriotes et l'exploitation des ressources rurales de l'île de Chypre' in *État et colonisation au Moyen Age*, ed. M. Balard. Lyons, 1989, pp. 145–52.

(ed.) *Crusade and Settlement: Papers read at the First Conference of the Society for the Study of the Crusades and the Latin East and presented to R. C. Smail*. Cardiff, 1985.

Enlart, C. *Gothic Art and the Renaissance in Cyprus*, trans. and ed. D. Hunt. London, 1987.

Fichtenau, H. 'Akkon, Zypern und das Lösegeld für Richard Löwenherz', *Archiv für österreichische Geschichte*, CXXV (1966), 11–32.

Folda, J. *Crusader Manuscript Illumination at Saint-Jean d'Acre, 1275–1291*. Princeton, 1976.

Forey, A. J. 'The Military Order of St Thomas of Acre', *EHR*, XCII (1977), 481–503.

'The Military Orders in the Crusading Proposals of the Late-Thirteenth and Early-Fourteenth Centuries', *Traditio*, XXXVI (1980), 317–45.

* Germain, A. C. *Histoire du commerce de Montpellier*. 2 vols. Montpellier, 1861.

Gill, J. 'The Tribulations of the Greek Church in Cyprus, 1196–c.1280', *BF*, V (1977), 73–93.

Gillingham, J. *Richard the Lionheart*. London, 1978.

Hamilton, B. *The Latin Church in the Crusader States: The Secular Church*. London, 1980.

Hill, G. *A History of Cyprus*. 4 vols. Cambridge, 1940–52.

Hillgarth, J. N. *Ramon Lull and Lullism in Fourteenth-Century France*. Oxford, 1971.

Holt, P. M. 'Qalāwūn's Treaty with Acre in 1283', *EHR*, XCI (1976), 802–12.

Housley, N. J. 'The Franco-Papal Crusade Negotiations of 1322–3', *PBSR*, XLVIII (1980), 166–85.

'The Mercenary Companies, the Papacy and the Crusades, 1356–1378', *Traditio*, XXXVIII (1982), 253–80.

'Pope Clement V and the Crusades of 1309–10', *Journal of Medieval History*, VIII (1982), 29–43.

The Italian Crusades. Oxford, 1982.

'Charles II of Naples and the Kingdom of Jerusalem', *Byzantion*, LIV (1984), 527–35.

The Avignon Papacy and the Crusades, 1305–1378. Oxford, 1986.

* Hubatsch, W. 'Der Deutsche Orden und die Reichslehnschaft über Cypern', *Nachrichten der Akad. der Wissenschaften in Göttingen. Philol.-Hist. Kl.* (1955), 245–306.

Irwin, R. 'The Mamlūk Conquest of the County of Tripoli' in *CS*, pp. 246–50.

The Middle East in the Middle Ages: The Early Mamluk Sultanate. London/Sydney, 1986.

Jackson, D. E. P. *see* Lyons, M. C. and Jackson, D. E. P.

Jackson, P. 'The Crisis in the Holy Land in 1260', *EHR*, XCV (1980), 481–513.
'The End of Hohenstaufen Rule in Syria', *BIHR*, LIX (1986), 20–36.
Jacoby, D. 'Jean Lascaris Calophéros, Chypre et la Morée', *Revue des études byzantines*, XXVI (1968), 189–228.
'The Encounter of Two Societies: Western Conquerors and Byzantines in the Peloponnesus after the Fourth Crusade', *American Historical Review*, LXXVIII (1973), 873–906.
'Citoyens, sujets and protégés de Venise et de Gênes en Chypre du XIIIe au XVe siècle', *BF*, V (1977), 159–88.
'L'expansion occidentale dans le Levant: les Vénitiens à Acre dans la seconde moitié du treizième siècle', *Journal of Medieval History*, III (1977), 225–64.
'The Rise of a New Emporium in the Eastern Mediterranean: Famagusta in the Late Thirteenth Century', Μελέται καὶ Ὑπομνήματα, I (1984), 143–79.
'The Kingdom of Jerusalem and the Collapse of Hohenstaufen Power in the Levant', *DOP*, XL (1986), 83–101.
'From Byzantium to Latin Romania: Continuity and Change' in *Latins and Greeks in the Eastern Mediterranean after 1204*, ed. B. Arbel *et al.* London, 1989, pp. 1–44.
Jenkins, R. J. H. 'Cyprus between Byzantium and Islam, A. D. 688–965' in *Studies Presented to David Moore Robinson*, ed. G. E. Mylonas. St Louis, 1951–3, II, 1006–14.
Jennings, R. C. 'The Origins of the Locust Problem in Cyprus', *Byzantion*, LXVII (1987), 315–25.
Jorga, N. *Philippe de Mézières (1327–1405) et la croisade au XIVe siècle*. Paris, 1896.
Kedar, B. Z. *Merchants in Crisis: Genoese and Venetian Men of Affairs and the Fourteenth-Century Depression*. New Haven/London, 1976.
Kedar, B. Z. *et al.* (eds.) *Outremer: Studies in the History of the Crusading Kingdom of Jerusalem*. Jerusalem, 1982.
Kedar, B. Z. and Schein, S. 'Un projet de "passage particulier" proposé par l'Ordre de l'Hôpital 1306–1307', *BEC*, CXXXVII (1979), 211–26.
Keen, M. H. *The Laws of War in the Late Middle Ages*. London, 1965.
Chivalry. New Haven/London, 1984.
Kohler, C. Introduction to 'Les Gestes des Chiprois' in *RHC Arm.*, II, pp. ccxix-cclxiv.
'Lettres pontificales concernant l'histoire de la Petite Arménie au XIVe siècle' in *Florilegium Melchior de Vogüé*. Paris, 1909, pp. 303–27.
La Monte, J. L. 'To What Extent was the Byzantine Empire the Suzerain of the Crusading States?', *Byzantion*, VII (1932), 253–64.
'John d'Ibelin: The Old Lord of Beirut, 1177–1236', *Byzantion*, XII (1937), 417–58.
'The Lords of Caesarea in the Period of the Crusades', *Speculum*, XXII (1947), 145–61.
La Monte J. L. and Downs, N. 'The Lords of Bethsan in the Kingdoms of Jerusalem and Cyprus', *Medievalia et Humanistica*, VI (1950), 57–75.
Landon, L. *The Itinerary of King Richard I*. Pipe Roll Society NS 13. London, 1935.
Lavagnini, B. 'I Normanni di Sicilia a Cipro e a Patmo (1186)', *Byzantino-Sicula*, II (1974) (= *Miscellanea G. Rossi Taibbi*), 321–34.
Lemerle, P. *L'émirat d'Aydin, Byzance et l'Occident. Recherches sur 'La geste d'Umur Pacha'*. Paris, 1957.
'Séance de clôture de la Section médiévale' in Πρακτικὰ τοῦ Πρώτου Διεθνοῦς Κυπρολογικοῦ Συνεδίου, II. Nicosia, 1972, pp. 153–6.

Leone, P. L. M. 'L'encomio di Niceforo Gregora per il re di Cipro (Ugo IV di Lusignano)', *Byzantion*, LI (1981), 211–24.

Little, D. P. *An Introduction to Mamluk Historiography: An Analysis of Arabic and Biographical Sources for the Reign of al-Malik an-Nāsir Muhammad ibn Qalā'ūn.* Wiesbaden, 1970.

Livi, R. 'Guido da Bagnolo, medico del re di Cipro', *Atti e memorie della R. deputazione di Storia Patria per le provincie Modenesi*, ser. 5, XI (1918), 45–91.

Lloyd, S. *English Society and the Crusade, 1216–1307.* Oxford, 1988.

Longnon, J. *Les Compagnons de Villehardouin.* Geneva, 1978.

Loud, G. A. 'The *Assise sur la Ligece* and Ralph of Tiberias' in *CS*, pp. 206–12.

* Lourie, E. 'An Offer of the Suzerainty and Escheat of Cyprus to Alphonso III of Aragon by Hugh de Brienne in 1289', *EHR*, LXXXIV (1969), 101–8.

Luttrell, A. T. 'Venice and the Knights Hospitallers of Rhodes in the Fourteenth Century', *PBSR*, XXVI (1958), 195–212.

'The Hospitallers at Rhodes, 1306–1421' in *HC*, III, 278–313.

'The Hospitallers in Cyprus after 1291' in Πρακτικὰ τοῦ Πρώτου Διεθνοῦς Κυπρολογικοῦ Συνεδίου, II. Nicosia, 1972, pp. 161–71.

'The Hospitallers' Interventions in Cilician Armenia: 1291–1375' in *The Cilician Kingdom of Armenia*, ed. T. S. R. Boase. Edinburgh, 1978, pp. 118–44.

'Gregory XI and the Turks, 1370–1378', *Orientalia Christiana Periodica*, XLVI (1980), 391–417.

'The Hospitallers in Cyprus: 1310–1378', Κυπριακαὶ Σπουδαί, L (1986), 155–84.

'English Levantine Crusaders, 1363–1367', *Renaissance Studies*, II (1988), 143–53.

Luzzatto, G. 'Capitalismo coloniale nel trecento' in *Studi di storia economica veneziana.* Padua, 1954, pp. 117–24.

Lyons, M. C. and Jackson, D. E. P. *Saladin. The Politics of the Holy War.* Cambridge, 1982.

Mango, C. 'Chypre carrefour du monde byzantin'. *Rapports et co-rapports du XVe congrès international d'études byzantines*, V. *Chypre dans le monde byzantin*, V. Athens, 1976.

* Martínez Ferrando, J. E. *Jaime II de Aragón. Su vida familiar.* 2 vols. Barcelona, 1948.

* de Mas Latrie, L. *Histoire de l'île de Chypre sous le règne des princes de la maison de Lusignan.* 3 vols. Paris, 1852–61.

'Le fief de la Chamberlaine et les chambellans de Jérusalem', *BEC*, XLIII (1882), 647–52.

* Mayer, H. E. 'Das Pontifikale von Tyrus und die Krönung der lateinischen Könige von Jerusalem', *DOP*, XXI (1967), 141–232.

* *Marseilles Levantehandel und ein akkonensisches Fälscheratelier des 13. Jahrhunderts.* Tübingen, 1972.

Bistümer, Klöster und Stifte im Königreich Jerusalem. Stuttgart, 1977.

'Die Kreuzfahrerherrschaft 'Arrābe', *ZDPV*, XCIII (1977), 198–212.

'Ibelin *versus* Ibelin: The Struggle for the Regency of Jerusalem, 1253–1258', *PAPS*, CXXII (1978), 25–57.

'Carving up Crusaders: The Early Ibelins and Ramlas' in *Outremer*, pp. 101–18.

'John of Jaffa, his Opponents and his Fiefs', *PAPS*, CXXVIII (1984), 134–63.

Mélanges sur l'histoire du royaume latin de Jérusalem. Paris, 1984.

Megaw, A. H. S. 'Saranda Kolones: A Medieval Castle Excavated at Paphos' in Πρακτικὰ τοῦ Πρώτου Διεθνοῦς Κυπρολογικοῦ Συνεδρίου, II. Nicosia, 1972, pp. 173–81.

Metcalf, D. M. 'The Gros grand and the Gros petit of Henry II of Cyprus', *Numismatic Chronicle*, CXLII (1982), 83–100, CXLIII (1983), 177–201.
Coinage of the Crusades and the Latin East in the Ashmolean Museum, Oxford. London, 1983.
'A Decline in the Stock of Currency in Fourteenth-Century Cyprus?' in *CS*, pp. 264–7.
'The Gros grand and the Gros petit of Hugh IV of Cyprus', *Revue numismatique*, 6th ser., XXVII (1985), 130–75.
Morgan, D. O. 'The Mongols in Syria, 1260–1300' in *CS*, pp. 231–5.
Morgan, M. R. *The Chronicle of Ernoul and the Continuations of William of Tyre.* Oxford, 1973.
Painter, S. 'The Lords of Lusignan in the Eleventh and Twelfth Centuries', *Speculum*, XXXII (1957), 27–47.
'The Crusade of Theobald of Champagne and Richard of Cornwall, 1239–1241' in *HC*, II, 463–85.
Papadopoullos, T. 'Chypre: frontière ethnique et socio-culturelle du monde byzantin'. *Rapports et co-rapports du XVe congrès international d'études byzantines*: v. *Chypre dans le monde byzanin*, part v. Athens, 1976.
* Papadopoulou, E. 'Οι πρωτες εγκαταστασεις Βενετων στην Κυπρο', *Συμμεικτα του Κεντρου Βυζαντινων Ερευνον*, v (1983), 303–32.
Paris, G. 'Les mémoires de Philippe de Novare', *ROL*, IX (1902), 164–205.
* Perrat, C. 'Un diplomate gascon au XIVe siècle: Raymond de Piis, nonce de Clément V en Orient', *MAHEFR*, XLIV (1927), 35–90.
Petti Balbi, G. 'La maona di Cipro del 1373', *Rassegna storica della Liguria*, I (1974), 269–85.
Prawer, J. *Histoire de royaume latin de Jérusalem.* 2 vols. Paris, 1969–70.
Crusader Institutions. Oxford, 1980.
Prestwich, J. O. 'Richard Coeur de Lion: *Rex Bellicosus*' in *Riccardo Cuor di Leone nella storia e nella leggenda.* Accademia Nazionale dei Lincei, quaderno 253. Rome, 1981, pp. 1–15.
Pryor, J. H. *Geography, Technology and War: Studies in the Maritime History of the Mediterranean 649–1571.* Cambridge, 1988.
Racine, P. 'Note sur le trafic Veneto-Chypriote à la fin du moyen âge', *BF*, v (1977), 307–29.
Rey, E. G. 'Les seigneurs de Giblet', *ROL*, III (1895), 398–422.
Richard, J. *Le comté de Tripoli sous la dynastie toulousaine (1102–1187).* Paris, 1945.
* 'Le casal de Psimolofo et la vie rurale en Chypre au XIVe siècle', *MAHEFR*, LIX (1947), 121–53.
'Un évêque d'Orient latin au XIVe siècle: Guy d'Ibelin, O.P., évêque de Limassol, et l'inventaire de ses biens (1367)', *MAHEFR*, LIX (1949), 98–133.
'Pairie d'Orient latin: les quatre baronnies des royaumes de Jérusalem et de Chypre', *Revue historique de droit français et étranger*, ser. 4, XXVIII (1950), 67–88.
'La révolution de 1369 dans le royaume de Chypre', *BEC*, CX (1952), 108–23.
'Un partage de seigneurie entre Francs et Mamelouks: les "casaux de Sur"', *Syria*, XXX (1953), 72–82.
* *Chypre sous les Lusignans. Documents chypriotes des archives du Vatican (XIVe et XVe siècles).* Paris, 1962.
'L'ordonnance de décembre 1296 sur le prix du pain à Chypre', *EKEE*, I (1967–8), 45–51.

* 'L'abbaye cistercienne de Jubin et le prieuré Saint-Blaise de Nicosie', *EKEE*, III (1969–70), 63–74.

'The Mongols and the Franks', *Journal of Asian History*, III (1969), 45–57.

* 'Le comté de Tripoli dans les chartes du fonds des Porcellet', *BEC*, CXXX (1972), 339–82.

'La situation juridique de Famagouste dans le royaume des Lusignans' in *Orient et Occident au Moyen Age: contacts et relations (XIIe–XVe s)*. London, 1976, XVII.

The Latin Kingdom of Jerusalem, trans. J. Shirley. 2 vols. Amsterdam, 1979.

'Le peuplement latin et syrien en Chypre au XIIIe siècle', *BF*, VII (1979), 157–73.

'Le royaume de Chypre et l'embargo sur le commerce avec l'Égypte (fin XIIIe–début XIVe siècle)', *Académie des Inscriptions et Belles-lettres: Comptes Rendus* (1984), 120–34.

* 'Les comptes du collecteur de la chambre apostolique dans le royaume de Chypre (1357–1363)' *EEKE*, XIII/XVI (1984–7), 1–47.

'La diplomatique royale dans les royaumes d'Arménie et de Chypre (XIIe–XVe siècles)', *BEC*, CXLIV (1986), 69–86.

'La lettre du Connétable Smbat et les rapports entre Chrétiens et Mongols au milieu de XIIIème siècle' in *Armenian Studies in memoriam Haïg Berbérian*, ed. D. Kouymjian. Lisbon, 1986, pp. 683–96.

'La cour des Syriens de Famagouste d'après un texte de 1448', *BF*, XII (1987), 383–98.

Riley-Smith, J. *The Knights of St John in Jerusalem and Cyprus c.1050–1310*. London, 1967.

'The Assise Sur La Ligece and the Commune of Acre', *Traditio*, XXVII (1971), 179–204.

The Feudal Nobility and the Kingdom of Jerusalem, 1174–1277. London, 1973.

'Peace Never Established: The Case of the Kingdom of Jerusalem', *TRHS*, 5th ser., XXVII (1978), 87–102.

Rudt de Collenberg, W. H. (Rüdt-Collenberg) *The Rupenides, Hethumides and Lusignans: The Structure of the Armeno-Cilician Dynasties*. Paris, 1963.

'Les premiers Ibelins', *Le moyen âge*, LXXI (1965), 433–74.

'L'empereur Isaac de Chypre et sa fille (1155–1207)', *Byzantion*, XXXVIII (1968), 123–77.

'Les grâces papales, autres que les dispenses matrimoniales, accordées à Chypre de 1305 à 1378', *EKEE*, VIII (1975–7), 187–252.

'L'héraldique de Chypre', *Cahiers d'héraldique*, III (1977), 86–157.

'Les Ibelin aux XIIIe et XIVe siècles', *EKEE*, IX (1977–9), 117–265.

'Les dispenses matrimoniales accordées à l'Orient latin selon les registres du Vatican d'Honorius III à Clément VII (1223–1385)', *MEFR*, LXIX (1979), 10–93.

'Etat et origine du haut clergé de Chypre avant le Grand Schisme d'après les registres des papes du XIIIe et du XIVe siècle', *MEFR*, XCI (1979), 197–332.

'Les Lusignan de Chypre', *EKEE*, X (1980), 85–319.

'The Fate of Frankish Noble Families Settled in Cyprus' in *CS*, pp. 268–72.

'Les *Bullae* et *Litterae* adressées par les papes d'Avignon à l'Arménie cilicienne, 1305–1375 (d'après les Registres de l'Archivio Segreto Vaticano)' in *Armenian Studies in memoriam Haïg Berbérian*, ed. D. Kouymjian. Lisbon, 1986, pp. 697–725.

Sáez Pomés, M. 'Un viaje del literato Felipe de Mézières a Catalunya, en 1367', *Estudios de Edad Media de la Corona de Aragón*, IV (1951), 432–5.

'Los Aragoneses en la conquista saqueo de Alejandria por Pedro I de Chipre', *ibid.*, V (1952), 361–405.

Schein, S. 'Gesta Dei per Mongolos 1300. The Genesis of a Non-Event', EHR, XCIV (1979), 805–19.

See also Kedar, B. Z. and Schein, S.

Schlumberger, G. *et al. Sigillographie de l'Orient latin.* Paris, 1943.

Servois, G. 'Emprunts de Saint Louis en Palestine et en Afrique', BEC, 4th ser., IV (1858), 113–31, 283–93.

Setton, K. M. (ed.) *A History of the Crusades.* 6 vols.. Philadelphia/Madison, 1955–89.

The Papacy and the Levant (1204–1571). 4 vols. Philadelphia, 1976–84.

Sinor, D. 'The Mongols and Western Europe' in HC, III, 513–44.

Smail, R. C. *Crusading Warfare (1097–1193).* Cambridge, 1956.

'The Predicaments of Guy of Lusignan, 1183–87' in *Outremer,* pp. 159–76.

Strayer, J. R. 'The Crusades of Louis IX' in HC, II, 487–518.

Thiriet, F. *La Romanie vénitienne au moyen âge.* Paris, 1959.

Thomas, A. 'Notice sur le manuscrit latin 4788 du Vatican contenant une traduction française avec commentaire par Maître Pierre de Paris de la *Consolatio Philosophiae* de Boèce', *Notices et extraits des manuscrits de la Bibliothèque Nationale et autres bibliothèques,* XLI (1923), 29–90.

Tibble, S. *Monarchy and Lordships in the Latin Kingdom of Jerusalem, 1099–1291.* Oxford, 1989.

Topping, P. 'The Morea, 1311–1364' in HC, III, 104–40.

Trenchs Odena, J. ' "De Alexandrinis" (El comercio prohibido con los muslmanes y el papado de Aviñón durante la primera mitad de siglo XIV)', *Anuario de estudios medievales,* X (1980), 237–320.

Troubat, O. 'La France et le royaume de Chypre au XIVe siècle: Marie de Bourbon, impératrice de Constantinople', *Revue historique,* CCLXXVIII (1987), 3–21.

Tyerman, C. J. 'Philip V of France, the Assemblies of 1319–20 and the Crusade', BIHR, LVII (1984), 15–34.

'Sed Nihil Fecit? The Last Capetians and the Recovery of the Holy Land' in *War and Government in the Middle Ages,* ed. J. Gillingham and J. C. Holt. Woodbridge, 1984, pp. 170–81.

'Philip VI and the Recovery of the Holy Land', EHR, C (1985), 25–52.

Van Cleve, T. C. *The Emperor Frederick II of Hohenstaufen. Immutator Mundi.* Oxford, 1972.

Vranoussi, E. 'A propos des opérations des Normandes dans la mer Égée et à Chypre après la prise de Thessalonique (1185–6)', *Byzantina,* VIII (1976), 205–11.

Zachariadou, E. A. *Trade and Crusade. Venetian Crete and the Emirates of Menteshe and Aydin (1300–1415).* Venice, 1983.

Zurita, J. *Anales de la corona de Aragon.* 6 vols. Saragossa, 1610.

INDEX

9 780521 458375